MAO TSE-TUNG
EMPEROR OF THE BLUE ANTS

By the same author:

THE UNDEFEATED
KHRUSHCHEV

George Paloczi-Horvath

MAO TSE-TUNG

EMPEROR OF THE BLUE ANTS

Doubleday & Company, Inc.
Garden City, New York
1963

CONTENTS

ABBREVIATIONS

The following abbreviations are used in references to sources.

CB: *Current Background*. Mimeographed translation service of Chinese Communist documents, statements and of articles on political, economic, social and cultural affairs. U.S. Consulate General, Hong Kong.

CCP: Chinese Communist Party.

CP: Communist Party.

CYN: *Chinese Youth Newspaper*.

FEER: *Far Eastern Economic Review*, Hong Kong.

FLP: Foreign Language Press, Peking.

NCNA: New China News Agency.

NPC: National People's Congress.

NYHT: *New York Herald Tribune*.

PD: *People's Daily*, Peking.

SW: Selected Works of Mao Tse-tung.

ACKNOWLEDGMENTS

This political biography of Mao Tse-tung could not have been written without the immense amount of original research of scores of historians, sociologists and economists, dealing with various aspects and periods of Chinese, Soviet and Comintern history. I wish to emphasise my special indebtedness to the following works:

I. The 1900-35 period: Tsi C. Wang, *The Youth Movement in China* (New York, 1937); Chow Tse-tsung, *The May Fourth Movement* (Harvard Univ. Press, 1960); C. Martin Wilbur and Julie Lien-ying How, *Documents on Communism, Nationalism and Soviet Advisers in China, 1918-1927*, papers seized in the 1927 Peking raid (Columbia Univ. Press, New York, 1956); Harold Isaac's classic, *The Tragedy of the Chinese Revolution*, 2nd rev. ed. (Stanford, Calif., 1961).

II. Comintern history and Sino-Soviet relations: Jane Degras, *Soviet Documents on Foreign Policy*, 3 vols. (Oxford, 1951-3); Jane Degras, *The Communist International, 1919-1943*, 2 vols. (London, 1956-60); Charles B. McLane, *Soviet Policy and the Chinese Communists, 1931-1946* (Columbia Univ. Press, 1958); M. S. Kapitza, *Sovietskoe-Kitaiskie Otnosheniya B 1931-1945 GG* (Moscow, 1956); Robert C. North, *Moscow and the Chinese Communists* (Stanford Univ. Press, 1953).

III. The 1940-60 period and general works: Max Beloff, *Soviet Policy in the Far East, 1944-1951* (London, 1953); Conrad Brandt, Benjamin Schwartz and John K. Fairbanks: *A Documentary History of Chinese Communism* (Cambridge, Mass., 1952); Jean-Jacques Brieux, *Le Chine: du nationalisme au communisme* (Paris, 1950); C. P. Fitzgerald, *Revolution in China* (London, 1952); Ygael Gluckstein, *Mao's China—Economic and Political Survey* (London, 1957); Ping-chia Kuo, *China—New Age and New Outlook* (London, 1960); Roderick MacFarquhar, *The Hundred Flowers* (London, 1960); Richard L. Walker, *China Under Communism—The First Five Years* (London, 1956).

I am greatly indebted to the biographers of Mao's youth and of his period before coming to power, particularly to Emi Siao, *Mao*

Tse-tung, His Childhood and Youth (Bombay, 1953); Siao-yu, *Mao Tse-tung and I Were Beggars* (Syracuse Univ. Press, 1956); Benjamin J. Schwartz, *Chinese Communism and the Rise of Mao* (Harvard Univ. Press, 1951); Robert Payne, *Mao Tse-tung, Ruler of Red China* (London, 1951), and to Mao's autobiographical account in Edgar Snow's *Red Star Over China* (London, 1937). I should have liked to have been able to quote a number of autobiographical passages from this book but was not able to obtain the necessary permission.

Last but not least I am most grateful to Professor Dennis Gabor for being able to quote from his essay on *Inventing the Future;* to the staff of the London Library and to that of the Royal Society of International Affairs; to the editors and translators of the *Current Background* and *Survey of the Chinese Mainland Press* (U.S. Consulate-General, Hong Kong), for their excellent translation service of Chinese documents, statements and articles.

MAO TSE-TUNG
EMPEROR OF THE BLUE ANTS

I

LEGEND AND REALITY

Nearly one-quarter of the world's present population is Chinese. According to demographic forecasts their number will grow to one thousand millions by 1980 and to around two thousand millions by the end of the century. These swarming millions are ruled by Mao Tse-tung, whom they are taught and forced to revere as omnipotent and infallible. The pattern of the most thoroughly total dictatorship the world has ever known was evolved by Mao and as long as Red rule lasts over China it seems unthinkable that even after his death there could be any serious deviation from the concept and commands of "Chairman Mao".

1. The legend and the outside world

From 1926 onwards Mao Tse-tung has been one of the most controversial figures within the Chinese Communist movement. The great news-agencies of the world became aware of him in 1927, after Chiang Kai-shek had renounced the Kuomintang-Communist alliance, executed many of the Communist leaders and forced the rest to go underground. Some of these leaders lived illegally in the coastal cities, while others—among them Mao—escaped to the provinces, where they organised peasant red armies and set up small Communist-run principalities, called "Soviet bases".

In the vastness of civil war torn China it was most difficult to get reliable information about these Red States within the State. For a while the Kuomintang press denied their existence or belittled their importance—in curious accord with the official leaders of the underground Communist Party who likewise denied the importance of the successes of their rivals. This jealous attitude of the Shanghai Communist Central Committee was partly responsible for the scanty and erroneous information Stalin and the Communist International had about the Chinese Soviets and the Red armies of the peasants.

Mao and the other Soviet and Red Army leaders were periodically reported dead by the anti-Communist Chinese press, and even the official organ of the Comintern published a long obituary of Mao Tse-tung "who died of consumption".[1]

[1] *Inprecor*, Vol. X, No. 14, March 20, 1930.

Stalin, who according to later legends was the devilishly cunning planner of the Communist revolt in China, had no trustworthy information about the Chinese Soviets or about Mao's Soviet government. At the Sixteenth Soviet CP Congress in Moscow, in June 1930, Stalin remarked:

It is said that a Soviet government has already been created there [in China]. I think that *if this is true,* there is nothing surprising about it. (Emphasis added.)

In fact, the first Chinese Soviet was set up in November 1927 in Tsalin, on the Hunan border. In 1928 a small Soviet was established in Central Kiangsi and subsequently the movement spread into Western Fukien. When in February 1930 a Provincial Soviet government was established under Mao's leadership in Kiangsi, several Red armies were already in operation, based on the Soviet areas of Central and Southern China. Yet Stalin and the Comintern were not certain of their existence.

Even after the rest of China, the Comintern and the outside world had finally agreed on the existence of the Chinese Soviets and their Red armies, wildly conflicting reports were in circulation about their leaders. According to some sources, these leaders of the "Red bandits" were agents of Moscow, while others depicted them as heretical Communists who were betraying the basic tenets of the Marxist creed for the sake of the revolutionary peasants.

Generalissimo Chiang Kai-shek led five "annihilation campaigns" against these Soviets. The Generalissimo had large armies, and an expensive and distinguished staff of foreign military advisers, at one time headed by General Von Seeckt, the former German Chief of Staff. Yet even after the fifth and largest offensive against them, the Red armies managed to escape from complete encirclement. The legendary Long March of 6,000 miles started from South-East China to the frontier regions of the North-West. Mao Tse-tung and his general, Chu Teh, emerged as the leaders of the fantastic Long March. They were regarded by Chiang Kai-shek's Government as the most dangerous of the "Red bandits". For the capture of Mao and Chu dead or alive they offered a quarter of a million silver dollars each. (Chou En-lai was at that time valued at only 80,000 dollars.) It was during the Long March which lasted nearly two years that Mao became the leader of the Chinese Communists.

From 1936 onwards the world press started to take notice of Mao. During the war against Japan he figured either as a patriotic and revolutionary war-lord, a Communist despot or an independently minded revolutionary peasant leader. After the victory over Japan, part of the world press was influenced by Communist propaganda about Mao, another part by the hostile propaganda of the Kuomintang. At times he was a heretical Communist, constantly at loggerheads with Stalin, at other times he was Stalin's most important agent. After the Communist victory on the Chinese mainland, the Western image of Mao still alternated between "the Tito of Asia" and "Stalin's Number One henchman in the Far East". All the while the Kuomintang press and a section of the world press kept on reporting that Mao had died, that he was mortally ill (cancer of the throat, of the lung, T.B., etc.), that he had mysteriously disappeared or had been summarily deposed.

Since he became the undisputed ruler of Red China, out of his thousands of aphorisms, hundreds of poems and many volumes of writings, a dozen short sayings have been most frequently quoted in the West, starting with his famous statement that "power grows out of the barrel of a gun". Most profiles of Mao tell the story of the sentimental intellectual who suggested to Mao that Communism is love. "No Comrade," Mao said "Communism is not love; Communism is a hammer which we use to destroy the enemy."

2. The metamorphoses of the Communist Mao-image

Since his emergence as military and political leader and chief theoretician of Red China, the Communist Mao-image has changed several times.

From 1934 till about 1944-5 he was the symbol and quintessence of the common man; a servant of the people; a military leader who lives, eats and dresses like the common soldiers; a student and scholar of frugal tastes; a representative of the masses mingling freely with peasants, soldiers, with everybody; a head of a fighting State, whose life is an open book.

Mao was often photographed, a tall, gaunt figure in worn, crumpled cotton uniform, indistinguishable from the common troopers. Most of this time he lived in a cave or in very simple quarters, his rough wooden table covered with books. After his work as head of the Government and Party was over, he retired and "pursued his studies", reading and chain-smoking often until dawn.

Towards the end of the Second World War when power over the entire Chinese empire was, for the Communists, no longer a wonderful dream but a not-so-distant possibility, the Communists'

Mao-image also changed. The man-of-the-people began to grow to superhuman legendary size.

Between 1944 and 1949 most of China heard the famous "Mao folk song" (first published in 1944 in a collection of popular Communist dance songs):

> *The sun is rising red in the East.*
> *China has brought forth a Mao Tse-tung.*
> *He plans blessings for the people.*
> *Aiyayo, he is the people's great saviour.*
>
> *Mao Tse-tung has a great love for the people.*
> *He is the man who guides us along the pathway.*
> *With him we shall build a new China.*
> *Aiyayo, he leads the people into the future.*
>
> *Mao Tse-tung is a son of the Chinese earth;*
> *He will lead us to fight the enemy.*
> *There will come a time when we will be masters.*
> *Aiyayo, all our enemies shall be beaten.*

In this period while both fights were still on, the war against the Japanese, and the struggle for Communist rule over China, Mao was the saviour, the rejuvenator, the remoulder of China, or—one of his most frequent appellations—the great saving star of the people.

Elementary school children learnt to sing rhymes like these:

> *Mao Tse-tung is like the sun:*
> *He is brighter than the sun.*
> *Little brother, little sister,*
> *Everyone clap hands, come and sing.*

A few days after the Japanese surrender, Mao wrote a poem, recalling the limited accomplishments of the Chinese emperors of the past and suggesting that the really great man would emerge in his own era: himself. He was proud of this poem, for he gave autographed copies to his friends:

> *. . . These lands, these rivers, their bewitching charm*
> *Inspired the conqueror-emperors of Chin and Han,*
> *Tang and Sung in splendour striving to expand.*
> *Alas! All short in stature! And Genghis Khan*
> *Knew only how to shoot a hawk for play.*
> *For the towering figure watch the scene today.*

During the last years of the war Mao put on weight. Instead of the thin, haggard revolutionary in his cotton tunic almost worn to shreds, the official photos showed a "towering figure": Mao Tse-tung wearing a general's greatcoat with fur collar and a military cap, standing up in a military car. He was photographed from below, giving the impression of a mighty war-lord, a giant of a leader.

Shortly before he left his humble dwelling, a new turn came. One of the first symptoms was a book by Chang Ju-hsin *On Mao Tse-tung*. In this official Party publication it was stated:

Mao Tse-tung is China's greatest theoretician, thinker and revolutionary. . . . Mao can truly be regarded as a genius such as never before has appeared in Chinese history . . . (He) . . . is the truest and most perfect representative of the Chinese people and *a leader of the people of the world.* (Emphasis added.)

The metamorphosis of the Mao-image was astonishingly great. Enormous pictures covering five, six or even ten stories of public buildings; songs, hymns, slogans, eulogies—all propagated the new Mao-image: a giant, a folk hero, a great warrior, a poet-emperor, an Emperor; a Great Emperor; the *omnipotent Mao.*

From this time onwards, his name was often treated like that of an emperor, that is to say it was printed at the beginning of a new line, raised two characters above the rest of the text.

After his move to the Imperial palace of the Forbidden City in Peking his public appearances became gradually more and more infrequent. He was rarely seen by ordinary mortals, save on great ceremonial occasions, surrounded by pomp, heralded by fanfares, on top of huge reviewing stands, high up above the people. From the Yenan cave and from life among the troops and the peasants, the step to the solitary splendour of the Forbidden Palace was very great. Not greater than the change in his public image. By 1950, one year after complete victory over the Chinese mainland, Mao was already well on the way to becoming God. The enormous pictures of his plump, benign, fatherly face (very reminiscent of the ancient fat gods) was seen everywhere. In the homes of simple people his picture ousted that of the kitchen god. The Chinese Communist press noted with approval that it was becoming a habit with the Communist devout among the peasants and workers to say this grace before meals: *"Thanks to Chairman Mao for our good food."*

On November 21, 1950 the report of the Peking Municipal People's Soviet published with manifest approval the suggestion of a peasant:

> Formerly we worshipped Kuan Kung who was said to be omnipotent. Where is his omnipotence? Whom shall we worship? To my mind, we should worship Chairman Mao.[2]

Meetings often started with silent bowing before the huge portrait of Mao which usually covered most of the backstage.

According to the Panchen Lama (October 14, 1959), Tibetans look upon Mao as "their sun, their lodestar and a living Buddha".

At the National People's Congress, the governor of the Yi national minority area said:

> The sun shines only in the day, the moon shines only at night. Only Chairman Mao is the sun that never sets.[3]

Shanghai Communist authorities notified Chinese Christians that

> Gods are those who liberate the people. This is why Stalin and Mao Tse-tung are greater than the empty, hypocritical and negative Jesus Christ.[4]

In the mid-fifties "Mao slept here" shrines were founded.

In a few years Mao—apostrophised by the poet-politician Kuo Mo-jo as "the sun of the human race"—became so Olympian that mingling again with ordinary mortals could no longer harm his cult. The Chinese Communist press and radio from this time onwards carried many reports on the tours of Chairman Mao all over the Chinese provinces. How people's eyes filled with tears of joy when they saw him in their midst! His benign smile, the infinite goodness emanating from him filled everyone with ecstasy!

During 1957-9 Mao's public image grew further. He was godlike, or in fact the greatest of the gods, omnipotent and infallible; and yet at the same time modest, ready to mingle with people. The Peking *People's Daily* summed up popular reaction to one of his tours in the following words:

> . . . This . . . sincere and fervent love for Chairman Mao is something rare in ancient and modern times, and in this country and in places outside China . . . Chairman Mao is like the sun,

[2] "General Report of the Peking Municipal People's Soviet", CB, No. 72, p. 9. Quoted by Ygael Gluckstein in *Mao's China*, London, 1957, p. 379.

[3] *NCNA*, Peking, July 26, 1955.

[4] *NYHT*, January 5, 1952.

giving light wherever it shines. This is a correct statement. Wherever Chairman Mao goes, tumultuous rejoicing follows him and is very much in evidence.[5]

On October 10, 1958, the *People's Daily* stated:

Today in the era of Mao Tse-tung, heaven is here on earth. Once the Party calls, tens of millions of the masses jump into action. Chairman Mao is a great prophet. Through scientific Marxism-Leninism he can see the future. *Each prophecy of Chairman Mao has become reality.* It was so in the past; so it is to-day.

The infallible Mao was getting on in years, and it became important to add to his public image the impression of physical perfection. Reports stated that he looked much younger than his age, that he was full of vigour. The portraits handed out for liturgical use (on giant posters, etc.), showed him stout but healthy, at variance with press photos of diplomatic occasions which showed him as he really is, flabby, enervated, with stooping shoulders.

China Youth News on May 17, 1957, reported that Mao swam across the Yangtze River from Wuchang to Hankow with a dozen young swimmers. Some of them could not complete the twenty-kilometres swim and had to climb on the accompanying launch. Not so Mao, who completed the distance in two hours, non-stop. Later it was reported that Mao swam across the Yangtze three times during this visit; later the figure was raised to seven times.

While the shops all over China were well-stocked with plaster busts, medallions, photographs, paintings and silk scarf images of the Olympian leader, in Communist press reports there were glimpses of him taking part in the work of ordinary people. Bursting with energy, kindness and wisdom, he was invariably the best swimmer, ploughman, shoveller—besides, of course, remaining "the brilliant sun that never sets".

On his resignation as head of the State and Chairman of the National Defence Council, in December 1958, he retained the Chairmanship of the Party. The time that has passed since this event has shown that the worship of Chairman Mao has become more intensive rather than less. All China is busy studying "Mao Tse-tung Thought", his books are the Great Texts and Founts of Wisdom for all ages. Every living soul in China must study them without fail. To make a not sufficiently enthusiastic remark about any of his actions or sayings is high treason. The compulsory ceremonial attitude

[5] *People's Daily*, Peking, November 4, 1958.

to Mao seems to be in harmony with the famous statement of a
renegade:

*"China is composed of five hundred million peasant slaves ruled
by a single God and nine million puritans."*[6]

It was "Mao's China" which announced a territorial claim (not
the last by any means) on Mount Everest in 1960. Soon afterwards
Chinese mountaineers duly erected a Mao Tse-tung statue on "the
summit of the world".

3. The not-so-hidden reality

This book is an attempt to give as detailed an account of "reality"
as possible in one volume. And it is possible to a surprising degree.

Mao Tse-tung—poet, journalist, Marxist theoretician and military
expert—has written a great deal. Besides the four volumes of his
official *Selected Works*, we can study his reports to Party congresses,
conferences, and military councils, not to speak of his very numerous newspaper articles and speeches. Some of his books, articles
and speeches can be studied in two or more versions: as they were
written or delivered originally and as they were "edited" at various
later dates.

Mao, Chu Teh and the other Communist leaders dictated autobiographical accounts to foreign journalists visiting the Red territories
between 1936 and 1945.[7] Mao himself dictated his autobiography
to Edgar Snow in 1936, covering the first forty-one years of his life.
This was published as part of Snow's *Red Star over China* and also
as *The Autobiography of Mao Tse-tung*, in English,[8] Chinese and
Russian.[9] Its trustworthiness can be checked against thousands of

---

[6] Former Communications Minister Chang Po-chun, deposed in January 1958.

[7] Agnes Smedley: *The Great Road, The Life and Times of Chu Teh*,
London, 1956, p. 461. Based on a series of conversations Miss Smedley
had with Chu Teh in Yenan in 1937, and on the notes and documents
given to her by Chu. Nym Wales: *Red Dust: Autobiographies of
Chinese Communists* (*As told to Nym Wales*) Palo Alto, Calif. 1952,
p. 238. Introduced by Professor Robert C. North. Robert Payne: *Mao
Tse-tung, Ruler of Red China* (London, 1951). Based partly on talks
Mr. Payne had with Mao's comrade and childhood friend, Emi Siao
in Kalgan, and on talks with other Communists. Since 1949 thousands of books, pamphlets and articles have been published in Red
China about various phases of Mao's career.

[8] Truth Book Company, Canton, 1938, rev. ed. 1949.

[9] See also: *Mao Tze-dun: Biograficheskiy ocherk* (Mao Tse-tung: A
Biographical Study) Moscow, 1939, p. 101.

various documents and against the accounts given by two close friends of the young Mao: the anti-Communist Siao-yu (*Mao Tse-tung and I Were Beggars*, Syracuse University Press, 1956) and the Communist Emi Siao (*Mao Tse-tung, His Childhood and Youth*, People's Publishing House, Bombay, 1953).

Siao-yu and Emi Siao were bosom-friends of Mao in his "sturm and drang" period. Emi Siao became a Communist who lived most of his life in the Soviet Union. Siao-yu became an anti-Communist who has spent much of his life in Western exile. And incidentally, Siao-yu and Emi Siao were brothers! Their conflicting accounts of Mao's early life were written decades later; they are distorted by the passage of time and by the respective political biases. Mao's autobiography, on the other hand, was dictated nearly twenty years earlier, at a period when Mao did not yet speak of himself as "the towering figure" of centuries. His account of his childhood and youth proves to be quite correct on the whole and the narrative is not devoid of some sense of humour, and even of some mild self-caricature.

Through a curious historical accident there are truckloads of secret documents at the disposal of Western scholars concerning the foundation and early history of the Chinese Communist Party. On April 6, 1927, Marshal Chang Tso-lin's Chinese police and gendarmerie raided the Soviety Embassy compound in Peking to seize the numerous Soviet agents and Comintern "instructors" whose headquarters were in the offices of the Soviet Military Attaché. While the search was proceeding in other parts of the compound, the gendarmes saw dense smoke coming from the former barracks of the Imperial Russian Embassy Guards, then used as the offices of the Military Attaché. It was discovered that the Soviet officials had locked themselves into this building and were systematically burning bundles of documents. The doors were broken down and, with fire equipment rushed to the scene, the flames were extinguished. By the evening seven truckloads of documents had been removed to a safe place. The revelations of these documents caused a real international storm at that time.

For the historians these documents offer a unique chance to study a revolution in action. Most of the documents were really "action-reports", written in great haste on the spot by various leaders and participants of the revolution. Reading them, it is perfectly clear that the writers never expected their reports to be made public, at least without most careful cutting and editing. Besides the action-reports of Russian and Comintern agents, and those prepared by

Chinese CP or Kuomintang members, there were minutes of secret conferences, confidential instructions sent from the Moscow Comintern headquarters, and the frank reports of the Soviet Military Attaché to the Kremlin.[10]

For the organisation of the Third (Communist) International, the Comintern, with its headquarters in Moscow, the Chinese revolution was supremely important. The two official organs of the Comintern, *The Communist International* and *International Press Correspondence* (Inprecor) printed thousands of essays, reports and news-items about the Chinese Communists. The minutes of Comintern Congresses, resolutions, and the instructions sent out to the Chinese CP are available and can be compared with the overt (non-conspiratorial) decisions of the Chinese CP at any given time. The Comintern was only disbanded in 1943. We have also several official histories of Chinese Communism, shorter and longer, and can see how the facts of the past were changed to fit the Party line of the moment.

Dealing with Mao's period of power a somewhat behaviouristic approach is both warranted and possible. Mao's statements about the motives and results of his actions can be checked against factual accounts of these actions. The Chinese Communist press, at least for some years, differed considerably from its Soviet counterpart. From the dailies and periodicals of Peking and the provincial cities and towns an astonishing wealth of trustworthy material can be extracted. From the press of the famous "hundred flowers" period for instance a far more realistic picture can be drawn of all aspects of Mao's tyranny than is generally known in the West. Visiting enthusiasts and even reasonably objective observers, who disregard the material contained in the Chinese Communist press (not only that of Peking but also that of the provinces) give a far more optimistic impression of the successes of the "Great Leap Forward" than the Chinese Communists themselves. Likewise, during the 1958–61 period, the Chinese Communist press, in its totality, contained a far truer account of the initial commune nightmare than any hostile report in the Western press.

During the first decade of Mao's rule, world public opinion has frequently been given two diametrically opposed pictures of the

[10] For the most important documents of the Peking raid, see: *Documents on Communism, Nationalism and Soviet Advisers in China, 1918-1927*, edited by C. Martin Wilbur and Julie Lien-ying How, Columbia University Press, New York, 1956.

Chinese dictator. According to one, Mao was a true successor of China's great scholar-emperors, visionary revolutionaries and warrior-poets; while the other depicted him as an inhuman despot murdering tens of millions in his vain attempts to force his outdated doctrines on reality. Faced with contradictory reports of these types, it was difficult to decide whether the Communist revolution in China, led by Mao, has been the most portentous event of the century or an interlude of pointless mass-suffering soon to be forgotten in the millennial flow of Chinese history.

II

REBEL IN THE FAMILY

Mao Tse-Tung was born on December 26, 1893, in the village of Shao Shan, Hunan Province. His father was a poor peasant who as Mao grew into boyhood, started out on small trading and gradually raised the family status to that of a well-to-do peasant.[1]

The Hunan peasants of Central China have had the reputation, all through their long history, of a sturdy, stubborn and very able people. When, more than 2,000 years ago, Hunan belonged to the feudal state of Ch'u, their neighbours described them as bellicose barbarians. At times Hunan was known as the land of heroes and bandits, at other times as the home of rebellious peasants. But Hunan is also one of China's richest granaries and its peasant-traders have sometimes been described as the Germans of China. According to a traditional saying "China can be conquered only when all the people of Hunan are dead".

Mao Tse-tung's father—a tall, sturdily built peasant—was often described as a typical man of Hunan.[2] To the non-Chinese he certainly seems to embody the traits of an age-old peasant type, with his passion for his land and his grim determination to better the status of his family.

The Mao family lived just as frugally and worked just as hard, if not harder, than the other families in the village. The fear of floods, droughts, famines was ever present in the minds of the peasant. The old ones, like Mao's grandfather, recalled many famines, and indeed a child of ten could remember at least one. No one knew how often the famines hit the countryside. Sometimes there was none for a decade, at times there were only three or four good years. Money and grain must be put aside, the precious tea leaves must not be squandered wantonly. There were mornings when a drink of warm water must suffice.

At the turn of the century, when Mao was seven years old, his

[1] *Bolshaya Sovietskaya Enciclopediya*, Vol. 26, p. 244, *The Autobiography of Mao Tse-tung* (op. cit.) Emi Siao (op. cit.), Siao-yu (op. cit.) Payne, op. cit., and Pierre Fromentin: *Mao Tse-tung—Le Dragon Rouge*, Paris, 1949.
[2] Emi Siao, *Mao Tse-tung, His Childhood and Youth*, p. 2.

family still shared their simple house in the high-walled courtyard with the Tsou family, the dividing line running through the exact middle of the "nice room", used only on ceremonial occasions.[3] At this time the boy Mao lived in their big room with his grandfather, his parents, and his younger brother. They rose at dawn and worked till dusk.

Soon another boy was born and, two years later, a girl. The whole family worked together. The boys gathering firewood, carrying manure to the fields, helping to plant rice seeds. They took turns in sitting on a wicker platform in the fields to frighten the birds away with their screeching.[4] They went barefoot all the year round and in mild weather their only clothing was a pair of blue linen pants.

In recollecting those early days Mao spoke of his father with dislike, saying that as he grew up he learnt to hate his father. Of his mother he had only pleasant memories. She was a gentle, silent, hard-working woman, completely illiterate, but refined in her feelings.[5]

Mao's communist biographer, Emi Siao emphasised the early revolutionary traits of Mao's awakening personality, and showed that, ever since he was five years old, he had been in permanent rebellion against his money-grabbing and cantankerous tyrant of a father.

The boy Mao rebelled against the oppression of his mother by his father, and the demonstration of this inequality between man and wife "sowed the seeds for his later all-out rebellion against the oppressive character of the feudal patriarchal system".[6] As he grew older he found ardent allies in his two brothers and sister in his incessant clash with his father.[7] In traditional Chinese language the mother was called the *Gentle One* while the father was the *Severe One*. In Shao Shan and all over the immensity of China in peasant households, and everywhere else, moral law, custom and etiquette demanded the utmost filial obedience of the children. Tension between the Severe One and his first-born was as usual as the little children's clinging to their meek and industrious mothers.[8] Moreover, we know from Mao that at this time he was just as devout a Buddhist as his mother.[9] And Buddhism is not a creed of rebels.

[3] Ibid.
[4] Robert Payne, *Mao Tse-tung, Ruler of Red China*, p. 26.
[5] Payne, p. 27, Emi Siao, pp. 5-6.
[6] Emi Siao, p. 16.
[7] Ibid., p. 27.
[8] Emi Siao, pp. 5-6.
[9] Payne, p. 25.

In Shao Shan most of the peasants were Buddhist by religion, while their entire life was conditioned by the teachings, customs and ceremonies of classical or Confucian China. The proverb was: "We must do everything as our ancestors did".

When the eight-year-old Mao enrolled in the local school, he started to learn the Chinese characters and, at the same time, "*Li*". This word is often translated as "propriety" or "ceremony", but it meant far more. This *Li* was the sum total of the moral rules, of the canons of proper conduct, the guide to approved behaviour in all the details of daily life. According to Confucius "all virtues have their source in *Li*".

The boys spent long, long hours in school, learning the Chinese characters, endlessly repeating their phonetic values, and later learning long passages from the classics. There they sat hour after hour reciting these passages in a parrot-like sing-song their bodies swaying in rhythm. The passages they had to read aloud as reading exercise and those they were expected to memorise, were maxims from the classics, full of *Li*. They learnt the doctrine of filial piety, for more than 4,000 years the basis of Chinese society. They learnt by heart the three grades of filial piety:

> The highest is to honour the parents by achievement, the lesser is not to disgrace oneself, thereby casting reflections on the father and the ancestors, and the least is to be able to support the parent.

> *Disloyalty to the Emperor is want of filial piety.*
> *Lack of self-respect is want of filial piety.*
> *Insincerity to friends is lack of filial piety.*
> *Lack of bravery in battle is want of filial piety.*

In every detail, *Li* admonished one to be obedient to one's father, to be respectful to one's elders. *Li* taught one the usages and ceremonies in the daily life of the village. (The Master, Confucius, said: "To cut a tree or kill an animal not according to season is want of filial piety".)

Mao has said repeatedly that he started to hate Confucianism at a very early age.[10] He felt that in the school they were persuading him all the time to be blindly obedient to his father. The Severe One reminded the boy all the time that it was his filial duty to study diligently. At the same time he made the boy work on the farm in the early morning before, and in the evening, after school.

---

[10] Ibid., p. 30.

But as, in time, Mao learnt enough characters to spell out simple romances, he rebelled against working after school and sneaked away with a book whenever he could. One of his favourite books was *Shui Hu Chuan* (*All Men Are Brothers*).[11]

Its heroes fought against the mighty to help the masses of poor peasants. They organised the oppressed peasants into guerilla-like bands, fearlessly attacked the landlords and shared out the spoils among the poor villagers. They meted out rough justice, helped the people and defied authority. The revolutionary strategy of these rebels indeed might have influenced Mao and the other Communist leaders, most of whom read *All Men Are Brothers* at an impressionable age.

The master who taught the Confucian *Analects* and the *Four Classics*, was a severe disciplinarian who often beat the boys.[12] Once, when he was ten years old, Mao ran away from school and did not dare to return home, fearing that his father would beat him even more violently. He wandered for three days before he was finally found and brought back to the village.[13]

There was no privacy at home or in the fields. Every word one uttered, every movement one made was constantly discussed, or at least noticed. He always felt his father's eye on him. He believed that his father viewed his thin, lanky figure with distaste. He was not as strong and sturdy as his father, and he failed to realise, at that time, that his father did not want him to become an even richer peasant, or even a "small landowner", but a successful merchant in the city. The elder Mao was glad his eldest son was a good scholar. Knowledge of the classics was of the most immediate practical importance to a trader. The elder Mao had once lost a lawsuit thanks to an astutely turned classical quotation by his adversary before the Chinese court. He wanted his first-born to raise the family status even higher with his knowledge—good, practical knowledge—and waxed furious when he found the boy reading romances.[14]

During the frequent scenes between father and son, young Mao was reproached for his laziness and his unfilial conduct. When his father showered curses and Confucian quotations on his head, the boy answered with other classical quotations urging elders to be

[11] Siao-yu, *Mao Tse-tung and I Were Beggars*, p. 6.
[12] Emi Siao, p. 8.
[13] Payne, p. 25.
[14] Payne, p. 33.

kind and affectionate toward their children.[15] When his father told him off for slowness while carrying two basketfuls of manure on a bamboo pole to the fields, or when the old man was dissatisfied with the amount of hoeing his son did, the exhausted boy again produced passages from the classics exhorting parents to set a good example by working harder than their children.

In the evenings the young boy nursed his grievances and read the classics just to equip himself with a new arsenal of Confucian quotations for further polemics with his father.

This constant nagging and hurling of classical maxims at each other often led to violent quarrels. All the male members of the Mao family were hot-tempered and violent. Storms flared up constantly without relieving the suffocating atmosphere.

In order to avoid his father's curt reprimands Mao had long bursts of working most diligently at farming or book-keeping tasks. Then, knowing that he had done all that was expected of him, he would relax in the shade of a tree, reading one of his favourite books. His father would "catch him being lazy" at such times and abuse him violently, while the young boy would be full of impotent anger and suppressed tears in the knowledge of the monstrous injustice of the attack. Self-pity, burning anger, great determination to master the situation alternated with periods of boyishly romantic day-dreaming.

Out of school, all his waking hours were controlled by his stern taskmaster of a father. In school where he was a respected member of the little school community he was happier. There he could forget about filial duties, learn about the China of the past and have long debates with his schoolmates about the present and the future.

It was fascinating to read of the overthrow of emperors and dynasties after they had "exhausted their mandates from heaven". Most of the twenty-four dynasties had come to an end during a "time of troubles", very similar to that in which Mao and his schoolmates were growing up. Change and reform and rebellion were in the air.

At the turn of the century when Mao Tse-tung reached his seventh year, the "Old China" of petrified traditions was in an advanced stage of decay. The Dynasty had "lost face" hopelessly. Since the middle of the nineteenth century China had suffered

[15] Ibid., p. 27.

humiliation after humiliation at the hands both of the European powers and of Japan. After the Anglo-Chinese opium war and the great T'ai P'ing rebellion of peasants in the middle of the century, certain high-ranking officials had tried to strengthen and modernise China by introducing the most important attainments of Western technology without even thinking of transforming China into a modern state.

Millions of young Chinese were still being taught the traditions, the customs and the world-view of the old Confucian and Dynastic China, when from the great coastal cities the powerful world of the "foreign devils" and the awakening China of the reformist rebellious intellectuals were mounting their manifold attacks.

At school the children learned that China was the centre of the world, the most splendid and powerful empire, vastly superior to the insignificant foreign countries of the barbarians. These barbarians were only fit to pay tribute to the Chinese Empire and acknowledge its suzerainty. Yet ever since the war with the British, China could not resist the onslaught of foreigners. In the Sino-Japanese war of 1894-5 China suffered a dismal defeat. The foreign barbarians proved to be superior in power and knowledge. Imperial China was forced to grant special privileges and rights one after the other to the British, the Russians, the Germans, the French and the Japanese.

In 1898 the Empress Dowager deposed the young Emperor who tried to reform that system of government which had hardly changed during the last 4,000 years. Filial piety had been the foundation of Chinese society since the time of the Emperor Shun (2285-2205 B.C.). The Empire itself was regarded as one great family and the authority of the Imperial Government was but an extension of that paternal authority to which all children were bound to yield absolute obedience. The rules and ceremonies of *Li* perpetuated the system by depriving everybody of any spontaneous public or private action.

The last fundamental reform in China had been introduced roughly around 200 B.C. when the feudal system and hereditary nobility were virtually abolished and replaced by the government of scholar-bureaucrats called *mandarins* since the time of the Manchus. From the Tang era onwards this ruling élite was selected by competitive examination. The candidates had to pass very stiff examinations, mainly in the Confucian classics and in the art and ethics of government. Excellence of taste, brilliance of style, gentlemanly moderation, serene conservatism were all just as important as thorough knowledge of the classics and the traditions.

For many centuries the Chinese mandarinate was regarded by the outside world as the most superior form of government. It seemed to be and often in fact was a real meritocracy, a rule of the intellectual élite. But this élite had the classics as guide to thought and action. It was a most static and conservative guide. Anyone who deviated from rigid Confucianism was disqualified from government office. The system and the subject of the examinations barely changed in 2,000 years. Neither did Chinese society.

All power, all virtue, all guidance emanated from the Emperor, who ruled by a mandate from Heaven. He was the Son of Heaven and the representative of all mankind (both the Chinese and the foreign barbarians) in his rôle as the only mediator between Heaven and Earth. He alone, with his ritual sacrifices, could influence the forces of nature. In paying homage to him, one paid homage to Heaven, to the gods, to the natural order of things and to the *mores* of Chinese civilisation. Everybody under the sun was a devout servant of the Emperor and performed the Great Kotow: the three kneelings and nine prostrations—Chinese and barbarians alike. All barbarians who had any sense wished to learn the civilised (that is: Chinese) ways. They sent delegations bearing tribute. They came "to be inwardly transformed" by remoulding themselves to the civilised pattern. The Son of Heaven was the great father of all mankind.

The Emperor ruled through the bureaucrats, the "keepers of the principles of civilised living". This small body of supreme administrators was recruited as was the military leadership from the large class of landed gentry. Only the members of the landlord class had the means and the leisure to learn the classics and prepare for the great examinations. Economically and also politically it was the landed gentry who controlled the peasantry which was conditioned to be loyal to the gods, to the Emperor, and to the *status quo*.

Since the great reform 2,000 years ago, whenever a new dynasty was established through a peasant revolt or a military *coup d'état*, some abuses in tax collection and in other matters were rectified, but the system went on. There was a return to "normal" times. "Abnormal" times came when because of a great population increase or natural calamities a series of famines swept through the land. Times of trouble followed and the dynasty was deposed. In normal times, as long as the people did not encroach upon the Emperor, the monarch would not interfere.

There is an oft-quoted song, recorded for the first time allegedly at the time of Emperor Yao in 2307 B.C. which runs:

> *When the sun rises I labour,*
> *When the sun sets I rest,*
> *I drink from the well I have dug,*
> *I eat from the fields I have tilled.*
> *What matters imperial power to me?*

The Chinese peasants truly felt that Imperial power had nothing to do with them. They were kept in their oppressed state and China was kept immutable, not by Imperial decrees but by the age-old ceremonial regulations of behaviour, by a universal conformity which was taken just as much for granted as the change of the seasons. Even the very industriousness of the peasantry was along the lines marked out by authority and tradition. The peasants were perfectly unaware of the fact that in obeying the rules and ceremonies of "proper behaviour", they were obeying the oppressive Imperial rule. Looking above them, they saw that everywhere in the social hierarchy, everyone obeyed the particular dictates of *Li*.

The Imperial Government was galvanised into manifestly oppressive action only when the need arose to suppress a rebellion or punish some non-conformist intellectual. Punishment was then extremely cruel.

In this static traditional system, science and technology could not develop. Chinese ingenuity invented gunpowder, paper, printing and the mariner's compass. But these inventions were absorbed by the traditional pattern. For centuries thousands of tons of gunpowder and paper were used annually to avert malignant *demons* by burning mock paper money and by exploding fire-crackers. The compass was used mostly to find auspicious grave sites for the family. The art of printing was used to perpetuate the system, not to improve or develop it. Public discussion—except the discussion of the beauty and wisdom of the classics—was anathema. The Empress Dowager in 1898 was inspired to an angry outburst when the introduction of modern newspapers was suggested to her. "The public discussion of affairs of State in newspapers is a monstrous impertinence and ought to be suppressed."

And now the fundamental change of the system was an urgent necessity if China was to avoid disintegration. After the collapse of the anti-foreign "Boxer" rebellion, foreign troops were permanently quartered in Peking as Legation guards. Foreign power was everywhere. Foreigners financed and built railways, roads, ports, they established and administered the customs, the network of posts and telegraphs. China could regain her complete independence only by complete modernisation. But this could be attained only through Western financial and technological help which entailed further debts and further entrenchment of Western influence.

In 1905 finally the old system of recruitment for the mandarinate was abolished by Imperial decree and a decision was made on paper to introduce a system of primary schools, middle schools and modern colleges. But Mao, and the overwhelming majority of Chinese youth, still studied for years in the traditional schools and heard only vague rumours about the wonders of modern education.

On October 10, 1904, when Mao was eleven years old, the birthday of the Empress Dowager was celebrated with the burning of incense. On the same day troops were marching through the villages to Changsha, where a rebellion had broken out.[16] Describing what he had heard of the revolt, and the massacre that followed it, to Edgar Snow,[17] Mao stressed the lasting effect that it had had on him and implied that it had started his eleven-year-old self on the road of a dedicated revolutionary. Yet both his own account and those of his childhood friends show that then and for two or three years afterwards he still took for granted the fundamental assumptions of Confucianism. Like most of the young peasant boys in the remote villages, he was a decent person in the traditional Chinese sense. He was "loyal". Along with being truly "filial", loyalty to the Emperor was one of the most important tenets in traditional China. Loyalty to the Emperor contained and expressed the feeling of devout patriotism, to the "natural order of things"; obedience to age-old customs; the love of peace and order and the contempt for dangerous and untidy disorder.[18]

At this time Mao Tse-tung still went with his mother to Buddhist ceremonies, singing the Buddhist hymns and making such a devout impression that his mother hoped he might become a priest. There are signs that the boy's fervent Buddhism was perhaps, in a way, an unconscious act of defiance against his irreligious father. The passivity of Buddhism, however, turned the boy slowly against his mother's creed. He dreamt of becoming a great hero who could save

[16] Payne, p. 28.
[17] Edgar Snow, *Red Star Over China*, pp. 131-2.
[18] Payne, p. 28.

China. As his scepticism increased, his mother hoped that he would be a great teacher some day.[19]

Another incident of his childhood which left a deep impression on Mao was a rebellion of a secret society in his own village.[20] Secret societies had existed in China since time immemorial. Most of them were conspiratorial defensive leagues of the common people to help their members against oppression by corrupt officials. Many societies were secret leagues of discontented peasants, labourers, vagabonds and bandits. Members had to swear never to betray the society and to carry out all of its commands. The oath of fidelity pledged loyalty until death. Betrayal or disobedience was punished by death. After the Manchu conquest, the most important secret societies worked for the overthrow of the foreign dynasty and the restoration of a Chinese one. There were others of a most rebellious nature. In one the ceremonial oath contained these sentences:

> The Supreme Being charged us to destroy the evil contrast between crushing poverty and excessive luxury. Father Heaven and Mother Earth had never given to the few the right to abuse—for their own satisfaction—the property of the millions.

The members of these societies were mostly ignorant and illiterate peasants and labourers. Propaganda among the people was conducted by oral tradition. Political propaganda was also conducted by means of crude, *commedia dell'arte*-like impromptu playlets. In these open-air theatre performances an actual situation then important would be enacted, mainly to cause discontent or to urge to revenge.

Towards the end of the nineteenth century, conservative mandarins, city merchants, rich villagers, revolutionary intellectual and all sorts of ambitious people started to join these secret brotherhoods. Some joined to defend themselves against possible attacks, some to gain power and influence, and the revolutionaries became members because it was next to impossible to organise insurrections in a given district without the active participation of these ubiquitous and most powerful organisations.

In Mao's village the schoolboys knew a lot about secret societies and they tried to guess who were the influential members.

A new and bitter period started for the boy Mao in 1906, when at thirteen he left elementary school. He was now completely at

[19] Ibid., p. 27.
[20] Ibid., p. 30.

the mercy of his father, having to work a full day on the farm and
keep the books at night.

At the age of fourteen Mao was very tall, almost as tall as his
father, and strong.[21] He could carry great basketfuls of manure,
slung at each end of a bamboo pole on his shoulders. The fields
were a long way from the house, yet Mao carried twenty basket-
loads of manure to the fields every day. He was always in a hurry
to finish his day's task, so as to be able to read at peace.

His father, worried by his son's frivolous reading, hoped that an
early marriage might set the boy right. The breeding of sons to
carry on the ancestral cult was anyhow a most important duty, and
marriage for boys had to be arranged at the earliest possible age.
The elder Mao chose for his son a plain and sturdy peasant girl.
Mao Tse-tung was not enthusiastic about acquiring a wife, whom
he naturally could not see before the wedding feast. He was not
yet fifteen when the day arrived. The last act of the very long and
elaborate marriage ceremony was the lifting of the bride's veil, so
that the young groom might at last see her face: and Mao did not
like what he saw. We do not know if the girl came to live with the
Maos or not.

In this period his interest shifted from the past to China's present
troubles. Of course no newspapers reached the village. Modern
newspapers had been but recently introduced into China and there
were very few even in the cities. Imperial edicts on payment of
taxes, conscription or special celebrations, were read aloud by the
schoolmaster to the assembled villagers and posted on the school
building. Real news was brought by occasional travellers or by
"radical" books and pamphlets. They all dealt with China's troubles,
humiliations and technological backwardness.

His grievance against his father merged with his grievance against
the foreigners humiliating China, and against the Emperor for not
being strong enough to withstand it. The foreigners with their troops
were there in the capital and in the great coastal cities. China was
not entirely subjugated, only constantly humiliated. It was not an
out-and-out colony, yet there was the oft-quoted notice put up in
the park of the Shanghai Bund: "Dogs and Chinese not admitted".

In 1908 when Mao was fifteen years old the Imperial government at last seemed to wake up. A "Nine Years Programme of Preparation" was promulgated. Between 1908 and 1917 China was to be
gradually modernised by reforms of administration, education, taxa-

[21] Siao-yu, p. 6.

tion, the introduction of local self-government, and similar measures. At the same time the proposed "Principles of Constitution" raised hopes of a constitutional monarchy. But all these proposed measures seemed to come too late. More famines and revolts in the district, news of further beheadings, of hunts for escaped rebels and of new national humiliations showed the urgency of the situation.

There was also news of the intellectual awakening and new schools in the distant cities. Mao Tse-tung hated his life as a farm labourer and part-time book-keeper, with less rights *vis-à-vis* his father than the hired farm-hand had. The family home, with its hundreds of monotonously recurring daily tasks, was for him like a prison. He wanted to escape and resume his studies. But Mao Senior resisted. Sending his son off to study meant double expense: his keep while studying, with school fees, books and all, and his replacement at the farm by a paid labourer.[22]

There were quarrels, the boy ran away from home again and lived for a time at the house of a school-friend. After his return his father offered to apprentice him to a rice shop in one of the neighbouring towns. At first Mao welcomed the idea as a chance to escape from paternal restrictions. But then he heard about a new modern school in the immediate neighbourhood where besides the classics they taught some of the new Western knowledge.[23] He argued with his father that by continuing his studies he would be of much more profit to the family than with his work on the farm. After days of discussion and heated quarrels the elder Mao at last gave in and the boy left his family for good.

[22] Siao-yu, p. 11.
[23] Ibid., pp. 9-10.

III

LOOKING FOR A ROAD

I

The sixteen-year-old Mao looked like a mature labourer when he presented himself at the gates of the "modern" primary school of the neighbouring town. He carried his belongings in two bundles, tied to the two ends of the bamboo pole carried like a yoke on his shoulder. His blue cotton tunic and trousers, his large sunburnt face, the inelegant pigtail on his head, his work-roughened hands were those of a peasant. The gate-keeper was at first reluctant to let him pass, and the well-dressed little boys, his later schoolmates, made fun of the adult labourer who wanted to study with them. Here he was not the son of a rich villager but a ridiculous and very poor country bumpkin. In order to learn the new knowledge of the West he had to swallow the humiliation of studying with much younger boys.[1]

After the first few days however he found his place. He made friends, among them the two Siao brothers. He did well in his studies and continued with his voracious reading. At school he studied new subjects such as natural science. His teachers seemed to approve of him, of his ambitious nature, and of his fervent patriotism. Mao's best friend of this period, Emi Siao, describes the political education of the school. Each morning when the students gathered for roll-call, the headmaster would speak of China's troubles, how she was "being bullied" by the foreign powers, firing his students with indignation and exhorting them to prepare for great efforts to save the Empire from decline.[2]

It was in this new school in 1909 that Mao first heard of the death of the Emperor and the Empress Dowager a year previously. The students, Mao apparently included, did not relinquish hope that the new Emperor would put things in order. They still took it for granted that all the problems of China could and should be solved from above by a genius of a ruler.

New worlds opened up for the sixteen-year-old boy. Like many

[1] Siao-yu, pp. 18-21.
[2] Emi Siao, p. 19.

of his friends, he too dreamed of great deeds, he too wanted to lead armies and "build up his nation". (At this time and for many years to come, the European concept "nation", for which no word existed in Chinese, meant for Mao and his contemporaries simply "race". He dreamt for years of making the Chinese race mighty and victorious again.) He told Emi Siao:

> We need more great people like these. We ought to study them and find out how to make China rich and strong and so avoid becoming like Annam, Korea and India.

Such sketchy information as he had gathered on the history of other countries weakened the boy's belief in the natural universality of Chinese customs and institutions. There were other and very strange ways in which human civilisation could develop. He learned that, though in culture China was by far the oldest and best developed country, there were quite important attainments in other parts of the world too. The students were warned, however, by some of their masters that the importance of the new knowledge of the West should not blind them to the superiority of Chinese civilisation. They were often reminded that Chinese civilisation was already old and highly refined at a time when most of Europe was still peopled by half-naked barbarians.

It was a shattering experience when it turned out that there could be other basic assumptions about the nature and purpose of Man and Society than those which had governed China for thousands of years.

In Confucian China it was quite naturally taken for granted that men were created unequal. The "inalienable rights" of individuals with which their creator was supposed to have endowed the foreigners was a most difficult concept to grasp. Government for the people by the people seemed to be quite an attractive maxim, but on closer examination it proved to entail many unnatural and disturbing elements. It seemed wrong, impractical and disorderly that government should be by the consent of the people, who hold a great variety of contrary convictions. There is obviously only one *right* way of doing things, only one *right* order and meaning of things. The professional ruling group has to have this right knowledge. The naturally omnipotent state has to enforce the right knowledge. Even according to the new knowledge of the Westerners there can be no two right solutions for a problem in mathematics or physics. Such a right solution has to be found and enforced in politics too.

The Western idea that states are sovereign equals, regardless of their age, size and importance, was also difficult to get used to. Surely it was in the natural order of things that smaller and less important states should be eager to acknowledge the suzerainty of great powerful states.

The histories of the Western countries were full of exotic ideas and concepts like "liberty" for which there was not even a word in the Chinese language.* The more one listened to explanations and descriptions of "liberty", the more confused one became. Some teachers equated it with the Chinese phrase for "unrestricted licence", while others said it was just as important as "wealth".

According to Emi Siao and to Mao himself, after about a year they grew dissatisfied with this provincial school. Siao-yu on the other hand maintains that Mao's cantankerous nature made him increasingly unpopular. During debates he would fly into violent rages. On one occasion a fellow student ridiculed Mao for his blind faith in anything printed. It turned out during the debate that Mao believed every word of the historical romances he read, seeing no difference between novels, legends and factual books on history. The debate turned into a quarrel and Mao, furious at finding himself in the wrong, threw a chair at his opponent.

As he was older and far stronger than his schoolmates, they not only disliked but also feared him:

> The feelings of fear and animosity which he had stirred up in the . . . school were so strong that Mao finally decided to leave for good. One day, he packed up his simple belongings and set off on foot for Changsha, the capital city.[3]

Mao does not mention this incident in his *Autobiography*, but states that he was longing for the city of Changsha so he *walked* there and gained admission at the modern secondary school there.[4] His Communist friend, Emi Siao, tells a different story. According to this, the two friends first walked to a senior primary school in Siangtan, but the headmaster there rejected Mao because of his height. The two friends then took a Siang River steamer to Changsha, where he was permitted to enrol as a student of the secondary modern school.[5]

Changsha, like the whole empire, was in a revolutionary ferment.

* See page 54.
[3] Siao-yu, p. 26.
[4] Snow, p. 136.
[5] Emi Siao, p. 22.

i

Here Mao Tse-tung read a newspaper for the first time in his life. Even its title filled him with excited enthusiasm. It was called *People's Strength* (Min Li Pao) and its pages emanated a strong faith in the possibility of regenerating China. The newspaper was the organ of the famous Dr. Sun Yat-sen's *Unity League*,* a secret league of various nationalist and democratic organisations. This league and the movement it led wanted to oust the Manchu dynasty, establish a republic and equalise landownership. The dynastical system would be replaced by that of "parliamentary democracy", a new concept difficult to grasp.

For Mao and for all the students who streamed to the cities from the backwoods, bringing with them their great respect for the printed word, such information on how to solve the problems of China was not so much points of view to be considered, as revelations of exact knowledge, vital "new knowledge", similar to the laws and discoveries of exact science.

And moreover there was none of the timidity and passivity of Confucianism, Taoism and Buddhism in the adherents of this national revolutionary movement. It already had its legends, heroes and martyrs.

The greatest hero was Sun Yat-sen himself. Everybody talked about him, legends grew up around his person. He was the man of the future with a great revolutionary past. And what was most important for Mao at that time, Dr. Sun was a master of the new knowledge of the West. Born in Southern China in 1866, Sun Yat-sen grew up in Hawaii and was educated at the American School in Honolulu, from which he went to Hong Kong to study medicine. He worked as a doctor in various hospitals there and gave up medicine only when he decided to dedicate his life to China's regeneration. He organised secret societies to save China. First he looked for help among the more enlightened and prosperous overseas Chinese communities. His activities were considered so dangerous that the secret agents of the Chinese imperial police trailed him across continents. Dr. Sun travelled a great deal in Europe and Asia, always hunted by the secret agents of Peking. In 1896 in London these agents kidnapped him and took him to the Imperial Chinese Em-

* Mao speaks about this League as "Alliance Society". Its full name was however Chung-Kuo Ko-Ming Tung-Meng Hui (The United Revolutionary Party of China), generally known as Tung Meng Hui (United League), the term "revolutionary" being omitted for obvious reasons. It was moreover not a party but a secret league, modelled on the secret societies of China.

bassy in Portland Place. He was to be smuggled out of England on a Chinese ship to be executed in Peking. But a Chinese servant at the Embassy conveyed a letter from Dr. Sun to his friends in London, who appealed to the British Government. There was an exchange of diplomatic notes and Dr. Sun was saved to resume his revolutionary activities. Until 1911 he led or inspired no less than thirteen revolutionary expeditions against the Manchu dynasty, mainly from Hong Kong and from French Indo-China. No failure could discourage him and now his victory seemed to be imminent.

All this inspired Mao to his first venture in journalism. He wrote an article, advocating that Sun Yat-sen should be at once recalled from abroad to become the first President of Republican China, and pasted it on the school wall.[6]

The brighter the republican future seemed to glow, the darker China's past appeared to the students. They pitied the millions and millions of peasants living for ages in abject poverty, ignorance and superstition. The people of China—so they thought now—were exploited by the luxury-loving, debauched Imperial administrators and by the bad landlords. In their most desperate revolutionary moods the students could even find words of contempt for the "oldest culture of the world". Chinese culture seemed to them to have been petrified through countless centuries. The genius and creative power of the Chinese people had been bound for ages and deformed, like the feet of Chinese girls. This culture was retarded by the princes, the scholar bureaucrats and their gentry, none of whom ever did any useful work. Their enormously long fingernails were the symbols of their contempt for useful labour and for the labouring masses. No wonder that the scientific ingenuity of the Chinese mind was never permitted practical expression. No wonder that Chinese inventions never led to the "new science of the West". The keepers of Confucian dogma wrote their delicate poetry, enjoyed their exquisite surroundings and delicious food, debauched themselves with their countless concubines. To these cultivated gentlemen any thought of change or development was abhorrent. Consequently the people remained in chains, the women remained slaves, the family was a prison, just like the whole of China. And now, when the Western onslaught made change and rebirth an absolute necessity, this system still resisted!

The symbol of the Manchu dynasty was the pigtail. By cutting

<hr>

[6] Emi Siao, p. 23.

off the ridiculous queues on their heads, the students could demonstrate their breach with the evil past.

The eighteen-year-old Mao Tse-tung took part in his school's rebellion against the pigtail. First he cut off his own pigtail, then "he and another student who had done the same thing began to work on others, and clipped off the queues of more than ten people who had previously entered into a 'queue-clipping pact' with them but lost courage at the last moment."[7]

This act was inspired just as much by nationalist as by republican sentiments. The dynasty which had now ruled China for more than 300 years, was by origin Manchu, a Northern people of Mongolian stock. And although the dynasty had quickly assimilated itself in both outward form and spirit to traditional China, many of the higher officials, military governors and even officers and troops, were still Manchus. The young patriots felt themselves to be like those European revolutionaries who rebelled against foreign oppression.

As well as to Dr. Sun's movement the hope of the young rebels was turned to the new National Army. In the disastrous Sino-Japanese War of 1894-5 China had no regular army in the modern sense. The organisation of a New Model Army was started in 1901 but ten years later it had still no more than thirty divisions. The divisions of this National Army, especially those stationed in Southern China, were infiltrated by thousands of "awakening intellectuals", and they represented just as revolutionary a break with traditional China as the newspapers or modern high schools and universities.

On October 9, 1911, there was a bomb explosion in Hankow and some revolutionaries were summarily executed. The next day the revolutionaries in the neighbouring town of Wuchang, on the other side of the Yangtze River, forced the local commander of the National Army to "raise the banner of revolt". In two days the National Army rebels had driven the Manchu governors out of Wuchang, Hankow and Hanyang. The rebellion spread like wildfire. In a few days, the great Southern city of Nanking was in rebel hands. Sun Yat-sen, who was in America, was recalled and on December 29, 1911, was elected provisional president of the Chinese Republic. In Peking, however, the Imperial Government still resisted.

Mao Tse-tung, a well-known revolutionary at his school since the pigtail episode, was one of the first to join the National Army. Be-

[7] Emi Siao, p. 25.

fore joining he witnessed a battle and saw the victorious National troops replace the Manchu Imperial flag with the white *Han* (Chinese) flag on the top of the military governor's headquarters.[8] A student army was also organised, but Mao joined the regulars. The Emperor had not yet abdicated and it seemed to Mao that only the regular army could liberate the whole of China. He went through basic training, waiting to fight for China.

Being a student, he helped to educate the other soldiers. In these days the traditional scrolls with classical maxims were replaced in China by placards and wall-newspapers. The most frequent slogans were: SET CHINA FREE! . . . OUT WITH THE MANCHUS! . . . SET UP REPUBLIC! . . . EQUALITY IN LAND! . . . FREEDOM FOR WOMEN! . . .

The road to follow seemed to be clear. It led to enlightenment, harmony, order through the application of the new knowledge and the liberal customs and morals of the West. But first the revolution had to be victorious all over China. The Imperial Government in Peking still wielded power over the north and parts of Central China. Everywhere armies were organised. There were enthusiastic preparations. Then came an anticlimax. Sun Yat-sen's victorious national revolutionary government in Nanking opened negotiations with the strong man of the Imperial Government, General Yüan Shih-kai. This Imperial general was the original organiser of the New Model Army, many divisions of which remained loyal to him. The majority of the Unity League forced Sun to negotiate with Yüan, although he warned them that this general could not be trusted. But Sun had to offer General Yüan the presidency of the republic if he persuaded the Manchu dynasty to abdicate. On February 12, 1912, the dynasty abdicated, the Imperial Government resigned, and Yüan became President of the Chinese Republic. China was "unified", the provisional government in Nanking was dissolved. Liberal democracy—so it seemed—was victorious throughout China. The Unity League—against Sun's advice—was transformed into a political party: the Kuomintang (National People's Party).

Mao, like countless thousands of other students, thought that the revolution was over, resigned from the army, and returned to Changsha.

The victorious new knowledge of the West was taught by now in hundreds of new schools. The mushroom growth of these institutions led to advertisement campaigns in the newspapers to catch

[8] Ibid., p. 27.

the eye of the demobilised students and the peasant boys streaming
into the cities. Mao recounts in his autobiography his own wavering
when faced with the many possibilities of study. Incidentally in so
doing, he shows the shallowness of his revolutionary fervour in the
nineteenth year of his life.[9] He registered in quick succession for
entrance to a police-academy, a soap-making school, a law school,
a business school, and lastly in a higher commercial school run by
the government.[10]

In the latter he actually spent a month and left only because
nearly all the lessons were in English and he did not think he could
learn the language quickly enough. He next tried the First Provincial Middle School where he stayed for half a year. Finally, he
decided to educate himself.[11] For the next six months he spent
his days at the Hunan Provincial Library, reading the most important books he could find. According to Emi Siao, the tall, pale,
plainly dressed Mao was there every morning when the library
doors opened and he read almost without interruption until closing
time. At noon he went out to buy two rice cakes which he ate at
the library table.

He was past nineteen when for the first time in his life he saw in
this library a map of the world. It was an experience which shook
him. A glance at the huge map hanging on the library wall showed
him why foreigners did not regard China as the centre of the globe;
it showed that there were other "great world-centres", great powers,
not as populous as China, but some of them, like Russia, apparently
larger in territory than the country of the Hans.

When Mao Senior found out that his son had left school and had
as yet found no regular employment, he cut off his allowance. Unwilling to become a manual labourer, he decided to study for a
profession his father would approve of. During the past years he
had often thought that he ought to become a teacher. So, happen-
ing to notice at this time an advertisement for the Hunan Normal
School, where tuition and board were free, he decided to take the
plunge.[12] He wrote to his father who agreed to support him for the
five years' course.

It was only with the utmost reluctance that he wrote asking for
his father's consent and support. During the political turmoil and
the many student discussions he had come to agree with those who

[9] Snow, pp. 139-41.
[10] Payne, p. 45.
[11] Emi Siao, p. 35.
[12] Ibid., p. 37.

thought that the Chinese family-system was the source of all evils. The fundamental way to attack the evils of society—they believed— was to begin with the "family-revolution".

How could there be individuality if the social unit was the family and the clan, not the individual? How could there be "freedom" of the individual if all adults had to be obedient to their fathers, if all property, all money belonged to the family, and even successful middle-aged men could not do what they liked with their property without their father's consent? Everyone was a prisoner in the traditional large family. According to Confucian ethics, and the petrified conventions, for a son to leave his parents and establish an independent small family of his own was immoral and unfilial. How could there be "progress" if all important matters were decided by the elderly "Severe Ones", clinging to the iron-clad laws of the old order, steeped in orthodoxy and cantankerous conservatism? It was through paternal authority, through ancestor worship, filial piety and domestic slavery that the old order had been kept intact for so many centuries.

His hatred for his father, the bitter years spent in "the prison of the family", made it difficult for him to write in a respectful manner to his father, who was to "buy an education for him". But being a realist, he saw no other road to a higher education.

II

"Awakened China" was also looking for a road to follow. During the five years from 1912 to 1918 that Mao Tse-tung spent in the Changsha Normal School, a long series of violent battles was fought out between the forces of old Confucian China and the adherents of democracy.

Very soon after the victory of their revolution, China's radical intellectuals found themselves again forced on to the defensive. In 1911 when their revolution achieved its formal victory, there was no doubt whatever as to which road to follow. China had to be modernised. This meant the introduction of modern railways, communications, modern industry and commerce, modern education and modern agriculture and of course—*the* modern political system. As there was only one medical science, so there was only one modern, effective and efficient system of government: *parliamentary democracy*.

It was this system, so the radical intellectual *knew*, that had made the Western countries rich and powerful. This system was spreading all over the world. It was obviously the system of the future, with every backward country progressing towards it. Liberal democracy had "enormous face" even among the conservative Chinese intellectuals. After all, it was successful everywhere. The great monarchies and republics of the West all had this system. It was safe and easy to live in constitutional states where the rule of law made everything smooth and orderly.

In 1911 and 1912, before the age of totalitarian régimes and long before the curious lessons of colonial liberation, parliamentary democracy and its humanely liberal ideas, seemed to the Chinese intellectuals to be a system likely to solve quickly all the problems of the country. Dr. Sun Yat-sen himself was not as naïve as most of the awakening intellectuals. He realised that constitutional democracy with a multi-party system could not be established overnight from scratch. According to his programme the victory of the revolution must be followed by a period of gradual transformation. The political revolution must aim at constitutional democracy, but this should be reached in three stages: military government, educative government, and only then constitutional government. Sun also warned his adherents against blindly imitating the various Western constitutions.

But Sun's warnings and qualifications were not generally known. When the revolution was unexpectedly victorious, the majority of Sun's closest followers decided to establish a parliamentary system at once, without going through the two preparatory stages. Sun's proposal to establish first a strong military government was rejected by the majority vote of his own League. This was not generally known either. The overwhelming majority of the "awakened" students, intellectuals and revolutionary citizens expected instant miraculous solutions from the formal introduction of constitutional democracy. Their disappointment was great and bitter when they found that their democratic revolution had let loose on the country a hierarchy of military despots, from the new president downwards.

In an effort to restore law and order General Yüan, as the president of the republic, tried to build up a centralised administration and a unified army. After the collapse of the Imperial Government, the vast country was in the hands of sundry new and not so new war-lords. These ruled the provinces quite independently, fought local wars, supported political movements of their liking and were mainly interested in enlarging the territories under their sway. Yüan's National Army was far from strong enough to defeat and disband the armies of the war-lords, nor was the treasury rich enough to bribe these generals to accept central rule. And although some of these war-lords were former bandit leaders, the only way out was to legalise their position. So President Yüan appointed them officially as governors of their provinces and they in return formally recognised the Central Government.

This was of course, nothing more than a face-saving manoeuvre. The only thing that was legal about these new governors was the governmental seal on their appointment papers. They disregarded most of the old and new laws, ruled at will, imposed taxes at will and withheld contributions from the central treasury. "Bad land-lords", money-lenders, corrupt entrepreneurs flourished, almost as healthily as the roaring trade in opium.

Real parliamentary government was abolished before it had even a chance to function properly. Yüan, the former Imperial general soon started to plot for the restoration of the monarchic system, with himself as Emperor. Radicals, republicans, national revolu-tionaries were out of favour in Peking. The Cabinet of the "Republic of China" was completely subservient to General Yüan. At the end of 1913 this Cabinet outlawed Sun Yat-sen's party as a seditious organisation. The liberals and radicals found themselves outlawed by the government which they had brought to power.

Early next year Yüan ordered all Chinese subjects to worship Heaven and Confucius formally. A series of press laws limited the freedom of writing. At the end of 1915 Yüan abolished the Republic and declared himself Emperor. His death in 1916 put an end to this first monarchical interlude, leaving behind an anarchy of war-lords under which China had to suffer during the next fifteen years. Yüan had been Emperor for only eighty-three days, and the next successful attempt at restoration, in 1917, kept an Emperor in power for twelve days. But these attempts indicated that many of the war-lords aspired to the throne.

These petty and not so petty despots with their ever-changing coalitions and campaigns against each other brought only chaos and suffering to the Chinese multitudes, and persecution, prison and execution to the radical intellectuals. In the dangerous state of anarchy, honest trade fell away. Commerce—outside the great coastal cities—was conducted by brigands and smugglers. Instead of progress, in many parts of the country, the worst practices of the old order were revived. The danger of famines became much greater because the war-lord governments failed to carry out even the one basic duty that all Chinese governments of the past had attended to: the upkeep of the irrigation system. Many of the important canals and their networks silted up.

Sun Yat-sen and his entourage had escaped to Japan in 1913, when their movement was banned by General Yüan. During the following years this small general staff of the national democratic revolution returned several times to power in the coastal cities whenever one of the war-lords offered them an alliance. Sun Yat-sen constantly appealed to the West for help. As his revolution was inspired by the political ideas of the West, he was convinced that the West would in fact help. Each time he returned to power, he set up a provisional government, and appealed for help for his political and military campaigns. Then the war-lord in question would realise that the democratic transformation would not serve his own quest for power, or he would be deposed by some other general hostile to the democratic leader. Dr. Sun's group would then go into exile or underground. They would again beg the Western governments to extend neither financial nor political support to the Peking reactionaries and the long series of war-lords. All his appeals were unsuccessful.

Towards the close of the First World War when the Wilsonian principles of the self-determination of nations were proclaimed, the followers of Dr. Sun and all the democratic intellectuals, became more optimistic again. They hoped that after the victory of the Western powers, China too would be "made safe for democracy". They hoped that China would regain her full sovereignty, that the Western powers would give up their extraterritorial rights in the Chinese cities and would renounce their various economic privileges while help would be forthcoming for China to regenerate herself on modern, democratic lines.

III

At sixteen Mao Tse-tung had been an overgrown peasant lad, with red knuckles, work-hardened hands and a face browned by sun and wind. He carried his belongings tied in bundles on a bamboo pole. When as a young man of twenty he entered the gates of the Changsha Normal School, he looked like the thousands of other earnest young intellectuals who were about to change the fate of China. His face was pale, the looseness of his features gone. His hands were white and soft, with very long sensitive fingers. He was dressed in an austere and very long grey gown, and carried carefully wrapped packages of books and newspapers. His unruly jet-black hair was constantly falling over his broad, high forehead.

Although many of his classmates were a year or two younger than he was, he no longer felt a ridiculous outsider in this community of young men, as he had felt in the other school four years earlier.

At first he found it hard to submit to the very strict school regulations. He had to get accustomed to a severely scheduled life. Sharp trumpet blasts marked the times for getting up, entering class-rooms, reading-rooms, the school canteen and the dormitory. Ten disciplinary officers looked after more than 1,000 students. Mao hated the trumpet calls, especially when they interrupted an interesting conversation. He complained about the regimentation, but the intellectual atmosphere of the school was so stimulating, and some of the subjects so fascinating, that he was able to resist the appeals of all other schools advertised in the newspapers.

According to Communist hagiographical writings about his youth, Mao emerged in school as an all-round genius. Emi Siao, the Communist of the Siao brothers, wrote at length about the fervour with which Mao studied the natural sciences. His anti-Communist brother, Siao-yu, on the other hand, recalls that Mao had very little talent or understanding for mathematics and the other exact sciences. He had no head for learning languages either. According to Siao-yu, Mao received no marks at all for English and only five out of a hundred for mathematics. He told Edgar Snow that he wanted to study the social sciences and got bad marks for the natural sciences which did not interest him.[13]

Mao was, however, so good at the then all-important essay-writing that he was considered a good student. This is recalled even by Siao-yu who has a far poorer opinion of Mao's talents than the enthusiastic Emi Siao.

The teacher who made the strongest impression on him during his first year at the Normal School, was Yang Chang-chi, who had taken his degree in philosophy at Edinburgh University. This man, a philosophical idealist, taught ethics, philosophy and psychology and under his influence Mao wrote the best essay of his school career entitled "The Energy of the Mind". This essay, completely alien to any sort of materialism, let alone Marxism, was based on a belief in absolute moral principles and in the power of the mind.

Professor Yang was in the habit of inviting some of his best students to his house for meals and long conversations. Mao Tse-tung soon became a member of this circle. Sitting at Professor Yang's table, eating the excellent meals prepared by Mrs. Yang, they were not quite immune to the charms of the professor's daughter.

---

[13] Snow, p. 142.

Although the Yang home was modern, when the ladies entered, they just bowed their heads, but never addressed them. The professor's daughter was small in stature, delicately built, with a charming face and pearly white skin. Siao-yu recalls:

> We ate our meals rapidly and in silence, not one of us ever uttering a word. Naturally we did not ignore each other. We could hardly act as if no one else were at the table, and sometimes our vision crossed, especially if two of us started to help himself (or herself) from the same dish at the same time. We communicated only by means of our eyes and eyebrows, but never smiled at each other.[14]

Moreover, at the Normal School they had several very talented and attractive girls as colleagues. Three of the most brilliant girls shared many of the convictions of Mao's group. Soon Mao fell in love with one of them.

In his autobiography Mao's purpose was to illustrate his political development. Understandably, he forgot his romantic moods, the long walks in the beautiful countryside, when two or more friends would compose poems on the beauties of nature. Ever since this period Mao has remained susceptible to poetry and all through his life he has gone on writing poems, even in the most unlikely circumstances.

It is true of course that in the urgency of the Chinese situation, driven by their ambition to take a leading part in the salvation of their country, he and his friends strove to be superhuman and talked mostly about "large matters".

Their ideal was the serene and dedicated philosopher-athlete. During the winter holidays they tramped through the fields, up and down hills, and crossed rivers. They slept in the open on frosty nights and swam in cold rivers. During one of the long summer vacations, Mao Tse-tung and Siao-yu in order to test and harden themselves, walked across the vast province of Hunan, quite penniless. Siao-yu described this curious venture in his book, *Mao Tse-tung and I Were Beggars*. But the young wandering scholars did not have to beg often, the peasants fed them and gave them a place to sleep in most villages. Next summer Mao and another friend went again on a "self-hardening" tour, in simple linen dress, sandals, and carrying umbrellas with towels wrapped around them.

During another summer holiday Mao lived with two of his friends

[14] Siao-yu, p. 42.

in a rickety little mountain hut. Professor Yang had brought back
from Edinburgh methods of living in a "democratic" and "scientific"
manner. He urged his students to mix with the people and lead an
austere life. He advocated meditation, deep breathing, cold baths
all the year round, and doing without breakfast. Consequently Mao
and his friends gave up breakfast *and supper*. They climbed on
empty stomachs each morning to the hilltop for long seances of
silent meditation and came down much later for a swim in the
river. Emi Siao describes their method of "voice training":

> They would go to the hills and shout, or recite the poets of the
> T'ang dynasty, or climb up the city walls and there inflate their
> lungs and yell to the roaring winds.[15]

These young men, studying furiously, forcing their minds and
bodies to harder and harder accomplishments, were an exceptional
group at the Normal School, but such exceptional groups sprang
up everywhere in China.

In 1915 a new periodical, called *Youth* (later *New Youth*) was
published in Shanghai, with a manifesto which launched a new
movement. It was called "Solemn Appeal to Youth" and was written
by Ch'en Tu-hsiu who years later became a Communist and the
first General Secretary of the CCP. Ch'en wrote:

> The Chinese compliment others by saying, "He acts like an old
> man although still young". Englishmen and Americans encourage
> one another by saying, "Keep young while growing old". Such is
> one respect in which the different ways of thought of the East
> and West are manifested. . . . The function of youth in society
> is the same as that of a fresh and vital cell in the human body.
> In the process of metabolism, the old and the rotten are inces-
> santly eliminated to be replaced by the fresh and living. . . . If
> metabolism functions properly in a society, it will flourish; if old
> and rotten elements fill the society, then it will cease to exist.
> According to this standard, then, is our society flourishing, or is
> it about to perish? I cannot bear to answer . . . I merely, with
> tears, place my plea before the fresh and vital youth, in the hope
> that they will achieve self-awareness, and begin to struggle.
> . . . What is the struggle? It is to exert one's intellect, discard
> resolutely the old and the rotten, regard them as enemies . . .
> keep away from them and refuse to be contaminated by their
> poisonous germs. . . . To use to the full the natural intellect of

---

[15] Emi Siao, p. 42.

man, and judge and choose among all the thoughts of mankind, distinguishing which are fresh and vital and suitable for the present struggle for survival.

. . . Oh, young men of China! Will you be able to understand me? . . . We must have youth if we are to survive.[16]

The manifesto, and the entire periodical, gave the programme and the basic principles which were to guide Young China in regenerating the country. Its effect was tremendous. The first issue was sold out instantly and it had to be reprinted several times. It was copied out in longhand, it was posted on walls, sent by post, each copy was read to shreds. "It came to us," one of the readers recalled later, "like a clap of thunder which awakened us in the midst of restless dream."

Mao Tse-tung was a faithful reader from the start. He was very proud when the April 1, 1917, issue published an article of his ("A Study of Athletics") on the importance of hardening one's body for the struggle of youth. The article, written in the classical style, was signed by the pen-name "The Man of Twenty-eight Strokes". (Mao's name is written with twenty-eight brush strokes.) In their violent revulsion against the Confucian family many students at this time discarded their family names. It seems that Mao, too, toyed with this idea.

During the summer of 1917 Mao wrote to a number of students in the various schools of China, asking them to contact him for patriotic work. By this means and through personal contact, Mao gradually built up a group of followers. He started to correspond with many students and young intellectuals in other cities of China and, in 1917, with a number of friends he founded the *New People's Study Society*.

The pattern with which the world was to grow more familiar later in the twentieth century, was already discernible in the China of 1917. Political revolts against the local despots led by students and intellectuals and brought to victory by the fight of the exasperated peasants resulted in the rule of some military figure or other, who soon turned into a despot himself. The students and intellectuals had their revolutionary experience, the soldiers had power. The masses proved to be unruly and cared more about the satisfaction

[16] *Youth*, Vol. I, No. 1, September 15, 1915. (Quoted in Chow Tsetsung; *The May Fourth Movement*, Harvard University Press, 1960, p. 74.)

of their concrete demands, than for the principles of liberalism and democracy.

There were many among the students who came to believe that the real and immediate need was not so much to learn a lot as to become good practical politicians. Sun Yat-sen could command country-wide enthusiasm, but his followers were not well enough organised for him to remain in power. The real task was to master the techniques of organisation and the techniques of *keeping power* after a successful revolution. Mao too regarded study as only a means to an end. Now that youth was clearly so supremely important, he wanted to become a youth-organiser and youth leader. He was eager to gather round him a large number of able, hardened and, last but not least, faithful followers. He already thought that his special talent lay in his knack of organising groups.

Although Siao-yu was elected secretary of the New People's Study Society, Mao was a prominent member and soon became assistant secretary. Of the more than seventy members of this group many became, years later, leading members of the Chinese Communist movement. For the time being, however, they were still enthusiastic adherents of "Mr. Democracy", just as the revered editor of *New Youth*, Ch'en Tu-hsiu was before his acceptance of Communism. As late as 1919, Ch'en still urged his readers to attack "Mr. Old China" for the sake of "Mr. Democracy". He wrote in one of his editorials:

> In order to support Mr. Democracy, we are obliged to oppose Confucianism, the code of *Li*, chastity, traditional ethics, old politics. And in order to support Mr. Science, we are compelled to oppose traditional arts, traditional religion; and in order to support Mr. Democracy and Mr. Science, we just have to oppose the so-called "natural quintessence and classical literature."[17]

Mao Tse-tung's *New People's Study Society* was only one of the innumerable new alliances and societies founded by the militant young intellectuals all over China. They were all ardent newspaper readers, Mao very much included, and bombarded each other, in letters and in articles, with various blueprints for the future. The last violent clashes between Mao and his father were caused by Mao's extravagance in spending a third of his allowance on newspapers and books.

During Mao's fifth and last year at the Normal School, his mother

[17] *New Youth*, January 1919.

died. Now the paternal home was for him nothing but the centre of the evil Confucian "big family", the prison of the individuals, a fortress of the bankrupt old order. He did not break with his father; he simply lost all interest in him.

Just as he was preparing to graduate, he read about a chance to study in France—a "work and learn scheme" which sounded most attractive. After graduation in 1918, Mao borrowed some money, as he could not or would not approach his father, and with a few other France-bound Hunanese students set off for Peking to learn a smattering of French.

It was this twenty-five-year-old self—open-minded, full of thoughtful uncertainty—which Mao described later as a confused person, still looking for a way.

IV

AT THE CROSSROADS

"Western people used to say that China has 'masses' but no 'society' and that since Chinese 'society' is more than two thousand years old, it is a type of society which does not meet modern needs. Facing the matter honestly, this is not untrue. Consider our evil and inferior customs which are dead rules for dead things cruel and contrary to human nature! There is no path left for human expression. We human beings are like dogs and sheep, not conscious whether we are living or dead. . . .

"Real learning gives one individuality and independence. The Renaissance and Reformation in the Western world show how scholars there declared their independence of tradition. . . . Through this magazine we desire to co-operate with students . . . throughout the country to fight for spiritual emancipation. Our hope is . . . that they will have personality enough to conquer our society rather than to be conquered by it."

(*New Tide*, Peking, January 1, 1919, quoted by Chow Tse-tsung, op. cit., pp. 59-60.)

I

The nine Hunanese students who travelled with Mao from Changsha to Peking in the summer of 1918, were full of excitement and enthusiasm. They were all bound for France under the work-and-study scheme. After learning a smattering of French they would go by steerage to France where they would earn their keep and school fees by working in factories, as dishwashers or anything. They would join the thousands of Chinese students who were already in France through similar schemes, and they would have an opportunity of organising the tens of thousands of Chinese labourers who had been sent to France as China's contribution to the war-effort of the Western powers.

But Mao who had helped to organise the France-bound work-and-study group was staying behind. He had borrowed enough money for his railway fare to Peking, but in the capital he had to look for work at once. He could not raise enough money to pay for his steerage passage to Europe. From his unsuccessful attempts at learning English, he knew that he was not a good linguist. So he decided to remain in China.[1] Although he was a little sad and even envious, he too looked forward to the years to come.

His plans had a lot to do with the political situation. The First World War was nearing its end. The adherents of New China all hoped for a Western victory, which would entail the restoration of China's sovereignty and the coming to power of the national revolution of the democrats. The Peking government and most of the war-lords were backed by the arch-enemy, Japan. In 1915 Japan had occupied Shantung Province, the "cradle of the nation", the "Holy Land of China" where Confucius and Mencius had been born and had taught; the Chinese masses felt its occupation deeply. Moreover Shantung was both economically and strategically most important. The victory of the Western democratic powers, the victory of the Wilsonian principles, would give Shantung back to China along with all the important coastal cities. After this, democracy would be even more popular and the anti-democratic governments and war-lords would lose face.

Most of the intellectual leaders of the democratic movement lived and worked in Peking, and Mao Tse-tung hoped that he would find scope there for his political and journalistic activities. He hoped to get many adherents for his New People's Study Society, to organise hundreds, nay, thousands of students. He looked forward to meeting the leaders of the various important "new thought" and "new tide" movements, to joining the most important societies and alliances. He wanted to go on with his independent studies, but first of all he wanted to test himself as an organiser of men.

Although he was quite penniless when he arrived in the capital, he was in high spirits. While his France-bound colleagues had to spend long weeks grappling with the French language, he was glad to be free for other and politically more profitable pursuits.

Peking was at first a shatteringly great disappointment. His former mentor in Changsha, Professor Yang, was now teaching at Peking National University, and through his help Mao was given a minor post in the university library. But it was a most unsatisfactory, even humiliating position. According to Siao-yu, Mao's task was to keep the library clean and the books tidy.

With his Hunanese friends he rented a miserable little two-roomed house near the university. One room was used as a study, the other as a bedroom. The bed was a *k'ang*, the typical Chinese peasant "stove-bed", a huge platform, made of bricks and heated

[1] Siao-yu, p. 170.

by a fire underneath, such as Mao had slept on in the parental home. And although the elder Mao was stingy, their *k'ang* was always passably warm in the winter. Now far up north in Peking, during the icy winter months, Mao and his friends had no money to keep their *k'ang* warm.

Siao-yu recalls that seven of them slept together on this cold bed, and that the seven of them had only one overcoat between them. They took turns to go out. By the end of the year two other collective coats were bought, but Mao did not manage to buy a coat for himself.

He was lonely, tired, morose and very conscious of the shabbiness of his only gown and of his "lowly" southern dialect. The others were progressing with their French studies, they were building their future, while he had not managed to establish any interesting new contacts. In his dark mood he was even too shy to visit Professor Yang's house.

His frustrated existence was in violent contrast with the hopeful ferment going on in Peking, just as his bleak surroundings seemed even more drab amidst the many splendours of the great Imperial city.

This was the setting of his short anarchist period. He read Bakunin and many anarchist pamphlets describing the twelve commandments of Chinese anarchism: atheism; renunciation of family names; refusal to hold government office, to join any political party, to become a member of parliament, or to enlist in the armed forces; abstention from alcohol, from nicotine, from hiring servants, from riding in rickshaws or sedan chairs; and vegetarianism. The anarchist proposals for the solution of China's problems were drastic: violent overthrow of the order and the rebuilding of the country without any central government and as little local government as possible. It is clear from his own account, given to Edgar Snow, that for a time Mao was much attracted by anarchist ideas.[2]

His interest in anarchism decreased after two or three months when he began to make more friends, and principally when he started to visit the Yangs. He was then already a member of the Philosophy and Journalism Societies and was attending classes in the university. He made friends with one of the lecturers in the Journalism Society, "a liberal, and a man of fervent idealism and fine character". His other new friends were adherents of the New Tide movement. These men, full of proselytising zeal, appreciated

[2] Snow, p. 149.

earnest young men of Mao's type. He no longer felt an outcast in Peking. And very soon he embarked upon one of the happiest periods of his life.

In the Yang home, as a sign of the new times, the ladies started to take part in conversation. Yang Kai-hui, who had developed into an attractive intelligent girl of original views, shared many of Mao's convictions, and she, too, wavered at this time between liberalism, anarchism and utopian socialism. The other students who occasionally visited the Yangs soon noticed that these two had fallen in love with each other.

Mao Tse-tung looked his best at this time. He was tall and very thin. His face was not yet fleshy; his high cheekbones, emphasised by the hollowness of his cheeks, his domed forehead, thick eyebrows, and earnest black eyes, gave an impression of strength and dedication. His well-moulded lips, small for a Chinese, were always tightly closed when he listened. Most of the time he was almost too austerely earnest. All the greater was the contrast when his eyes suddenly softened and a boyishly enthusiastic smile lit up his face, exposing his small, very white teeth. It was an engaging smile.

Mao's friends also noticed that the "thing" was serious between Kai-hui and Mao, that they were planning to marry, although they did not announce their engagement.

After his hard and unhappy childhood and the privations of his youth, after the grim loneliness of his first Peking months, Mao was happy. He would marry a girl of his own choice, an emancipated, modern girl, and would set up a small, independent family of his own.

It was during this happy period that on November 11, 1918, the First World War ended with the victory of the Western powers. All China was jubilant. Even the Peking government declared a three-days' holiday. On November 17, there was a victory parade in which many tens of thousands took part, among them all the rebel intellectuals, like Mao and his friends. The day after the victory parade the Peking intellectual leaders founded the *New Tide Society* to guide and organise the intellectual revolution which was to sweep over China.

Mao Tse-tung's New People's Study Society was counted upon to work for the New Tide in the important Hunan province. During the next few months Mao had an increasingly important rôle as student organiser and a member of the New Tide movement.

II

On January 1, 1919, when the editor of the *New Youth* called on young China to fight for "Mr. Democracy", the New Tide Society brought out the first issue of its monthly, *New Tide*, which had the English sub-title: *Renaissance*. The programme of the movement left no doubt that it was to be a democratic renaissance, aiming at a society of independent individuals.

During this period of hope hundreds of more or less important periodicals were launched all over China. Some of them became quite influential, others had an all too short existence. Their titles were characteristic of the times: *The Dawn, New Hope, Citizens, Weekly Critic, New Society, New Man, Freedom, Save the Nation, Progress of Youth, New Woman, Woman's Clarion, Hope,* etc.

But all too soon "Mr. Democracy" gave China its first great shock. At the end of January 1919 the Japanese delegate to the Paris Peace Conference reminded the Big Four in plenary session that in 1917 Great Britain, France and Italy had signed a secret treaty with Japan, pledging "support to Japan's claims in regard to the disposal of Germany's rights in Shantung". They were rights of the colonialists!

The cradle of the nation was in danger. And moreover if Great Britain, France and Italy supported Japan's claims to a great sphere of influence in China, what of Chinese sovereignty? What about China's general demands to the Peace Conference?

China was demanding from the great Western powers the renunciation of all spheres of influence or interest; the withdrawal of all foreign troops and police forces from China; the relinquishment of the "leased territories"; and the return to China of all foreign concessions and settlements.

Everything depended now on Woodrow Wilson, the President of the United States and his democratic principles. Would America, and the public opinion of the Western world, support China or her enemies? Would they, in effect, support democracy or the enemies of democracy in China? Would the Western powers, by the betrayal of their often proclaimed democratic principles sentence China to perpetual loss of sovereignty and to a continuation of the horror of the war-lord era?

On the first two days of May 1919 the news came that the Peace Conference had decided against China. Woodrow Wilson was one of those responsible for this decision. A typical quotation gives an impression of the impact of this news on Chinese youth:

> When the news of the Paris Peace Conference finally reached us we were greatly shocked. We at once awoke to the fact that foreign nations were still selfish and militaristic and that they were all great liars. . . . We could no longer depend upon the principles of the so-called great leaders like Woodrow Wilson for example.[3]

China was shocked by other revelations too. It turned out that in 1918 the Peking government, in exchange for a secret loan from Japan, had "gladly agreed" to Japan's position in Shantung. This "glad agreement" made it far easier for the Big Four at the Peace Conference to back the Japanese side.

On May 3, 1919, a meeting of student representatives of all the universities and colleges of Peking decided on an all-out struggle against the Paris decision, and for the return of Shantung, of Tsingtao and all the Chinese cities. One of the students cut his finger deeply with a knife and wrote on the wall with his own blood the slogan: *Return our Tsingtao!* The students decided on a mass demonstration to be held the next day. Next morning about 5,000 students and others marched to the legation quarter to get American and European diplomats to intercede for China. The demonstrators shouted such slogans as: "Down with power-politics", "Down with secret treaties", "Down with Japan". But the legation quarter was guarded by foreign troops who refused the demonstrators entrance. Infuriated by this reminder that Chinese citizens were debarred from entering a quarter of their own capital city, the demonstrators set out to find the traitors, those members of the Peking government who were primarily responsible for selling out to Japan. One of these was the Minister of Finance, whose house the demonstrators wrecked and set on fire. They attacked other houses, beat up various officials, threw stones and clashed with the police. The traitors escaped to the Japanese Embassy.

All the time the demonstration grew in numbers and in fury. The police had fired once or twice into the air and used their rifle butts on the demonstrators. Groups of students were dragged away to police custody. The sound of firing, the news of the arrests, and the stupendous news of attacks against government buildings, set the

[3] Quoted in Tsi C. Wang, *The Youth Movement in China*, New York, 1937, pp. 161-2.

city in turmoil. The fighting lasted till the evening. The government declared martial law in parts of Peking.

The "May Fourth Incident", which soon grew in retrospect to a tremendous historical occasion, and came to be regarded as a starting point of the second stage of the Chinese revolution, had an immediate effect on the rest of the country. Students in Shanghai, Nanking, Tientsin, Wuhan and all the other cities and provinces rose in solidarity and indignation over the arrests.

Although the main fury of the movement was directed against Japan and the pro-Japanese Peking government, and against its supporting clique of reactionary bankers, landlords and former mandarins, the infatuation with the "new learning of the West" too came to a sudden end.

It was not only that with the Paris decisions China was to remain a semi-colony shared out among a handful of great powers, or that Japan could encroach upon very large and important territories of the country. The lethal chaos of the war-lord era had hit China like a long series of irregularly recurring typhoons. A way had to be found out of the chaos.

People had turned to democracy at the start of this period as a technique for escaping from chaos and anarchy. But democracy as a technique and a method did not help. Neither did the great democratic powers. Respect for the right to free expression of individuals, of the various political groups and parties was a fine democratic thing. But it made the democratic camp in China into a huge mass of "loose sand". This camp could inspire the people to heroic fight, to great mass-demonstrations; but it found no method of preventing ambitious generals from grabbing political power. Parliamentary democracy in China was barely beyond the infant stage. Her modern press, her modern education were also in their infancy. This democracy had as yet found no method for keeping political power.

III

Mao Tse-tung had left Peking four months before the May Fourth incident. In January 1919 he had suddenly decided to accompany some France-bound students to Shanghai and then to get somehow to Changsha, the capital of Hunan, where he hoped to start his large-scale political activities. The New Tide Society did not send him officially. They were glad to hear that this eager and earnest young man was returning to Hunan with plans for important work for the cause, but they did not finance his trip. Mao had no idea how he would cover the enormous distance between Peking and Changsha. He had a railway ticket for less than one-tenth of the way. During the trip he borrowed some money and soon found himself in Shantung province, where for some days he travelled on foot as a wandering scholar. He could not resist the opportunity of visiting the holy places of China.[4]

From Shantung it took him nearly six weeks to get to Changsha where he arrived in March 1919. He had to borrow money twice to cover his railway fares. In Changsha he found the cheapest lodgings possible and, living on one meal a day, of broad-beans and rice, he started his activities.

His real chance came when the news of the May Fourth Uprising threw Changsha into a ferment. Mao at once assumed the rôle of the student leader. He had an organisation, the New People's Study Society, which had gained scores and scores of new members since his return: he could talk about his connections with the Peking leaders of the New Tide movement, he had journalistic abilities. People forgot that he was only a high school graduate and looked upon this twenty-six-year-old man as a seasoned radical. He founded the *Hsiang River Review,* as the organ of the revolutionary students of Hunan and, as editor and leader writer, his name soon became known in revolutionary circles. The editor of the Peking *New Tide* wrote that the *Hsiang River Review* was one of the five or six best magazines of China, ranking with the famous *New Youth* and the important *Weekly Critic.* Mao's editorial in this paper, entitled "The Great Alliance of the People" advocating the unification of all the radical organisations of students, workers, merchants and intellectuals, had a real influence in South China.[5]

Mao was also the co-founder of the Changsha *Cultural Book Store* for the sale of radical newspapers, pamphlets and books.

From then on Mao Tse-tung had some standing in national politics as one of the revolutionary leaders of the large and important Hunan province. *His* organisations attacked the Hunan war-lord, demanded his removal, sent delegations both to Peking and to Dr. Sun Yat-sen in the south for support. After a student strike in protest against the war-lord, Mao's *Review* was banned.

During the latter half of 1919 Mao went to Peking and to Shanghai as the delegate of his organisation to negotiate with various

[4] Payne, pp. 60-1.
[5] Cf. Chow, op. cit., p. 348.

leaders of national importance. The Hunanese revolutionaries
wanted autonomy for their province. In Shanghai he again met
Ch'en Tu-hsiu, the famous editor of *New Youth,* and head of the
department of literature at Peking National University. Ch'en had
been arrested by the government shortly after the May Fourth Incident and was released only in September 1919, thanks to waves
of mass-protest against his imprisonment. Ch'en gave advice on
Mao's planned *League for Reconstruction of Hunan.* Ch'en, later
the co-founder and first General Secretary of the Chinese Communist Party, was still far from being a Marxist. Two months after
his release from prison he drafted the famous "Manifesto of the
New Youth Magazines", which was approved by all the editors and
published in the December 1, 1919 issue. It was still a democratic
manifesto as the excerpts below will show:

> . . . Our ideal new era and new society are to be honest, pro-
> gressive, positive, free, equal, creative, beautiful, kind, peaceful,
> full of universal love and mutual assistance, and pleasant labour;
> in short, happiness for the whole society. We hope that the hypo-
> critical, the conservative, the negative, the bound, class-divided
> . . . all these phenomena will gradually diminish and disappear.
> . . . We believe that in a genuine democracy, political rights must
> be distributed to all people.[6]

The Hunanese revolutionaries were also working at this time on
the establishment of a democratic régime in their province. After
his return to Changsha, Mao found a teaching job and at the same
time became the head of an "anti-militarist" news-agency. This
propaganda was directed equally against the militaristic governments of foreign countries and against the militarism of the despotic war-lords. The slogan was: "If the world refuses to give up
militarism, China must lead the way in non-violent-resistance."

The movement in Hunan for the United Autonomous States of
China received the support of a "democratic" general. But as soon
as this general managed to oust the hated Hunan war-lord with
the help of the revolutionary democrats, he started to turn against
them. Mao, as one of the editors of the *New Hunan,* and as the
leader of the Changsha revolutionaries, reacted quite violently: he
organised an attack on the provincial parliament.

---

[6] *New Youth.* December 1, 1919, quoted and translated by Chow
Tse-tsung, in his *The May Fourth Movement,* Harvard University
Press, 1960, pp. 174-5.

This frightened the "democratic" general who turned out to be a war-lord like the rest. Betraying his allies who had helped him to power, he became as viciously anti-democratic as his predecessor.[7]

Mao Tse-tung, who had taken part in the negotiations with this general while the latter was still making himself out to be a democrat, had the same sense of personal disillusionment that Sun Yat-sen had experienced so many times. He, too, saw that with this type of mass-movement nothing could be gained as long as the democrats had to rely on generals.

1920 was a year of fulfilment for Mao Tse-tung. He *emerged*. The village boy, who a few years ago had toyed with the idea of becoming a soap-maker, a police officer or a commercial expert, was now a well-known political figure in Hunan, above all in Changsha, the city of his student years. As a radical editor, a student leader and political organiser he was known in important revolutionary circles in Peking and Shanghai. After his friends had departed to France, he became the sole head of the New People's Study Society. He had a large group of enthusiastic and loyal followers. The thousands of students in Changsha respected and liked him. They all knew stories about his student years when with iron determination he had hardened his body and cultivated his mind. And yet he was not simply a grim ascetic functionary, there was romance in his life.

In 1920 he married Yang K'ai-hui, the daughter of his former professor. All of his student friends regarded this as an important event. They spoke of his marriage as an "ideal modern romance". It was in Changsha that these two first started a "trial marriage", which they formalised only when they saw that their marriage would "not interfere with the free development of their personalities". K'ai-hui was not only a lovely girl, but a real revolutionary comrade, a university graduate who could and did discuss all the "isms" with her husband's friends and took part in most of their activities.

In Changsha, Mao Tse-tung was directly or indirectly the mentor and political leader of hundreds of young men and women in their teens or early twenties, who all led the same hectic, almost too full and intellectually and emotionally tense existence. Their childhood and early youth had been spent in a China of civil wars, insurrections and famines. Very few of them had reached their twentieth

[7] Payne, pp. 70-1.

birthdays without seeing emaciated corpses by the roadsides or the heads of decapitated insurgents stuck up on bamboo-poles. Many of them had experienced starvation and danger. People known to them had been executed or arrested. When news came of politicians being assassinated by the agents of some war-lord, it was not something distant and difficult to imagine, for assassinations happened in their own city or district. The constant war between the various military governments and the politicians and intellectuals of New China was *their* war. Its ups and downs affected their own struggle against the local military dictator.

In this situation the various "isms" were considered by Mao Tse-tung and his followers in Changsha not as abstract political theories but as possibly decisive weapons in their own political war. Their revolution—like that of other groups and even of Dr. Sun Yat-sen's Kuomintang—had as yet no clear-cut political programme. Their revolutionary war, fought with physical and political weapons, was also a struggle for the survival of China and for their own personal survival.

No doubt, the leaders and members of the various revolutionary movements and groups had great political ambitions. They all wanted their own movements to become the governing party (which political movement does not cherish such ambitions?). But their hunger for power was for them not only a question of satisfied ambitions but also the question of survival.

In considering the various political "isms", Mao Tse-tung began to pay more and more attention to their effectiveness in helping to build up closely knit, efficient and dynamic organisations. In the last few years Mao had grown convinced that his own particular talents lay in organisation and propaganda. And like all the political and intellectual leaders of awakening China at this time, one question was uppermost in his mind: which of the "isms" offered the revolutionary élite the best programme and method for the dynamic mobilisation, control and direction of the masses? How could this élite transform the ocean of Chinese people into a single tidal wave which would sweep away the old evil system? How could *they* lead the masses to victory for the good of all China?

The mistakes and distortions of the first Chinese translators and popularisers of Western works had influenced the thought of several Chinese generations. The monosyllabic Chinese language, differing as radically as it does from the languages of the West, is an awkward vehicle for the transmission of Western ideas. The absence in

Chinese of hundreds of more or less important words, abstract terms and "self-evident" Western generalisations, made the task of the translators and popularisers extremely difficult, and some of them when coining new Chinese words to express Western ideas unconsciously retained many of the principles and basic assumptions of traditional China. The popularisers of Western knowledge could not but render somewhat distorted versions of various Western teachings. In the 1919-20 "crossroads-situation" the effects of all this could be clearly observed.

Liang Ch'i-ch'ao, the Darwinist and "Spencerist", for instance, was worshipped not only by Mao Tse-tung in his teens but by thousands of other intellectuals who were now active in politics. Liang taught his adherents that in the struggle for survival the individual must be sacrificed:

Whether it be a struggle between individual and individual or race and race, the outcome is that the unfit is defeated and perishes while the superior who is equal to the situation flourishes. . . . In this movement of evolution *there must be a sacrifice of the individual for society, of the present for the future. Therefore the man who grasps at his own immediate profit entirely misunderstands the theory of evolution.*[8]

Liang was for years Mao Tse-tung's favourite author. His actions and writings show that Mao was really guided by Liang's teachings. But in the general disillusionment of the early nineteen-twenties the great democratic leader, Sun Yat-sen, also turned against the idea of individual liberty and the multi-party system.

When in 1905, Dr. Sun had organised his revolutionary Unity League, the oath of the League contained this sentence: "The spirit and the binding principles of our various aims are Liberty, Equality and Universal Love." In his writings and speeches between 1905 and 1915 Dr. Sun showed himself a champion of individual liberty. The next years turned him away from these principles which he had formed and cherished for a lifetime. His disillusionment and great change is indicative of the change in a great many Chinese intellectuals, Mao Tse-tung included. One year before his death, Dr. Sun gave a series of lectures to his adherents in the Kuomintang. Then he had this to say about liberty:

[8] Quoted by E. R. Hughes, *The Invasion of China by the Western World*, New York, 1938, p. 211. (Emphasis in the original.)

If we speak of liberty to the average man . . . he surely will not understand us. The reason why the Chinese really have attached absolutely no importance whatever to liberty is *because that word is but a recent importation into China*. It is understood now only by young people and by those who have studied abroad. . . . But even those do not know exactly what is really meant by liberty.[9]

The Chinese do not know anything about liberty; they are interested merely in acquiring wealth. . . . We have too much liberty, no cohesion, no power of resistance; we are "loose sand". Because we have become "loose sand", we have been invaded by foreign imperialism and oppressed by an economic and commercial war on the part of the Powers. Now we are unable to resist. If, in the future, we want to repulse foreign oppression, we shall have *to break down individual liberty;* we shall have to form a very solidly organised body, and so to say, add cement to the "loose sand" so as to make it into a solid stone.[10]

The liberty of the individual must not be too great, but that of the nation must be unrestricted. When the nation will have freedom of action, China will become a strong nation. In order to attain this end, *all must sacrifice their liberty*.[11]

In 1919 and 1920 study groups and societies for the study of the various "isms" mushroomed in the Chinese university cities. Separate societies were founded for the study of socialism, anarchism, syndicalism and guild socialism. No society was as yet founded for the study of Communism and Bolshevism. The Chinese word for "Communism" (kung-ch'an-chu-i) had been coined by a Chinese anarchist in the early nineteen-tens. Some students and intellectuals had only very vague notions in 1919 and 1920 about Communism and Bolshevism. Political essays were published according to which Bolshevism was a faction of the anarchists while others wrote that the two main branches of socialism are: *Marxist collectivism* and *anarchistic Communism*.

Mao and many of those intellectuals who a year or two later became co-founders and early members of the Chinese Communist Party, in retrospect put a curious smoke-screen around the origins of the Chinese Communist movement. Contrary to the facts, they

[9] Sun Yat-sen, *Triple Demism,* Second Lecture, March 16, 1924, para. 419. (Emphasis added.)
[10] Para. 456. (Emphasis added.)
[11] Para. 462. (Emphasis added.)

tried to show that the future Communist leadership was first converted to Communism by the grandiose intellectual revelations of Marxism-Leninism, and that they proceeded to found the party only after they became convinced Marxists. In fact, among the many factors which drove them toward Communism, the most decisive was information on the methods and techniques through which the Communists seized and kept power.

When the Russian revolution came, the awakening intellectuals were glad to hear of it, vague though the news was. Sun Yat-sen was glad that *"a hundred and fifty million Russians broke away from the Whites and disapproved of the White race's encroaching behaviour"* (Fourth Lecture). But both he and the radical intellectuals, who knew next to nothing about Communist theories, started to pay attention to Russia only when, nearly three years later, the Soviet revolutionary régime still seemed to be secure.

V

THE TURN TO COMMUNISM

I

Nineteen hundred and twenty is one of the Orwellian years in Chinese chronicles. "Facts" and "unfacts" abound, the dates of events are often changed in retrospect and are mixed with "word-facts", to borrow Mr. Galbraith's term for a fictional event that is so often talked about that it becomes a fact-in-words, even though it has never been a fact-in-fact. Communists and anti-Communists all played their part in slight falsifications of history, often without any ulterior motive. Western diplomats and Japanese secret police officials, hypnotised by the Red Bogy, reported Bolshevik machinations at a time when there were none. Chinese conservatives dubbed suspected intellectuals "Communists" when these were still in their liberal or anarchist period. The various Russian agents sent by Moscow to the Chinese cities sent biased progress reports, while the Chinese Communists themselves did their best to hide the reasons why and how they originally became Communists.

Whether the first *Chinese Society for the Study of Marxism* was founded in 1918 (as many Communists assert) or in 1920 (as the documents show), does not seem to be very important. But it is significant for two reasons: China was the first non-white country in which Moscow succeeded in introducing a Communist movement. The methods applied were the same as those used in the case of all non-white and colonial countries. Secondly, the factors which caused Mao Tse-tung to become a Communist, played and are still playing an important rôle in his life, in the Chinese Communist movement, and even in the drama of international politics in the second half of the twentieth century.

Not all Mao's recollections of his own conversion to Marxism, as given to Edgar Snow, are borne out by other evidence. According to Mao it had been largely the influence of Li Ta-chao that had turned him to Marxism at the time that Mao had been working under him in the Peking University Library.[1] But Li Ta-chao was still far from Marxism at the time when he was supposed to have

---

[1] Snow, p. 159.

had this effect on his assistant Librarian. Mao worked under him from September 1918 until January 1919, yet in his first serious study on Marxism, published in the May 1, 1919, issue of *New Youth*, Li Ta-chao was highly critical of Communist theories:

Marx's theory was a product of his time; in his time it was indeed a great discovery. However, *history should not be interpreted forever by this theory* which was formulated at a specific time and under specific circumstances, *nor should Marxist theory be accepted as a whole* and applied uncritically to modern society. On the other hand, we should not disregard its historical value and specific findings. (Emphasis added.)

According to Li, one of the main defects of Marxist Historical materialism was its deterministic, indeed fatalistic aspect. In this, it contradicted the theory of class struggle. Another defect—according to Li—was that Marx did not consider the significance of the Humanist movements in the course of history and disregarded the function of ethics. Thus Li Ta-chao, several months after Mao had ceased to work under him, was in Communist terminology an out-and-out "revisionist". For years Lenin attacked the revisionists as traitors of the working class and enemies of Marxism. Yet Li wanted to "rectify" Marxism. In the same article he stated: "Recently there has appeared in philosophy a neo-idealism which may rectify Marx's materialism and remedy its defects."

For Lenin and his followers any form of philosophical idealism was of course obnoxious bourgeois ideology. Until the spring of 1919, Li Ta-chao either had not read Lenin's philosophical works or did not think of following the Communist road. We had documentary evidence for asserting the same about the editor of *New Youth*, Ch'en Tu-hsiu, whose Marxist conviction was supposed to have had such a deep impression on Mao. Ch'en too, was far from being a Marxist at the time when his Marxist faith was supposed to be so infectious. This can be seen in the December 1919 Manifesto of *New Youth* (see p. 50.)

Li and Ch'en who barely a year later played the decisive rôle in the foundation of the Chinese Communist Party had read only a few of the most important works of Marx and Lenin at the time of their conversion to Communism. None of the founders had read even the first volume of Marx's *Das Kapital* or Lenin's *Materialism and Empirocriticism*. Very few of them knew about Lenin's other works on the strategy and tactics of the Bolsheviks in the "age of imperialism".

This is illustrated by the fact, that according to Mao's auto-biographical account three books were decisive in building up his faith in Marxism: *The Communist Manifesto, Kautsky's Class Struggle* and a *History of Socialism* by Kirkupp.[2]

Mao then was deeply influenced by Kautsky, whom Lenin denounced as an enemy of Marxism. It seems that neither Mao, nor his mentors in Marxism, Li and Ch'en had even heard of the title of Lenin's work published in 1918: *The Proletarian Revolution and the Renegade Kautsky*.

Most Communist sources assert that the first Chinese Society for the Study of Marxism was founded in 1918 in Peking. The articles and manifestoes of the supposed founders show, however, that they did not study Marxism at that time. Moreover, we know that this Society was initiated in March 1920 and after a network of provincial branches had come into being, it was formally established in October 1921, *after* the founding of the Chinese Communist Party.[3]

Most of the founders of the Chinese Communist Party could read no foreign language, and up to 1920 very little Communist literature was available in Chinese.* Lenin was known to Chinese readers only from quotations and a very few articles.

A careful examination of the sequence of events and publications indicate that all those who became the founders of Chinese Communism in 1921 *were converted not so much by what they had read about Communist theory, but far more by what they had learnt about Communist practice.*

They appear to have been converted only after having long discussions with the first two agents of the Communist International who were sent to Peking in the spring of 1920. The two Comintern

[2] Snow, p. 153.

[3] *Peking University Daily*, November 17, 1921.

* A very small part of the *Communist Manifesto* was published in Chinese in 1906. A larger part was published in the students' monthly, *The Citizens*, in the November 1, 1919, issue. The full *Manifesto* was published only in April 1920. Marx's *Wage, Labour and Capital* was serialised in the 1919 May 9-June 1 issues of the Chinpuntang daily, *The Morning Post;* Marx's preface to *Das Kapital* in *The Citizens*, October 1, 1920; Marx's preface to *The Critique of Political Economy* in *Eastern Miscellany*, January 1921.

Apart from these, until 1921 only the following works were translated into Chinese: Engels, *Socialism Utopian and Scientific;* Engels, *Part III of Anti-Dühring;* Kautsky, *Karl Marx's ökonomische Lehren*.

instructors, Grigori Voitinsky, head of the Eastern Department of the Comintern, and Yang Ming-chai, a Moscow-trained Chinese emigrant, arrived in Peking with the aim of contacting left-wing intellectuals and possible Marxist sympathisers.

The two Comintern instructors contacted first of all Li Ta-chao, who a year previously had still been highly critical of Marxist theory. Voitinsky and his colleague gave Li detailed information on the revolutionary experience of the Bolsheviks. Li heard from them a great deal about the methods of Party organisation, about the technique with which a minority group of utterly dedicated and disciplined individuals seized and kept power. The practice of the dictatorship of the proletariat was explained in detail. For Chinese ears it was not at all repugnant to hear about the minority group of Communists (the central leadership of the Party), who establish a firm dictatorship for the good of the country and the good of the people. The Party is justified in dictating because it realises those aims which the majority of the people would desire if they were mature enough and educated enough to see where their true interests lie.

In the frank discussions on Party practice it emerged that the Central Party leadership was in essence a conspiratorial group, very much like the leadership of the Chinese secret societies. This Communist élite had found the strategy and tactics for establishing order out of the post-war chaos in Russia. The Comintern men analysed for their Chinese friends how Lenin succeeded in persuading, cajoling and forcing the masses to pursue his policies.

Li was sufficiently impressed. He introduced Voitinsky to Ch'en Tu-hsiu and his Shanghai group. Voitinsky's headquarters were then set up in Shanghai, where in the foreign settlements meetings could be arranged without danger from the Chinese police.

Voitinsky, and the other Comintern agents who came later to China, taught the Chinese sympathisers Leninist strategy and tactics, methods of penetrating other political associations, of dividing and whittling down all the parties and groups opposed to Communism; the art of tactical compromise and tactical retreat, of exploiting antagonisms within "enemy groups" and the practice of setting up Communist cells.

What Li and Ch'en, and through them the others, learnt about Communism was really a revelation. The Russian Communists—so it seemed to these radical intellectuals—spoke and acted like adults, like master strategists and tacticians of political warfare. They were professors of the revolutionary struggle. With the monolithic Communist Party apparatus, with adroitly manipulated mass-organisations and the Communist methods of dictatorship, there would be no danger of some war-lord grabbing power after a successful revolution.

That the greatest appeal of the Communist message was in Leninist practice, is shown not only by the actions and writings of leftish leaders, but also by those of Sun Yat-sen and his Kuomintang. Dr. Sun and his party were essentially anti-Communist; but when Sun learnt about Communist practice and party-organisations, he rebuilt his Kuomintang on these lines. The Kuomintang took over Communist Party practice without its ideology. It became a monolithic dictatorial party.

Among Sun's followers in the Kuomintang there were conservative nationalists, liberals, radicals and men with socialist leanings. But in the critical period of Chinese history from 1920 to 1925 most of them believed that the dictatorship of a monolithic party-apparatus was the best way out of chaos and anarchy. If a man with Dr. Sun's Western liberal background, and long career as a democratic-nationalist revolutionary, could be converted to the Soviet method, it is no wonder that young men like Mao Tse-tung were eager converts. Sun and his followers on the one hand, and the founders of the Chinese CP on the other, saw nothing unethical in the dictatorship of a small minority in the name and for the good of the vast majority.

The founders of the Chinese CP were by no means a homogeneous group as far as Marxist theory or general political ideals were concerned. Among the many documents seized in the 1927 Peking raid on the Soviet Embassy was the carbon copy of a report sent to Moscow. The title of this Russian document was: "A Brief History of the Chinese Communist Party", and it dealt with the Party's development up to 1926. It was written in the autumn or winter of 1926.

According to this report, at the time of the Russian revolution it was impossible to find anything that could have served as the foundation of a Chinese Communist Party:

Even an embryonic organisation was lacking, since there was no organised group of comrades for the study of Marxism who could at some future time serve as the nucleus of a new mass organisation. China did not even have an organised Social democratic party from which men most devoted to the revolutionary cause could be detached. . . .

Of course there were revolutionaries in China, but they were ideologically far from Marxist. Most of them were either followers of Dr. Sun or anarchists. There were also socialists, however. . . .[4]

The first task of the Comintern agents was to start "embryonic organisations". As there were no real Communists, the first nuclei of the future Party were formed of various leftish intellectuals, mainly anarchists, guild socialists and "a few prominent revolutionaries, most of them old but some young, [who] were interested in Marxism". It was planned in 1920 to organise a group of students under the direction of Ch'en Tu-hsiu to "plant the seeds of a Communist Party in Shanghai".

By the summer of 1920, in Shanghai and Peking, mixed groups of anarchists, socialists and Marxist sympathisers had started to plan the establishment of a Communist Party. According to the report, in Peking "of the eight comrades in the group, six were anarchists and two Communists".

The Comintern agents did not demand ideological conformity, or even knowledge of Marxism. They were satisfied that these embryonic groups started to organise trade unions, study circles, youth leagues, Russian language schools and various front organisations.

Once Mao Tse-tung had been convinced by Li and Ch'en that the revolution could succeed only by Communist methods, he returned to Changsha to convert his own adherents in the New People's Study Society. He founded a Youth Library and formed action groups for "the organisation of the masses". His most advanced adherents helped him to form the "Changsha Society for the Study of Marxism" and the Hunan branch of the "Socialist Youth Corps". Mao had to train a growing number of propagandists and agitators to convince the students of the necessity of a violent revolutionary upheaval. The propagandists were to explain that through the various organisations inspired by the Russian revolutionary experiences and led by Marxists the revolutionaries could seize power by force.

Mao's Study Society organised a demonstration in Changsha to celebrate the third anniversary of the Russian October Revolution. The demonstrators tried to raise the Red Flag, but were prohibited

[4] *Papers Seized in the 1927 Peking Raid, etc.*, Columbia University Press, 1956, p. 42.

from doing so by police, who then suppressed the whole sympathy march. It was Mao's first attempt at political organisation of the workers on Marxist principles.

When, in May 1921, Mao Tse-tung travelled to Shanghai to attend the inaugural congress of the Communist Party, he was already secretary of eight trade unions in Changsha and had succeeded in converting the majority of the New People's Study Society to Communist policies. Mao was one of the handful of delegates who took part in the foundation of the Chinese Communist party.*

The Congress reflected the real condition of the Party at that time. Men of divergent ideas, political outlooks, and frames of mind assembled. The situation of heterogeneity previously characterising the local groups in Peking, Shanghai and Canton repeated itself once more at the Congress. Among the eleven delegates there were: (1) students of socialism; (2) democratic socialists; (3) anarchists; and (4) Communists.[5]

The majority of the Congress, to which Mao Tse-tung belonged, approved Ch'en Tu-hsiu's proposals on Party centralisation, discipline and the Party's ultimate objective: "Seizure of political power by proletarian organisations under the leadership of the Party."

Only two of the eleven delegates disagreed with these proposals, showing that nine Chinese revolutionaries of divergent ideas and political outlook attached far more importance to revolutionary practice than to the intricacies, or even some of the principles, of Communist revolutionary theory. They, Mao included, agreed on the slogan of the dictatorship of the proletariat. In the last ten years they had taken part in a great many "struggle-movements" and now easily accepted Lenin's thesis that a real Marxist extends the recognition of the necessity of class-struggle to that of proletarian dictatorship. From the Party statutes they had just accepted, it was clear to them that proletarian dictatorship would be exercised by the Party leaders (themselves) in the name of the proletariat.

Mao Tse-tung, now twenty-eight, had every reason to feel satisfied with himself. He was momentarily one of the few leading per-

---

* According to Mao (Snow, p. 154), there were twelve founding members; Chen Pan-tsu (*Communist International*, October 1936, pp. 1,361-4) speaks of nine; others maintain that there were eleven, thirteen or fifteen.

[5] Report to Moscow, "A Brief History of the CCP", *Papers Seized in the 1927 Peking Raid*, p. 52.

sonalities of what he thought to be China's most dynamic political movement. He was convinced that he was taking part in a historic meeting.

During the long congress he did not speak often. He listened to the heated debates on points of Marxist theory and on the questions of strategy and tactics. For him, the debates on Party structure, on methods of organisation, had immediate practical importance, for on his return to Changsha he would have to help in the foundation of the Hunan Party, and in the setting up of trade unions and other mass-organisations. His ambition was to become the leader of the Hunan Communists, with sufficient standing and influence in the All-China CP.

His accomplishments during the next twelve months make it easier to understand why he has so little to say in his reminiscences about his private life. He had virtually none. With his wife taking her full share in the work, mainly in organising students and women, and helping to run the cultural front organisations, Mao Tse-tung took Hunan really in hand. By October 1921 the first provincial branch of the CP was set up in Hunan and by May 1922, when Mao made his report as its secretary, the Communists under him had organised twenty-two trade unions, mainly among miners, railway workers, printers, municipal employees and students.

The work was as dangerous as it was difficult. The Hunan warlord government did all it could to suppress revolutionary activities. Two trade unionists were executed in this period. Mao and his staff had to organise innumerable conspiratorial meetings, with security measures against possible police raids.

He rose early, went to bed very late and had to work very hard all the time. He had many trade union and other positions in addition to his editorial activities and his Party secretaryship. And in his "private time" he had to read Marxist theoretical works. He sensed that his organisational skill, and his standing as one of the founders of the Party, would not secure him a leading position without some theory as well. The Party had ordered the translation of certain Marxist works likely to help the Party in winning adherents. Mao tried to overcome his handicap in not knowing foreign languages by reading all the Marxist works that were available in Chinese. But for tactical reasons the Comintern advised the Chinese CP against the translation of many basic Marxist-Leninist works, thereby incidentally ensuring that Mao would remain ignorant of them.

As the Chinese Communist movement grew, Mao's position and importance in the Party started to diminish. From the rank of one of the handful of founding members, he lapsed temporarily to that of one of the 100 or 200 second-echelon leaders. Above him were some Shanghai and Peking intellectuals, some "Muscovites" and already a few representatives of a very important category of leaders: that of the "returned students". Most of these types and categories had initially a sounder theoretical basis than Mao had. Moreover, many of them spoke English or French and so could take part in vital discussions with the chief Comintern delegates. For a long time to come Mao had a barely veiled dislike for both the arrogant Comintern representatives and the well-educated returned students devoid of revolutionary practice.

The Chinese CP is "the most often founded Party". Chinese student-groups in France, Germany, Japan and America "founded" *the* Chinese CP and tried to get in touch with the Comintern through the French, German or other local parties. Two of Mao's trusted lieutenants of later years belonged originally to the returned-student group. Chou En-lai was one of the founders of the Paris Chinese CP, while Chu Teh, later the Commander-in-Chief of the Chinese Red Army, organised the Chinese CP in Germany.

II

On Lenin's instructions, the Comintern agents also approached Sun Yat-sen. The leader of the Kuomintang was first visited by Voitinsky in 1920 and then by some other Moscow representatives. The Comintern's line during the 1920-5 period was to work on many levels in the colonial, semi-colonial and other backward countries. The policy was to support local capitalists against foreign capitalists, to support all "bourgeois-democratic" and "bourgeois-nationalist" movements against the imperialists and against local conservative governments; to teach *some* revolutionary methods to non-Communist nationalist or democratic parties, conclude tactical alliances with these and, at the same time, to form Communist fractions within them. The bourgeois parties and national liberation movements were to draw even the most backward masses into politics, thereby making them sufficiently "politically conscious" to be later receptive to Communist mass-propaganda.

The Comintern representatives, however, took quite a different line with Sun Yat-sen and the Kuomintang leaders, telling them that according to the Soviet Government and the Russian CP *the*

Chinese conditions were not suitable for the Communist system.
What China needed was independence and unity. The Comintern
offered to help Dr. Sun in annihilating the war-lord governments
and establishing his own version of a democratic system. They
cleverly exploited Dr. Sun's thesis that constitutional democracy
could be established in China only in three stages, the first two
being that of a military government and then an "educative government". Clearly, for these two transitional stages Dr. Sun needed
to organise an authoritarian party, a party apparatus capable of
exercising dictatorship—in short, a party modelled on Soviet lines.

In July 1922 the Chinese CP had official negotiations with Dr.
Sun and in August the Communist Central Committee decided
to offer Sun a Communist-Kuomintang alliance. In January 1923
there was a formal agreement between Sun and the Communists,
by the terms of which the two parties formed a united front. Each
Party kept its identity but the Communists could and should join
the Kuomintang as individuals.

Dr. Sun had the assurances of the Soviet envoys and the Comintern representatives that the Communists did not want to introduce
a Soviet-type proletarian dictatorship into China. He was also convinced that he would be able to control the Communist members
of his Kuomintang.

While the Soviet Government and the Chinese Communists
courted Sun and the national revolutionaries, the Western powers
and groups of Western banks supported the Northern war-lords
and their so-called Peking government which at no time had effective control over the majority of the most important provinces,
let alone the whole of China. In 1920 power over the northern
half of the country was divided between three war-lord confed-
eracies* and several lesser war-lords. In the southern half of China

---

* The Fengtien group headed by Marshal Chang Tso-lin, the Anhwei group led by Tuan Chi-jui and the Chihli group controlled by
Wu Pei-fu and Tsao Kun. In addition to innumerable minor clashes,
there was the Chihli-Anhwei war in 1920, the Chihli-Fengtien war
in 1922, and the second Chihli-Fengtien war in 1924. In the same
year there was a major war between the Kiangsu and Chekiang war-
lords. In 1925 war broke out between the Fengtien and Chekiang war-
lords, and there was a split in the Chihli group after which part of the
Chihli group in alliance with the Fengtien group attacked the "National
Army" of the other part of the Chihli group. Most of the wars
among the Northern war-lords were fought in the Jehol, Liaoning,
Hopei, Shantung, Kiangsu, Chekiang and Hopei provinces. The mobilised forces on each side ranged from 100,000 to 400,000 men.

the situation was similar. In Peking itself the "central government" changed hands several times. Between 1920 and 1926 the number of "independent" and effectively controlled war-lord territories fluctuated between fifteen and thirty, and within several of these territories reigning war-lords were ousted by their rivals.

Sun Yat-sen's movement could count on very wide popular support because it aimed at wresting power from all the war-lords. Sun's programme—the *People's Three Principles*—was ridiculed by the propagandists of the war-lords. Sun was called a "madman paraphrasing a dream". In the eyes of the Western governments of the time, Dr. Sun was either a harmless lunatic or a dangerous rebel. Only Lenin saw that Sun was the man who could arouse China, although Sun's principles were quite opposed to Communism. The first of Sun's principles was that of nationalism, through which China was to be a free and independent nation. The second principle was that of democracy. The third was the principle of "people's livelihood", and it consisted in essence of a moderate, gradual land reform, some State control of private capital and industry, and the development of State-owned industry and "State-capital".

Western progressives and democrats were antagonised by Sun's "racism". The Soviet leaders, however, were quick to see that the backward Chinese masses could be drawn into politics by this sort of propaganda:

> If we want to save China, if we wish to see the Chinese race survive forever, we must preach nationalism. . . . What is the present standing of our race in the world? When we compare all the races in the world, we see that we are the most numerous, that our race is the greatest, and that our civilisation dates back more than four thousand years. . . . But . . . our actual position at this time is extremely dangerous. If we do not promote nationalism and weld together these four hundred million people into one strong race, China will face the tragedy of being destroyed as a nation and extinct as a race.[6]

In his Fourth Lecture, Sun Yat-sen told his audience that "the whites try to weaken the yellow race, by attacking nationalism as too narrow and unsuited to the present age", and by preaching cosmopolitan theories.

[6] Sun Yat-sen, First Lecture, Sections 21-23.

But these theories are not to be accepted by a race which has been the victim of injustice. We, the abused race, must first of all recover the liberty and equality of our race, and then we shall be ready to talk cosmopolitanism.[7]

About the same time he sent a young army officer of his entourage, Chiang Kai-shek, to lead a delegation to Moscow to study the Red Army. He asked for military and political advisers and for material help from the Soviets. He particularly wanted an expert in the organisation of an efficient party apparatus.

The Comintern representatives readily agreed with Sun's reiterated statement that "the white race wants to swallow up the coloured races" and that "the yellow race is now oppressed by the whites" (Fourth Lecture, para. 198). Sun for his part agreed that the whites were doing all this from imperialist motives, so, in this phase, Chinese nationalism was given an anti-imperialist and anti-Western character.

In February 1923, Sun Yat-sen again returned to power in South China. He organised a military government in Canton, assumed the position of Generalissimo and proceeded to consolidate his army bases. In these circumstances he needed every kind of help.

Instead of Soviet arms and financial help, the Comintern sent to Canton a man who proved to be far more valuable to Sun Yat-sen than several well-armed divisions. This man, whom Mao Tse-tung learnt to hate, became—under his assumed name, Michael Borodin —one of the most controversial figures of modern Chinese history.

The real name of this veteran revolutionary was M. M. Gruzenberg. The Bolshevik Party had often entrusted him with dangerous work, requiring diplomatic skill and adventurous spirit and very quick wits. Borodin, after graduating from Czarist prisons, worked in the United States, Mexico, Great Britain and other countries. For his activities he had been imprisoned for six months in Glasgow; he smuggled jewels to finance revolutionary activities, worked in the Comintern, travelled as a journalist, a merchant and in many other capacities.

When Borodin arrived in Canton in October 1923 Sun Yat-sen found out within a few days that his new adviser was a veritable walking encyclopedia of practical revolutionary knowledge. Having absorbed the innumerable reports on China and the Kuomintang which Moscow had received during the past few years, Borodin

[7] Fourth Lecture, para. 203.

arrived with concrete plans. A week after his arrival the Kuomintang leadership accepted his suggestions for transforming their party into a disciplined army of political shock-troops, a Party under totally centralized direction, in which the members sacrificed their individual freedom and contributed to the Party all their capacities.

The new Kuomintang Constitution was written by Borodin in English and, after Sun had approved, it was translated into Chinese.

Just as in the Leninist Party, the Kuomintang Party organs at each level had to render absolute obedience to the higher party organs. The Party leader (Sun Yat-sen) was given power of final decision on all resolutions of the Central Executive Committee. Party members were forbidden to discuss any question once a decision had been reached on it, and had to carry out the Party's decisions with unquestioning obedience.

Borodin and his staff organised Sun's government apparatus and his armies on the Soviet pattern. In May 1924 Borodin and the Soviet General Galen (V. Blücher) helped to organise the Kuomintang General Staff School, the Whampoa Military Academy. The first military commander was Chiang Kai-shek, and the academy's political department was directed by the "returned student", Chou En-lai, one of the founders of the Paris Chinese Communist Party.

In 1923 at the time of the third congress of the Chinese CP, Mao was already Secretary-General of the All-Hunan Labour Syndicate. He was the successful organiser of a First-of-May general strike in Hunan, which had shown the increased power of the labour movement.[8] At the Congress Mao was elected to the Communist Central Committee and subsequently moved to Shanghai where he worked in the headquarters of the Communist movement. In January 1924 he attended the First National Congress of the Kuomintang, and from then on he combined his work in the Communist executive bureau with that in the executive bureau of the Shanghai Kuomintang.

His existence as one of the leading members of the Communist fraction within the Kuomintang was a continuous tightrope walk. As a disciplined Communist he had to give limited obedience to his Kuomintang chiefs, while pretending to be fully loyal. The fractions and intrigues in the Moscow Comintern, within the groups of Soviet advisers in China, in the Chinese Communist leadership, and within the Kuomintang—enveloped all the functionaries in var-

[8] Payne, p. 76.

ious more or less dangerous webs. At the same time the Communist-Kuomintang "organisation-men" had to fight the national revolution against the northern war-lords as well as carrying out their manifold daily tasks as politicians, propagandists, trade-union chiefs or heads of educational departments.

It was during the years of the Communist-Kuomintang alliance that Mao Tse-tung first clashed with his erstwhile mentor, Ch'en Tu-hsiu, the head of the Chinese Communists, with Michael Borodin, and, at first indirectly, with Stalin.

VI

THE PEASANTS SHOW THE WAY

"The rise of the present peasant movement is a colossal event. In a very short time . . . several hundred million peasants will rise like a tornado or tempest, a force so extraordinarily swift and violent that no power, however great, will be able to suppress it . . . They will send all imperialists, war-lords, corrupt officials, local bullies and bad gentry to their graves. All revolutionary parties and all revolutionary comrades will stand before them to be tested . . . To march at their head and lead them? Or to follow at their rear, gesticulating at them and criticising them? Or to face them as opponents?"

(Mao Tse-tung, *Report of an Investigation into the Peasant Movement in Hunan*, March 1927.)[1]

Stalin and his Comintern agents on the spot directed the Chinese Communist leaders to follow the peasants, to gesticulate at them, at times even to oppose them. Mao decided to march at their head.

According to the legend carefully fostered by Communist propaganda and credulously accepted in the West for a very long time, Stalin's political foresight and insight were unsurpassable and infallible. This master-strategist of world revolution was supposed always to foresee events correctly and always to adopt the precisely correct course. Even nowadays the fact that in 1949 the immensity of China came under Communist rule is sometimes cited as proof of Stalin's genius in long-term planning. *The fact points to the exact opposite*. Stalin's directives to China very often had catastrophic consequences, and several times very nearly wrecked the Chinese Communist movement. Although Soviet representatives and Comintern agents were tremendously active all over China, the Chinese Soviets emerged not because of them, but in spite of them. And much evidence goes to show that Stalin was not at all eager for the emergence of a strong Communist China.

After Lenin's death, the struggle for power between Stalin and Trotsky began. Trotsky was the advocate of world-revolution, Stalin of "socialism in one country". Trotsky was against the Kuomintang-Communist alliance, Stalin almost fanatically supported it. Trotsky

[1] Mao, *Selected Works*, Lawrence and Wishart, London, 1954, Vol. I, pp. 21-22.

wanted to have Soviets established in China, Stalin was against this. At times Stalin's attitude to various questions in China became more rigid for the simple reason that Trotsky attacked it.

The struggle for personal power in the Kremlin was camouflaged by endless theoretical debates, conducted in scholastic Marxist-Leninist verbiage. Tons of paper were filled with explanations and analyses of various principles, or even of fine doctrinal nuances. In Chinese Communist headquarters, and in the offices of the Comintern instructors, the twists and turns of this scholastic debate were seized upon as intellectual tools, or indeed weapons in the local struggles for personal power.

This was part of the background of Mao Tse-tung's activities during the 1924-34 decade. But the decisive background was the ocean of peasantry which reacted to the civil war, *coups d'état*, massacres, strikes, famines and to the suicidal anarchy, with ever larger and more dangerous waves of unrest. Mao felt the enormous power of these waves and tried to ride on their crest.

I

However Machiavellian were the reasons for the Communist-Kuomintang alliance, in 1924 it presented the only hope of beating the war-lords who ruled over most of China. Only a broad national front under Sun Yat-sen could hope to raise armies and unite all the patriotic elements from the Chinese bankers, merchants and landowners who were tired of the war-lords, to students, intellectuals, workers and peasants. Sun Yat-sen's name became the symbol of national liberation. Borodin's blueprint for transforming the Kuomintang into an effective apparatus of the national revolution was excellent. But it was the task of Sun's ablest adherents, and of Communists, like Mao Tse-tung, to realise the plan in all its details.

In addition to his membership of the Communist Politbureau, Mao also worked in the Executive Bureau of the Shanghai Kuomintang and later became a candidate member of the Kuomintang Central Committee. So in principle he belonged to the entourage of the supreme policy-makers of both parties. His practical tasks were legion. For a while in Shanghai he co-ordinated the various measures of the two parties. As the aim was to start a nation-wide revolutionary movement against the war-lords, the differences between the Kuomintang and Communist policies were at first not too important in Mao's work. The growing national armies planned large-scale military expeditions to liberate the north. People like

Mao, as propagandists and peasant-organisers had to instil patriotic enthusiasm and revolutionary fervour into the population. They had to persuade the people that the armies about to launch their northern offensive were *their* army, that their victory would be China's victory.

Mao threw himself so wholeheartedly into this work that even his hardened physique could not withstand the strain. By the winter of 1924 he was so thin and exhausted that when he caught a cold it developed into lung-trouble. He returned to Hunan to be cured and to take a long rest.* His illness forced him to be idle for almost the first time in his life. For a while he could not even read. This enforced long rest was a most important stage in his development as a politician. During his convalescence he could read quietly, think over all the thousands of problems he had had to cope with while engulfed in the feverish activities of the last few years. He convalesced in his birthplace, in the village of Shao Shan. He was again at home, in the peasant country which he knew so well. The peasantry was in ferment. As news came of strikes, shootings and massacres from all over China and the local military bosses grew bolder with every success scored by the war-lords anywhere, the anger and determination of the peasants grew. In the spring of 1925 Mao saw the chance, and the necessity, of organising the nucleus of a great peasant movement in Hunan.

On May 30 a protest demonstration of students and workers in Shanghai attacked a police station in the foreign settlement demanding the release of arrested workers. The British officer in charge lost his head, gave the order to fire and twelve students were killed. This led to general strikes and anti-foreign demonstrations in many cities.

In Hunan Mao was in enemy territory, not only as a Communist but also as an official of the Kuomintang, for the province was ruled by a war-lord, one of the most vicious military despots. The war-lord's police and the gendarmery of the landlords hunted down and executed all agitators. Mao, looking like a peasant, speaking the Hunan dialect, could, however, live inconspicuously among the peasants. But the effect of the May 30 incident increased the militancy of the peasants, and Mao was drawn into feverish activity.

Troops were sent out after him, a price was put on his head, and

* According to other sources Mao was not ill at all, but because of his pro-Kuomintang tendencies was not re-elected to the Communist Central Committee and so retired to Hunan.

Mao had to escape to Canton where he was soon given work of national importance by the Kuomintang.

Dr. Sun Yat-sen died on March 12, 1925, but his policy of national unification and rebuilding went on being effectively applied at first by his successors. The same cannot be said about Dr. Sun's revolutionary aims. The most powerful of the Kuomintang leaders were Wang Ching-wei, the politician, and General Chiang Kai-shek, the military chief. At first, they concentrated on defeating the warlords. The technique of dictatorial party rule learnt from the Comintern agents had brought great initial results. The Kuomintang also started on an extensive programme of national construction and reconstruction.

The centuries of an impotent social system and the ravages of the war-lord era had left the immensity of China in an impossibly primitive and feeble state. It was a roadless country. It was a country in which for hundreds of miles one could not find water fit to drink. A country attacked by the sands of Asia in the form of advancing deserts; almost yearly huge tracts of the country were flooded and devastated by its enormous rivers. Famine and pestilence, ignorance and superstition enfeebled the country. In good years the peasants could not produce enough with their primitive tools and backward farming methods. For the peasantry, indeed for the whole of China, the most urgent tasks were the repair and rebuilding of the neglected, silted-up irrigation system, the introduction of modern agricultural tools and methods, the building of modern roads.

As the Kuomintang armies—with their Communist political commissars and propagandists—liberated the war-lord territories one by one, a start could be made on this gigantic work. When Mao arrived in Canton, the political leader of the Kuomintang was the new Prime Minister, Wang Ching-wei, with whom he had worked for a time in the Shanghai Kuomintang. Wang now gave Mao important positions as editor of the Kuomintang's *Political Weekly*, head of the training of peasant organisers, and head of Kuomintang agitation and propaganda.

In the second part of 1925 when Mao took on his really important responsibilities, there were signs that the Kuomintang-Communist alliance was going to be more short-lived than either side had thought a year previously. General Chiang Kai-shek learnt a great deal about Communist aims and methods during his sojourn in Moscow. After his return, he very soon discovered the true

nature of the Communist factions within the Kuomintang. Stalin
and the Comintern, while paying lip-service to the alliance, were
making too many propagandistic statements about industrial and
agrarian revolts. The Communist commissars in the national armies
antagonised the commanding officers. The right-wing of the Kuomintang made overt moves to oust the Communists. The successes of the national armies emboldened the peasantry, and the
Kuomintang centre feared that new revolutionary outbreaks would
again lead to chaos before Kuomintang rule could be safely established all over China.

It came as a surprise to no one, save Stalin and his entourage,
when on March 20, 1926, a year after Sun Yat-sen's death, General
Chiang Kai-shek made his first anti-Communist *coup*. He declared
martial law in Canton, arrested the Communist commissars attached
to his command, closed the trade unions and put a military guard
around the houses of his Russian advisers. Under Chiang's rule the
individual Communists within the Kuomintang were forbidden to
follow the orders of the Communist Party; in the Kuomintang headquarters Communists could no longer become department heads,
and Communist membership in other executive positions was limited
to one third.

Borodin and the scores of other Comintern representatives in
China tried to minimise the significance of this *coup* and, on instructions from Stalin, accepted the restrictions. The true account
of Chiang Kai-shek's *coup* was denounced by Moscow as imperialist
propaganda. The Comintern agents told General Chiang that some
of the Communist commissars and agents in his armies were career-
ists who gave a mistaken impression of Communist policies. Stalin
wanted to placate Chiang Kai-shek until the Communists could
succeed in preparing the way for a Communist take-over by a much
slower and more prudent penetration of his armies. Chiang, in his
turn, was willing to pretend that all was well with the Kuomintang-
Communist alliance. He too was buying time till he should have
enough power to make a total break with the Communists.

So Chiang was able in July 1926 to lead the Kuomintang armies
against the northern war-lords with Communist backing. His forces
soon discovered that their advances were greatly helped by peasant
revolts and sudden strikes behind the enemy lines. While the strikes
were mostly the work of Communist agents, the peasant revolts
flared up thanks to the organisational and propaganda activities
directed, mainly through Kuomintang channels, by Mao Tse-tung
and others. The propagandists worked so well in the war-lord armies

also, that Chiang's nationalist divisions were joined by thousands of deserters from the other side.

Mao's first indirect clash with the Stalin line was in his attitude to these peasant revolts within the war-lord territories. The movement was swiftly gaining strength and momentum, when *on Stalin's instructions* the Comintern ordered Borodin and the Chinese Communists to stop, or at least to restrain the peasants, as their revolts were antagonising some of the Kuomintang leaders, and above all the Kuomintang generals in charge of the offensive against the North.

As reports came in from China that the peasants could not be restrained, Stalin sent a half-hearted cancellation some months later.

Mao's attitude can be documented from a pamphlet he wrote in March 1926: *Analysis of the Classes in Chinese Society*.

The pamphlet pointed out that in China the modern industrial proletariat numbered only about two million, and could not win without its "staunchest and most numerous ally, the peasantry". Mao advocated a radical land policy and the vigorous organisation of the peasantry. Communist Party headquarters, following the Stalin line of the time, opposed this policy and refused to allow the publication of the article in the official Party organs.

It was the first time that Mao had come up against the Marxist dogma that Communist revolution can only be led by the industrial workers of the cities, and that the peasantry—the "staunch ally" of the workers—cannot win the decisive battles of a revolution. Although many Marxist-Leninist quotations can be found to prove the view that the dogma was not rigid on this point, the fact remains that the Soviet CP and the Comintern acted rigidly. They could not believe that a significant initiative could come from the peasantry.

The "northern expedition" of the Kuomintang armies met with singular success. Between July and October 1926 several powerful war-lords were beaten and Kiangsi, Hunan, Hupeh, Anhwei and Kiangsu came under Kuomintang rule. In November the Kuomintang central government was set up in the important Wuhan cities, Wuchang, Hankow and Hanyang. This gave Borodin and his staff a chance to organise further masses of the industrial proletariat.

This success only strengthened Stalin's belief in the importance of the Kuomintang alliance. His policy was to placate General Chiang Kai-shek whose armies could capture further cities which could serve as bases for a dogmatically proper Communist revolution.

When an alliance was important for Stalin, he refused to believe
that his partners were untrustworthy or about to turn against him.
A dismal illustration of this was in 1941 when he refused to believe
that Hitler was attacking Russia, and at first forbade a counterattack. It was the same with Chiang Kai-shek. In the winter of
1926 Stalin sent the Indian Comintern agent M. N. Roy to China
with the Comintern directive to transform the Kuomintang "into
a real people's party, a solid revolutionary bloc of the proletariat,
peasantry, the urban petty bourgeoisie, and other oppressed and
exploited strata".[2]

At this time it was already perfectly obvious that the Kuomintang in fact was heading towards a split. Chiang Kai-shek was the
leader of the right wing of the Party, backed by the Shanghai
bankers and powerful secret societies. The centre and left wing of
the Kuomintang, under Wang Ching-wei's leadership tried to placate
Chiang. In the spring of 1927 this already seemed hopeless. Chiang
was planning to crush the trade unions, the labour and the peasant
movements and annihilate the Communists. It was equally clear
that he intended to assume leadership of the Kuomintang.

In March Chiang's troops were moving against war-lord-held
Nanking and Shanghai, where the Communist trade unions had
organised strikes and insurrections. Chiang's method was simple.
He slowed down his advance and gave his enemies time to massacre
his allies. The Shanghai General (Li Pao-chang), in obvious agreement with Chiang Kai-shek, executed as many Communists and
trade unionists as he could find. After Chiang took the city, Li
Pao-chang was given an important command by Chiang Kai-shek.
From this and many other incidents it was obvious that Chiang was
moving against the Communists. Yet on March 31, 1927, the Comintern's *Inprecor* wrote:

> A split in the Kuomintang and hostile sentiment between the
> working class in Shanghai and the revolutionary soldiers
> (Chiang) are absolutely out of the question. . . . A revolutionary
> like Chiang Kai-shek will not act in co-operation with counter-
> revolutionaries. . . . The only danger for the working class in
> Shanghai consists in the provocation by the imperialists.

Pravda wrote in the same vein, and Stalin went on to act in
this belief. The Comintern telegraphed to the gravely worried
Shanghai Communists to hide or bury all the workers' weapons

---

[2] Resolution of the Seventh Plenum.

in order to avoid military conflict with Chiang Kai-shek. At a Moscow rally Stalin attacked the opponents of his China policy:

Why drive away the Right when we have the majority and when the Right listens to us? . . . The people of the Right have relations with the (war-lord) generals and understand very well how to demoralise them and induce them to pass over to the side of the revolution, bag and baggage, without striking a blow. . . . So they (the Right) have to be utilised to the end, squeezed out like a lemon, and then thrown away.[3]

Although Stalin's speech was not published at the time in the Soviet press, the candidates for "squeezed-out-lemonship" promptly heard about it. Stalin's colossal imprudence speeded up developments. Chiang Kai-shek arrived in Shanghai and, on April 12, 1927, started on a systematic massacre of Communists, leftish intellectuals, strike pickets and Communist-led trade unionists. Those who resisted were executed instantly, others were shot a few hours later. Similar measures were taken in Nanking and Canton. The Communist organisations in the most important cities were annihilated and many of the leaders executed.

At the same time Chiang Kai-shek openly broke with the Wuhan government and, splitting the Kuomintang, he set up his rival government in Nanking. The Wuhan government, the so-called "Kuomintang left" kept up for a while the alliance with the Communists. During this short period Stalin urged the Communists not to antagonise the Kuomintang left and the generals under its direction. The Communists were again ordered to restrain the peasants. They were again instructed to base everything on the industrial proletariat, the "vanguard of the revolution".

II

At the end of 1926 the signs that the peasant revolution would get out of hand alarmed the Kuomintang and worried the Communist leadership in the Shanghai Party Centre. Mao Tse-tung, as director of the Communist Party's peasant department, was sent off to the storm centre of the revolt in Hunan, to inspect the peasant organisations and report on them to the Party.[4]

Leaving behind the Shanghai offices of the Communist Political

[3] Trotsky, *The Stalin School of Falsification*, pp. 389-90.
[4] *A History of the Modern Chinese Revolution*, p. 133. See also SW, Vol. I, p. 21.

Bureau and Central Committee, and the scholastic debates on
Marxism, on Comintern instructions, sick of the theoretical-bureau-
cratic approach to the rebellions of flesh and blood human beings,
Mao Tse-tung no doubt set out in a most perceptive frame of mind.
He had faith in the peasants and expected important actions from
them. But what he found greatly surpassed his wildest expectations.
In Hunan from which the Kuomintang chased away the war-lord
government, the peasants found the way and the means to smash
utterly the old order of things.

He spent only thirty-two days in visiting the five most important
counties of Hunan, but this was beyond a shadow of doubt the
most decisive period of his political existence.

He expected to find a "revolutionary movement" and "revolutionary organisations". Instead, he found a revolutionary tempest.
He expected that the vaguely rebellious peasants would need
guidance from professional revolutionaries, instead he found that
the peasants were the ones who could give guidance. They had
found the methods with which the revolution could triumph all
over the country. He wrote later in his report: "What Dr. Sun
Yat-sen wanted to do in the forty years he devoted to the revolution but failed to accomplish, the peasants have accomplished in a
few months."

They also accomplished something else. They taught Mao Tse-
tung the methods with which he tried to remould China after coming to power in 1949. The Hunanese peasants were the inventors
of the "terror with fanfare", of the mass brain-washing sessions, of
public accusation and "struggle" meetings, of collective confessions
which Mao was later to apply on the greatest possible scale.

After describing these methods, in his report to the Party, Mao
summarised the significance of the peasant revolt:

The peasants attack as their main targets the local bullies and
bad gentry and the lawless landlords, hitting in passing against
patriarchal ideologies and institutions, corrupt officials in the cities
and evil customs in the rural areas. In force and momentum, the attack is like a tempest or hurricane; those who submit to it survive, and those who resist it perish. As a result, the
privileges which the feudal landlords have enjoyed for thousands of years are being shattered to pieces. The dignity and
prestige of the landlords are dashed to the ground. With the fall
of the authority of the landlords, the peasant association becomes
the sole organ of authority, and what people call "All power to

the peasant association" has come to pass. Even such a trifle as a quarrel between man and wife has to be settled at the peasant association. Nothing can be settled in the absence of people from the association. The association is actually dictating in all matters in the countryside, and it is literally true that "whatever it says, goes".

Crowds of people swarm into the homes of the local bullies and bad gentry who oppose the peasant association, slaughtering their pigs and consuming their grain. They may even loll for a minute or two on the ivory beds of the young mesdames and mademoiselles in the families of the bullies and gentry. At the slightest provocation they make arrests, crown the arrested with tall paper-hats, and parade them through the villages: "You bad gentry, now you know who we are!" Doing whatever they like and turning everything upside down, they have even created a kind of terror in the countryside. This is what some people call "going too far" or "going beyond the proper limit to right a wrong", or "really too outrageous".

The opinion of this group, reasonable on the surface, is erroneous at bottom.

First, the things described above have all been the inevitable results of the doings of the local bullies and bad gentry and lawless landlords themselves. For ages, these people, with power in their hands, tyrannised over the peasants and trampled them underfoot; that is why the peasants have now risen in such a great revolt.

Secondly, a revolution is not the same as inviting people to dinner, or writing an essay, or painting a picture, or doing fancy needlework; it cannot be anything so refined, so calm and gentle, or so mild, kind, courteous, restrained or magnanimous.* A revolution is an uprising, an act of violence whereby one class overthrows another. A rural revolution is a revolution by which the peasantry overthrows the authority of the feudal landlord class. If the peasants do not use the maximum of their strength, they can never overthrow the authority of the landlords which has been deeply rooted for thousands of years.

To put it bluntly, it was necessary to bring about a brief reign of terror in every rural area; otherwise one could never suppress the activities of the counter-revolutionaries in the countryside or

* Allusion to the analects of Confucius.

overthrow the authority of the gentry. To right a wrong it is necessary to exceed the proper limits, and the wrong cannot be righted
without the proper limits being exceeded.[5]

The section of the report dealing with the poor peasants bears
the title: "Vanguard of the revolution". According to Mao the leadership of poor peasants was absolutely necessary: "Without the poor
peasants there can be no revolution. To reject them is to reject
the revolution. To attack them is to attack the revolution. *Their
general direction of the revolution has never been wrong.*[6]

This most unorthodox sentence remained in the 1951 official
Chinese publication of the *Selected Works;* only the following sentence from the original Chinese edition was left out:

> To give credits where they are due, if we allot ten points to the
> accomplishments of the democratic revolution, then the achieve-
> ments of the urban dwellers and the military units rate only three
> points, while the remaining seven points should go to the peas-
> ants in their rural revolution.

Mao's report, with his proposals for a widespread redistribution
of land, was accepted by an interprovincial meeting of peasants in
Wuhan. The meeting decided to submit Mao's proposals to the
Fifth Congress of the CCP. The Central Committee, guided by
the Comintern directions, rejected them. The Congress was held
in April-May 1927. According to the *History of the Modern Chinese
Revolution* (p. 158), Mao attended the Congress but "he was excluded from the leadership . . . and illegally deprived of the right
to vote."

Mao and the official Chinese Party-line put all the blame for this
on Ch'en Tu-hsiu, the then leader of the Chinese CP and not on
Stalin or the Comintern:

> The Right opportunists in the Party, headed by Ch'en Tu-hsiu,
> were unwilling to accept Comrade Mao's views and persisted in
> their erroneous opinions. Their chief mistake was that, scared by
> the reactionary current of the Kuomintang, they dared not sup-
> port the great revolutionary struggles of the peasants that had
> broken out or were breaking out. To appease the Kuomintang,
> they preferred to desert the peasantry, the chief ally in the revo-

[5] *SW*, Vol. I, pp. 23-27. (Emphasis added.)
[6] *SW*, Vol. I, p. 32.

lution, and thus landed the working class and the Communist Party in helpless isolation.[7]

The truth is that Ch'en, though he had to carry out Stalin's instructions, nevertheless valued Mao's work and hence made him leader of the peasant movement.

At the end of his report Mao likened the opponents and restrainers of the peasant revolt to the legendary Lord Sheh who was so fond of dragons that he adorned his whole palace with drawings and carvings of them. But when a real dragon heard of his infatuation and paid him a visit, he was frightened out of his wits:

If one shouts every day about "arousing the masses of people", but is scared to death when the people do arise, what is the difference between that and Lord Sheh's love of dragons?[8]

Stalin, the modern Lord Sheh, continued to shout orders about arousing the masses and send out instructions to restrain them when events developed in an undogmatic way.

China was at this time roughly divided into four main camps: (1) the northern war-lords and their provincial allies; (2) Chiang Kai-shek's Right Wing Kuomintang régime in Central China; (3) the southern "Wuhan régime" consisting of the Left Wing Kuomintang government, still in temporary and very uneasy alliance with the orthodox Communists; and, last but not least, (4) the rebellious countryside in the territories "governed" by the three other camps. For a time all three governments agreed more or less, that the peasants ought to be restrained.

Stalin was doggedly defending his new pet idea of the Left-Kuomintang-Communist *entente* against the criticism of Trotsky and against actual developments.

In Mao's Hunan the left-wing Kuomintang commander started to arrest the peasant leaders in Changsha and to reorganise the local Kuomintang on safe non-revolutionary lines. Many peasant organisers and Communists were executed. In retaliation, about 20,000 revolutionary peasants led by Communists moved against Changsha. They had reached the outskirts of the city when the Communists received instruction from headquarters to retreat and

[7] Introduction to Mao's report, SW, Vol. I, p. 21. See also Snow, p. 158.

[8] SW, p. 59.

dissolve the peasant troops. They obeyed, whereupon the "left" Kuomintang general attacked the retreating peasants and started a general massacre.

Stalin's obsession then was to preserve for the time being the Left Kuomintang-Communist *entente* at all costs. Mao Tse-tung, working in the Chinese countryside, just like Stalin's opposition in Moscow, wanted to end this *entente* which only weakened the Communists and threatened the revolutionary peasants with extinction. Attacking the opposition, Stalin said at the June 1927 Comintern meeting:

> What does the withdrawal of the Communist Party from the Kuomintang mean at the present moment? . . . It means to weaken the Communist Party, to undermine the revolutionary Kuomintang . . . and to deliver the flag of the Kuomintang, the most popular flag in China, into the hands of the Right Wing members of the Kuomintang. . . . It follows therefore that the Opposition . . . is playing into the hands of the enemies.[9]

The continued alliance with the Wuhan régime of the so-called Left-Kuomintang actually meant that the Communists were ordered to curb the peasant revolt which broke out like a tornado in Hunan, Hupeh and Kiangsi. In June 1927 Mao's All-China Peasant Union had nearly ten million members. The peasants were everywhere confiscating and redistributing the land owned by the landlords. Mao was not following the Stalin-line. He insisted on "marching at the head" of the peasants. Finally, the Party Centre explicitly ordered him not to organise peasant uprisings, and then recalled him from Hunan. Even more serious disciplinary action would have been started against him, had not the Left-Kuomintang government in Wuhan turned with increasing vehemence not only against the rebellious peasants but also against the trade unions and the Communists.

The two rival Kuomintang governments in Nanking and Wuhan were also rivals in this respect. They competed with each other in executing Communists, labour leaders, peasant organisers. The armies of both governments attacked the rebellious peasant districts and staged massacres in their territories.

In this situation Stalin still sent firm orders to the Chinese Communists not to "provoke" the Left-Kuomintang. At this time Ch'en Tu-hsiu, the Communist leader suggested to Stalin's representative,

---

[9] *Inprecor*, June 16, 1927, p. 737.

Borodin, that the Communists withdraw from the Kuomintang and start defending themselves. Borodin said: "I quite agree with your idea, but I know that Moscow will never permit it."[10]

A few days after this the "Left-Kuomintang" government renounced the alliance with the Communists and ordered the annihilation of all Red organisations. About 25,000 Communists were executed. The Party had to go underground.

Stalin now put the blame for the bankruptcy of his policies on those Chinese Communist leaders who had carried out his instructions to the letter. The Secretary-General, Ch'en Tu-hsiu was deposed early in August 1927. Mao became a member of the Politbureau. Stalin sent new Comintern agents to direct the new Secretary-General of the CCP. All hope of working with the Kuomintang was relinquished and Stalin ordered an open struggle for power, with uprisings in the cities and the countryside.

Mao Tse-tung was sent by Stalin's new agents, and by the new Communist leadership, to Changsha to organise a peasant revolt, which later became known as the Autumn Crop Uprising. His task was to organise a peasant-worker revolutionary army and to set up the power of the Communist Party in Hunan, independent of the Kuomintang.

Mao was at first quite successful. Widespread uprisings were organised and the first units of the peasant-worker army were formed. But the uprising was not dogmatically correct. The Red Army consisted mainly of peasants and deserters from the Kuomintang armies. The workers were represented by some Hanyang miners. Communist headquarters and the Comintern agents were dissatisfied. The uprisings and the Red troops were not based on the cities, the proletarian and Communist elements were not strongly enough represented, and action was often initiated without first giving the distant party headquarters a chance to discuss it. Furthermore Mao organised local Soviets although this was against the party line and against Comintern instructions.

Orders from the Party Centre were again confusing. Some of the local Communists, obedient to the distant party leaders, opposed Mao's moves and sabotaged what they called "the rifle movement". Some of the former Left Kuomintang generals deserted their command in the new Red Army, and went over to Chiang Kai-shek

[10] Ch'en Tu-hsiu, *Letter to the Comrades of the Chinese Communist Party*, Shanghai, December 10, 1929. English text in *Militant*, New York, November 15, 1930 to January 15, 1931.

whose troops were closing in on the Hunan peasant troops. Repudiated by his own superiors in the Communist Party, attacked by local Communists who were jealous of his growing personal power, Mao continued to struggle.

As the Communist leadership in the Red Armies was wavering, the Communist cause suffered many defeats in other parts of China, and there were many desertions from its ranks. The loyal core of Mao's troops were led by him to an impregnable mountain stronghold on the Hunan-Kiangsi border at Chingkangshan. In November 1927 the first Soviet government was set up on the Hunan border. But Mao was deposed by the Party, and dismissed from the Politbureau. His peasant Red Army was denounced as a "rifle movement".

The uprisings in the cities, in Nanchang and Canton, also failed. Chiang Kai-shek occupied Wuhan, the Left Kuomintang government ceased to exist. Communists were executed all over China. The leaders escaped to Russia or went underground. General Chiang Kai-shek established his dictatorship in Nanking.

Dealing with this débâcle in his autobiography, Mao criticised Stalin only indirectly. He blamed Ch'en Tu-hsiu, and criticised his policies.[11] But Ch'en had merely been following Comintern orders.

Mao knew very well that Ch'en bitterly blamed himself for carrying out Comintern instructions. After his expulsion from the CP, Ch'en Tu-hsiu wrote on December 10, 1929 his *Letter to the Comrades of the Chinese Communist Party:*

> Since the time when I followed the appeal to organise a Chinese Communist Party in 1920, I have sincerely carried out to the utmost the opportunistic policy of the leaders of the Communist International, Stalin, Zinoviev, Bukharin and others, who led the Chinese Revolution to a shameful and terrible defeat. . . . I whose understanding was not sufficiently clear, whose opinion was not sufficiently resolute . . . unconsciously became an instrument of the narrow Stalin faction. . . .
>
> Dear Comrades! The Party's present errors do not refer to particular problems; they reveal, as in the past, the whole opportunistic policy which Stalin has conducted in China. Responsible functionaries of the Chinese Central Committee and the CCP who have agreed to become Stalin's phonographs have since lost whatever political conscience they had, they have got worse and worse and can no longer be saved.

[11] *Autobiography.*

We must . . . struggle under the banner of real Marxism-Leninism . . . against the opportunism of the Comintern and the Central Committee of the Chinese CP.

As Mao must have known that Stalin and the Comintern gave almost daily telegraphic instructions and orders to the Chinese Communist leadership through Stalin's two main agents, Borodin and Roy, his criticism of these two is really directed against their master.

If—as Edgar Snow reports—Mao regarded Roy as a "fool" and Borodin as a "blunderer",[12] what was his opinion of their master, whose orders they always carried out faithfully?

[12] Snow, p. 161.

VII

THE GUERILLA LEADER

> *The enemy advances: we retreat*
> *The enemy halts: we harass*
> *The enemy tires: we attack*
> *The enemy retreats: we pursue.*

"The phenomenon that within a country one or several small areas under Red political power should exist for a long time amid the encirclement of White political power is one that has never been found elsewhere in the world."

(Mao, *Why can China's Red Political Power Exist?*)[1]

The irregular plateau of Mao Tse-tung's mountain stronghold was about 40 kilometres wide and 250 kilometres in circumference. It was protected by thick pine forests and steep cliffs and only five narrow paths linked it to the outside world. Mao established his army base here with the remnants of three regiments, barely 1,000 men. At the beginning they were really nothing more than a "rifle movement", because they had no machine-guns, no wireless transmitters or field telephones, let alone guns or mortars. The only buildings on the plateau and on the mountain-sides were Buddhist temples which could be used as dormitories and hospitals.

In this curious bandit-lair at Chingkangshan Mao Tse-tung had his first taste of real power. For the first time in his life he had all the power and responsibilities of a military commander and civil governor. He was out of touch with Party headquarters and the innumerable committees which until then had hampered his decisions. The Party had repudiated him, and in his diminutive mountain command there was no one with whom he had to contend for leadership.

He was a dictator in Chingkangshan in the sense that a bandit chief is a dictator over his territories. Regular contact with party headquarters was not established until the winter of 1928, so for about a year he exercised such power as he had independently. As there is ample documentation of his actions during this period, we have an authentic portrait of the thirty-five-year-old Mao Tse-tung as a ruler of men.

[1] Party report, October 1928, SW, Vol. I, pp. 64-65.

I

Chingkangshan was truly a bandit stronghold, at that time occupied by two groups of peasant-bandits numbering about 600. Their leaders were at first prepared to welcome Mao's small Red Army only on the condition that it was incorporated in their bands. After some uneasy weeks Mao persuaded the two leaders to accept regimental commands in his army. This settled, Mao organised military and political courses for his whole army. The former peasant-bandits were persuaded that in the victory of the revolution lay their only hope. The lands of the great landowners would be divided among the poor peasants and they too would be able to settle down peacefully on their farms. But first they had to transform themselves into real revolutionaries and into disciplined Red Army soldiers. In this army the officers and commanders wore the same uniform and led the same lives as the troops. But the troops were taught that obedience to the higher command was the essential pre-condition of success. By teaching them discipline, Mao convinced the former bandits and their leaders of the necessity of accepting him as their supreme commander.

He was an effective commander. He knew the importance of army morale. The troops were kept busy at hundreds of evidently useful and important tasks, from digging concealed entrenchments on the mountain slopes and cutting timber for houses, to learning from their scholarly commander-in-chief the science of guerilla warfare. They knew that he was a peasant like themselves, born not very far from their mountain lair, that for many years he had amassed both knowledge of the ancients and the new knowledge of the West, that he was a seasoned revolutionary and that he was a man who thought of everything. They could hear him talking to the men of the surrounding villages, telling the peasants to share out the land of the escaped landlords; they saw the couriers leaving and arriving to and from other revolutionary bases. There was always something going on, something planned; there was always hope.

In his military lectures, Commander Mao spoke of Sun Wu, the great Chinese military thinker who lived about 2,500 years ago and quoted some of his sayings such as, "If you have ten times as many troops as the enemy, surround him; if five times as many, attack him; if equal in numbers and superior in fighting power, engage him; otherwise avoid the conflict." Out of this and similar sayings Mao formed his famous guerilla maxims quoted at the head of this chapter. In Chinese these consist of four lines each of four syllables only, easy to memorise and chant.

The troops planted rice wherever possible on the mountain plateau and went down to help the peasants or to work on abandoned lands; they took part in courses and some of them started to learn to read and write. The Red base had soon its own primitive printing press and crude army newspaper. Mao and his comparatively small staff of Communists trained the ablest Red Army men to become agitators and peasant organisers. Chingkangshan was in the border area of three provinces: Hunan, Kiangsi and Kwantung and if Mao's Red Army was pursued by the local troops of one province, they could always slip over into another. Moreover they tried to organise around their stronghold an ever widening area of sovietized districts where the revolutionary peasants ruled themselves under the guidance of the Red base. The villages had their local Red Guards and the peasants of the sovietized districts formed the base of Mao's intelligence network. His peasant-spies covered enormous distances, bringing news about enemy movements.

In the early spring of 1928 after a very hard winter the morale of Mao's troops was low. Some units mutinied and had to be disciplined. The army was listless, uneasy, the prospects dark. It was at this time that Mao made one of the most important decisions in his life. He sent his younger brother to invite a fantastic war-lord-revolutionary to join forces with him.

This man, General Chu Teh was at that time forty-two years old. He came from a wealthy Szechuan landed family and, as a graduate of the first modern military academy of China, became an officer of the Yunnan Army which caused the downfall of the Manchu dynasty in 1912. He was brigadier-general in 1916 when General Yüan attempted to restore the monarchy. Chu Teh became famous as one of the "four fierce generals" who foiled the restoration attempt. This helped him to political and military power: he became one of the war-lords ruling Szechuan province.*

In 1920, in his thirty-fourth year, Chu Teh was a very fat, exceedingly corrupt, opium sodden war-lord. His subordinates plundered the public funds to enrich him, while he, in his palatial residence divided his time between opium smoking, reading the classics and visiting his sizeable harem of wives and concubines. But news of the utter chaos in China kept pouring in. The literate war-lord started to read confiscated revolutionary books and

* According to Communist accounts Chu Teh came from a poor peasant family.

pamphlets, and one day towards the end of 1921, in a clear moment, he decided to start a new life. He pensioned off his wives and concubines, left his riches behind, and went to Shanghai. By a most radical treatment he cured his addiction to opium in three weeks and then joined some Europe-bound revolutionary students. The reformed war-lord became a student himself. In Germany he helped to establish the Chinese Branch of the Communist Party there, then went to study in France, and finally studied Marxism under Chinese teachers in the Eastern Toilers' University in Moscow. After his return in 1925, the Kuomintang made him Chief of Public Safety in Nanchang (Kiangsi Province). The August 1927 uprising in that city, in which 30,000 former Kuomintang troops took part, was led by Chu Teh and Chou En-lai. After the defeat of the uprising Chou En-lai joined the underground Party Centre while Chu Teh led part of the rebel army towards the South. He took and lost cities and finally, with his troops in rags, reached the Kiangsi-Kwantung border district where, with some bandits led by a revolutionary student, he established a Red base. It was here that Mao's invitation reached him.

As he himself was distrusted by his Party superiors, it was a daring move of Mao's to join forces with a former war-lord of most unsavoury past, whose Communist convictions were doubted by Party headquarters. But Mao, a firm believer in the possibility of remoulding men, admired Chu Teh's tremendous will-power. And Mao had pressing need of his professional military skill. He wanted a brilliant and courageous general who neither would nor could take part in Communist intrigues against him. Mao knew well that Chu Teh wanted to be accepted by the Party leaders as a true Communist. For Chu Teh, Mao Tse-tung was a real Communist, a good Marxist theoretician, from whom he hoped to get his "Party blessing". This was the basis of the Mao-Chu Teh alliance and friendship which, at the time of writing, is more than three decades old.

In May 1928 Chu's and Mao's forces were united in Chingkangshan. Mao was the political, Chu Teh the military head. Their combined forces with new recruitment numbered about 10,000 men. They had by now trench-mortars, machine-guns and some other equipment, mainly captured from the enemy.

Mao and Chu Teh were in complete agreement concerning their future tasks and possibilities, but their plan was less ambitious than the Party Centre recommended.[2]

[2] See Snow, p. 166.

After the recall of Roy and Borodin, Stalin sent two new Comintern agents to China: the Georgian, Besso Lominadze, and the German, Heinz Neumann. They brought instructions for a rapid expansion of the revolutionary movement. They had concrete instructions for the urgent staging of the Canton and Nanchang uprisings, which failed, led to a White terror and to the decimation of the Communists. The Chinese Communists on the spot tried to convince the Comintern that the time was not ripe for such uprisings. But Stalin needed victories in China as weapons in his fight against his own opposition. He was most impatient, and had the Comintern cable almost every day to the Chinese CP urging immediate insurrections in the cities. One order stated that it was necessary for strategic reasons to start an insurrection *"even if it were certain to fail"*.

The revolts did fail. In Canton alone more than 6,000 Communists and sympathisers were executed; but Stalin could point out to his critics that the Canton affair was evidence that the "Chinese revolution was still alive".

In the summer of 1928 the Comintern urged a revolutionary upsurge in the countryside. The peasant armies were to roll in great revolutionary waves towards the cities, to ensure the success of the uprisings to be staged there. At the same time the Comintern was uneasy about the "Communist movements of the peasants". The Comintern spokesman, Lozovsky, said in July 1928 about China:

> The workers' movement lags behind that of the peasants and this is fraught with tremendous dangers to the further development of the Chinese revolution.[3]

Because of the general chaos and the enormous distances, the Shanghai centre and the Comintern in Moscow had only vague information on the appearance of Red Armies in several districts of Central and Southern China. Various "Soviet districts" large and small came into being and the Sixth World Congress of the Comintern declared that a new revolutionary upsurge was imminent in China; hence the Communists were to win over the peasants and organise revolutionary armies of *workers* and peasants. The aim was the establishment of a powerful Red Army under the direction of the Chinese Politbureau (and the Comintern). The new Comintern-line was naturally adopted by the Chinese leadership in Shanghai and this gave Mao and Chu Teh, and the leaders of the

[3] *Inprecor,* July 19, 1928.

other Red Armies and Soviet district leaders a chance to "normalise" their relationship with Party headquarters.

Mao and Chu Teh were by no means the only leaders distrusted by the Shanghai Party Centre. The Sixth Red Army of the "Hunan-Western Hupeh Base" for instance was commanded by a famous former bandit leader, Ho Lung, who later became a Kuomintang officer and joined the Communists only after the defeat of the Nanchang uprising. The Fifth Red Army of the "Hunan-Hupeh-Kiangsi base" was commanded by Peng Teh-huai, also a former Kuomintang officer. In the other Soviet districts* too, the leadership, including the political commissars of the Red units, the chairmen of the local Soviets, and even the secretaries of the local Party organisations, consisted of men who were not appointed by Party headquarters, but elected by various front committees or local soviet conferences. This was of course against Communist Party principles and practice.

The territory of these Red enclaves, at the beginning, usually encompassed a county or two. After the first year, Mao's base was the largest when it stretched over most of six counties on the border between Hunan and Kiangsi provinces. The size of these territories naturally fluctuated according to the military situation and, after a sudden expansion, the Party organisation grew too, together with the number of responsible Communist officials. It was simply impossible to wait for their appointment until the Party Centre's blessing was given. Besides the lack of "workers", in the leadership and in the ranks, this was one of the sources of friction.

II

In November 1928 Mao wrote a report to the Central Committee of the Chinese CP, entitled "The Struggle in the Chingkang Mountains". This report gives a true portrait of Mao as a ruler during this period and shows how and why the Red Armies of Mao and Chu Teh could survive twenty-one years of incessant fighting under enormous difficulties until their victory in 1949. It is one of the most important documents of modern Chinese history:

The majority of the Red Army soldiers came from mercenary armies; but once in the Red Army, they changed their character.

* The Hupeh-Honan-Anhwei base, the Fukien-Chekiang-Kiangsi base, the Kwangsi (Yukiang River-Tsokiang River) base, to mention only the most important ones.

First of all the Red Army has abolished the mercenary system, making the soldiers feel that they are not fighting for somebody else but for themselves and for the people. . . . Land has been allotted to all Red Army officers and men who are natives of the border area, but it is rather hard to allot land to those from distant areas. . . .

As the casualties among the lower cadres are heavy, soldiers captured from the enemy a short time ago have often been made platoon or company commanders and some of those captured only last February or March are now battalion commanders. . . .

The average soldier needs six months' or a year's training before he can fight, but our soldiers, though recruited only yesterday, have to fight today with practically no training to speak of. Exceedingly poor in military technique, they fight by courage alone. As a long period for rest and training is impossible, we shall see whether we can find ways to avoid certain battles in order to gain time for training. . . .

The Hunan Provincial Committee has asked us to attend to the material life of the soldiers and to make it at least a little better than that of the average worker or peasant. At present the very reverse is the case, for, besides rice, each man gets only five cents a day for cooking oil, salt, firewood and vegetables, and it is hard even to keep this up. *The monthly cost of these items alone amounts to more than ten thousand silver dollars, which are obtained exclusively through expropriating the local bullies.* We have now obtained cotton for the winter clothing of the whole army of five thousand men but are still short of cloth. Cold as the weather is, many of our men are still wearing two suits of clothes of single thickness. Fortunately we are inured to hardships. Furthermore all alike share the same hardships: everybody from the army commander down to the cook lives on a daily fare worth five cents, apart from grain. In the matter of pocket money, if two dimes are allotted, it is two dimes for everybody; if four dimes are allotted, it is four dimes for everybody. Thus the soldiers harbour no resentment against anyone. . . .

The officers do not beat the men; officers and men receive equal treatment, soldiers enjoy freedom of assembly and speech; cumbersome formalities and ceremonies are done away with; and the account books are open to inspection of all. The soldiers handle the messing arrangements. . . . All these measures are very satisfactory to the soldiers. *The newly captured soldiers in particular feel that our army and the Kuomintang's army are worlds apart.* They feel that, though in material life they are worse off in the Red Army than in the White army, spiritually they are liberated. The fact that the same soldier who was not brave in the enemy army yesterday becomes very brave in the Red Army today shows precisely the impact of democracy. *The Red Army is like a furnace in which all captured soldiers are melted down and transformed the moment they come over.* In China not only the people need democracy but the army needs it too. *The democratic system in an army is an important weapon for destroying the feudal mercenary army.* . . .

The local armed forces are the Red Guards and the workers' and peasants' insurrection corps. The insurrection corps is armed with spears and fowling-pieces and organised on a township basis with a contingent in every township, the strength of which is proportional to the township population. Its job is to suppress counter-revolution, to protect the township government, and, when the enemy comes, to assist the Red Army and the Red Guards in war. . . .

In the propaganda directed to the enemy forces, the most effective means are releasing the captured soldiers and giving medical treatment to their wounded. Whenever soldiers or platoon, company or battalion commanders of the enemy forces are captured, propaganda is immediately carried on among them; they are divided into those who wish to leave, and the latter are given travelling expenses and set free. This immediately shatters the enemy's calumny that "the Communist bandits kill every one on sight". . . . The comfort given by Red Army soldiers to the captured soldiers and the farewell made to them are extremely warm-hearted, and at every "Farewell Party to New Brothers" the captured soldiers make speeches to express in return their heartfelt gratitude. Medical treatment for the enemy wounded is also a very effective means. . . .[4]

Mao used the same tactics toward rich peasants as he used towards captured enemy troops. In the sovietized areas the land was redistributed. Most of the land belonged to large and small landlords and this was divided up among the poor peasants. Usually there was complete redistribution of land, so that the rich peasants also lost some of their land. When war-lord troops managed for a time to reoccupy a Red district, most of the rich peasants put on

[4] SW, Vol. I, pp. 79-86. (Emphasis added.)

white ribbons and became "Whites", helping the war-lord troops to arrest the Red peasants, pointing out to them the houses of the escaped Red leaders which were promptly burnt down, and supporting in every way the White Terror in their districts. When the Red troops reoccupied these districts, the rich peasants and their allies fled, fearing Red Terror. But the Red troops, on Mao's instructions arrived with these slogans: *"Do not kill peasants who have become turncoats!"*; *"Peasants who have become turncoats are welcome home to reap their crops"* and even: *"Turncoats are also given land when they return"*. The result of this line, according to Mao's report, and also according to independent accounts, was that some of the peasants did in fact return. The news of the prudently human treatment of the captured enemy troops, and of former turncoats, started slowly to spread.

Almost every main section of Mao's report ends with pleas to headquarters for Party activists, officers, physicians and other trained personnel. A true picture is given of the strength and of the possibilities of the Red areas and their armies. Although Mao states that the Chingkangshan leadership fully agrees with the new Comintern resolution concerning China, and with the Shanghai party directives, he goes on to say: "The area in which the Party's Central Committee has instructed us to develop guerilla warfare is too extensive; . . . this is probably due to an over-estimation of our strength."

The report tried to appeal to the feelings of the Central Committee in passages which also give a truer picture of the real situation than the doctrinaire Communists in Party headquarters could see:

> Having fought in various places in the past year, we are keenly aware that the revolutionary upsurge in the country as a whole is subsiding. . . . Wherever the Red Army goes, it finds the masses cold and reserved; only after propaganda and agitation do they slowly arouse themselves. We have to fight the enemy forces hard whoever they are, and scarcely any mutiny or uprising has taken place within the enemy forces. . . . *We have an acute sense of loneliness and are every moment longing for the end of such a lonely life.*[5]

In spite of this, Mao Tse-tung tries to convince his Party superiors that the only hope lies in the strengthening of the Red Armies and of the Soviet areas; and first of all, the main area: his own.

[5] SW, Vol. I, p. 99. (Emphasis added.)

For a whole year the Red Flag has been kept flying in the border area . . . this is of great significance in national politics. That is why we have always held that it is entirely necessary and correct to build up and expand Red political power in the . . . mountain district.[6]

The Chinese Central Committee and the Comintern instructors could not trust a Communist movement which was not firmly under their control and in which not the industrial workers but the peasants played the leading rôle.

Nor was Stalin in the Kremlin prepared to believe that the Soviet districts and Red Armies, formed without his blessing, could represent the main force of the revolution. He wanted to base the revolution on the cities and the working class. Mao Tse-tung and many other Communists who worked in the Red areas did not agree. They knew that in the immensity of backward and politically divided China the conditions were ripe for the existence of Red governments and guerilla armies.

Even had China then had a strong centralised government, with a single powerful modern army, the backwardness of the country and its geographical conditions would have made it most difficult to annihilate these pockets of Red rule. The lack of modern roads and communications, of sufficient bridges on the gigantic rivers, of well-built passes over mountain-chains, was the best defence of the guerillas. Marshes and ravines, flooded districts and wild mountainous regions, forced regular armies to make detours of hundreds of miles, while the guerilla-type Red Army, helped by the local population could always make its escape. And most important of all: their enemies, the Chiang Kai-shek forces and the war-lord armies, were all the time waging wars against each other. Between August 1927 and 1930 there were six major civil wars between Chiang's Kuomintang and various war-lord coalitions,* while the war-lords in Kweichow, Yunnan and Szechuan waged wars among themselves. The minor clashes between various war-lords were innumerable all over China.

[6] Ibid., p. 104.
* The war between Chiang and Li Tsung-jen on the one hand and Wang Ching-wei and Tang Sheng-chih of Wuhan on the other in October 1927; the war between Chiang and the Kwantung war-lords in December of the same year. In 1928 Chiang in alliance with several war-lords conducted a major offensive against Chang Tso-lin and the Fengtien group. In 1929 Chiang fought the Kwangsi war-lords for the control of Central China; in 1929 and 1930 there were two wars between Chiang and the united forces of Feng and Yen.

Chiang's Kuomintang and the allied or hostile war-lord régimes were based on the cities. Under Comintern instructions the official leadership of the Chinese Communist Party was too. But the Party Centre—the Political Bureau and the Central Committee offices— led a precarious underground existence in Shanghai, just as the provincial bureaux did in the provincial capitals. Living illegally, most of the time in great danger, the Shanghai Communist leaders were most intolerant of breaches of Party usage and discipline. According to the Party constitution everything had to be controlled, directed and initiated by the Party Centre. This was clearly impossible as far as the distant Red enclaves were concerned. The Centre looked with misgivings on these rural organisations, and did its best to concentrate on the cities. Stalin urged them to go on with "classical" Communist activities. The result was a series of more or less pointless small uprisings in the cities, leading to the execution of thousands of Communist workers. The rest of the workers in the factories seeing how senseless this all was, withdrew from the Communist organisations. Soon the Shanghai Party Centre and the provincial centres were comparable to the rural soviets in having precious few of the industrial proletariat, so indispensable for a "proper" Communist movement.

The Hunan-Kiangsi border region was only about 600 miles southwest from Shanghai as the crow flies, but as to attitude and approach it could have been on another planet.

Living in one of the greatest and most intriguing cities in the world, the Shanghai Communist leaders, immersed in their endless scholastic debates and inner-Party struggles, were cut off from reality. Mao Tse-tung, when he retired to his cell in one of the former Buddhist monasteries on Chingkang mountain, had to make do with some quite old newspapers if he wanted to form any idea of national and international developments. Yet he it was who saw the main trends; he, who was not isolated from reality. Very little Communist literature was translated into Chinese. Not reading foreign languages, he could not compete in Marxist-Leninist scholasticism with his Party leaders, and yet (or for this very reason?) he mastered the broad outlines of Leninist tactics and strategy far better than they did.

Having been concerned all his life with political power, he understood Stalin's strange behaviour. Stalin first wanted to consolidate his dictatorship in the USSR and to make that country powerful, before he could welcome the emergence of strong Communist countries. If several other strong Communist countries existed, Stalin's Russian opposition could turn for help to other Communist leaders. So Stalin was not anti-Chinese or anti any country; he simply wanted to remain Number One in world Communism. In Stalin's eyes the Chinese and other revolutions had one task: to help the USSR and to weaken and harass its enemies. Mao knew that he could not count on help from any quarter. If he wanted to lead the Red revolution to victory, he had to fight his way to the top.

In his monkish cell, isolated from his family and from intellectual equals, Mao read the classics, pondered on tactical and strategical problems, or, taking brush and paper, wrote poems. And curious poems they were. Written in the classical style, they mirrored the Olympian calm of a patient war-lord sure of victory. Early in 1928 Kuomintang troops attacked the Huangyang-chieh district on the road to Mao's mountain stronghold, but were ambushed and defeated by the Red guerillas. After the battle, Mao wrote this poem:

> Below the hill were our flags and banners,
> To the hilltop sounded our bugles and drums.
> The foe surrounded us thousands strong,
> But we were steadfast and never moved.
>
> Our defence was strong as a wall and already,
> Now did our wills unite like a fortress.
> From Huangyang-chieh came the thunder of guns,
> And the enemy army had fled in the night!

The "we" of this and similar poems stands for more than the entire Red Army, for more even than the present generation of Chinese workers and peasants. The "we" who "were steadfast and never moved" were not the few regiments who fought under Mao and lost hundreds in dead and wounded, but the simple people of China in revolt. At times the "we" expands and refers to eternal China, to the invincible flow of hundreds of Chinese generations. Their leader is serenely patient because he is certain of the victory of this eternal China. This is the reason why—in such moments of millennial perspective—Mao does not seem to be touched by the fate of his fallen comrades.

The death and suffering of thousands of soldiers are rarely mentioned in these poems. Blood, filth, hunger and pain are ever-present in the life of his ragged troops, yet their leader, after each bloody battle, has idyllic visions of serene calmness following the storm of death.

III

Historical perspective tends to magnify out of contemporary context the rôle of those personalities whose activities prove in retrospect to be important or successful or both. Mao Tse-tung of course was not the only one among the Chinese Communists who disagreed with the vacillating and frequently too doctrinaire Comintern line, nor was he alone in recognising the colossal dynamism of the peasant movement. In the years after the break with the Kuomintang several Red areas were established. Within the political and military leadership of each Red base there were struggles for personal power, while the heads of the various Soviet districts also manoeuvred for the leadership of all the Soviets. Many of these temporary leaders died during the innumerable battles and local skirmishes during the next few years, others either sooner or later accepted Mao's leadership or were ousted by him. In 1955 Mao conferred the title of Marshal on ten of his outstanding army leaders. Most of them had fought with him or in alliance with him since 1927, commanding the various Red Armies. To mention only the best known: Chu Teh; Peng Teh-huai, of Korean war fame; Ho Lung; Chen Yi, who became Foreign Minister after Chou En-lai; and the famous "young general" Lin Piao.

Even if we discount the magnifying effect of historical perspective, the events of these fighting years show that Mao emerged as the head of the Chinese Soviets thanks to his manifold talents and great capacity for hard work and in spite of the misgivings and disapproval of Stalin, the Comintern and the Chinese Party leadership. Between the deposing of Ch'en Tu-hsiu in 1927 and 1934, Stalin, through the Comintern, appointed five leaders of the Chinese CP. They never even considered Mao for leadership, and all of the successive General-Secretaries were highly critical of Mao Tse-tung. He became Party leader only when he had effective power, and he was the first Chinese Party leader to achieve this position without the blessing, or even the previous knowledge, of Stalin and the Comintern.

Mao's leading position depended on the success of his own Soviet districts, and on the successes of Chu Teh's armies, which were, in the last analysis, under his direction. But it also depended on getting the heads of the other Soviet areas to accept his supreme political leadership; and his position depended last but not least on his skill in avoiding an open break with Shanghai and the Comintern. He had to, and did in fact, combine the qualities of successful war-lord, bandit leader, provincial governor, head of state, spy-chief, agricultural organiser, propagandist and diplomat.

While Shanghai criticised the class proportion of his armies, his own main worry was that they had no winter uniforms and that food was extremely scarce. When a most dangerous intrigue was developing against him at Party headquarters, his first concern had to be the local military reality, such as finding a safe way back from a sortie with some army detachment he happened to be leading. At times when his troops were desperately trying to defend themselves against concentrated enemy attack, couriers would arrive with news of a new manoeuvre directed against him by the Shanghai Bureau of the Comintern.

Although for many years Chu Teh and Mao shared power in their own enclave and acted almost always in agreement, it was clear that Mao was the overall leader and that Chu Teh was his choice for military commander. During these turbulent years Mao tied to his leadership several other very able Communist generals, who were later to prove themselves masters of guerilla warfare, like the brilliant young general Lin Piao. During his first period in power then, Mao chose all his staff well, and knew how to delegate power, and to whom.

His guerilla armies were trained to carry out political and economic tasks, as well as military. The three main rules of discipline were: prompt obedience to orders; no confiscation whatever from the poor peasantry; and prompt delivery directly to the Soviet government, for its disposal, of all goods confiscated from the landlords. The fighters were also ordered to be courteous and polite to the people and help them when they could; to return anything they borrowed and replace all damaged articles, to pay for everything. If they slept in a peasant house, they were to clean up and put in order everything before leaving, and "be sanitary, and especially establish latrines a safe distance from people's houses". Everything was done so that the poor peasants, the overwhelming majority of the population, should learn not to dread the Red Army.

From Shanghai, and from the Hunan provincial Party committee, special commissaries arrived, urging the intensification of the Red Terror in the sovietized areas. Mao's troops executed landlords, "local bullies", usurers and all sorts of "class enemies". They often went to excesses. But the critics were not satisfied with this:

In March (1928) the representatives of the Southern Hunan Special Committee arrived in Ninkang and criticised us for leaning to the Right, *for having not done enough burning and killing.*[7]

Mao was intent on changing the "ultra-left" line, not because he was against Red Terror in principle but because he knew that too much burning and killing would jeopardise the successes of his armies. As it was, the mass-executions of class-enemies horrified the countryside. In the villages there were not only "classes" of large and small landlords, rich, medium, and poor peasants, but there were, above all, clans—and the very strong clan-ties cut across the class barriers. For these reasons poor peasants often turned against the Red rule.

The Shanghai Party Centre was against the establishment of "areas of Red political power" in the provinces. Mao's Front Committee complained of the Party Centre's letter of February 9, 1929, disapproving of the plan to seize Kiangsi Province and wanting the Red Army to engage only in guerilla activities without trying to set up larger districts of Red power. In reply, Mao wrote in the name of the Front Committee that "the letter of the Party Centre gives too pessimistic an appraisal of the objective situation".

He pointed out that Chiang Kai-shek had mounted three offensives against Chingkangshan which had failed, and that the Red areas were growing. He agreed that the Party should go on organising the workers in the cities, but "in our opinion it is . . . a mistake for any of our Party members to fear the development of the power of the peasants lest it become stronger than that of the workers and hence detrimental to the revolution. . . . The establishment of Red political power in small areas and the creation and expansion of the Red Army, are in particular the main conditions for helping the struggle in the cities and accelerating the revolutionary upsurge."[8]

Not only some Party members, but the Party Centre itself feared the growing power of Mao's peasants. The Secretary-General of the Party Central Committee at that time was Li Li-san, who carried out Stalin's instructions faithfully—if somewhat reluctantly. From the foreign settlement of Shanghai, he and his staff directed a propaganda war against the leaders of the Soviet bases and the Red Armies.

How well informed they were about events in these areas is illustrated by the fact that the official organ of the Comintern Centre, which was in wireless contact with the Shanghai Comintern repre-

---

[7] *SW*, p. 99. (Emphasis added.)
[8] *SW*, Vol. I, p. 122.

sentatives, published in March a long obituary of Mao Tse-tung who had "died of consumption".[9]

The Stalin line of the time was summarised by Li Li-san in the official *Red Flag*. The Secretary-General complained that "the forces of the peasantry, particularly of the Red Army, have far out-stripped the forces of the workers". This is a deviation which proves "a lack of faith in the strength of the working class . . . [for] simply to rely on the Red Army to take one or several provinces in order to set up a national revolutionary régime would be a most serious error. Not only is such an idea preposterous but it might even lead us to neglect our most vital activity—the organisation of the workers' struggle and the organisation of political strikes by armed workers' units."[10]

Moscow left no doubt that this was the official line. *Pravda* (April 28, 1930) attacked the same deviation, while the Comintern journal had this to say:

Powerful as the partisan movement already is at present, the counter-revolution which stands under the protection of the im-perialists in the industrial and trading centres *cannot be finally crushed with the partisan forces of the Chinese villages and small districts alone.*[11]

At the same time Li Li-san quite openly attacked the Mao-Chu Teh strategy as expounded in Mao's report to the Central Committee:

The leading rôle of the proletariat in the revolutionary struggle is not simply a basic principle in the line of any proletarian party but is, in fact, the only guarantee of the success of the revolution. The Proletariat is the leader of the revolution—the peasantry is its ally. No strategic line can ever depart from this principle.[12]

Among historians of Chinese Communism there has been much debate whether or not, in 1927 and later, Mao Tse-tung violated basic principles of orthodox Marxism-Leninism.[13]

[9] *Inprecor*, March 20, 1930.
[10] *Red Flag*, No. 88, March 29, 1930.
[11] *Inprecor*, May 22, 1930.
[12] *Red Flag*, No. 104, May 24, 1930.
[13] See for instance the recent debate between Professors K. A. Witt-fogel and Benjamin Schwartz in Nos. 1, 2 and 4 of *The China Quarterly*, London, January-March, April-June and October-December, 1960.

As a Communist theoretician, Mao Tse-tung was no "peasant-deviationist". Even during the years of the peasant revolution, Mao insisted that his aim was to establish a Communist state based on heavy industry and the leadership of the proletariat. He was attacked by the dogmatists because of the unorthodox means by which he wanted to reach the most orthodox Communist ends. But as a Communist Party member and functionary, he most certainly was a deviationist, for the simple reason that he did not obey the instructions of the Comintern and his own Party superiors. He did not carry out to the letter the Party line of the day; on the contrary, he opposed it in action. It is beside the point that events proved him right; he was disobedient for a long period.

The Comintern ruled that the Chinese Communists could not crush their enemies "with the partisan forces of the Chinese villages and small districts alone". Mao disregarded this ruling. The Comintern instructed the Chinese Communists to concentrate on the cities and to launch the main assault against capitalism with the revolution of the workers. Mao successfully put into practice his theory that the Communists could come to power through the revolution of the countryside. As long as the Comintern rejected this theory, Mao was not only a disobedient party member, but also a theoretical heretic.

Mao and Chu Teh left their mountain stronghold at the beginning of 1929. Chiang's main armies were engaged in wars against various war-lords, the offensives against the Red enclaves had temporarily ceased, so expansion was possible. Fighting against the militia of local landlords and some weak units of the war-lord forces, Mao's Red Army moved into southern Kiangsi and set up their headquarters in the small village of Juichin. Mao's "Central Soviet base" soon encompassed several counties of southern Kiangsi and western Fukien. In February 1930 the first Provincial Soviet Government was formally established in Juichin under Mao's chairmanship. He was, at the same time, political commissar of the First Army Corps, consisting of three Red Armies under the supreme command of Chu Teh. As political commissar, Mao took part in many military expeditions.

We have a glimpse of his everyday life in the early nineteenthirties from the reminiscences of his former orderly, Chen Changfeng. Chen recalled that it was at the end of March, 1930 when he was transferred to the Revolutionary Front Committee to be Mao's orderly:

At that time we called him "Commissar", not "Chairman" Mao. He had only the simplest of belongings. Two cotton and wool mixture blankets, a sheet, two of the ordinary uniform jackets and trousers, a sweater, a patched umbrella, an enamel mug which served as his rice-bowl, and a grey brief-case with nine pockets. On the march he used to carry the brief-case and the umbrella himself, and I made a roll of the rest of the things. When we made camp I used to get hold of two boards for a bed, and make it up with the blankets and sheet. He used the rest of his belongings as a pillow.

He never did spend much of the nights in sleep, though. Directly the evening meal was over he would get out his maps, papers and pen and start working by lamplight. . . . He would often wake me up around midnight, saying to me "Let's have some cold water". We had a little bucket we had brought with us from Kiangsi, and I used to get cold water in that for him to freshen up in. We hadn't got a basin—he just used the bucket. He'd feel hungry after that, and I would get him the "three-level-rice" in his mug—that is, rice in first, then whatever vegetable was going, and then another level of rice. The rice was left over from the afternoon meal, and I would heat it for him. If he didn't finish it he would cover it up with a piece of paper and eat it at the next mealtime—he would never let me throw food away. After this midnight snack he went on with his work. It was under such conditions that he wrote the famous *On the Land-Investigation Campaign.*

ʳ Later on, when the Central Workers' and Peasants' Democratic Government was set up at Juichin, Kiangsi, and he was elected Chairman of the Republic, he still lived just as simply.[14]

Mao was by this time one of the most wanted men in China. The Kuomintang and the various war-lord governments offered rewards for his capture dead or alive. There were horrible reprisals against his family. We have no direct documentation as to how he reacted then to the tragedies in his personal life. The testimony of his autobiography shows only how he dealt with these events six years later, in 1936 when he dictated his memoirs.

Mao Tse-tung had married Yang K'ai-hui in 1920. She was executed ten years later. They were lovers, sharing the same obsessions, the same tastes and very often the same dangers. They had their home together whenever the hectic existence of two professional

[14] *Stories of the Long March,* Foreign Language Press, Peking, 1958.

revolutionaries made this possible. Party work often separated them for months in such a way that they could not even write each other. Their two children were often left with friends or Party comrades, and from 1925 onwards there were only rare periods when the family lived under the same roof for any length of time. Party eulogies and hostile accounts alike imply that in K'ai-hui, Mao Tse-tung had a true companion, an "understanding friend and brave comrade". Yet K'ai-hui figures only twice in Mao's autobiographical accounts. One sentence reports their marriage, while her arrest and execution (and that of his sister) is mentioned later in a long paragraph as one of the illustrations of the growing prestige of the Red Army and its leaders.*

If a non-Communist Westerner mentioned the prestige of the Red Army immediately after mentioning the execution of his wife and sister, it could be taken as affected cynicism or callousness. Mao was neither callous nor a cynic when he dictated his reminiscences in 1936. He was a man who could write in an official party report: "We have an acute sense of loneliness and are every moment longing for the end of such a lonely life." It was only for the sake of his friendly Western interviewer that he mentioned private matters at all. As there is no record of the date of his wife's execution, it is impossible to tell whether he received the news during one of the innumerable battles or the rare periods of comparative calm.

Although his entire existence was on "war-footing" and how to fight became the central problem of his daily life, he remained all through the twenty-one years of continuous warfare a reader and writer of poetry. In the enforced lulls in his governmental and military activities he read the classics and books on Chinese history. He was not too shy to write about sentiments when they had to do with "the cause". In a long letter written in January 1930 "to a comrade", he wrote:

> Those of us working in the Red Army, especially when defeated in battle, encircled on all sides or pursued by strong enemy forces, often unwillingly universalise and magnify what are after all only momentary, particular and local conditions, as if the whole situation in China and throughout the world was dark and gloomy, and the prospects of victory dim and remote.[15]

He was in love with Yang K'ai-hui and in his lonely, hard, guerilla

---

* Snow, p. 173-7.
[15] SW, Vol. I, p. 119. (Emphasis added.)

existence, her execution must have been a cruel shock. But it is a mistake to conclude—as some writers do—that the execution of his wife and sister made him harder and more inclement. He was a professional revolutionary accustomed since childhood to the spectacle of executions. His attitude, or rather his indifference, to death changed little through the years. He was a military commander who had to send his troops into mortal battles. He was the head of an armed régime, used to signing execution orders and to dealing summarily with political enemies. He ordered the first "rectification campaign" of his life in December 1929, dealing severely with deviations and mistakes of Communists in the Red Army. He was the leader of a mighty faction in the All-China Communist Party and was not choosey about means when he had to fight against his enemies within the Party. Communists in the Soviet areas who formed factions against Mao's leadership were simply arrested as members of an "Anti-Bolshevik Corps" and summarily executed.

Chang Kuo-t'ao who was a member of the Chinese Political Bureau in 1921-3, 1925-7* and 1928-38, the last three years under Mao's leadership, later broke with the Party. In an article entitled "Mao—A New Portrait by an Old Colleague", he wrote that in December 1930 Mao executed hundreds of anti-Mao Communists who were "falsely dubbed anti-bolsheviks". According to Chang, Mao was "a hero of the grass wilderness, a rough-hewn rural Robin Hood" who had "a mind in which Chinese monarchical concepts, Marxist-Leninist ideas and dreams of glory existed side by side".[16]

Another former colleague, Li Ang, has repeatedly asserted in writing that even a slight personal quarrel would induce Mao to kill people, whether Communists or not. Other writers maintain that Communist emissaries from Shanghai were apt to die in suspiciously large numbers during the military campaigns. It is impossible to check these accounts. But Mao's writings, his governmental and army directives, give ample evidence that he was by no means a "bourgeois sentimentalist". At the same time, he was of course far more than a "rough-hewn rural Robin Hood". He worked out pragmatically the blue-print of Chinese Communist rule during these years, he wrote original and important treatises on strategy, and

* According to Conrad Brandt, *Stalin's Failure in China*, Cambridge, Mass. 1958, p. 215, until 1927 there was no political bureau in the Chinese C.P. However, Comintern and Chinese Communist reports mention the Politbureau also between 1921 and 1927.

[16] New York, *Time Magazine*, August 2, 1953.

he was certainly an exceptionally able Chairman of the junta of Communist war-lords whom he transformed, through the years, into most obedient subordinates.

The Chairman's "office" was at times under a tree, his "desk" a board on two stones; at times it was in a primitive army tent, in a peasant hut or in a cave in the mountain-side. The Chairman, his office, his government, were often on the move; most of the time having far less comfort, privacy and safety than a small field-command during a battle. The Chairman's government sometimes administered small districts with a few hundred thousand inhabitants, sometimes huge tracts of land populated by millions. In addition to the areas under direct Red rule there were the very large and numerous guerilla zones. Here the people were peasants during the day and guerillas after dark—their actions planned and directed from the current headquarters of the Soviet government.

Mao's entourage liked to quote an old Chinese saying: "A plan prepared in an army tent beforehand decides the victory to be won thousands of miles away."

By the end of 1930 when the strength of the Red Army was growing and it was clear that the provincial Kuomintang armies were unable to crush them, Moscow realised the propaganda value of the Soviet areas, and, forgetting about orthodoxy, gave the Chinese Soviets an official blessing, without waiting for the capture of large cities.

At this time Mao was working on the realisation of several plans. First he had to become acknowledged governmental leader of all the Soviet areas. This he achieved in November 1931, when the first All-China Soviet Congress elected him Chairman of the Chinese Soviet Republics Central Executive Committee. Secondly, he had to become official leader of the Chinese Communist Party. The first step towards this goal was the transfer of the Central Committee and the Politbureau of the Party from distant Shanghai to the headquarters of Soviet China, where Mao and Chu Teh had more power. This was caused by the fact that in Shanghai the underground Communist leaders were in a most dangerous position. But at first, the transfer of the Party Centre made Mao's life and work incomparably more difficult. The Party leaders, inspired by the Stalin line and immersed in dogmatic squabbles, interfered with the running of the Red Army and the Soviet Government. Meanwhile General Chiang Kai-shek unleashed his campaigns of "encirclement and extermination" against the Red districts. Not counting three smaller offensives before 1930, and not counting the constant attacks against the Red bases by the troops of various war-lords, Chiang Kai-shek's central government conducted five "extermination" offensives against the central Red base in Southern China.

In the first campaign, about 100,000 front line troops attacked from December 1930 until the end of January 1931. They were defeated by the Mao-Chu Teh strategy: to lure the enemy deep into revolutionary territory, concentrate superior forces to attack the weakest units of the invader and destroy his forces piecemeal by mobile guerilla tactics.

For his second offensive, during May and June 1931, Chiang used 200,000 troops, with similar result. In the third annihilation campaign, ending in October 1931, as many as 300,000 troops were concentrated—and defeated. The growing Red Armies were by now armed to an ever increasing degree with captured military equipment. During 1932, while the fourth annihilation drive was being planned, General Chiang Kai-shek tried to blockade the Red districts with an army half a million strong. In this fourth offensive (April-October 1933), General Chiang used a quarter of a million troops, far better equipped than those in the first three drives. For the fifth campaign Chiang mobilised nearly a million men and, from October 1933 till October 1934, there were almost always 400,000 troops engaged in the anti-Red offensive. This last annihilation campaign was planned by Chiang's chief military adviser, the late General von Seeckt, a former Chief of Staff of the German Army. Three lines of fortifications, consisting mainly of small blockhouses, were built around the central Red base, to make it difficult for the Red Army to apply guerilla tactics.

Chiang had modern arms, communications, military aeroplanes, well trained staff officers, hospitals, plenty of medicine, doctors, money and food. The Red Army was short of everything.

It was in the atmosphere of these ceaseless annihilation campaigns that Mao had to run his government, direct the distant guerilla zones, defend himself against internal intrigue and work out the political and propaganda strategy for Red victory over all China.

For Mao Tse-tung this normal "campaign-existence" lasted for two decades. In the shorter or longer intervals of comparative safety and comfort he had his "private life". A year or two after the execution of his first wife, he married Ho Tzu-ch'en,* a former school-

---

* In some other accounts her name is given as *Ho Tzu-ch'en* or even as *Ho Tze-nien*.

teacher who had studied for a time in the Changsha Normal College, where the Mao legend was still alive. Seventeen years younger
than her husband, the third Mme Tse-tung was a good-looking,
slender woman and an ardent Communist. She bore Mao five children, three of whom had to be left with peasants during the perils
of the Long March. These children, and indeed their peasant foster-
parents, could not be traced in later years. Ho Tzu-ch'en was one
of the thirty women who survived the Long March. Whenever
possible, she was at her husband's side.

Dressed in the faded cotton tunic of the ordinary soldiers, chain-
smoking, the Red war-lord sat at his ever-changing "desks", planning, composing speeches and essays on strategy, reading the
classics, writing poems in traditional style, signing execution orders,
directing his government—surviving all possible political and military dangers and bent on surviving all the dangers yet to come.

After the arrival of the Shanghai Communist leaders at the Juichin headquarters of the Central Soviet Government, Mao Tse-
tung was for years like a tight-rope walker, whose ropes are being
slackened by some of his enemies, while others throw stones at him,
or try to make him fall by emitting sudden blood-curdling screams.

The Moscow-directed Party leaders tried to reduce Mao's status,
as head of the Soviet Government, to that of a figure-head, and Chu
Teh's to that of a field commander.

Most of the Party leadership were returned students from Moscow where they had been taught Marxism-Leninism under Comintern direction. They insisted that the supreme direction of the Soviet Government and the Red Army was to be conducted by the
Standing Committee of the Party's Political Bureau. Each governmental and Red Army department was to be directed by an ap-
propriate department of the Party Centre. The system of multiple
controls was to ensure that all decisions should originate in the executive organs of the Party. Mao Tse-tung, Chu Teh and their like
were regarded as "within-the-party-fellow-travellers", adventurers,
right-wing deviationists, who denied the leading rôle of the industrial workers in the revolution. According to some sources, in 1931
Mao and Chu Teh were not even elected to the Party Central Committee, let alone the supreme Standing Committee of the Politbureau. Political power at Party headquarters was in the hands of
Po Ku, while the Chairman of the Party's Military Affairs Bureau
was Chou En-lai, who had managed ever since 1924 to serve in and
survive all the vicissitudes of the Chinese Party leadership.

But the Party Centre, freshly arrived at Mao's headquarters in Juichin, had simply not enough power to depose Mao from his governmental position, or to squeeze Chu Teh entirely out of Red Army leadership. Mao had the Soviet "governmental" network sufficiently in hand to retain considerable powers. His allies and supporters were Red Army leaders like Chu Teh and a few other generals. In the Party apparatus of the Soviet areas he had many loyal disciples and supporters.

Such theoretically unimportant practical details as the feeding and clothing of the Soviet population and the Red Armies were left to Mao's government. Attacked or at least blockaded most of the time by the Kuomintang armies, the Soviet territories had to rely on "village-self-sufficiency" and on black-market trading with neighbouring Kuomintang districts. Ideologically it was, of course, all wrong to engage in illicit trade and undercover deals with rich Kuomintang merchants, these "nasty lackeys of the imperialists", but the alternative was starvation or freezing to death. The Party line called for a resolute class struggle against the rich peasants in the Soviet territories, but as such a struggle would have cut the rice production in these areas, Mao Tse-tung, as head of the Soviet government, decided against it, a decision which his rivals and enemies used in an attempt to show that Mao was a deviationist. This was not so. The struggle against the rich peasants would have led to their burning their rice stocks, to their escaping to Kuomintang territories. Faced with extermination the rich peasants would not have bothered to work their fields. The Central Committee of the CP in January 1934 officially instructed Mao's Soviet Government to "conduct a clear and decisive class-line in the matter of liquidating the landlords and kulaks (rich peasants)". Mao disregarded this directive to save the physical existence of the Soviet base and the Red Army.

In the same way, Mao was not against proletarian leadership in the Soviets. It was he who proposed that the 1934 Constitution of the Soviet Republic should give an almost four-to-one electoral privilege to workers. (One delegate to thirteen workers, while it required fifty peasants to elect one delegate.) But in practice Mao had to work with the people who were at hand.

The Party Centre, by moving nearer to the real issues and detailed practical problems of Chinese Soviet existence, exposed its own trusted apparatus to the "infection of reality". The colossal blunders committed in the defence of ideological purity only enlarged Mao's camp of supporters.

Since 1931 Japanese armies had been invading Northern China. Chiang Kai-shek, who held the view that "domestic rebellion must be suppressed before fighting a foreign foe", ordered his Kuomintang armies to retreat. After taking Manchuria, the Japanese armies crossed the Great Wall and attacked on a broad front. General Chiang Kai-shek did not resist. He temporised, negotiated armistices, tried to gain time. In 1932 his own Nineteenth Route Army resisted for more than a month an all-out attack against Shanghai. General Chiang did not support the defenders, on the contrary, he disowned them, by signing a truce agreement with the Japanese concerning the complete demilitarisation of the Shanghai district. This, and similar "truce" and "armistice" agreements gave Japan power over large territories in Northern China. Meanwhile Chiang Kai-shek's Central Government *prohibited all anti-Japanese agitation and "conspiracy"*. Anti-Japanese organisers were executed or imprisoned in their tens of thousands.

In this situation the rigid "ultra-left" policy urged by the Chinese Party leadership was really catastrophic. In November 1933, in the important maritime province of Fukien, three Kuomintang military leaders rebelled with their armies against Chiang Kai-shek's "traitor régime". They organised a "People's Government" based on liberal democratic reforms and preached militant resistance to the Japanese. Mao, Chu Teh and other "right-wing opportunists" wanted an alliance with the Fukien rebel régime. But the Comintern and the Chinese Party Centre were against an alliance with such "middle roaders" as the "bourgeois democratic" leaders of the Fukien revolt. The Party leadership made it impossible for Mao, Chu Teh, and other Soviet and Red Army leaders to link up with the non-Communist rebels in the neighbouring Fukien province. Without allies and help, the Fukien armies were beaten by Chiang Kai-shek. But the Comintern in Moscow looked upon the Fukien revolt as "a fresh swindle from the counter-revolutionary camp" and gave its blessing to the Chinese Communist Party for its "sharp struggle against the right deviation as the principal danger in the present period".[17]

That the suppression of the Fukien revolt was a victory for Chiang Kai-shek and a great loss of opportunity for the Chinese Soviets, was soon obvious to everybody concerned.

By that time Chiang Kai-shek had launched his fifth and largest extermination offensive. According to Mao the Red régime made

[17] *Inprecor*, February 5 and 23, 1934.

two fatal errors during this period. The first was the failure to unite with the armies of the Fukien rebellion in 1933, the second and more serious mistake was to meet Chiang Kai-shek's vastly superior forces in positional warfare, abandoning the guerilla tactics of manoeuvre.

For both errors partial or perhaps main responsibility lay with the Comintern military expert whom Stalin sent in 1933 to the Chinese Soviets. This Comintern representative assumed the Chinese name "Li Teh", although it was well known that he was a former German officer, who turned Communist, served as cavalry officer in the Soviet Army, and after graduating from the Moscow Red Army Academy, became commander of a Soviet division. There is no trustworthy evidence as to the real name of this German general. After arriving in China Li Teh, as Comintern representative, could not help coming under the influence of the official Communist Party leadership, who were opposed to Mao and his generals in the field. It was this German general who worked out plans for positional defensive warfare to meet the onslaught of Chiang Kai-shek's fifth annihilation campaign, planned by another German, Chiang's adviser, General von Seeckt.

The Chinese members of the Party's Military Affairs Bureau, all opposed to the Mao-Chu Teh leadership, accepted Li Teh's plan.

When the ring tightened around the Kiangsi Soviet base, the Party Centre ordered passive defence. This gave time and possibility for the Kuomintang armies to depopulate the surrounding guerilla zones. The peasants of these zones were deported or executed. The Red frontier districts were bombed and machine-gunned from the air. According to Kuomintang sources, during the fifth annihilation campaign nearly one million people were killed, or starved to death in the hermetically sealed "Red pockets".

As it was impossible to repulse the Chiang Kai-shek armies, a decision was reached to break through the rings of fortifications and retreat to the interior of China where a new Soviet base could be set up under better conditions. The First Front Red Army and the population of Soviet Kiangsi (the "Central base") was secretly alerted. Moving only at night, about 100,000 men were concentrated in the south and at the end of October 1934, in a sudden offensive, they broke through the lines of entrenchments and blockhouses. Through this gap poured the entire Soviet republic. Hundreds of thousands of peasants' carts, of mules and ponies, carried weapons, ammunition, machine-tools, whatever was portable from the dismantled factories, State papers, office equipment, silver dollars, food, seed, printing presses. The cities and towns of Soviet China were stripped bare of everything useful and portable. The families of Red Army men and government functionaries, entire peasant households, children, old and young women, everyone was on the move.

The Long March had begun!

VIII

THE LONG MARCH

The farthest distance covered by the Red Army was 25,000 *li*, extending over . . . eleven provinces. Chiang Kai-shek had exerted his utmost efforts to mobilise his crack army and air force units, to unite with the troops of war-lords' and landlords' armed forces, and to set up defence works at natural barriers along the route of advance of the Red Army, while never letting-up in his attacks. To avoid an enemy which was far better equipped and in much greater numbers, the Red Army had to advance along desolate regions, crossing lofty mountains and turbulent rivers, as well as dangerous shoals and treacherous paths, particularly in western Szechuan with its snow mountains rising 5,000 metres above sea level, and its murderous marshlands: These regions were marked by their universal poverty, sparse population and shortage of food. The national minorities of these areas . . . were full of animosity towards the Hans (Chinese) . . . All these difficulties and hazards, however, did not prevent the Red Army from achieving victory in the Long March.*

I

The main body of the March, led by Mao, was for 368 days constantly under reconnaissance, machine-gunning and bombing from the air. They were pursued, obstructed and intercepted, attacked and encircled by several hundred thousand Kuomintang troops, and in addition had to fight the armies of ten war-lords in twelve different provinces. The distance they travelled was similar to that from Mexico to Alaska, with the difference that the natural barriers on their way were more formidable. They crossed eighteen mountain ranges, twenty-four rivers, several deserts, swamplands and six territories inhabited by wild and hostile aborigines. They fought more than 200 battles, and hardly a day passed without a skirmish or two. The troops covered about 6,000 miles on foot.

They passed through twelve provinces, inhabited by 200,000,000 people. They occupied more than sixty cities, and several hundred towns. While parts of the Red Army pursued the local troops, in

* *Stories of the Long March*, Foreign Language Press, Peking, 1958, pp. ix-x.

the cities and towns political instructors taught the people how to
form Soviets and start to govern their own districts. The travelling
theatres of the Red Army gave performances. Posters proclaimed
the liberation of the slaves, the abolition of taxes, the "expropriation" of the landlords, the destruction of land-deeds, the distribution
of the lands of the absentee landlords. Before they left a district,
guerilla zones and peasant partisan units were organised. Some of
the rifles confiscated from the war-lord arsenals were distributed
among the peasantry.

The statistical summaries of the Long March give a rough impression of what the troops had to suffer, but give no hint of the
agonies of the leaders.

Of the 100,000 men in Mao's main column 80,000 died during
the March. They were killed in battle, starved or frozen to death,
drowned in turbulent rivers, fell off mountain precipices, or perished in epidemics. But the soldiers were spared the mental anguish
of the leaders. The troops had to fight for their physical survival.
*The few dozen leaders had in addition to fight the most bitter and
dangerous battles of their lives for their political survival.*

Most of the time they were just as hungry, tired and ill as the
troops. They were tormented by cold, by disease, by dirt, by lice.
But, hunted from the air, pursued, harassed, ambushed, encircled
on land by the Kuomintang forces—their most dangerous enemies
were riding or wearily trudging along near by. The enemies who
caused Mao Tse-tung most of his anxiety were some of his own
comrades. He had to cope with all the "normal" dangers of the
fugitive Red Army, but in addition there were around him his rivals,
ever ready to ambush him, ever ready to exploit one of his mistakes
in order to oust him from leadership. Natural calamities, from sudden landslides to snowstorms, endangered him like any other
trooper. But political calamities could originate any day in the distant offices of Stalin and the Comintern or in the headquarters-on-
the-move of the other Red Armies.

The statistical summary of the Long March as far as Mao, Chu
Teh, Chou En-lai and the other leaders are concerned, should also
include a frighteningly long list of political clashes, of Party infighting, of violent battles for leadership. Mao himself had to survive
two main onslaughts and hundreds of smaller attacks against his
leadership, not to mention the perpetual crop of hostile intrigues.

At the outset, the Long March had no acknowledged leader. In
war and at times of utmost national danger even democracies produce if not a dictator at least a generally accepted supreme leader.

The migrating Chinese Soviet Republic, fighting for its life, did not and could not have such a leader. Committees, cliques, and outstanding individuals were fighting for supreme power and none of them were either fully backed or fully repudiated by Stalin and the Comintern. As the authorised oracle on Marxism-Leninism and as the leader of world Communism, Stalin was at this stage reluctant to give his supreme blessing or to excommunicate any one of the rivals for Chinese leadership. As the struggle for personal power in China was also expressed in clashing ideological lines, he wanted to back the line which proved itself successful and fairly stable.

In retrospect, the 6,000 miles trek of Mao's First Front Army turned out to be the most important of the "Long Marches", indeed it was *the* Long March. But other Chinese Soviets and their armies were also on the move, and at that time it was still an open question which of these would prove to be most important. General Ho Lung commanded the Second Front Army which was to start its Long March only in November 1935 from the recently established Hunan-Hupeh-Szechuan-Kweichow Soviet base. Mao's rival, the Vice-Chairman of the Soviet Republic, Chang Kuo-t'ao had his own Soviet base and Fourth Front Red Army in the Szechuan-Shensi area. Other Soviet bases and Red Armies were also on the move. Some of these were annihilated, other established new Red enclaves in various parts of the country. But during the Long March of Mao's First Front Army no one could foretell which of the armies and Soviets would survive.

Moscow's ambiguous behaviour made it even more difficult for the Chinese Reds to agree on firm, long-term plans, and on supreme political and military leadership. The rivals and their cliques were in conference at each halt. Committees and subcommittees discussed the hundreds of problems which cropped up daily and, as Mao was to complain later, they paid less attention to the immediate situation than to various theoretical lines and clique-policies. Tactical and strategical plans had to be approved by committees of Moscow-trained Marxist scholastics and theoreticians.

At the beginning of the Long March, Mao Tse-tung was decidedly not in Stalin's favour. Since 1931 he has always been mentioned in Moscow as one of the leaders of the Chinese Soviets, but never as a Party leader. At the time of the Long March he was not a member of the Chinese Party's Political Bureau, so in principle he had many Party superiors. During the Long March his position as leader of the Chinese Soviet Government was also endangered. He was the Chairman of the Central Executive Committee of the Soviet Republic, embracing some fifteen Soviet base areas. The Vice-Chairman, Chang Kuo-t'ao, leader of the Fourth Front Army was, moreover, in principle Mao's Party superior. During the Long March Chang made several attempts to oust Mao from leadership.

Another dangerous rival was Chou En-lai, the most versatile tight-rope walker in the Red leadership. He was most unlike Mao in appearance, background, nature and upbringing. Coming from a family of mandarins, he started out on his career in the Communist movement with the versatility and talent for intrigue of his ancestors. His background was urban middle class. He grew up in Mukden and Tientsin, the great mercantile port of the North. After graduating from a Western style middle school, he studied in Japan, Britain, Germany and France and was co-founder of the Paris branch of the Chinese CP. On his return to China in 1924, he was instantly given a high Party post as Secretary of the CP in Kwantung Province, and deputy head of the Political Department of the Whampoa Military Academy during the alliance with the Kuomintang. From 1927 onwards he was continuously a member of the Chinese Politbureau. With his great talent for political survival, he managed to keep his position each time the Party leader was deposed, although he seems to have served each one of them faithfully. In 1930 he had to confess his "rotten cowardly opportunism" before the CentCom Plenum, but again received a high Party appointment. From 1931 onwards he was Central Committee representative at Mao's Soviet base, and during the first few months of the Long March, as head of the Party's Military Affairs Bureau, he tried to oust Mao from the direction of the Red Army. In 1932 Chou took over from Mao the post of political commissioner of the First Front Army.

Moreover Chou En-lai's wife, a leading woman Communist official, made several public attacks in the early nineteen-thirties against Mao's "antiproletarian line". Chou, who had already visited Moscow, had good connections at the Comintern centre. With his international background, and knowledge of foreign languages, Chou En-lai wanted to be acknowledged as an expert in foreign affairs. Having helped to train the Kuomintang army as one of the heads of the Whampoa Military Academy, he was also regarded by the Party as a military expert. In fact, he knew a great deal about the Kuomintang armies and was later a useful adviser of General Chu Teh.

Another rival was Po Ku, the nominal head of the Party. There were also the returned students from Moscow, who had the best connections in the Comintern, and the on-the-spot backing of Li Teh, the only Comintern agent taking part in the Long March.

The average daily distance covered by the marchers was twenty-four miles. Main roads or frequented tracks were rarely used. In most of the territory crossed they did not exist at all. Across muddy plains, up and down mountain-ranges, over stony hillsides, through swampy valleys, and thick forests, the March went on. The leaders rode horses, donkeys, or mules, whenever this was possible. But to spend eight to twelve hours a day in the saddle, in slashing rain, in snowstorms, in heat, or even in good weather—and afterwards to spend long hours in staff conferences or in Party committees, was an exceptionally hard test of endurance. And at least a third of the distance the leaders had to cover on foot.

In terribly tight and dangerous situations, when everything turned on a swift decision, the Standing Committee or Military Bureau wasted hours in ideological and dogmatic squabbles. The ideological clash was still between the dogmatically correct Muscovite line and the "too realistic" Mao practice. The Muscovite Chinese leaders at first opposed the move away from the vicinity of the great cities, from the more industrialised maritime provinces towards the interior and the Tibetan and Mongolian border regions. They were worried by the fact that the Red Army could only make good its losses by recruiting tens of thousands of peasants. They disapproved of "countryside Communism", and of the lack of industrial workers in leading army and government positions. They criticised and attacked the "ideologically weak comrades" in the leadership of the Party and the Soviet Government.

At first none of the leaders anticipated a "long march".* They simply wanted to escape from Kuomintang encirclement and thought of joining the nearest large Soviet base a few hundred miles to the North. Advancing towards this base in an almost straight line, they made it easier for their enemies to anticipate their movements. After terrible losses, they changed direction and sent out several diversionary columns to mislead the enemy.

The futile dogmatic debates were often cut short by a sudden enemy attack, giving Chu Teh or some other commander a chance to make a quick decision. The squabbles caused very heavy losses at the beginning. In the first two months the main column suffered

* Although ever since 1927 there were discussions about moving the Party Centre to the North-west.

more than 20,000 casualties, in front-line soldiers, Party or governmental officials, women and children.

The Red leaders could not risk leaving their families behind for
fear of their capture by Kuomintang or war-lord forces. But the
presence of these families during the innumerable battle hazards
and hardships of the Long March, added to the anxieties of the
leaders. Among them, Mao Tse-tung suffered most in this respect.

During a dive-bombing attack a few weeks after setting out from
Kiangsi Mao's wife was unable to reach safety quickly enough.
About twenty bomb splinters penetrated her body and she almost
died. For the next ten months—most of the March—she travelled on
one of the peasant carts for the wounded, or was strapped to the
back of a mule during difficult mountain crossings. The children
and Mme Mao travelled with the medical corps. In one of the
perilous situations that arose the following year, they had to aban-
don the three youngest children to the care of local peasants. Whenever he could, Mao rode back to the medical corps to see his wife
and during the brief periods spent in captured cities, they shared a
room or an apartment.

Like all of the marchers, Mao had little and mostly inferior food.
When the army captured a city or a rich estate, after weeks of near
starvation, the troops feasted themselves on cured ham, ducks,
geese, and suckling pigs. Mao and the other leaders could not afford
to relax and eat their fill, for they had to be fit for the dangerous
political infighting which flared up most vehemently during such
rare intervals of comparative rest and safety. The troops and most
of the officers could sleep off some of their weariness. The leaders
spent days and nights in conference, in committees, staff meetings,
governmental sessions.

After more than three months of fighting advance, in January
1935 the First Front Red Army crossed the Wukiang and captured
Tsunyi, the largest city of Northern Kweichow. Here the main force
of the Red Army rested for twelve days, recruited more than 4,000
soldiers and proceeded to attack the war-lord armies of the province,
spending some weeks in fighting. During the twelve days' rest period Mao Tse-tung fought one of the hardest political battles of his
career, and emerged as the *Party* leader of the First Front Army
and, in principle, of the entire Chinese Communist movement.
Years later the "Tsunyi Conference" was described as one of the
great events of Chinese Party history, but as most of the Communist records were lost during the Long March, and as contemporary Russian and Comintern accounts did not mention it at all, it

is impossible to know the exact details. It is clear that with the war situation as it was Mao managed to override the then Party leadership and succeeded in calling together an enlarged meeting of the Political Bureau. In plain English, the *nominal* leaders were obliged to meet Mao and other *actual* leaders, and accept them as equals, with equal rights of vote. Mao's followers were in the majority among the actual leaders. That Mao's political move had great chances for success from the outset, is attested by the fact that the brilliantly flexible Chou En-lai suddenly decided to join the Mao-Chu Teh bandwagon. This assured Mao's success locally.

The present official version of the Tsunyi Conference in *A History of the Modern Chinese Revolution*,[1] is as follows:

> In January 1935, after the Red Army had taken Tsunyi an *enlarged meeting* of the Political Bureau of the Central Committee of the Party was held to save the imperilled Red Army and China's revolutionary cause. . . . Thanks to the resolute struggle put up by Comrade Mao Tse-tung and many other comrades and to the support of the majority of the comrades, the Tsunyi conference repudiated the wrong "Left" military line and approved the correct line of Comrade Mao Tse-tung. . . . Thereafter, the Chinese Communist Party and the Chinese Revolution, remaining under the Marxist-Leninist leadership of this great, outstanding and completely reliable leader, pushed ahead from victory to greater victory."

But at that time and for some years afterwards Mao's leadership of the Chinese Party was not acknowledged in Moscow. The Comintern correspondent with the Long March did not mention a change of Party leadership.[2] Seven months later, at the August 1935 Comintern Congress in Moscow, Mao was mentioned as one of the fifty heroes of the Chinese revolution, *but no Party rank was coupled to his name.*

Agnes Smedley and Edgar Snow, who less than two years later spoke to most of the Chinese Party and Army leaders, make no mention at all in their books of the "Tsunyi Conference". It was probably a clever *coup* through which Mao and some other *actual* leaders, disregarding Party statutes and usage, managed to get the upper hand. But it is clear that at the time Mao had the backing of

[1] Foreign Language Press, Peking, 1958, pp. 264-5.
[2] M. Fred, "At the Front with the Chinese Red Army", *Communist International*, No. 14, July 20, 1935.

Chu Teh, of other powerful army leaders and of certain outstanding Communists like Chou En-lai and Liu Shao-chi. Liu, one of the most conformist Chinese bolsheviks, was political commissar of the Ninth Army group during the Long March. He had previously spent some time in Moscow headquarters of the Comintern and in Kiangsi became Chairman of the All-China Labour Federation. In this work as organiser of Red trade unions, Liu clashed with the Moscow-trained theoreticians in the leadership, who opposed his method of combining legal and illegal forms of work in Kuomintang areas. This clash between Liu and Mao's enemies also helped the emergence of Mao Tse-tung as *de facto* (if not yet *de jure*) leader. It also seems that Mao was not effectively opposed by the Comintern representative Li Teh, who was partially responsible for the Kiangsi débâcle when events proved him wrong when he opposed Mao. This is also indicated by the fact that after the Long March Mao gave him a teaching position in the Red Academy in Yenan, and that Li Teh was not criticised publicly until his recall to Moscow in 1939.

The main factor was of course that Mao held actual power through the loyalty of his generals and enjoyed great prestige among the middle and lower functionaries, who were not supposed to know anything about a Party split.

However, the struggle for power went on. A few months later Mao's leadership was openly challenged when the First and the Fourth Front Armies linked up. Official excommunication by the Comintern was still hanging over his head.

Meanwhile in Kweichow Province the Red Army was facing 200,000 troops of Chiang Kai-shek and his war-lord allies. Most of the hostile troop concentrations were in the north, blocking the shortest way to the Yangtze River which they had to cross on their way to the interior. While the main body of the Red Army fought a series of battles, destroying five Chiang Kai-shek divisions, Mao's government overhauled the economy of the republic-on-the-move.

The Red industry in Kiangsi had been mainly based on handicrafts, on small industrial co-operatives and on home industry. When the Long March started, turning machines, stampers, dies, lathes, light printing machines, duplicating machines, village smithies, sewing machines—everything movable was packed on peasant carts, mules and ponies. During longer halts, as now in Kweichow, Red detachments conducted many guerilla raids with the sole object of replenishing their mobile industry. At times even pitched battles were fought to get scrap iron, new lathes and badly needed pieces of machinery. The Red Army and the population of the migrating republic were clothed by the mobile textile and shoe "factories". The crude summer and winter uniforms were manufactured during the halts.

The next aim, to say nothing of the final aim, of the Long March was still uncertain. After a month's fighting in Kweichow, most of the northern half of the province was taken. The cities and villages were sovietized; thousands of new recruits were added to the army and the treasury was filled by confiscating gold, silver and banknotes, from the banks, the moneylenders and the local landlords. The Red Army still paid the peasants and small merchants for everything.

The long halt in Kweichow gave Chiang Kai-shek time to blockade all routes save those leading towards the south-west or into the arid deserts of the Tibetan highlands. The Red Army was forced to turn southward into Yunnan, the frontier province bordering on the then Indo-China and Burma. While several Red detachments made diversionary manoeuvres, the main body marched towards the Gold Sand River (as the Upper Yangtze is called there) in the mountainous wastelands of the west, where the river flows in the depths of mile-deep canyons.

Although General Chiang and his troops occupied the few possible crossing points, and ordered all boats to be transferred to the other side, the guerilla tactics of the Reds defeated him. As a diversion, the Red Army started to build a bamboo bridge over the perilous gorges. While this site was bombed by General Chiang's air force and while Chiang's intelligence was led to believe that the main column was concentrated there, Red Army men dressed in Kuomintang uniforms, and helped by peasants speaking the local dialect, captured a ferry-crossing eighty miles distant from the bridge site. During the next nine days the entire republic with army, mobile industry, hospitals, offices, and all, was ferried over the gorges.

II

On this occasion Mao crossed over with his staff at dawn. His orderly recalls that while the Chairman went to a General Staff Conference to plan the next stage of the march, he set about looking for a temporary office and home for the head of the republic:

It didn't look hopeful. The river bank was nothing but bare rocks, with a few holes in the cliffs, dripping with moisture, hardly big enough to be called caves. I sought in vain for a plank or even straw to use for a bed. In the end I had to lay out a piece of oiled cloth and put the blanket on that, feeling that that would at least give him something to lie down on—he hadn't rested at all the whole night.[3]

Then Mao's personal secretary would arrive, carrying the most confidential documents. The main Party and Government departments usually set up their temporary quarters near the Chairman's "home". Red Army G.H.Q. would not be too distant either. If the halt was for any length of time, field telephones were installed. By the time the Chairman returned from the General Staff Conference, the orderly and the personal secretary had rigged up some kind of table from wooden boxes or planks. Then, the documents spread out in front of him, Mao, chain-smoking as ever, would deal with the most urgent business, while awaiting the next emergency of the day—usually one of many. Orderlies would arrive on ponies or mules, bringing urgent reports from various army groups; sleep might be interrupted by a squadron of Kuomintang bombers, or by a courier overtaking the Long March with vital messages from other Soviet areas or from some Communist bureau working illegally in Kuomintang territory.

On this day, after the successful crossing, Intelligence sent detailed reports about the aboriginal Lolos, whose mountainous and thickly forested lands had next to be crossed. The Lolo peoples had never been entirely subdued by previous Chinese governments. Their two main tribal groups, the Black and the White Lolos were constantly at war with each other and with the Chinese of the surrounding territories. In order to reach central Szechuan on its way towards the North, the migrating republic had to march right through the whole Lolo country.

Once Mao had satisfied himself that the general chosen to befriend the Lolo chieftains was well-suited for his task, he could deal with routine governmental matters. Working in caves, under a tree or on horseback, he had to absorb at least in broad outlines all the relevant information at the disposal of the Red Ministry of Interior, the Foreign Office, the War Office and other departments. In addition to the information available to the whole Red leadership about the latest developments—in war-torn and chaotic China; within the Kuomintang leadership, in Japan, the USSR and the

[3] Chen Chang-feng in *Long March*, pp. 1-2, Foreign Language Press, Peking, 1958.

world in general—there were the intelligence reports from his own trusted men. Through these, as far as humanly possible, he had to keep himself informed about latest moves and intrigues in Stalin's entourage, in the Comintern offices, and of course in the offices and mobile HQs of his rivals, leading other Soviets and Red Armies.

He developed at this time a singularly un-Napoleonic disregard for details. With the enormous amount of information he had to absorb daily, he got used to ignoring everything of secondary importance. He was interested in broad outlines, and main trends only. After forming a brutally simple yet realistic judgment on a given situation, he left the details to his subordinates. His talent for delegating power and for choosing able men for its exercise, gave him time to think about long-term plans. Whenever he could, during the Long March, he read a lot of Chinese history. In temporarily taken cities or towns, his orderlies had to search for books. During the March another of the orderly's duties was to look out for various leaves which when dried, might serve as a substitute for tobacco, as the Chairman was almost constantly short of cigarettes.

His hectic, hard existence—one fight for survival within another —in which the danger of physical and/or political extinction was the main constant factor, was coupled with very little sleep, a great deal of nervous irritation due to overlong dogmatic discussions in tight situations, and the numerous lice under his cotton uniform. (During the Long March everybody was plagued by lice.) Yet, according to all accounts written about this period, Mao was most of the time the calm, unruffled and patient Chairman, a good listener and prudent talker. But most accounts also agree that on rare occasions Mao would erupt in fits of furious anger, throw fearful scenes and indulge in unrestrained invective.

But his general mood seemed to be that of the poet war-lords of China's past. For him, thinking not in terms of months or years, but rather in decades and centuries, the hazards, dangers and the sordid details of day-to-day guerilla existence faded into oblivion. The poems he wrote during this period indicate something of this mood. The following poem for instance was written shortly before the crossing of the gorges of the Upper Yangtze:

Loushan Pass
(to the melody of "Remembering the Beauty of China".)
Cold is the west wind;
Far in the frosty air the wild geese call in the morning moonlight
In the morning moonlight!

The clatter of horses' hooves rings sharp,
And the bugle's note is muted.
Do not say that the strong pass is guarded with iron.
This very day in one step we shall pass its summit,
  We shall pass its summit!
There the hills are blue like the sea,
And the dying sun like blood.[4]

Some of these poems were written in especially difficult classical forms. This short poem, for instance, also written during the Long March contains only sixteen words (characters) in the Chinese original:

Mountains!
Faster I whip my speeding horse, never leaving the saddle;
I started as I turn my head,
For the sky is three foot three above me![5]

III

In the land of the fierce Lolos the Long March had to cope only with the difficulties of the terrain and the vagaries of the climate. In captured border-towns the Red Army found Lolo chieftains who had been held by the local war-lord as hostages. These were sent home, with the information that the army which was now about to pass through their territories was that of the Red Chinese, who hated the White Chinese just as much as the Lolos did. An alliance was offered to and accepted by the supreme Lolo chieftain, and the Red Army handed over to the Lolos some of its surplus arms and ammunition. As a result, the Red Army was joined by hundreds of Lolo scouts who guided the Red vanguard to the next great obstacle, the turbulent Tatu River, flowing through huge gorges. Here a boat crossing was impossible and the Red Army had to use a centuries old chain-bridge, guarded by large Kuomintang detachments. The bridge—a number of heavy iron chains stretched out between the two banks and boarded over with thick planks of wood —had been partially destroyed. The wooden planks had been removed from two-thirds of the bridge and Red volunteers had to work their way across, hanging by their hands—all the while under machine-gun fire from the other side. Dozens were killed, before a

---

[4] Mao Tse-tung, *Nineteen Poems*, Foreign Language Press, Peking, 1958.
[5] Ibid.

few reached the bridgehead on the other side. Hurling hand grenades and supported by Red machine-guns, they managed to take the bridgehead, and rout the Kuomintang troops in ferocious fighting. New boards were placed on the crazily swinging chains and, while Kuomintang bombers attacked from the air, the migrating republic again crossed a great natural obstacle, only to be faced with the next one: the 16,000-foot Great Snowy Mountain.

Clad in cotton uniforms these southerners froze as they struggled up the precipices. It was the middle of the summer and a few days before, in the lowlands, they had been plagued by extreme heat. Now they had to endure the icy gales coming from Tibet, the mountains of which were visible from the crest of the Great Snowy Mountain. At this great altitude many men had heart-failure. The young general Lin Piao almost died. Mao Tse-tung himself was weak and feverish and had to be carried over the crest.

Thousands of men and pack animals perished during this mountaineering feat, and even more in the process of crossing several other mountain ranges. The melting snow and torrents of water covered the mountain slopes with lava-streams of mud. When the march reached north-western Szechuan at the end of July 1935, the First Front Red Army numbered 45,000 men. It had started out 100,000 strong and recruited nearly 30,000 men on the way, so the losses were severe indeed. True, some 5,000 seasoned troops had been left behind in small groups in the various provinces crossed, to organise peasant guerillas. The loss in transport animals, in machinery and all sorts of equipment was also very great.

In Szechuan the First Front Red Army, which had set out under the leadership of Mao and Chu Teh, was joined by the Fourth Front Red Army, headed by Chang Kuo-t'ao, Mao's most dangerous rival. This army originated in the Hunan-Hupei-Anhwei Soviet district and in 1933 marched to Szechuan and established a Soviet base in the north of the province. The Fourth Front Army numbered 50,000 men, so Chang had a somewhat larger army at his disposal than Mao.

While the troops rested for some weeks and the mobile industry was replenished and started to work, the Red leadership sat in continuous conference. The anti-Mao men in the Central Committee who had travelled with the First Front Army were now joined by Chang and the anti-Mao Communist leaders in the Fourth Front Army. The struggle for personal power was expressed in a series of violent disputes over the general policies of the Chinese Communists, the final aim of the Red armies, the possibility of setting up a large permanent base in the north, and, lastly, over the rôle the Red armies could play in the defensive war against the Japanese invaders. The disputes led to a temporary but very serious split in the Communist Party and the Red Army.

Since Mao reached undisputed power the history of this period has been effectively rewritten. The present official account of this interlude maintains that the majority of the Central Committee and of the Red generals supported Mao. Contemporary accounts show, however, that Mao was in the minority. According to the official history Chang's "deviation" became manifest at these Party conferences:

It was then that Chang Kuo-t'ao, who had been working in the Fourth Front Army, showed a serious tendency towards flight-ism and war-lordism in the face of enemy attacks. . . . A serious dispute [thus] arose between him and the Central Committee of the Party. The Central Committee held that the Red Army should march north and open up a base in the Shensi-Kansu-Ningsia area to co-ordinate with the daily growing nation-wide anti-Japanese movement. But Chang Kuo-t'ao opposed this policy and advocated instead the defeatist line of withdrawing to the national minorities areas in Sikang and Tibet . . . Chang Kuo-t'ao . . . ordered the troops of the Fourth Front Army . . . to recross the grasslands and march south with him. He took his troops to the Kantze area in Sikang, and established a bogus "Party Centre", undermining the solidarity of the Party and the Red Army. Besides, he plotted to place the Central Committee of the Party in danger.

Part of the Red Army, led by Comrade Mao Tse-tung, resolutely marched northwards in the direction of Kansu and Shensi. . . .[6]

This account glosses over the fact that of the joint Red armies, some 100,000 men strong, only a "detachment" accepted the leadership of Mao Tse-tung. Mao was accompanied by Chou En-lai and the generals Lin Piao and Peng Teh-huai. Chu Teh, however, remained in the rival camp. Later accounts have it that Chu Teh was more or less physically detained by Chang and his entourage. At the time there were many reports of a split between Chu and Mao, and it is a fact that part of the First Front Army

[6] A History of the Modern Chinese Revolution, Foreign Language Press, Peking, 1959, pp. 267-8. (Emphasis added.)

under Chu Teh remained with Chang, instead of following Mao.

As for Chang's "bogus Party Centre", Stalin and the Comintern did not repudiate or acknowledge either of the Party centres. Although Mao and his followers accused Chang of "anti-Party activities", the Comintern passed no decision on the personal question. The Seventh Congress of the Comintern in July-August 1935 elected *in absentia* a number of Chinese Communists to the new Comintern Executive Committee. Mao and Chou En-lai became full members of the International Executive, but so did Chang, the head of the "bogus Party Centre", while Po Ku, another rival of Mao's, was made candidate member.

No minutes were ever published of the debates leading to the split in the Party and the Red Army. Probably no such minutes exist. Mao's standpoint, and his version of the debates, can be fathomed from his lectures delivered a year later, in which he dealt with the "left-deviationists", and other opponents, without naming them.

He had to assert his views against adherents of "pure military science", and those who wanted to copy the Russians in everything:

> . . . They declare that it is enough to study Russia's experiences of revolutionary war or, specifically, that it is enough to follow the guiding laws of the civil war in the Soviet Union and the military directives published by the military leadership there. *They do not see that these laws of war and military directives in the Soviet Union embody the special characteristic of the civil war and the Red Army of the Soviet Union;* if we copy them and apply them mechanically and allow no change whatsoever, it will also be like whittling down the feet to fit the shoes, and we shall be defeated. Their argument is: our war, like the war in the Soviet Union, is a revolutionary war; since the Soviet Union has won victory, how can there be any alternative but to follow its example? *They do not see that although we must especially cherish the Soviet experiences of war . . . we must also cherish the experiences of China's revolutionary war, because there are a great number of conditions special to the Chinese revolution and the Chinese Red Army.*[7]

Mao's interpretation of the theoretical foundation of Communism, according to his opponents, reduced it simply to a method of anal-

---

[7] *SW*, Vol. I, pp. 176-7. (Emphasis added.)

ysis. Blaming the "ultra-Left" for the loss of the Kiangsi base after
Chiang Kai-shek's fifth annihilation campaign, Mao wrote:

> Advocating a return to conditions of a general nature, they re-
> jected the experience in the history of the Red Army's bloody
> fights. . . . As a result . . . we received an extremely great
> historical punishment. This group of people called themselves
> Marxist-Leninists, but had actually not learnt even an iota of
> Marxism-Leninism. Lenin said that "the most essential thing in
> Marxism, the living soul of Marxism" is *the concrete analysis of
> concrete conditions*". These comrades had forgotten exactly this
> point.[8]

"Concrete analysis of concrete conditions" of course meant that
men on the spot have to decide and not the distant Comintern
offices or Stalin's Moscow bureau.

Mao did not know whether the then leaders of the Hunan-Hupeh-
Szechuan-Kweichow border area and their Second Front Army and
of the Red Army in northern Shensi would support his leadership
or that of Chang. So when he started out with his detachment on
the last and most perilous lap of the Long March, his position
was quite insecure.

This last lap led through the border areas between Tibet and
China, inhabited by the primitive Mantzu tribes. The Mantzus
could not be placated as they would permit no Chinese to approach
them. In their wild mountainous country the Mantzu warriors persistently harassed the marchers. They waited on both sides of the
deep, narrow mountain passes, to roll down boulders as soon as the
Red column entered them. On the plateaus it was not safe to leave
the road. After innumerable skirmishes, and eating nothing but raw
vegetables for days, the marchers left the Mantzu territory to be
confronted by the most formidable natural barrier on their way.
In order to penetrate into Kansu Province, they had to cross the
swamp-infected grasslands.

> Treacherous bogs were everywhere, which sucked a man down
> once he stepped off the firmer parts, and more quickly if he tried
> to extricate himself. We could advance only with minute care,
> stepping on grass-clumps. Even so, one could not help feeling
> very nervous, for the great grass mounds sank with the pressure

[8] *SW*, Vol. I, p. 193.

and black water would rise and submerge the foot. . . . It was really like traversing a treacherous quicksand.[9]

In the central part of the grasslands the marchers came across no human habitation for ten days. There was almost continuous rain, a torture for the marchers who carried no tents.

They had to cover ground quickly, pursued as they were by Kuomintang troops. These, however, soon gave up the chase, deterred by the swamps. Mao's detachment pressed on, losing many men and transport animals on the way. But at last they reached Kansu; and after three more major battles and many skirmishes, they arrived at the end of their journey—northern Shensi, near the Great Wall of China. Their number, civilians included, was less than 20,000. The date was October 29, 1935. For Mao's column the Long March was over.

A few weeks later Mao said of the significance of the Long March:

It is a manifesto, an agitation corps and a seeding-machine. . . . It proclaims to the world that the Red Army is an army of heroes and that the imperialists and their jackals, Chiang Kai-shek and his like, are perfect nonentities. It announces the bankruptcy of the encirclement, pursuit, obstruction and interception attempted by the imperialists and Chiang Kai-shek. The Long March is also an agitation corps. It declares to the approximately two hundred million people of eleven provinces that only the road of the Red Army leads to their liberation. Without the Long March, how could the broad masses have known so quickly that there are such great ideas in the world as are upheld by the Red Army? *The Long March is also a seeding-machine. It has sown many seeds in eleven provinces, which will sprout, grow leaves, blossom into flowers, bear fruit and yield a harvest in the future.*[10]

[9] *The Long March,* Foreign Language Press, Peking, 1958, p. 91.
[10] SW, Vol. I, p. 161. (Emphasis added.)

IX

A FOOTHOLD IN THE NORTH

> When societies first come to birth, it is the leaders who pro-
> duce the institutions of the republic. Later, it is the institutions
> which produce the leaders.
>
> (Montesquieu.)

I

Late in 1935 the newspapers of China from Peking and Shanghai
to Nanking and Canton reported that Mao Tse-tung, the Number
One Red Bandit had died. Detachments of his unfortunate followers were allegedly trying to escape annihilation in the north-western
frontier province of Shensi, near the Inner Mongolian border. All
over the interior and in the regions of the Tibetan frontier other
detachments of Red bandits were supposed to be struggling to escape mopping-up operations.

Moscow knew that Mao had reached northern Shensi safe and
sound at the head of a small detachment. But it was also known
that the bulk of the Red armies were still on the move. Indeed, it
was only in November 1935 that Ho Lung's Second Front Army
started out on its Long March from its base in Central China to
join up in June 1936 with the Fourth Front Army (led by Mao's
rival, Chang Kuo-t'ao) and with the First Front Army under General Chu Teh. These forces then started to move northward to
Shensi; but in October 1936 there was again a split, Chu Teh
continuing northward to reach Mao's forces, while Chang led his
army towards Sinkiang. A large part of this army was annihilated
on the way, the rest, together with Chang, only reached Shensi in
1936; and it was somewhat later that General Ho Lung arrived
with the remnants of the Second Front Army.

The fate of the Red armies and of Chinese Soviet power seemed
to be most uncertain in the winter of 1935; yet Mao was utterly
convinced that the seeds sown by his Long March would yield a
great harvest in the future. The rival Party Centre was working
against him, the majority of the Red armies were not under his
command, Stalin and the Comintern did not back him, the future
of his leadership was insecure. Yet living in a "residence" hewn out

of the rock, Mao started to create "the institutions of the republic" which were to produce the leaders of the future—while the fatigue of the Long March was still in his limbs. This man who for years could not be certain if he would live to see the next moment, yet was kept going by his vision of future decades, had now a fixed point from which to turn the axis of the Chinese world.

This stronghold in one of the most remote and backward parts of China could, he believed, be built up into a strong Soviet base. His lectures and theoretical writings of the 1935-7 period show that, while hoping for Red China's victory over Japan and over Generalissimo Chiang Kai-shek's armies in a decade or two, Mao Tse-tung was already planning the colossal task of "remoulding" the whole of China after these victories. His most systematic lectures on strategy and tactics, on various problems of Marxist theory or political practice, delivered in this period, gave glimpses of Mao's millennial vision of the future. The politician-warrior of the Shensi caves, whose local rule was still not entirely safe, appeared calmly and gigantically convinced that all the ideas on the nature and purpose of Man, accepted by the rest of humanity, were wrong; that victorious China would lead the whole of mankind in a thorough remoulding of all human beings and institutions.

Speaking in December 1936, he foresaw a great war in which China would have the leading part:

> The greatest and most ruthless of all unjust counter-revolutionary wars is pressing on us; and if we did not raise the banner of a just war, the majority of mankind would suffer destruction. The banner of a just war of mankind is the banner for the salvation of mankind; . . . A war which will be waged by the overwhelming majority of mankind and of the Chinese people will undoubtedly be a just war—it will be incomparably the most honourable undertaking *for saving mankind and China and will form a bridge leading world history* into a new era.[1]

In the same lecture he pointed out that "the ten years' revolutionary war we have fought may be surprising to other countries, but for us it is only like . . . the preliminary exposition of a theme in an . . . essay."[2]

In July 1937 lecturing at the Yenan Military and Political College,

[1] *SW*, Vol. I, p. 179. (Emphasis added.)
[2] *SW*, Vol. I, p. 248.

he said that the struggle of revolutionaries *"in changing the world* consists in achieving the following tasks":

> To remould the objective world as well as their own subjective world—to remould their faculty of knowing as well as the relations between the subjective world and the objective world. . . . The people of China and the rest of the world are either passing, or will pass, through such a remoulding process.
>
> And the objective world which is to be remoulded *includes the opponents of remoulding, who must undergo a stage of compulsory remoulding before they can pass to a stage of conscious remoulding.* When the whole of mankind remoulds itself and changes the world, the era of world Communism will dawn.[3]

This is by no means the first or the last indication that the terrible "rectification drives" between 1950 and 1960, the compulsory self-remoulding through physical labour to which Chinese intellectuals had to submit, were planned by Mao during and after the Long March.

Mao Tse-tung was at this time intent on completing his own self-remoulding. He retained the supreme direction of the military, political and economic affairs of the Soviet republic in his own hands, but delegated ever more power to his close associates. The Red Armies were fighting not only defensive battles but offensive ones also, to enlarge the Red territories. By the end of 1936 Mao ruled over nearly ten million people. But as contemporary evidence shows, he developed an increasing distaste for being consulted on daily developments and problems. Reports were sent to his residence and he periodically issued overall instructions; but most of the time he was engrossed in studying, writing, and long-term planning.

During the Kiangsi period and the Long March Mao Tse-tung had not had much opportunity to retire to his own room for days for study and meditation. But this he did whenever there was a chance. In Shensi he could and did indulge in long bouts of retirement, when no one could see him, save his wife of the time, who shared his residence. After 1936 these periods of retirement grew longer and more frequent. It was often reported that the Chairman liked to study all night or most of the night. Part of the day he slept. It is obvious that his private inclinations lay in this direction, and there is no doubt that he read and studied a great deal. His ambition was to develop into an all-round Marxist theoretician. In Shensi

[3] Ibid., p. 297. (Emphasis added.)

he again read omnivorously. He studied philosophy, the theory of knowledge, formal and dialectical logic and, as a relaxation, the history of China. And it was in Shensi that, for the first time, he worked his way systematically through the main works of Marxism-Leninism. His lectures on strategy and on political theory delivered in this period and his philosophical essays, show that by the end of 1937 his basic self-remoulding was accomplished. He had cast off from his thinking all sentimental, subjective, humanistic considerations. The immense trials of the Long March had largely immunised his nerves against the effect of momentary setbacks, against shocks and dangerous situations. He had grown used to regarding all setbacks as momentary—even if they obviously meant additional years of struggle. He managed to blend his millennial visions of China and mankind with his version of Marxist theory and Marxist knowledge.

He subjected the Marxist classics to painstaking, yet most one-sided analysis. He was convinced that his reading of Chinese and world history proved the correctness of the Marxist theory of class-struggle, of Lenin's theory of imperialism as the last stage of dying capitalism, and of the "law of the development of social forms" put forward by Marx and Engels. He took it for granted that progress from primitive Communism to slave-owning societies, then to feudalism, capitalism and finally to socialism, with the lower and higher form of Communism at the end, was not merely a hypothesis but the discovery "of the objective process", and that this process, from primitive Communism at the dawn of history to mature Communism at the pinnacle of historical development, was just as inevitable as the fact that winter is followed by spring.

Never having been abroad, and ignorant of foreign languages, he was limited for his knowledge of the outside world and of recent history to the "facts" endlessly repeated in Soviet Party publications and in Comintern reports on the international situation. He *knew* that social-democratic parties are opportunistic and inevitably betray the working-class; that the Western democracies are imperialist class-dictatorships; that colonies can be liberated only through violence and war. He *knew* that "class hostile" elements like landlords, bankers, manufacturers and "petty bourgeois intellectuals" cannot act as individual human beings because they are fully determined by their class-status.

Nearly two decades of his own experience had, unfortunately, provided him with many instances when these and a great many similar dogmatic and highly biased views had been borne out by reality. While he often attacked those whose Marxism was "a col-lection of petrified dogmas", he regarded his own dogmatic convic-tions as unassailable and well-tested facts, and proofs of Marxist "universal truth". By 1937 his thinking was already petrified in the sense that he accepted a great number of biased views as facts. He accepted furthermore a long string of Marxist-Leninist "basic prin-ciples", dialectical laws, methods of analysis and conceptual tech-niques from which he never meant to, and rarely could, deviate.

Accepting the inevitability of the victory of Communism as the highest stage of the social forms possible for mankind, his thinking had already at this time achieved a three-dimensional quality: for him not only the past and the present were concretely given but also an inevitably approaching stage of the future.

He was convinced, as his lectures and books show, that he *knew* what sort of future is being prepared in the present. To work against this progress towards the inevitable future, was pointless, reaction-ary, harmful. As a revolutionary leader guided by the "science of sciences" (Marxism) he had to remould his brain into a precise and rationally sensitive instrument with the sole aim of finding the best day-by-day tactics and long-term strategy for bringing about the inevitable future as quickly as possible.

It seems that in this period he matured, in the sense that an electronic computer is "mature", that is ready for operation, once it has been fully instructed. By being "programmed" with all the rele-vant information and the equations and methods for solving prob-lems, the electronic computer is furnished with its patterns of "think-ing" and its basic principles. The trouble in Mao's case was that some of the "instruction" and "programming" material happened to be faulty. He was more or less erroneously "programmed" as to his-tory, international affairs and sociology, but he had an excellently functioning "mechanical brain" when it was applied to guerilla operations, to the strategy and tactics of civil war and of war in general. He had more than a decade of most intensive practice as a Chinese war-lord, not to speak of his much tested skill in the art of organising and manipulating masses, or of his rich experience in intrigues within the Comintern and the Chinese Communist Party. And, as he was mostly successful in the matters on which he was well "programmed", he naturally trusted his other—as yet untried—programming too. We shall see later to what consequences all this led.

Now, in 1936, he was intent on teaching his disciples the method of dialectical thinking, which he himself had just mastered:

To reflect a thing fully in its totality, to reflect its essence and its inherent laws, it is necessary, through thinking, to build up a system of concepts and theories by subjecting the abundant perceptual data to a process of remodelling and reconstructing,— discarding the crude and selecting the refined, eliminating the false and retaining the true, proceeding from one point to another, and going through the outside into the inside; it is necessary to leap from perceptual knowledge to rational knowledge. . . . But . . . the most important problem does not lie in understanding the laws of the objective world and thereby becoming capable of explaining it, but in actively changing the world by applying the knowledge of its objective laws.[4]

The "objective laws" were naturally those promulgated by the Marxist-Leninist teachings.

The aims set before the Yenan Communists in 1936 and 1937 were similar to the tasks of the modern computers which, by trying various possible solutions, through a method of trial and error, can profit from objective experience:

Generally speaking, whether in the practice of changing nature or of changing society, people's original ideas, theories, plans or programmes are seldom realised without any change whatever. This is because people engaged in changing reality often suffer from many limitations: they are not limited only by the scientific and technological conditions, but also by the degree of development and revelation of the objective process itself, (by the fact that the aspects and essence of the objective process have not yet been fully disclosed). . . . It does happen that the original ideas, theories, plans or programmes fail partially or wholly to correspond to reality and are partially or entirely incorrect. In many instances, failures have to be repeated several times before erroneous knowledge can be rectified and made to correspond to the laws of the objective process, so that subjective things can be transformed into objective things, viz. the anticipated results can be achieved in practice.[5]

These instructions to his disciples sound quite sober, objective and scientific. The trouble is that by "objective process" Mao Tse-tung means a process leading to the practical achievement of the

[4] SW, Vol. I, pp. 291-2.
[5] SW, Vol. I, p. 294. (Emphasis added.)

"anticipated results". He means finding ways by trial and error, new trial and so forth, to achieve the various tactical and strategical aims of the Chinese Communist Party (set by himself). Whenever a method of land reform, a drive for remoulding intellectuals, or certain guerilla tactics, produced the required and anticipated result, its truth and absolute correctness were held to be "proved by practice". If the anticipated result did not materialise, one had to go on trying until it did.

Mao's disciples were impressed by the scientific objectivity of his teachings. Yet neither their master nor they had any experience or even correct idea of scientific investigation. Although they treated China as an immense laboratory in which they had to experiment, in doing so they were not *testing* their hypothesis and discarding it if it was proved wrong. They regarded their Marxist hypothesis as a fact, as a well-established "scientific law". They experimented only to find out what method led in the quickest possible way to the required (and inevitable) result. As Communists—always and everywhere—they refused to accept present reality and therefore one of the tools in their laboratory was naked force itself. Knowing the future strategical end, it was only a question of finding the right means (tactics) to accelerate the "objective process" leading to the Communist millennium.*

These "objective scientists" were also firm believers in the dictatorship of the proletariat, that is the dictatorship of the Party leadership representing "the real interest of the proletariat". Granted that the salvation of mankind can be attained only through this dictatorship, the dictators only served the latent "objective process" in submitting "the opponents of remoulding . . . to a stage of compulsory remoulding".

In this Mao Tse-tung's mentality did not differ from that of his

---

* "The present really exists only by virtue of the fact that the past and the future exist, the present is the form of the unnecessary past and of the unreal future. *Tactics are the future appearing as present*." (J. Revai, "Das Problem der Taktik"), in *Kommunismus*, Zeitschrift der Kommunistischen Internationale, 1920, Vol. II, p. 1,676. (Emphasis added.)

I am indebted for this quotation to the late Professor Karl Mannheim (*Ideologie und Utopie*). Professor Mannheim comments that the utopian mentality in this case is based on the conviction that an insight into the tendencies latent in the present "can be obtained only if the present is understood in the light of its concrete fulfilment in the future".

comrades in the Chinese Party's Politbureau. They accepted him by now as their leader and agreed with him on the main lines of policy. For the last fifteen years all of them had led the same hard life, all of them had undergone the trials of the Long March, all of them had devoted their best years to the cause. Mao was the acknowledged and approved leader in this junta of seasoned warrior politicians because by 1936 he had proved himself as a master of political and military strategy. They worked under him almost like a normal cabinet under a premier. Each leader had very great tasks and responsibilities. Chu Teh, Lin Piao and other generals were organising, training and commanding the armies. Liu Shao-chi directed all underground Communist activity in the vastness of Kuomintang China. Chou En-lai dealt with foreign policy and was the Number One diplomat and negotiator of the Red State. Other leaders had the very hard task of directing agricultural and industrial production in the Red areas, to feed and clothe the population and the armies. The tasks and responsibilities were so immense that even the most overweening of ambitions could be satisfied by them. As events generally showed Mao's overall policies to be right, there was no objective need to question his supreme leadership. But there was as yet no "cult of personality" around the Chairman.

The capital of the Chinese Soviet Republic, which until December 1936 was in Pao An, was then moved to the town of Yenan, in a valley between loess hills. For years many dwellings, offices, schools, hospitals and institutes of the republic were in the caves cut into the hillside.

In Pao An and in Yenan Mao lived and dressed very simply. He went about dressed as a private, with nothing on his crumpled cotton uniform to distinguish him from any other trooper. No retinue followed him when he went to deliver one of his periodical lectures, and in the crude Yenan theatre he made a point of not sitting in the first row. His lectures, speeches, writings and political actions of the period seem to indicate that there was no *folie de grandeur* in him at that time, only the objective and non-personal megalomania of a cause-addict, who is supremely convinced of the ultimate victory of his cause.

The Western visitors to Yenan, coming from Kuomintang China, could not but be impressed by the dedication, modesty and simplicity of the Red leaders. The contrast after the conspicuous luxury, haughty manners and corruption of the Kuomintang leadership, was very great. Generalissimo Chiang Kai-shek had the manners of a Chinese Emperor and his entourage was full of officials who amassed fortunes or were about to amass them. The Red leaders were truly uninterested in wealth and in the outward signs of power. They wanted as yet only power for the sake of their cause.

And the cause identified itself at this time with saving China from annexation by the Japanese. For Westerners, gravely worried by the spreading of Japanese power, the patriotism of the Communist leaders was most appealing. These Western visitors looked on Mao and his comrades as potential allies in a coming war with Japan, which made them understandably biased in favour of the Chinese Reds.

Western visitors to the Soviet base during the Yenan period came away with conflicting impressions of Mao. On some he made a feminine, on others a "darkly masculine" impression. To some he seemed a twenty-year-old student, to others a heavy shouldered peasant, rough and uncouth. Some were impressed by the refined intellectual wearing the uniform of an army private. All were impressed by Mao and the other leaders, who had experienced more and more grievous hardships and more and greater successes than most of their contemporaries anywhere in the world.

II

An alleged explosion on the South Manchurian Railway on September 19, 1931, had been the pretext for the invasion of Manchuria by the Japanese forces who installed the last Manchu Emperor, Henry Pu-yi as nominal ruler of the puppet state of Manchukuo. This had happened during one of Chiang's annihilation campaigns against the Reds. From that time onwards, Japan had gone on invading and occupying important Chinese cities and provinces, while Chiang continued his extermination campaigns. In 1935 the Japanese made preparations to create a new puppet state from the five North China provinces.

On August 1, 1935—during the Long March—the Communist Party proclaimed an anti-Japanese People's United Front for all China. The conference urged all Chinese patriots to "unite as one man in spite of differences of political opinions, strivings and interests".

It was clear from the proclamation and subsequent Communist statements that they were appealing to the patriotic elements in the Kuomintang, not to the Kuomintang leadership. Generalissimo Chiang was still called the arch-traitor, while the Kuomintang leadership was regarded as agents of Japanese imperialism.

In 1935 the National Salvation movement launched by the Chinese Communists had limited aims to begin with. The slogan "Chinese Do Not Fight Chinese" was meant to stop the Generalissimo in his extermination drives against the Soviet bases. It was also thought that the Generalissimo, in forbidding resistance to Japan before he had exterminated the Chinese Reds, had weakened his position and that a new, leftish Kuomintang leadership would eventually be prepared for a new Kuomintang-Communist alliance. A further aim of the proclamation was to inspire anti-Japanese guerilla activities. The maximum aim—an all-out Chinese war of resistance against Japan—was at this time vague. But such a war would obviously stop the Kuomintang offensives against the Communists and, what was even more important for Moscow, it would divert the Japanese threat away from the Far Eastern provinces of the USSR.

The National Salvation movement had its greatest successes in the Kuomintang territories most directly exposed to Japanese expansion. On December 9, 1935 for instance 10,000 students demonstrated in Peking, shouting slogans such as: "Stop Civil War and Unite Against Foreign Aggression", "Down with Japanese Imperialism". They were met by the swords, batons, and fire-hoses of the police. Two hundred students were wounded and there were rumours of hundreds of arrests. The news of this event sparked off even bigger demonstrations in all of the major cities. There were anti-Japanese strikes, student demonstrations, and attacks on the Kuomintang police, who were ordered by the Generalissimo to stop all anti-Japanese propaganda. The demand for resistance spread.

The Long March was now given a new explanation. According to Communist propaganda the Chinese Red armies had fought their way across thousands of miles of almost impossible terrain only to be on the spot to defend China against Japan. The official name of the army was soon changed from "Workers' and Peasants' Red Army" to "Chinese People's Anti-Japanese Vanguard Red Army".

The intentions of the Communists can be fathomed from the following excerpts from the December 25, 1935 resolution of the Chinese Politbureau, written by Mao:

The current situation makes it clear to us that the Japanese attempt to annex China has shocked the whole country and the whole world. . . . Therefore, the Party's *tactical* line is to arouse, unite and organise all the revolutionary forces throughout China to fight the main enemy confronting them—Japanese imperialism and Chiang Kai-shek, the arch traitor. All people, all parties, all armed forces and all classes, *in so far as they are opposed to Japanese imperialism and the traitor Chiang Kai-shek,* must unite to extend the sacred national revolutionary war to drive the Japanese imperialists out of China. . . .

As to the broad masses in the anti-Japanese war, it is necessary to satisfy their demand in the matter of their basic interests (the peasants' demand for land and the demand for better living conditions on the part of the workers, the soldiers, the poor people and the intellectuals). Only when their demands are satisfied can we mobilise wider sections of the people to join the anti-Japanese front, keep up the anti-Japanese movement, and lead the movement to complete victory. Only thus can we win leadership in the anti-Japanese war.[6]

After this resolution the Party line underwent a gradual change. Everything was done to win all classes of Chinese society over to the idea of the united front. The class line was temporarily shelved, the lands of the rich peasants were not confiscated, and a propaganda barrage was kept up against continuation of the civil war.

Those Manchurian armies which had been driven out of their country by the Japanese were operating in the territories adjacent to the Soviet base. When Chiang directed them against the Chinese Communists, instead of against the Japanese, he encountered criticism and even some resistance. The Red Army men fraternised with the Manchurian troops and infiltrated their own propagandists into their ranks.

On May 6, 1936 the Yenan government announced that the Red Army would voluntarily cease fighting against the Manchurian armies because "in the present national crisis a decisive battle between the two sides, no matter which side should come out the victor, would only add much to the delight of the Japanese imperialists and reduce China's strength for national defence."

Announcing this decision, Mao sent a circular telegram to Chiang Kai-shek's government in Nanking, to *"all land, sea and air forces; all parties; all groups, all organisations, all newspapers, and all fellow countrymen unwilling to be slaves of a foreign nation":*

The Revolutionary Military Committee of the Red Army hereby solemnly advises the gentlemen of the Nanking government that at this critical moment of the threat of immediate destruction to

[6] Cf., SW, Vol. I, pp. 328-30. (Emphasis added.)

the nation and the people, you ought, in all reason, to break with your past and, in the spirit of the maxim, "Brothers quarrelling at home will join forces against attacks from the outside", to stop the nation-wide civil war. . . . This will not only be for your own good, but also a blessing to the nation and the country. If, however, you obstinately refuse to awaken to reason and want to become collaborators and traitors, then your rule will certainly collapse in the end, and you will certainly be spurned and over-thrown by the people of the whole country. The old saying has it, "Pointed at by a thousand accusing fingers, one dies even though in perfect health". And again, "The butcher becomes a Buddha the moment he drops his cleaver". These are words for you gentlemen to digest and ponder.[7]

Everything possible was done to see that all China should know of this telegram. And it was addressed to a China driven to despair and fury by Chiang's dictatorship.

Had Chiang Kai-shek's Kuomintang régime carried out reforms at the outset, his anti-Communist campaigns would not have be-come unpopular. Had the Kuomintang made China richer, healthier, safer and freer, Communist propaganda would have had far less success. But the Kuomintang one-party dictatorship had a sorry record indeed. Soon after the split with the Communists, Chiang's Kuomintang took over the methods and institutions of other dictator-ships. The Government had a terrorist secret organisation (the Blue Shirts), that was later reorganised as the secret military police. As the Kuomintang ceased to be a nationalist democratic movement, the number of its critics grew. They were dealt with by the dreaded Blue Shirts, whose task was to wipe out all opposition to the Kuo-mintang. Students and intellectuals were terrorised by the system of "thought control". The Kuomintang tried to restore the worst aspects of Confucianism, precisely those aspects which had been denounced by all Chinese democrats during the first two decades of the cen-tury. The old feudal *pao chia* system for fighting subversion and en-forcing collective responsibility was reintroduced in the villages. First set up a thousand years ago under the Sung dynasty, it evolved into a method of military and labour conscriptions and a means of suppression. Groups of peasant households were held collectively responsible, and were collectively punished, for any single indi-vidual's "subversion". The Japanese also used this system in the territories occupied by them.

[7] *SW*, Vol. I, pp. 330-1. (Emphasis added.)

The Kuomintang suppressed the free press and the free trade unions. Those who resisted or criticised were imprisoned in one of the many political jails or concentration camps.

In vain did Chiang Kai-shek's propagandists denounce the Communist one-party dictatorship and atrocities; the Kuomintang dictatorship was guilty of far greater atrocities at this time.

The Japanese invaders in Manchuria and North China instituted an even worse terroristic régime. Yet in the Kuomintang territories it was the gravest crime to indulge in anti-Japanese propaganda. While the invaders went on with their piecemeal occupation of China, the Generalissimo's Blue Shirts imprisoned thousands and thousands for anti-Japanese activities.

In all the former Red enclaves in South and Central China the Kuomintang repudiated the Communist land-reform; and lands were taken from the poor peasants and given back to the landlords. All this made it easier for the Communists to find adherents and sympathisers. All through the past decade the *tactical* line of the Communists (in Kuomintang territories) had been to demand freedom of speech, of press and of association—rights which the Kuomintang régime firmly denied.

The economic and agricultural policy of the Kuomintang made it easier for the Communists to act as the advocates of Sun Yat-sen's famous programme for the "People's Livelihood". The extreme poverty of the people in all of the Kuomintang territories, and the fact that Chiang Kai-shek's régime seemed to be firmly aligned with the privileged groups, made the Kuomintang look like the betrayer of Sun's "People's Livelihood". Chiang Kai-shek still maintains that history has shown he was right to see in Communism the greatest danger to the Chinese people, but he certainly used wrong and mistaken methods in his fight against the Reds. And, in 1936 the Kuomintang was still prohibiting resistance to the Japanese invaders until the Communists were annihilated, while the Communists were demanding a united front against Japan.

The famous circular telegram was the first sign that Mao and the Communist leaders were prepared to make considerable temporary political concessions for the sake of a united front and resistance to Japan. On August 25, 1936 the Communist Party sent an open letter to the Kuomintang declaring that if a Chinese democratic republic were formed, the Soviet regions were willing to become a component part of it:

The Chinese Communist Party declares that it actively supports the movement for a democratic republic. It also declares that when the democratic republic embracing the whole nation is established and a parliament elected by universal suffrage is actually convened, the Red areas will be made a component part of the republic, the people of the Red areas will elect their representatives to the parliament, and one and the same democratic system will be put into practice in the Red areas.[8]

During the next few months many declarations were made, many more circular telegrams and open letters were sent to the Kuomintang, which of course omitted to stress the determination to strengthen the Communist Party and the Red Army. This propaganda barrage aimed at convincing the entire country of the patriotic zeal of the Communists and their readiness to make concessions.

General Chiang Kai-shek refused even to consider these offers. Instead, he stepped up preparations for a great "final annihilation campaign" against the Red bases. In December 1936 he flew to Sian in southern Shensi in order to supervise the final preparations for an all-out offensive against the Reds in the north of Shensi province.

His arrival led to the "Sian Incident", one of the most momentous and controversial events of the twentieth century, which led to the cessation of the civil war and ultimately to Communist rule over the Chinese mainland.

The Sian incident, furthermore, revealed a clash between Mao and Stalin, a clash which was to have a lasting effect on the relations between the Russian and the Chinese Communist Parties.

III

Sian was the headquarters of Marshal Chang Hsüeh-liang, Deputy Commander-in-Chief of the Kuomintang armies, who had 170,000 Manchurian troops under his direct command. The Marshal's general staff officers and the divisions under his command were in a rebellious mood, wanting to fight the Japanese, not the Chinese Reds. That summer and autumn the Marshal himself had begged the Generalissimo several times to permit him to defend the national frontiers instead of preparing for anti-Communist campaigns. Chiang however was adamant. Instead, he sent to Sian in the autumn 1,500 of his dreaded secret police, the Blue Shirts, to arrest

[8] SW, Vol. I, pp. 331-2. (Emphasis added.)

Communists, anti-Japanese agitators and rebellious students, and to spy on the army.

In Sian, the capital city of Shensi province, the governor was a trusted Chiang follower who had under his command the provincial gendarmery and the city police force. The Generalissimo felt safe in Sian and again refused even to consider the ending of the civil war. On December 10, 1936 at a General Staff Conference he gave mobilisation orders against the Communists and threatened the Marshal that if the orders were not carried out he would be dismissed and his armies disarmed by loyal troops.

When the other officers of the Manchurian armies learnt about the decision they decided to mutiny, and appealed to Marshal Chang Hsüeh-liang to arrest and try the Generalissimo as a traitor. The Marshal agreed with his officers in deploring Chiang's decision, but he was reluctant to turn against his Commander-in-Chief. He decided to do so only when it became obvious that he could not avert a mutiny, and when the only chance of saving the Generalissimo's life seemed to lie in his taking personal leadership of the mutiny. He hoped to be able to persuade the Generalissimo to agree to a patriotic war. So the Marshal ordered a division of his troops to the capital. By dawn on December 12, the Blue Shirts, the gendarmes and the city police were disarmed by the Manchurian troops and, after a brief fight put up by his bodyguard, the Generalissimo was arrested.

Marshal Chang Hsüeh-liang now informed his Commander-in-Chief that he would be set free only if he agreed to end the civil war and to lead China against the Japanese invasion. A telegram was sent to the Nanking government giving assurances of Chiang's safety provided that he and his government agreed to the immediate cessation of the civil war, to a democratic reorganisation of the government, to the release of political prisoners and to the convocation of a National Salvation Conference.

At first the Generalissimo staunchly refused to negotiate under duress. The Nanking government also refused to negotiate with the rebels. Meanwhile the Marshal invited Communist plenipotentiaries to take part in deciding the fate of the Generalissimo. It was in this situation that Mao Tse-tung sent Chou En-lai to Sian with *firm instructions to save Chiang Kai-shek and obtain his release*.

In trying to save Chiang, his hated and despised enemy, whom he regarded as the murderer of his wife and his sister, Mao was moved by strategical and political considerations. He feared that without Chiang Kai-shek the Kuomintang régime might split into rival groups. The right wing would organise even fiercer anti-Communist campaigns than the Generalissimo did and the pro-Japanese faction would hand over further Chinese provinces to Japan. The centre and the left would split into war-lord governments and armies. While part of the Kuomintang forces fought the Communists and other parts fought each other, Japan would be able to invade and occupy the whole country, and the Red armies and Soviet bases would be wiped out.

His most important reason—to be discussed in the next chapter—was to steal a march on Stalin who was at that time conducting various negotiations which could not but deal a mortal blow to the existence of the Chinese Soviet bases and their Red Army.

The Generalissimo was shaken by the mutiny of an army of 170,-000 men under his own Deputy Commander-in-Chief. He knew that his life was at stake. His captor told him that the questions between them "should be referred to the people for verdict".

When I heard "the people's verdict", I realised that it was a malicious plot to kill me by using the mob as their excuse.[9]

He was also shaken by the news coming from Nanking, where several Kuomintang leaders were all set to step into his shoes. His own Minister of War was planning to send twenty divisions against Sian as a punitive expedition, no doubt hoping that this action would lead to the Generalissimo's execution. Ten provincial governors were against the continuation of the civil war, while the generals ruling Shantung and Hopei provinces demanded a peaceful settlement between the Generalissimo and his captor.

While Chou En-lai negotiated with the Generalissimo, these and similarly alarming items of news came streaming in. In the end Chiang Kai-shek gave a verbal promise to fulfil the demands made of him. The Marshal was willing to release the Generalissimo and even accompany him to Nanking, to save his face. But the difficulty now was that the officers in the Marshal's entourage and all those who had effective power in Sian, wanted to bring the Generalissimo to public trial and sentence him to death for his crimes. Chou En-lai and the other Communist negotiators had to argue with the rebellious officers for days, before they agreed to Chiang's release.

Once negotiations had started, the rebel Marshal permitted Chiang to call for his wife and political advisers. So Mme Chiang

[9] General and Mme Chiang Kai-shek, *China at the Crossroads,* an account of the fortnight in Sian, etc., London, 1937, p. 163.

Kai-shek, Chiang's brother-in-law, T. V. Soong, and Chiang's chief political adviser, the Australian W. H. Donald, went to Sian and stood by the Generalissimo during the discussion. Most non-Communist sources from Donald to Mme Chiang Kai-shek agree that only the Communists were able to persuade the Manchurian rebels not to execute Chiang but let him go.* Writing about the Communists, Mme Chiang Kai-shek stated that, "quite contrary to outside beliefs, they were not interested in detaining the Generalissimo."[10] Donald gave the same version to his biographer and he wrote in an article that Chou En-lai was "actually the one man who enabled General Chiang to depart unharmed".[11]

On December 25, 1936, the Generalissimo, accompanied by his wife, by Donald and by Marshal Chang Hsüeh-liang, returned to Nanking. Although he denied upon his arrival that he had made any promises, during the ensuing months he gradually fulfilled them. Slowly and reluctantly he agreed to the cessation of the civil war and to the nominal formation of a United Front. In the end, he even started to resist the Japanese. But he could not forgive his captor, the symbol of his humiliation; Marshal Chang Hsüeh-liang was sentenced to ten years' imprisonment. When Chiang escaped to Formosa, he took his prisoner with him.

On August 31, 1961, the Taipeh garrison command announced that Marshal Chang Hsüeh-liang had been freed after twenty-four years of strict surveillance. The marshal served two years for each of the twelve days he held Chiang Kai-shek a prisoner.

---

* Cf. "Adopting from the outset the position that Chiang's release was essential to Chinese unity, Communist negotiators in Sian, flown in a few days after the *coup*, persistently pressed their—and Chiang's—case with the insurgents", McLane, *Soviet Policy and the Chinese Communists, 1931-1946*, Columbia University Press, 1958, p. 82.

"Ironically, the Communists, instead of taking the opportunity to do away with their arch enemy, came into the picture as mediators", (A. K. Wu, *China and the Soviet Union*), Methuen, 1950, p. 319.

See furthermore: J. Burnham, *First Act in China;* North, *Moscow and the Chinese Communists;* Rosinger, *China's Wartime Politics, 1937-44;* Selle, *Donald of China,* etc.

[10] Generalissimo and Mme Chiang, *Sian, A Coup d'État,* Shanghai, 1937.

[11] In *New York Times*, February 18, 1937, as quoted by McLane, *Soviet Policy and the Chinese Communists.*

X

MAO AND STALIN DURING THE SINO-JAPANESE WAR

The background and the consequences of the Sian incident.

1931. Japan invades Manchuria. The Soviet Government promises to maintain strict noninterference. Stalin permits Japanese troop transports over the partly Soviet-owned Eastern Chinese Railways, enabling the swift occupation of North Manchuria.

The Chinese CP (Sept. 20, 1931) and the Chinese Soviet (Sept. 25) denounce Japanese aggression in Manchuria. The First Congress of the Chinese Soviets announces that Japanese seizure of Manchuria will be resisted.

1932-5. The USSR negotiates with Japan and the Japanese puppet state of "Manchukuo" and sells its share in the Eastern Chinese Railways to the Japanese puppets. This is *de facto* recognition of the puppet state. Anti-Communists "campaigns" are launched in Manchukuo.

1932-5. The Chinese Soviet Republic declares war on Japan (April 5, 1932). The Chinese Reds repeatedly declare their solidarity with the partisans fighting against Japanese-Manchukuo troops. Mao offers alliance to anti-Japanese volunteer units in Manchuria (Jan. 1933 and Jan. 1934).

1932. The USSR resumes diplomatic relations with Chiang's Republic of China, declaring that "all sincere friends of peace . . . will learn with satisfaction that resumption of diplomatic relations between our two great States has taken place".

Mao's Soviets and Red armies have by this time withstood three annihilation campaigns directed against them by the leader of this "great State". Mao's line: the reactionary Kuomintang régime must be destroyed before China can turn against Japan.

June 1936. Some Kuomintang generals stage an uprising in Canton to force Chiang to fight Japan. *Izvestiya* denounces this as a Japanese manoeuvre to start civil war (June 10). *Pravda* declares that the insurrection is "hindering the anti-Japanese movement" (June 23, p. 5).

The Red Chinese press greets the news of the uprising with approval. Mao declares his readiness to conclude an anti-Japanese alliance with the Cantonese generals. (In "Letter to the Leaders of the All-China Association for National Salvation", Aug. 10, 1936, text in *China: The March Toward Unity*.)

August 1936. Comintern spokesman warns Mao: "Communist
must not place the Kuomintang and
Chiang Kai-shek on the same foot-
ing with the Japanese aggressors!"
(In *Communisticheskiy International*, Aug. 1936, pp. 88-89.)

Chiang insists that the Chinese
Communists must be destroyed before fighting Japan (December 10,
1936). Mao tries to avert the campaign.

I

STALIN AGAINST MAO'S ALLIES

This summary brings the chronicle to the eve of the Sian incident. By this time secret negotiations had already been going on
for several months between Moscow and Chiang Kai-shek's Nanking Government concerning a non-aggression pact between the
two powers. When this pact was signed in August 1937, spokesmen
of the two contracting powers made no secret of the fact that
negotiations leading up to it had been in progress for more than a
year. According to Chiang Kai-shek, negotiations opened in the
spring of 1936, while *Izvestiya* in its editorial on this pact wrote
that negotiations for it had been going "for more than a year".[1]

Stalin and the Kremlin leadership certainly knew of Chiang Kai-
shek's preparations for the culminating annihilation campaign
against the Chinese Communists in the autumn of 1936. Yet the
negotiations went on.

At the end of November 1936, in one of his lectures at the Red
Army College, Mao Tse-tung said:

Our fight against Chiang Kai-shek has become a war between
one state and another, between one great army and another.[2]

During and after the *coup* against Generalissimo Chiang Kai-
shek, there was daily evidence of the divergences between the
Mao and Stalin lines. Mao Tse-tung and the Chinese Communists
not only regarded the Sian insurgents as true patriots but were in
fact their allies.

On the day of Chiang's arrest (December 12), the Sian insurgents telegraphed their "eight demands" to the Nanking Govern-

[1] Chiang, *Soviet Russia in China*, pp. 69 and 71. *Izvestiya*, August 30,
1937, p. 1. See also: Wu, *China and the Soviet Union* and Abend,
My Life in China. Soviet Ambassador Bogomolov told the American
newspaper correspondent, Abend, that the Soviet Government was able
to convince Nanking at once that it had no part in the Sian incident,
since negotiations were going on previously.
[2] *SW*, Vol. I, p. 214.

ment and to the people of China and seven of these eight demands were identical with the demands of the Communist Party's circular telegram of December 1.

On December 14, two days after Chiang's arrest, the delegates of the insurgent armies and of the Chinese Red Army held a joint meeting and announced the formation of a United Anti-Japanese Army. Nearly a hundred thousand Red troops came under the command of the United Military Council.

Marshal Chang Hsüeh-liang, the head of the insurrection, sent his own plane to Yenan for the Chinese Communist plenipotentiaries. On December 19, 1936, five days after Chiang's arrest, the Nanking Government made preparations for a large-scale punitive expedition against the Sian insurgents—with the hearty approval of the Soviet press, as we shall see later. On the same day, Mao Tse-tung sent a telegram in the name of the Chinese Communists to all concerned, suggesting an immediate truce, to be followed by a peace conference. He stated that the "Sian leaders acted with patriotic zeal".[3]

In a note to a speech delivered in 1937, Mao wrote:

Prior to the Sian incident, the North-Eastern Army was . . . in direct contact with the Red Army in northern Shensi. *Profoundly influenced by contact with the Red Army*, it finally staged the Sian incident. To cut off its contact with the Red Army . . . the Kuomintang reactionaries ordered it to move eastward.[4]

The first volume of Mao's *Selected Works* was published in China in 1951. The above-quoted note appears in this and in all subsequent editions, proving that in this case no attempt has been made to rewrite history by refraining from mentioning the contradictory attitudes of Moscow and Yenan. Even the official *History of the Modern Chinese Revolution*, published in 1959, states that the Sian insurgents and their armies

. . . had come under the influence of the Red Army and the People's Anti-Japanese Movement, and stopped fighting against the Red Army. *Accepting the Communist Party's policy for an Anti-Japanese National United Front*, Chang and Yang [the insurgent leaders] urged Chiang Kai-shek to unite with the Communists against Japan. Chiang Kai-shek rejected their demands

---

[3] *China: The March Toward Unity*, pp. 122-3.
[4] SW, Vol. I, p. 335. (Emphasis added.)

and stepped up military preparations for "annihilating" the Communists. . . . *Spurred on by the People's Anti-Japanese Movement*, Chang and Yang detained Chiang Kai-shek in Sian on December 12, 1936 and *compelled him to stop the anti-Communist civil war*, which could only end in the destruction of the country. . . .[5]

The Soviet Government organ, *Izvestiya*, the Soviet Party organ, *Pravda*, and the Comintern papers *knew* on the other hand immediately that Marshal Chang Hsüeh-liang was a pro-Japanese reactionary and that Chiang's arrest was the result of Japanese machinations and instigations.

Moscow learnt of the arrest of Chiang Kai-shek on December 13. The editorials written for publication next day in *Izvestiya* and *Pravda*, contrary to all the facts and to every declaration of Mao and the Chinese Reds, credited Chiang Kai-shek with a readiness to fight Japan. After stating that the insurgent Marshal was a willing accomplice of Japan, *Pravda* wrote:

The Japanese military clique . . . correctly considers that the process of unification in China around Chiang Kai-shek's government, which has been moving forward strongly, constitutes a mortal danger to its plans.[6]

Izvestiya insisted that the Sian *coup* had been staged because the anti-Japanese united front movement was developing well:

During the last year there has been a significant rallying around the Nanking government by all social forces in China; the Nanking government, despite its . . . indecisions and campaigns against the united front movement, has nevertheless shown its readiness and ability to lead the defence of the country against Japan.[7]

The Moscow press went on for days denouncing the Sian insurrection and praising Chiang Kai-shek. *Inprecor* expressed anger that the punitive expedition against Sian was called off. This article was published ten days after the formation of the United Anti-Japanese Army of the insurgents and the Reds.[8] A few days later the same paper stated:

[5] *A History of the Modern Chinese Revolution*, Peking, Foreign Language Press, 1959, pp. 300-1.
[6] *Pravda*, December 14, 1936, p. 4.
[7] *Izvestiya*, December 14, 1936, p. 1.
[8] *Inprecor*, December 24, 1936, p. 1,514.

The rebellion of the traitor Chang Hsüeh-liang in Shensi has come to a miserable end. This is a real defeat of the Japanese intrigues directed against the unity of the Chinese people. Nanking was not impressed and sent troops against the rebel marshal, who was compelled to release Chiang Kai-shek.[9]

There is sufficient evidence that Stalin and the Soviet Government were ready to make any deal in the Far East to secure the USSR from Japanese attack. This will become even clearer as the events of the next eight years are examined.

That Stalin could turn viciously against insufficiently obedient foreign Communists is well known from such things as the extermination of the Polish Communist leadership; the execution of many Communists who took part in the Spanish Civil War; the sad fate of General Markos, the Greek Communist Partisan leader; and the campaign against Marshal Tito. On the evidence of the Stalinist purges in the thirties, when thousands of Communists were executed for much slighter disagreements, "deviations", disobedience or simply differing attitudes—there is little doubt that Mao too would have been executed, had he been within Stalin's reach.

In 1944, Molotov, speaking about the Sian incident, told Donald Nelson that the "Soviet Government had turned its back on the Chinese revolutionary groups". Donald Nelson reported:

He [Molotov] said that the Soviet Government had turned its back on the Chinese revolutionary groups led by Chang Hsüeh-liang and Wang Ching-wei [!] which included many Communists who looked to the Soviet Union for sympathy and aid, and had issued a statement to the effect that Japanese provocation had been the cause of the uprising in Sian.[10]

The anti-Stalin tract read by Khrushchev at the secret session of the Twentieth Party Congress in 1956, stated that Stalin had been prepared to break with the Chinese Communists.*

A non-aggression pact between Stalin and Chiang would have meant just this: Stalin's open break with the Chinese Communists. Such a pact, concluded *before* the cessation of Chiang's anti-Communist offensive, would have been an open repudiation of the Mao leadership and of the Chinese Soviets and their Red Army.

---

[9] *Inprecor*, January 2, 1937, p. 4.
[10] *United States Relations with China*, U.S. Government, Department of State, Washington, 1949, p. 72.
* The reference to China is omitted in some versions of the anti-Stalin tract published in the West.

Instead, Mao manoeuvred Chiang into a Kuomintang-Communist United Front.

It is a fact that the negotiations between the USSR and Chiang's China went on in a favourable atmosphere *before* the Sian incident, while after it Chiang Kai-shek was far less eager to see it concluded. It seems one of his reasons for this pact was to acquire an additional weapon against the Chinese Reds.

II

The Sian incident ended with virtual armistice between the small Soviet base and Chiang's Republic of China. The mortal threat to the Red base was averted. During and immediately after the incident, the Red Army expanded the Soviet area to nearly a hundred thousand square miles. Moreover, this Red area had in its rear Sinkiang and Inner and Outer Mongolia, so it could not be attacked from behind by the Japanese, nor could they completely blockade its sources of supply.

In the first half of 1937 the agreement between the Communists and the Kuomintang was completed. Generalissimo Chiang Kai-shek ceased to attack the Red areas and lifted the blockade. Communications and trade relations between the two territories were restored. The "Special Region" (later Border Region) was included in the "national defence area" and for a while the Kuomintang made regular payments to Yenan as the Central Government's contribution to defence expenditure. As a result of some very mild reforms in the Kuomintang areas, the Communist agitators and organisers had greater opportunity for their work.

On July 7, 1937, a new Japanese attack near Peking led to the All-China War of Resistance against Japan. The negotiations between Mao and Chiang and between Chiang and Stalin were speeded up.

On August 23, 1937, a treaty of non-aggression was signed in Nanking between Chiang Kai-shek's government and the USSR. Next month the Kuomintang government proclaimed the United Front in China.

The Communists ceased to be outlawed Red Bandits. Chiang Kai-shek in a widely publicised statement hailed the Communist offer to support Sun Yat-sen's "Three People's Principles", formally to abolish the Soviet government, and to redesignate the Red Army as one of the armies under the control of the Central Government. This action of the Communists, he declared, was "an out-standing instance of the triumph of national sentiment over every other consideration". The Generalissimo expressed his hope that the Communists would fight faithfully "shoulder to shoulder with the rest of the nation for the successful completion of the National Revolution".[11]

Before the United Front was formally established, Mao told the national conference of the Communist Party (May 1937), that the next task was to establish "the Communist Party's political leadership over the people of the whole country".[12]

This statement led to the next—and last—serious dispute in the Chinese Communist leadership. The minority, with some backing from Stalin, represented the "Victory for All!" policy—meaning that both parties, the Kuomintang and the Communists should emerge victoriously from the war with Japan. The "Victory for All!" group was against upsetting Chiang Kai-shek in any way and thereby weakening his determination to fight Japan. This minority felt that if they enlarged too blatantly the area of Communist influence, Chiang might again turn against them, instead of concentrating everything on the war against Japan. Mao's line was dubbed by his opponents a "Defeat for All!" policy, i.e. defeat for both Japan and Chiang's Kuomintang régime.

The "Victory for All!" group was first led by Chang Kuo-t'ao, Mao's erstwhile rival, a member of the Chinese Politbureau in 1937. He was expelled from the Party on April 17, 1938, by a Central Committee resolution for "right opportunism" and Trotskyist activities. Chang by this time had escaped to Kuomintang territory, and became a "counter-revolutionary traitor".[13]

Some time before this happened, Stalin had sent his Number One Chinese agent, Wang Ming back to China. A member of the Comintern Presidium since 1935, Wang had been Stalin's principal expert on China for a number of years, and he was briefed by Stalin before his departure. Wang was, incidentally, the author of the Comintern warning to Mao "not to place Chiang on the same platform with the Japanese".

Wang Ming arrived in China at the end of 1937, with the declared aim of negotiating with Chiang Kai-shek. It seems that he (and Stalin) still supported the "Victory for All!" line because, like

[11] Chiang, *Revolution and Reconstruction*, New York, 1942, pp. 20-21.
[12] SW, Vol. I, p. 281.
[13] SW, Vol. I, p. 336.

Chang Kuo-t'ao, he too was attacked by Mao for urging too many
concessions to the Kuomintang, thereby giving up the independence of the Communists within the United Front. Wang Ming was
charged furthermore with having "published a number of declarations, decisions and articles without the consent of the Central Committee".[14]

During Mao's fight against Chang Kuo-t'ao and Wang Ming, the
Soviet and Comintern press was lavish in its praise for Chiang
Kai-shek and the Kuomintang armies. Although these armies had
suffered defeat after defeat since the start of the all-out war with
Japan, and the only victories had been won by the Communists,
the main credit was consistently given to the Kuomintang armies.
Even the history of the Chinese Civil War (1927-37) was rewritten
in Moscow and Chiang's anti-Communist annihilation campaigns
and the Long March itself became "unfacts". Without mentioning
the war between the Kuomintang and the Communists, the Moscow
line was this:

> Until very recently the Chinese Republic had no central au-
> thority. Each province had its own authority, centered in the
> generals of local armies who gave only formal allegiance to the
> central government organised by *the party of national unity—the
> Kuomintang*. These generals fought among themselves as much as
> against the central government. . . . As a result, continuous civil
> war tore China apart.[15]

By July 1938 it was obvious in Moscow that the Chinese Communists under Mao Tse-tung represented a significant force in the
anti-Japanese war. Stalin, obsessed by the Japanese threat to his
Far Eastern frontiers, now saw that Mao's armies and guerillas were
pinning down an ever growing number of Japanese divisions. So
from then on he recognised Mao's leadership among the Chinese
Communists, but he continued to give active support only to Chiang
Kai-shek.

Mao well knew why he wanted the cessation of the civil war
and an all-out war against Japan. After the Sian incident, and even

---

[14] Hu Chiao-mu, *Thirty Years of the Communist Party of China*, London, 1951, pp. 53-54. The official Party history was published in China
and in Russia in 1951 and 1952 respectively.

[15] "On Japanese intervention in China", *Vlast' sovyetov*, No. 8, April
1938, p. 24; quoted by McLane, *Soviet Policy and the Chinese Communists*.

more after the outbreak of the anti-Japanese war, every month enlarged the military and political power of the Reds.

His generals, Chu Teh, Peng Teh-huai and Lin Piao, won victories over the Japanese forces, while the Red guerillas, steeled by a decade of stern practice, created many large anti-Japanese guerilla bases. Meanwhile Chiang Kai-shek's Kuomintang armies went on suffering defeat after defeat. The Eighth Route Army and the new Fourth Army of the Communists, and their numerous guerilla units, grew steadily, while Chiang lost his very best divisions one after another.

At first most of the might of the Japanese armies was directed against the Kuomintang forces, which were defending the most important cities, industrial districts and seaboard provinces. During the first fifteen months of the war the Kuomintang lost Peking, Tientsin, Shanghai, Canton, Nanking and the important Wuhan cities and, cut off from the sea, they had to retreat to the southwestern provinces in the interior. With its capital in Chungking, Generalissimo Chiang's Kuomintang-China was a far less significant power than it was at the time of signature of the pact with the USSR.

While the Japanese held the newly conquered cities and the railway lines, the countryside throughout vast territories of northern China came gradually under Communist rule. With the technique perfected during the Kiangsi period and the Long March, Mao's men organised their new guerilla base areas. Mao's directives were simple:

> We must spread a guerilla war all over these vast enemy-occupied areas, converting the enemy's rear into his front and forcing him to fight ceaselessly throughout his occupied areas.[16]

The Central Red base, renamed Border Region, with Yenan still as the capital, was greatly enlarged and had become since the end of the civil war a far more secure, prosperous and in a way even peaceful, territory than ever before. Up to the Sian incident this Red base had lacked everything—money, materials, machinery, weapons, medicine, trained personnel. Now for a time it had financial backing from the Kuomintang. With the lifting of the Kuomintang blockade, men and materials came streaming in. Engineers, physicians, scientists, students and all sorts of intellectuals came in their thousands to Yenan. The Red Academy was renamed Anti-Japanese

[16] SW, Vol. II, p. 135.

University and soon it had 5,000 students. Most of this university was housed in the Yenan caves.

Yenan was now used by Mao and his colleagues as a secure base in which to indoctrinate, train and discipline thousands upon thousands of new Communist functionaries and all sorts of Red specialists.

Yenan, the capital of Red China, was almost totally pulverised by Japanese bombing. But in the surrounding cliff-sides caves mushroomed to such an extent that Yenan soon became a bomb-proof cave-city; it continued to be the capital and its population even grew. The thousand-foot-high loess cliffs on the two sides of Yenan valley became human honeycombs. The streets were levelled out from the cliff-side tier above tier. Each tier had its rows of caves for offices, schools, hospitals or homes. These streets were connected by steep paths, steps or zigzagging hairpin footpaths. Mao's cave residence was similar to, if somewhat more spacious than, the homes of the other functionaries.

The cave-city of Yenan soon became a legend in China. A growing number of people outside the Red areas regarded it as the real centre of anti-Japanese resistance.

The political tactics for this period—elaborated by Mao—aimed at convincing China that the Communist offer to democratise their régime was sincere and genuine. The class-line was dropped in practice. Equal rights were given in principle to all citizens, regardless of their actual "class-status" or "class-origin". Communist rule in the central base and in the other base territories became much milder and much more democratic. The only lands confiscated were those of collaborationist absentee landlords. The new rules provided for a reduction of the rent and interest collected by the landlords and also ensured the payment of these by the peasants. It was laid down that rent should be cut generally by twenty-five per cent, but that the rate of interest should not be reduced to the point where nobody would be willing to give loans. Thus, both the landlord's ownership and the peasant's tenant rights were recognised. Communists helped to organise "anti-Japanese democratic" local governments and village councils with the inclusion of all classes. Private enterprise in commerce and industry was encouraged. In many guerilla areas and "liberated" bases, all classes of the population were better protected from the Japanese and led a freer existence than in most of Kuomintang China.

Mao's aim was that most of the rural population should benefit from the reforms brought about by his "Anti-Japanese Vanguard

Armies". The result of this policy was that the rural masses living
behind the Japanese lines accepted Communist directions and gave
all the help they could to the guerilla operations.

Communist teams were organised on the "three-in-one" principle:
they were to fight as troops, carry on political work on behalf of
the (Red) government, but act like the common people in ordinary
times. These teams would appear or disappear unexpectedly in the
very heart of Japanese occupied territories.

III

The propagandists directed from Yenan did everything possible
to convince the Chinese people that the Communists were the most
determined fighters in the patriotic war of resistance. Chiang Kai-
shek on the other hand claimed that Mao said his real policy was:
"to devote seventy per cent of our efforts to our own expansion,
twenty per cent to coping with the (Kuomintang) Government and
ten per cent to fighting the Japanese".[17]

It is true that, after the initial battles, the Communist armies
were far less active in regular warfare than in guerilla campaigns.
It is also true that during the first two years of the war they concentrated mostly on the formation of rural guerilla bases in Japanese-
occupied territories. But it is also a fact that from 1937 till the
end of 1940 they had liberated and organised under their government 150 counties. By this time the liberated Red territories and
the guerilla areas had a population of nearly a hundred million and
the membership of the Communist Party had reached 800,000.
From the end of 1940 onwards there were long periods when the
Japanese regarded the Communists as their main enemies in China
and used more troops against them than against the Kuomintang.

Mao Tse-tung never tired of reminding his Party of their real
aim in the anti-Japanese war. In a speech, not published at that
time, he said this to the Central Committee plenary session on November 6, 1938:

As a national war resistance is going on, we must further contend
for military power for the nation. . . . Every Communist must
grasp the truth: "Political power grows out of the barrel of a gun."
Our principle is that the Party commands the gun, and the gun
will never be allowed to command the Party. *But it is also true
that with guns at our disposal we can really build up the Party*

---

[17] Chiang, *Soviet Russia in China*, p. 85.

organisation, and the Eighth Route Army has built up a powerful Party organisation in North China. We can also rear cadres and create schools, culture and mass movements. Everything in Yenan has been built up by means of the gun. Anything can grow out of the barrel of a gun. According to the Marxist theory of the state, the army is the chief component of the political power of a state. Whoever wants to seize the political power of the state and to maintain it must have a strong army. . . . Experience in the class-struggle of the era of imperialism teaches us that the working class and the toiling masses cannot defeat the armed bourgeois and landlords except by the power of the gun; *in this sense we can even say that the whole world can be remoulded only with the gun.*[18]

Generalissimo Chiang Kai-shek for his part also hoped to exploit the anti-Japanese war to weaken and finally to crush the Communists. His policy right from the outset of the nominal United Front was to put the Communist areas and armies under his control. In July 1937, before he even announced the formation of the United Front, he told the Kuomintang Party Training Course at Kuling that the aim was "to reduce the strength of the Communist Party by two-fifths in the course of the anti-Japanese war". After the war started, the Kuomintang authorities began to restrict the Red areas and Red armies. There were isolated clashes from the outset between Kuomintang and Communist troops. The Kuomintang was alarmed by the growth of the Communist-inspired "Anti-Japanese democratic government" territories in occupied China. They charged the Communists with overrunning districts where Kuomintang forces were operating, and incorporating these forces in their own guerilla armies.

The Kuomintang too organised guerilla forces behind the enemy lines, but these had none of the vast experience of the Communists and soon came under Communist control. Both sides had ample reason for accusing each other of breach of the United Front pact. From the outset neither side meant to keep it. Early in 1939 Chiang ordered the blockade of the Yenan government region. Blockhouses were set up, communications were interrupted and it was only due to wartime conditions that this new anti-Communist blockade was not really effective.

In many parts of occupied and unoccupied China the situation soon became as chaotic and dangerous as during the era of the war-

[18] SW, Vol. II, pp. 272-3. (Emphasis added.)

lords. Besides the Kuomintang-Communist bickering, and often open hostility and pitched battles, the military governors of some of the outlying provinces, still nominally under Chiang's rule, became independent or semi-independent war-lords, engrossed in securing greater power for themselves in post-war China. The Japanese set up a Chinese puppet-government with Nanking as the capital. This puppet-government had its own troops, police and intelligence network, under Japanese control. Both the Kuomintang and Communists had their agents in the puppet territories. Many divisions of the Kuomintang armies went over to the Japanese and served under direct Japanese command. Chiang acknowledged after the war that some of these generals and armies deserted to the Japanese with Kuomintang approval in order to turn against them "when the time came". Meanwhile these Chinese puppet troops fought side by side with the Japanese against the Red guerillas and armies. During the first anti-Communist upsurge (January 1939-April 1940), the Kuomintang launched offensives against the Red Border Region, against various bases and even against the headquarters of the Eighth Route Army, which was nominally under Chiang's own command.

Mao and his colleagues made innumerable public complaints against Chiang Kai-shek and his armies. The Russian press meanwhile went on praising Chiang Kai-shek and giving the Kuomintang armies credit for most of the fighting against Japan. In addition to this moral support, Stalin helped Chiang Kai-shek with large shipments of arms under a series of loan agreements. Chiang's government acknowledged the following loans from the Soviet Union:[19]

March 1938	50,000,000	US dollars
July 1938	50,000,000	" "
June 1939	150,000,000	" "

The same sums and dates are mentioned in official Soviet publications.

A further loan of fifty million dollars in November 1940 cannot be documented from official Kuomintang and Soviet sources, although in view of the circumstantial evidence one can hardly doubt that it was made. These loan agreements were signed at a time when it was obvious that Chiang Kai-shek was fighting against

[19] *China Handbook, 1937-1945,* published by the Kuomintang Government; revised edition, 1947, p. 209.

Mao's regions and armies. Soviet shipments of arms were sent through Sinkiang to the Kuomintang areas at the very moment when Chiang was launching his offensive against the Communists.

Although Chiang Kai-shek later accused Stalin of all sorts of duplicity, *he never charged him with helping the Communists in any way during this period.* No Kuomintang source ever accused Mao of having received supplies from the USSR, and Chiang's brother-in-law and chief economic expert, T. V. Soong, told Edgar Mowrer in 1941 that the Chinese Communists received no material aid from the Soviet Union.[20] All through the anti-Japanese war the Chinese Communists fought with arms captured from Kuomintang or Japanese troops or manufactured by themselves. There is no indication in the Kuomintang, Soviet or Western press, nor in any other reports that Stalin accorded material aid to Mao at any time during the eight years of the Sino-Japanese war.

The Chinese Communist press was full of Mao's pronouncements on the proneness of Chiang's régime to capitulate. Stalin, on the other hand, in a letter sent to Chiang Kai-shek on July 9, 1939 complimented the Generalissimo on the Kuomintang war effort.[21]

In August 1939 Stalin concluded the pact with Hitlerite Germany. Whatever his private views, Mao Tse-tung publicly acclaimed this as a step leading to Japanese isolation in the Far East, and to thwarting the machinations of the Western powers to provoke war between the USSR and Germany. He assured the people of China that this pact would not diminish Soviet aid given to China. In view of the fact that Generalissimo Chiang Kai-shek also applauded the Nazi-Soviet pact saying it "will benefit even more our national cause",[22] Mao could not have said anything else. His writings, declarations and propaganda directives at the time all go to show that Mao understood Stalin's manoeuvres to keep the USSR out of the war as long as possible. He even foresaw the possibility of a Soviet-Japanese pact. Discussing the Nazi-Soviet pact, he wrote in an article on September 29, 1939, that for many years the Soviet Union had been proposing to Japan a non-aggression pact,

but Japan has rejected it all along. At present a clique within the Japanese ruling class is offering to conclude such a pact, but whether the Soviet Union is willing to conclude it depends on the basic principle—whether such a pact fits in with the interests of

[20] Mowrer's interview quoted in Rosinger, *China's Crisis*, p. 228.
[21] Chiang, *Soviet Russia in China*, p. 90.
[22] Chiang, *Collected Wartime Messages*, I, p. 323.

the Soviet Union and the majority of mankind. . . . Should a
Japanese-Soviet non-aggression pact be concluded, the Soviet Union will surely see to it that nothing in this pact limits its help
to China.[23]

In this article, written twenty months before the Soviet-Japanese
non-aggression pact was actually concluded, Mao tried to convince
the Chinese people (or Stalin?) that there was a "unity between
the interests of the Soviet Union and the interest of mankind". But
it was written in a country suffering from Japanese aggression. It
was written by a man who never ceased to denounce Japan for her
policy of "burn all, kill-all and loot all", in a country where thousands of villages had been razed to the ground by Japanese troops,
where everyone had heard of the raping, looting and massacres
perpetrated by the Japanese forces. In fact Mao feared the consequences of the new pact. A few days after publicly hailing the
Stalin-Hitler pact, Mao Tse-tung warned his party in the new
magazine, *The Communist*, "to make preparations for coping with
possible emergencies, so that, in case they occur, the Party and the
revolution will not suffer unexpected losses".[24]

The Nazi-Soviet pact and the outbreak of the Second World War
made Generalissimo Chiang Kai-shek more optimistic. He knew
very well that, ever since committing himself strongly to the support of the Kuomintang in the nineteen-twenties, Stalin had welcomed any chance of proving in retrospect the correctness of his
pro-Chiang Kai-shek line. Chiang's diplomats and Soviet experts
reported continuously all the signs indicating Stalin's dislike for
the Mao leadership of the Chinese Communist movement. The va-
lidity of these reports is proved by the fact that Stalin kept on sending shipments of arms and of bomber planes to the Kuomintang
even after a series of widely reported anti-Communist campaigns.

Late in 1940 Chiang ordered that the units of the Eighth Route
and New Fourth (Red) Armies operating south of the Yellow
River should be transferred to the north of the river. Preferring to
avoid an open break, the Communists agreed to shift some units.
As part of the New Fourth Army, some 10,000 men, moved northward they were ambushed on January 4, 1941 at South Anhwei by
a numerically superior Kuomintang contingent. The fighting lasted
for a week, and according to Yenan reports more than 6,000 Red

[23] *SW*, Vol. III, p. 5. (Emphasis added.)
[24] *SW*, Vol. III, p. 53.

soldiers were killed. The Communist Commander was arrested.*

In Moscow, *Pravda, Izvestiya* and the Comintern organs treated the South Anhwei Incident as the outcome of the intrigues of the Japanese and/or Anglo-American imperialists and their lackeys in the Kuomintang. Some "narrow-minded Kuomintang generals" were also blamed. But nowhere in the press directed by Stalin was there even an illusion that Chiang Kai-shek was to blame. In fact, Stalin's press and radio still treated Chiang Kai-shek as the personification of anti-Japanese resistance. This was of course in direct contradiction to the Chinese Communist line which treated Mao Tse-tung as the leader and symbol of anti-Japanese resistance.

The January 22, 1941, statement of Mao's Military Council alleged that the South Anhwei Incident was part of a plot to make a deal with the Japanese against the Communists:

> Japan is to bring troops originally stationed in Central and South China to North China as reinforcements and to launch most ruthless attacks on the Eighth Route Army, attempting in co-operation with the Kuomintang forces, to annihilate completely the Eighth Route and the New Fourth Armies. . . . A state of cease-fire like that of last year is to continue between the Kuomintang and the Japanese troops on all fronts . . . [the plotters want to] launch attacks on the . . . Border Region and capture Yenan.[25]

In 1941 Japan started to concentrate its main forces in China against the various Red areas. The Chinese Red Armies were engaged in battle with the Japanese on several fronts during April 1941 when Stalin signed the Japanese-Soviet neutrality pact, and publicly embraced the Japanese Foreign Minister, Matsuoka, whom he called his "fellow Asiatic". The USSR pledged itself to respect the "territorial integrity and inviolability" of Manchukuo (taken by Japan from China) in exchange for Japanese recognition of the territorial integrity and inviolability of Outer Mongolia (taken by the USSR from China).

Mao Tse-tung gave his public endorsement to the Russo-Japanese neutrality pact, although he knew that it was a grave shock to the Chinese masses fighting against Japan or suffering under Japanese occupation. At this time Stalin's period of "friendship" with Hitler was not yet over. But whereas the Hitler-Stalin pact was only of ideological concern to the politically articulate leftist

---

* Chiang Kai-shek maintains that the Communists refused to obey his orders and that they attacked first.

[25] SW, Vol. III, p. 227.

and Communist minorities in China, the Soviet neutrality pact with Japan awoke Chinese national resentment. It was clear, of course, that the leaders of the USSR were merely attending to the security of their Far Eastern frontiers; but it was equally clear that this neutrality pact increased neither the security of the Chinese Communist regions, nor any affection Mao and the Chinese Communists might feel for Stalin and the Soviet Union.

IV

There is no such thing as abstract, only concrete Marxism . . . expressed in a *national form*. It means utilising Marxism in the concrete struggle taking place in the concrete Chinese environment . . . to *make Marxism Chinese*, to see to it that in every manifestation it bears a *Chinese character*, that is to say, that it is applied according to *China's special characteristic*.[26]

Stalin's main and only preoccupation was with the interests of the USSR. Mao Tse-tung's sole aim was to build up a Communist China.

For Stalin's Far Eastern interests it was essential then, and continued to be important even after the war, that the Chinese United Front should exist under Chiang Kai-shek's leadership. The Soviet and Comintern press continued to refer to Chiang throughout 1942 and 1943 as "the leader of the Chinese people and the symbol of Chinese unity."

According to the Stalin-Comintern line, feudal or semi-feudal China had a long transition period to go through—the stage of the *bourgeois revolution*,—and could only thereafter progress to the higher stage of socialist revolution. This was in accordance with one of the basic tenets of Marxism: the necessity of the "capitalist stage" which would produce modern industry and with it the "grave-diggers of capitalism", the industrial proletariat, who would then lead the socialist revolution. In 1940, Mao published the new programme of the Chinese Communists, the theoretical blueprint for the next period, called *On New Democracy*. In this he declared that the stage the Chinese Revolution had then reached was not a bourgeois revolution, but one of "several revolutionary classes". It should no longer be led or controlled by the bourgeoisie (the Kuomintang), but should be under "the joint dictatorship of all anti-

[26] Mao to the Sixth Central Committee plenary session, November 6, 1938. (Emphasis added.)

imperialist and anti-feudal people led by the proletariat" (the Communist Party). Mao, it seemed, proposed to leave out the "capitalist stage".

One of the most revealing passages dealt with the question of what to absorb from foreign examples, including *socialist* (i.e. Soviet) examples:

> New-democratic culture is national. It opposes imperialist oppression, and upholds the dignity and independence of the Chinese nation. . . . We must absorb whatever we now find useful, not only from the present socialist or new-democratic cultures of other nations, but also from the older cultures of foreign countries, such as those of the various capitalist countries in the age of enlightenment. However, we must treat these foreign materials as we do our food, which should be chewed in the mouth, submitted to the working of the stomach and intestines, mixed with saliva, gastric juice and intestinal secretions, and then separated into essence to be absorbed and waste matter to be discarded—only thus can food benefit our body; *we should never swallow anything raw or absorb it uncritically.* So-called "wholesale Westernisation" is a mistaken viewpoint. China has suffered a great deal in the past from the formalist absorption of foreign things. *Likewise, in applying Marxism to China, Chinese Communists must fully and properly unite the universal truth of Marxism with the specific practice of the Chinese revolution; that is to say, the truth of Marxism must be integrated with the characteristics of the nation and given a definite national form before it can be useful,* it must not be applied subjectively as a mere formula. Formula-Marxists are only fooling with Marxism and the Chinese revolution, and there is no place for them in the ranks of the Chinese revolution.[27]

The "formula Marxists", those who were intent on following the Stalin line and tried to oppose Soviet Marxism to Mao's "Chinese Marxism", soon had good reason to be shocked by Mao's unorthodox political tactics. The number of large and small "democratic anti-Japanese government" regions, controlled by the Communists, grew. Mao wanted to increase their appeal by the introduction into the electoral procedure of a new "one-in-three" principle according to which the Communists limited themselves to one-third of all elected government posts, council memberships, etc. In the "anti-

[27] *SW*, Vol. III, p. 153-4. (Emphasis added.)

Japanese government" or council areas, effective armed power was in the hands of the regular or guerilla forces of the Reds. Yet Mao instructed them to allot two-thirds of assembly, government and council-posts to non-Communists of all classes. In areas inhabited by non-Chinese nationalities (Mongols, Uigurs, etc.), these were given the right to elect their own representatives.

From 1941 until 1947, this "one-in-three" principle was rigorously adhered to. If in any election the Communists received more than one third of the votes, they had instructions from Yenan to give up the "excess" positions.

By initiating this "one-in-three" practice Mao aimed at expanding Communist-guided areas. By courting all classes of the population, by giving governmental and council posts to thousands upon thousands of non-Communists, by conferring the title of "labour hero" on thousands of peasants (and by courting all sorts of middle-class people), Mao demonstrated to them, and to China that unlike the Kuomintang the Communists did not exercise a one-party dictatorship in the territories where they had effective power. They were not supposed to know and in fact did not, of Mao's declaration on the temporary character of these measures.

The platform of the Communist candidates for the "People's Political Council" in the 1941 elections, was written by Mao:

> The Communist Party desires to safeguard civil, political, and *property rights* equally with the rights of freedom of speech, press, assembly, organisation, belief, residence and movements of all anti-Japanese people . . . *including landlords, capitalists, peasants, workers, etc.*
>
> The Communist representatives will propose measures designed to develop industrial production and trade, *encourage private enterprise, and protect private property*. They believe the Border Region should welcome investments from outside and abroad, *foster free trade*.[28]

The long election manifesto pledged clean and honest government and promised even to the "traitors, except those hopelessly unchangeable, a policy of magnanimity", irrespective of their past history. Efforts would be made to instruct and convert them. Even Party renegades and former "anti-Communist plotters and wreckers" were promised similar treatment.

[28] Harrison Forman, *Report from Red China*, London, 1946, pp. 57-61. (Emphasis added.)

The application of the "one-in-three" principle did not endanger
effective Communist control over all activities. The Communist third
was directed according to a central plan. All the information on
which decisions were based came from Communist sources. The
Army, the Red militia and the Red guerilla units were led by Communists. And lastly "public safety" (i.e. the secret political police)
was in Communist hands. As civil, political and property rights
were guaranteed *for anti-Japanese citizens only*, it was up to the
authorities to decide who was anti-Japanese and who was not.

These and similar political tactics made it even easier to expand
the Communist-controlled areas. The non-Communists on the whole
had not much reason at that time to doubt the sincerity of the
"New Democratic" period. It lasted for roughly eight years. Compared with Kuomintang dictatorship, and Kuomintang secret police
activities, the Communists did not break many of their promises.
Compared with Western democratic countries, the New Democratic
rule as practised by the Communists was a more or less cleverly
camouflaged military dictatorship.

Within the Party this policy of Mao's met with opposition or
misunderstanding from two sides. The "returned student" type of
Communist, the "Muscovites" and their adherents, saw revisionism
and opportunism in it, while more than half a million new Party
members interpreted it in too "bourgeois-liberal" a way. The success of the Reds was indicated also by the growth of Party membership from 40,000 in 1937 to nearly 800,000 by the end of 1941.
In 1942 Mao Tse-tung therefore launched a large-scale purge and
rectification campaign within the Party.

With the exception of a handful of the main Party and Army
leaders—the most loyal adherents of Mao—all Party members were
subjected to a rigorous examination before the public session of
their own particular Party organisation. Mao's leadership changed
and perfected the Soviet technique developed during the Party
purges. Party members had to exercise "self-criticism" in reviewing
their entire past, confessing their shortcomings and deviations. Then
their comrades and superiors criticised them in turn, exposed further
shortcomings and past deviations, pointing out unrevolutionary and
un-Marxist traits, demanding fuller and more concrete confessions.
These "criticism-self-criticism" sessions generally developed into accusation meetings, the entire organisation "struggling" against the
not sufficiently "self-critical" comrade, that is hurling accusations at
him or her, forcing the culprit to "turn resolutely against the enemy

within his or her skull", as the first step of real Communist self-remoulding and inner rectification.

During this very large-scale rectification campaign the old and new Party members had a taste of what Mao had learnt from the Hunanese peasants in 1926 and what the world was to learn after 1950 about "brain washing", mass accusation and mass struggle meetings. Many Party members were expelled, and some thousands arrested.

Besides forging an absolutely hardened and disciplined Party apparatus, the rectification campaign was used to purge from the Party all those who wanted to follow dogmatically the Soviet Party line, and in doing so were not sufficiently loyal to the Mao leadership. Chinese Communists were persuaded that in making Marxism Chinese they were only following the example of Lenin and Stalin. The official Russian line, however, until 1956 was that the Soviet road to Socialism must be followed by all Communist parties. There are signs that Mao and his colleagues had to cope with a vocal minority in their own Party, which wanted to follow the Soviet line.

Liu Shao-chi, the later Head of State of Red China, was by this time already the second chief ideologist of the Chinese Communists. He still attacked those who did not regard the Chinese Party as the foremost Party of the world Communist movement. Liu wrote:

If we cast aside the rich experience of the revolutionary struggle of China, if we despise the experience of the struggle of our Party in the great historical events in these twenty-two years, if we do not study such experiences carefully and learn from them, but *merely confine our study to the experience of foreign revolutions far away from us,* then we shall be reversing the true order of things and we will have to traverse a much more tortuous road and suffer more setbacks. . . . The Chinese Communist Party has in its twenty-two years passed through many more great events than *any other Party in the world* and has had richer experience in the revolutionary struggle.[29]

Stalin could not very well denounce this line since in May 1943 he had disbanded the Comintern. It was only after the war that he once more asserted that Communists must follow the Soviet road.

[29] Liu Shao-chi, *Liquidate the Menshevist Ideology within the Party,* written in 1943. English translation published in Peking, in 1951[!], pp. 2-4.

After the outbreak of the Russo-German war in June, and of the American war against Japan in December 1941, and the consequent Anglo-American-Soviet alliance, both the Kuomintang and the Communists intensified their preparations for seizing power as soon as the war was over. Chiang Kai-shek maintained that the Communist guerillas were fighting against Japan only in order to expand their own liberated areas. On the other hand, Chiang's armies did even less fighting against Japan. Two hundred thousand of his troops were engaged in trying to blockade the Communist Border Region, against which Chiang launched a large-scale offensive in June 1943. This was the start of the short-lived "third anti-Communist upsurge".

The last two years of the anti-Japanese war followed the pattern developed since 1937: a Kuomintang blockade of the Red areas and offensives against the Border Region, Japanese mopping-up operations against the Red enclaves and offensives against the remnants of Kuomintang China. During the first eight months of 1944 the Japanese army took from the Kuomintang the major part of six provinces in central and southern China. The Kuomintang Army lost over half a million troops and abandoned to the Japanese a population of well over sixty million. The Communists on the other hand regained the losses they had suffered in 1941, and by 1944 Mao Tse-tung was head of a large state consisting of nineteen very large liberated territories and innumerable guerilla base areas, from North China and Inner Mongolia to Hainan Island in the extreme south, with a population of a hundred million. The combined strength of the Red armies and Red militia was well over three million.

In the second part of 1944 it was obvious that the outbreak of the civil war could not be long avoided. Mao wrote in an editorial in October 1944:

Chiang's attitude is getting more and more anomalous, as witness his stubborn opposition to the people's demands for political reform, his bitter hatred of the Chinese Communist Party and his hint at the pretext for the anti-Communist civil war he is preparing.[30]

At the end of the Sino-Japanese war, Mao and the Chinese Communists could have made the same complaint as Tito and the Yugoslav Communists were later to voice. The Yugoslav partisans

[30] SW, Vol. IV, p. 224.

persistently denounced General Mihailovic for collaborating with the Germans and Italians and attacking the Yugoslav partisans, yet

> In the USSR . . . they spoke only of Draja Mihailovic. . . . The whole uprising, our entire efforts, were ascribed to Draja Mihailovic. . . . Stalin . . . was displeased by the fact that we established a new form of authority against his will. . . . Stalin never wanted a new progressive movement to be created with roots of its own. . . . It was for that reason Stalin did not encourage the development of the uprising in Yugoslavia, Soviet propaganda never mentioned the partisans, although Stalin received detailed daily reports on the situation.
>
> . . . Relationships with the Soviet Union had begun to deteriorate from the very first day of the war. Moscow refused to tolerate any movement independent of itself, any movement that had primarily the interest of its own country and of its own people in view; it wanted a movement which would be blindly obedient and in fact a weapon of Russian foreign policy, an unjust foreign policy . . . since it was only concerned with great-power expansionist interests.[31]

And the post-war period showed that the Chinese Communist movement was not a weapon in the hands of Soviet foreign policy, but a danger to it.

[31] Vladimir Dedijer, *Tito Speaks*, London, 1953, pp. 170-1, and p. 259.

XI

RULER FROM THE YENAN CAVES

I

Life in Yenan, where Mao Tse-tung lived for more than twelve years before becoming the ruler of China, was in many respects similar to that of the communes Mao was to set up in 1958. Everyone led a hard and austere existence. As in the communes, workers and peasants were expected to become intellectuals, while the latter were to live, think and feel like workers and peasants. Human nature was being remoulded into "class nature". The Red Army men worked as peasants between battles and the peasants were part-time guerillas.

The thousands of Communists who had survived since the Kiangsi days went through precisely the same remoulding during their long struggle for power. Forced out of the cities, they had given up civilised urban existence nearly ten years ago. Organising and leading peasant guerillas, they became peasant guerillas themselves. Living in army tents, peasant huts or caves, they created a regular army in which each soldier had to become a student, organiser of men, agitator and administrator. The leaders of the Party and the army, and the rank and file, leading the same life, fighting the same battles, became members of a closely knit brotherhood, with the solidarity and mutual loyalty of seasoned veterans. All of them were poor; much of their life they had less comfort than ordinary peasants in backward Chinese villages. For decades they were not exposed to the influence and temptations of urban existence.

Yenan was a large city. It had a large population, a university, schools, theatre, hospitals, newspapers and all the rest. But in its way of life it was more like a backward village. Surgeons and actresses, writers and professors wore the same crude uniform and lived like peasants. The electricity of the Yenan radio station was produced by foot-pedal and the hospitals had to make do with the crudest instruments, with very little in the way of medical supplies from the outside world. Physicians, biologists and chemists experimented with local herbs to replenish their store of medicine. All over the cave-city washing was hung up in front of the dwellings.

Mao worked for years by candle-light. His cave dwelling was sparsely furnished and badly protected against heat and cold. The yellow dust that filled this valley between the loess hills got everywhere. People often had to wear gauze masks over their faces as a protection. Food was primitive and scarce. On little clearings in front of the caves, or on small terraces cut into the cliff-side, people grew their own vegetables. Visitors reported catching a glimpse of Chairman Mao as, towards sunset, the ruler of nineteen soviet governments all over China worked in his garden where he grew his own tobacco and tomatoes.

Other visitors saw him walking in his dusty uniform through the narrow passages in the cliff-side, "looking like any other peasant soldier". This life—he maintained—remoulded him.

He spoke of his own self-remoulding to a Yenan conference of writers and artists in 1942:

If you want the masses to understand you and want to become one with them, you must be determined to undergo a long and even painful process of remoulding. In this connection I might mention the transformation of my own feelings. I began as a student and acquired at school the habits of a student; in the presence of a crowd of students who could neither fetch nor carry for themselves, I used to feel it undignified to do any manual labour, such as shouldering my own luggage. At that time it seemed to me that the intellectuals were the only clean persons in the world, and the workers and peasants seemed rather dirty beside them. I could put on the clothes of other intellectuals because I thought they were clean, but I would not put on clothes belonging to a worker or peasant because I felt they were dirty. Having become a revolutionary I found myself in the same ranks as the workers, peasants and soldiers of the revolutionary army, and gradually I became familiar with them and they with me too. It was then and only then that a fundamental change occurred in the bourgeois and petty-bourgeois feelings implanted in me by the bourgeois schools. *I came to feel that it was those unremoulded intellectuals who were unclean as compared with the workers and peasants, while the workers and peasants are after all the cleanest persons, cleaner than both the bourgeois and the petty-bourgeois intellectuals, even though their hands are soiled and their feet smeared with cow dung.* This is what is meant by having one's feelings transformed, changed from those of one class into those of another. If our artists and writers from the intelligentsia want their works to be welcomed by the masses, they must transform and remould their thoughts and feelings. Without such transformation and remoulding they can do nothing well and will be ill-adapted to any kind of work.[1]

Mao's life in Yenan was stripped to the barest of essentials. He ruled over fifty, then a hundred and later nearly a hundred and fifty million people, his armies grew to three million, but still he did not live like the ruler of a mighty state. He only worked like one. There were no receptions, no ceremonial occasions, state visits, splendid banquets or any of the other formal functions that take up a great deal of the time of heads of states or Prime Ministers. He had his personal staff who sifted the thousands of reports streaming in daily from the fronts and from all parts of China and the world, so that the Chairman should not waste his time on unimportant matters. The Chairman was a member of all the supreme committees directing the various departments of the Party, the government and the army. Each department, army group, each major political or economic campaign had its responsible director under Mao. The Chairman formulated the broad outlines of policy and intervened only if some change in the situation necessitated a change in military or political tactics. The rest of the time he spent in complete seclusion in his cave-dwelling, studying, writing, working on his long-term plans.

The absence of any kind of representative function saved Mao a great deal of time. So did his habit of working at night and sleeping through most of the day.

Yenan morals were as strict as in a puritanical village, or as in a beleaguered fort. Men and women—as in the communes of today—wore the same crudely cut uniforms. Everybody—whatever his or her function—had to do a certain amount of physical work, gardening and household chores, in addition to the multifarious army, governmental, Party and civic tasks. Furthermore, and again as in the communes, everybody was studying, lecturing and listening to lectures. No one was exposed to the softening influence and temptations of urban "gracious living"; on the contrary, everyone was under the spell of patriotic wartime fervour, of revolutionary dedication, of the *esprit de corps* of a persecuted minority, fighting with its back to the wall. Japanese planes paid frequent bombing visits to the city. With people packed closely together, in caves and huts, a strict code was evolved to avoid sexual chaos.

[1] *SW*, Vol. IV, pp. 67-68.

The wives, all of whom had their Party or governmental functions, were also cooking for their husbands, doing the washing, preserving fruit for the winter. Mme Chu Teh and Mme Chou En-lai had shared the hazards of the Long March with their husbands, like Mme Mao and the wives of many other Red leaders. Now they were functionaries by day and peasant wives in the evening. In Mao's terminology, they became "clean like the workers and the peasants".

Some visitors reported that at times Mao appeared to be bored by the year-in year-out monotony of Yenan life. It was at such times that he relaxed by visiting the workshops and joining in the discussions of the Yenan artists and intellectuals.

If Red Yenan was without running water, pavements and many of the comforts which city-dwellers take for granted, its cultural atmosphere was quite interesting. Since the United Front agreement, the university, the Lu Hsün Art Academy with its theatre workshop, the schools and scientific institutions, the hospitals and the Red publishing house had been filled with many of the finest artists, scientists and intellectuals in the whole of China. These— whether Communists, or sympathisers, or simply leftish patriots— came to Yenan and offered their services to the "builders of new China". Some came out of curiosity, others because the Japanese had occupied their cities. They made the intellectual and artistic life of the cave-city livelier.

One of Mao Tse-tung's pet projects was the Art Academy, especially its theatre workshop. New dramas and operas were produced, with revolutionary themes. It is said that Mao himself took part in the writing of some of these. Allegedly he is one of the authors of a play based on the favourite book of his childhood, *All Men Are Brothers.*

It was at the theatre workshop that Mao met Lang Ping, a popular Shanghai film actress, who had given up her film career in 1937 when the truce in the civil war made it possible to go to Yenan. Lang Ping, a dedicated revolutionary, had joined the Communist Party in 1933 and, ever since her arrival in Yenan four years later, she had worked at the Lu Hsün Art Academy. As an attractive and talented actress and an interesting intellectual, she soon became one of the leading figures of the Red theatre movement.

Mao Tse-tung fell in love with her, so much so that he was prepared for her sake to divorce his third wife, Ho Tzu-ch'en, his companion since the Kiangsi days. It will be recalled that Mao had married Ho Tzu-ch'en after the execution of his second wife, and that she had nearly died from the wounds she received during the Long March. Ho Tzu-ch'en had borne Mao a girl in Pao An, shortly after the Long March.

Divorce is a rare thing in the upper reaches of the Communist hierarchy. For a Party leader, who is supposed to live an exemplary life in all respects, it is a grave step. To divorce a Long March companion is even graver. Yet the forty-six-year-old Mao took this step, and in the spring of 1939 he married Lang Ping.

Ho Tzu-ch'en moved out from the cave-dwelling and the new Mme Mao moved in. Ho Tzu-ch'en went on working in Yenan and is now a functionary in Peking.

As the Yenan years went on, Mao and some of the leaders seem to have had enough of their own "remoulding". They went on wearing the clothes of the peasants, they did not change their living quarters, they still took care that everyone should be impressed with their austere way of life—which in fact seemed to become less ascetic from 1940 onwards. We do not know exactly what sort of exceptions and privileges they accorded themselves. But some of the revolutionary writers who came to the Red Region during the last two years were plainly disappointed and disillusioned by some aspects of Yenan life. The *Liberation News* of the Red capital published several exceptionally critical articles during the first four months of 1942.

The most daring one was written by a Moscow-trained Party writer of very high standing. He was Wang Shih-wei, the official Chinese translator of Marx and Lenin, a Party member since 1926. His article gives a curious and ominous glimpse of Yenan conditions:

> I am not a follower of egalitarianism . . . to have clothing in three colours and meals in five kinds may not be absolutely necessary or reasonable. But if on the one hand sick comrades have nothing to eat and young students have but two meals of thin congee a day; on the other hand perfectly healthy "big shots" are given to flagrant and senseless pleasure, with the result that those below are likely to think that those above consider them not as human beings and that they not only show no love for them but also—well, to think of it all, cannot but cause despondent feelings.[2]

[2] Wang Shih-wei, "Wild Lily Flower", Yenan *Liberation News*, March 13, 1942. Translation in Chao Chung, *The Communist Programme for Literature and Art in China*, Hong Kong, 1955, p. 53.

Highly critical articles were written by the famous woman novelist, Ting Ling, by Chou Yang and others. This was at the time of the Party rectification campaign, and soon the Party decided to correct the "erroneous ideology" of the writers too. The *Liberation News* stopped printing critical articles and Mao Tse-tung in opening the Yenan literary forum on May 2, 1942, said:

> The task of art and literature has always been to expose. This sort of argument . . . arises from the lack of knowledge of the science of history. For the revolutionary artists and writers the objects to be exposed can never be the masses of the people, but only the aggressors, exploiters and oppressors. . . . If we treat our comrades like enemies, then we are taking the standpoint of the enemy.[3]

After the literary forum some writers, like Ting Ling and some of her colleagues, confessed their errors. Wang Shih-wei was expelled from the Party as a member of a "Trotsky bandit gang", and was never heard of again.[4]

We do not know who were the "perfectly healthy big shots given to flagrant and senseless pleasure". But this article and the most violent reaction to it seem to indicate that at least some of the great austerity of *all* the Yenan leaders was a sham. Wang may have been too stern a bolshevik himself and too severe a critic, the Yenan pleasures and luxuries may not have been very great compared to ordinary urban life, but still there must have been some cynics and hypocrites among the Yenan great ones.

It is also true that they expected very great sacrifices from the rank-and-file of the Party and the army. The population of the Border Region and the guerilla areas was courted in order to get their backing. But observers such as Wang Shih-wei could have noticed, of Mao and his colleagues, that their great love for the toiling masses changed into an abstract "love" of humanity, of future generations. They made propaganda to show that they love the present generation of humans too, but in fact treated them as expendable material. Wang's exposure of the "big shots" is in strange contrast with the impressions of visitors from the outside.

Harrison Forman describes an evening in 1945 with Mao and his actress wife at their home:

---

[3] *SW*, Vol. IV, pp. 87-88.
[4] Chao Chung, op. cit., p. 54.

Both were plainly dressed, she in a pyjama-like outfit belted at her slim waist, he in a rough homespun suit with baggy, high water pants. I was taken to the "parlor"—one of the caves with a simple brick floor, whitewashed walls, and solid, rather lumpy furniture. It was evening, and the only light was furnished by a single candle fixed on an upturned cup. For refreshments I was served with weak tea, cakes and candy made locally, and cigarettes. Mao chain-smoked his abominable Yenan cigarettes, while youngsters ran in and out during the whole conversation. They would stand and stare at me for a few moments, and then, seizing a piece of candy, race out again. Mao paid no attention to them.[5]

This was the parlour of a man who at that time ruled well over a hundred million people, who directed negotiations with the great world powers, and who was rounding off his blueprint for the transformation of China.

It was during the Yenan period that Mao Tse-tung wrote most of his important theoretical works on politics and on military tactics and strategy. It was in Yenan that he worked out the detailed pro-gramme for the transition period until the Communist victory (which he took for granted) and for the subsequent stage when he was to remould his country on "Chinese Marxist" lines. Three vol-umes of his *Selected Works* contain the products of the Yenan days, although he left out speeches, reports, memoranda and other works of his which would fill another three or four volumes.

II

To the participants in the 1942 Yenan forum on art and literature, Mao talked about the "new epoch of the masses":

Since we must adapt ourselves to the new epoch of the masses, we must thoroughly solve the question of the relationship be-tween the individual and the masses. Lu Hsün's couplet should be our motto: "With frowning brows I coldly defy the thousands pointing their accusing fingers at me; with bowed head I meekly submit as an ox for the child to ride on". The "thousands" here re-fer to the enemy, and we will never succumb to him no matter how fierce he may be. The "child" here refers to the proletariat and the broad masses of the people. All Communists, revolu-tionaries, revolutionary artists and writers, should follow the ex-

[5] Harrison Forman, *Report from Red China*, London, 1946, p. 178.

ample of Lu Hsün and be the "ox" for the proletariat and the broad masses of the people, bending their shoulders to the task unto death. The intellectuals must go through a process of getting acquainted with the masses before they can unite with them and work for them. Although this process can be, and is bound to be, fraught with suffering and conflict, once you have made up your mind you will be equal to the task.[6]

The words "the new epoch of the masses" should by no means be understood in a general Western sense! Mao, who was a master in coining slogans, was this time not trying to put over a slogan. His audience knew very well that he was referring to a most concrete change in Chinese history, a change brought about by Mao and his comrades.

For thousands of years in the past, and in Kuomintang China of the wartime present, ninety per cent of the population stood outside of and below the State and the nation. The machinery of State administration reached down only to the *hsiens* (counties). The Central Government's lowest outpost was at the county seat, below which virtually all the functions of government were carried out by the local landlords, who even had their own local troops. The Central Government controlled and directed the country administrators while the landlords ruled over the countryside. In effect, the base of the social pyramid, the peasantry, was outside and below public affairs. In speaking of the masses, Mao Tse-tung meant these masses of peasants, the ninety per cent of the Chinese population. With his peasant associations, peasant Red guards, and village councils Mao Tse-tung was the first Chinese revolutionary who succeeded in basing his revolutionary strategy on the bottom of the social pyramid. Ousting the landlords, he evolved the pattern of Chinese Soviets and of "democratic anti-Japanese governments".

His armies had won many battles for him against Chiang Kai-shek. But his greatest victory over his enemy was in the battle fought for the minds and hearts of the vast sea of Chinese peasantry. He won this battle because he had learnt to live, feel and speak like the peasants. His slogan "Learn from the masses!", so often repeated, meant all this and also to learn from the masses how to treat them, how to discipline and inspire them.

Chiang Kai-shek's régime was by this time a military dictatorship, based on the cities, on the landlords, on the upper classes, and entirely divorced from the masses. In the Kuomintang armies

[6] *SW*, Vol. IV, p. 93.

soldiers were never allowed to fight in the provinces from which
they were recruited. The Kuomintang Army in its requisitioning,
billeting and other activities had no regard for the needs and interests of the local population. This was the reason why contact between the troops and the people was strongly discouraged. Mao on
the other hand had built his armies up from the peasantry, and
his troops were taught to help the peasants in their work whenever
possible.

Mao did not and could not hope for foreign aid. Chiang gambled
everything on it and on the victory of the Western powers over
Japan. American aid came streaming in, first along the Burma road,
later in the airlift over the Himalayas. American generals and officers helped to train his armies, and the Kuomintang's war in the
air against Japan was fought entirely by General Chennault's American air force stationed in China. The American government backed
Chiang even against American generals. When the American General Stilwell protested against the corruption, inefficiency and in-
action of the Kuomintang armies, and asked to be given field command over Chiang's forces, he was recalled.

Chiang's extremely strict censorship kept foreign correspondents
in Kuomintang China from reporting in detail the graft and embezzlement, the general corruption and inefficiency of the régime
and the terror and misery in which the people lived. Instead,
Chiang's Western propagandists were successful in putting over the
picture of the Kuomintang armies fighting heroically. The Generalissimo took it for granted that Washington would back him even
more resolutely after the war than during it.

Mao's only hope lay in his own armies and in the Chinese countryside. He could only rely on the masses. He tried to transform
and use all the human resources of the masses.

In November 1943 he was able to report:

In all the armed units of the border region that have been allotted land this year, the soldiers . . . can make or produce practically everything—foodstuffs like vegetables, meat and cooking
oil; things to wear like cotton and woollen clothing, shoes and
socks; shelters like caves, houses, big and small meeting-halls;
articles for daily use like tables, chairs, benches and stationery;
and fuel like firewood, charcoal and coal. With our own hands
we have attained the end of being "well-clad and well-fed". In
each year every soldier needs only to spend three months in pro-

duction and can devote the remaining nine months to training or fighting. Our troops depend for their pay neither on the Kuomintang government, nor on the Border Region government, nor on the people, but can provide for themselves.[7]

The cruelty of Japanese military operations and the heavy taxes the puppet régime imposed, made the peasants receptive to these young men and women who arrived in their midst from one of the Red bases and taught them how to defend themselves against the enemy and the oppressor. Mao's entire system of government was based on the countryside, as was his armed struggle against the Japanese and the puppet troops.

The regular (Red) army defended the base areas as a whole, while the guerilla units looked after the counties and districts, and the peasant militia the villages and townships. The militiamen comprised five to eight per cent of the population. Trained by the Red soldiers or guerillas, they were the full-time warriors of the villages. They acted as scouts and, when enemy troops were approaching, they led the peasants in burying and hiding all grain, firewood and fodder, leaving nothing to the enemy except vacant houses and empty fields.

In China, from time immemorial, peasants have produced homemade fireworks for festive occasions. It was easy for the guerilla instructors to teach them how to make mines and booby-traps out of bottles, teapots, all sorts of cans, earthenware jugs, stuffed full of gunpowder and detonated by a crude fuse. These mines and booby-traps were planted in the approaches to the villages, empty huts, peasant carts abandoned on the road, fallen trees across a footpath, pumpkins in a field, and so on and so forth—all could be booby-traps. The villagers manufactured thousands of "wooden bazookas", made of hardwood logs loaded with scrap metal and stones and ringed with metal or tightly bound wire, to keep them from blowing apart.

In thousands of villages the local jack-of-all-trades, his imagination fired by the guerilla instructor, produced all sorts of crude but ingenious instruments to protect the village. Japanese columns were ambushed on mountain paths, and when they took cover on the mountain-side they would run into a veritable mine-field.

On the plains, the militiamen led the peasants in digging up main roads and transforming them into ditches, which held up enemy vehicles and served as cover for the guerillas. They also

[7] SW, Vol. IV, pp. 149-50.

learnt the practice of tunnel warfare. On the plains, secret tunnels connected villages, passing under strategic roads or well-guarded county borders; in mountainous areas they were dug through the hills. In many places the people, the Red guerillas and militiamen, even the regular units, could move about without exposing themselves to the Japanese. The militia was not only organised in base and guerilla areas, but also in isolated villages and townships behind the enemy lines. These secret militiamen in Japanese or puppet territories furnished intelligence and conducted sabotage. The normal militia—according to the Maoist principle—formed mutual aid teams with the villagers. Their hours of fighting counted as workdays in the team. When there was a lull in the fighting, they would work on farming tasks.

By the end of the war there were two and a half million militiamen all over China. Throughout the years of war with Japan, these militiamen were used to fight in co-ordination with the Red guerillas and the regular Red forces, and ties of loyalty and comradeship were forged between these peasant warriors and their Communist instructors. Together, they fought, suffered and won. They were comrade veterans of thousands of battles. And these militiamen defended their own villages run by the Communist-inspired and controlled "Anti-Japanese Democratic Councils". Thousands upon thousands of villages, from Hainan Island in the south to Manchuria in the extreme north, belonged to military, political and economic organisations which were centrally directed by the ruler from the Yenan caves.

Mao Tse-tung used the eight years of war with Japan to link a very large part of the Chinese countryside to Yenan with real —not bureaucratic or arbitrary—ties. For these tens of millions of peasants the "Chairman" was the wise and tough war-lord who guided them in their patriotic war. Clever Communist propaganda —and Kuomintang counter-propaganda—helped to fix this Mao-image in the mind of the rural millions: the Chairman—the friend of the peasants, who has endured decades of fighting and the hardships of the Long March to fight against the landlords and corrupt officials for the rights of the peasants. He it is who reduces taxes, who instructs his soldiers not to live off the countryside, he it is who means to share out the lands of the rich among the poor.

At the end of the war against Japan, Mao was confident of ultimate victory over the Kuomintang; he thought that whatever happened in the cities, the peasant millions tested and hardened by war, were on his side.

The combined war effort of the Red Army, guerilla and militia forces made it clear to Japan as early as 1943 that the main enemy was not the Kuomintang but the Communist Party. The Tokyo daily *Asahi Shinbun* published a communiqué of the Japanese North China Army, stating that:

> Instead of the Chungking Army, the Communist Army has become the central object of mopping-up operations. . . . 75% of the 15,000 engagements have been against Communist forces, and more than half the enemy troops were party troops, half the corpses collected were also Communists, while among the 74,000 prisoners captured (in 1943) only 35% were Communists. This clearly exposes the weakness and abasement of the Chungking Army (Kuomintang), and at the same time shows the apparent increase of the morale and fighting will of the Communist forces. . . . After the (1943) Taihang campaign . . . the Chungking Army has lost its will to fight.[7a]

There were many similar reports in the Japanese press in this period. According to a US Military Intelligence report, Chiang Kai-shek's government had concluded a virtual truce with the Japanese and puppet troops and was using most of its forces to blockade the Chinese Communists and to build up Kuomintang strength for postwar times.[8]

US Military Intelligence reported in 1945:

> All observers agree that the greatest cause of the poor showing made by the Chungking forces last year during their defence against the Japanese was *the hostility of the people toward their own army,* and the hopeless disunity between the regular Kuomintang or Central Army and the Provincial Armies.[9]

III

Mao Tse-tung opened the Seventh National Congress of the Chinese Communist Party on April 23, 1945. This was the first full congress since 1928. The delegates represented 1,210,000 Party members, and the Party now ruled over a territory far larger than France and Italy together, with a population of a hundred

[7a] Tokyo, January 15, 1944.

[8] *The Chinese Communist Movement,* McCarran Hearings, 7A US Government Printing Office, Washington, 1952, pp. 2, 354-5. As quoted by North, *Moscow and the Chinese Communists,* pp. 203-4.

[9] Ibid., p. 2,396, North, p. 205.

million people, and it had its own powerful army. It thought itself invincible. The task of the next period was promulgated by Mao in these words:

> To defeat the Japanese aggressor, liberate the whole people and build up a new-democratic China under the leadership of our Party.[10]
>
> No enemy can crush us but we can crush any enemy and overcome any difficulty so long as we rely on the people, firmly believe in their inexhaustible creative power and consequently trust them and become one with them.[11]

The Congress accepted Mao's political report—*On Coalition Government*—proposing that the Party should demand a leading part in a new Chinese coalition government. In this report, new Marxist-Leninist theses were promulgated concerning the transition to socialism in backward, semi-colonial and colonial countries.

This Congress was a major political event both from the Chinese and from the international standpoint and was certainly a most significant development in the international Communist movement. Yet the Soviet press which always reported the congresses and meetings of Communist parties all over the world in great detail, and which was even then devoting extensive space to the activities of the French, Italian and even of the Albanian Communist Party, did not in so much as a single line refer to the Chinese Congress. A "brother" Communist Party announcing its bid for power over the most populous country in the world was officially and completely ignored by the centre of world Communism for several months afterwards. This in spite of the fact that Mao Tse-tung and the Congress went out of their way to demonstrate to Stalin and to the world that they were enthusiastic followers of Stalin, and that they thought and acted in Stalin's spirit. The resolution on Party history stated that Mao had "brilliantly developed Lenin's and Stalin's teachings on the revolutionary movement in the colonial and semi-colonial countries as well as Stalin's teachings on the Chinese revolution".

The minutes of this long Congress, which took up much of April and May, 1945, indicate that the Chinese Red leaders hoped that Stalin would forgive them for the unorthodox means by which

[10] *SW*, Vol. IV, p. 316.
[11] Ibid., p. 313.

they had so successfully approached the mutual and most orthodox Communist end.

The realisation that Stalin and the Soviet leadership meant to ignore them was a bitter pill for Mao and his colleagues. The most important textbook of the world Communist movement at that time, and indeed until 1956, was the *Short History of the Communist Party of the Soviet Union (Bolshevik)*. This was officially regarded as "the best synthesis and summary of the world Communist movement . . . a model of the unity of theory with practice and the only perfect model of its kind in the whole world". This Communist catechism was first published in Russian in 1938 and came out in later years in more than fifty languages. Every Party member the world over learnt Communist history, ideology and practice from this textbook. In subsequent editions history was changed in retrospect to fit the Party line. The latest Russian edition before the Congress, however, did not differ from the original edition in ignoring the Chinese Communists. No mention was made of Chiang's annihilation campaigns, of the Long March, or of the Chinese Soviets, but Chiang's National Government came in for praise:

> The heroic struggle of the Chinese people and their army against the Japanese invaders, the tremendous national revival in China, her huge resources of man-power and territory, and lastly, *the determination of the Chinese National Government to fight the struggle for emancipation to a finish* . . . show beyond doubt that there is no future for the Japanese imperialists in China.[12]

Several reasons can be adduced to explain why Stalin, the Soviet leaders and the Soviet press were not mollified in 1945 towards Yenan by Mao's avowal of Stalin's and Moscow's leadership.

1. All governments—in most cases quite rightly—acted on the assumption that Communist action everywhere in the world was centrally directed from Moscow. Stalin expected complete and immediate obedience from all Communist parties whenever he took a major ideological turn (the pact with Hitler, with the Japanese, etc.), so as not to be compromised by some parties taking a different line from his own. The Communist Parties had to accept, and did in fact accept, Stalin's thesis that the interests of the Soviet

---

[12] *Short History of the Communist Party of the Soviet Union (Bolshevik)*, authorised English translation reprinted in London, 1943, p. 305. (Emphasis added.) *This text was not changed in subsequent Russian or Western editions.*

Union were identical with that of the world Communist movement. The first loyalty of every Communist was to the Soviet Union. It was often promulgated from Moscow that even if some Soviet action in the international field was temporarily detrimental to a local Communist Party, the general Communist front must not be weakened by disobedience. Even parties with the most orthodox Muscovite-Party line got into trouble if they did not give complete and immediate support to a new turn of Soviet policy. Parties which had a tendency (or could be suspected of a tendency) to be too independent and pay too much attention to the interests of their own movement and own country, were overtly or covertly admonished or attacked by Stalin, (the Spanish, Polish, Yugoslav, Greek and other parties). This was one of the general reasons for his ignoring the Chinese Communists.

2. During the last months of the war with Japan, Mao's party and army were quite specially an inconvenience, even a danger to Soviet foreign policy. In the Teheran and Yalta agreements Stalin obtained from the United States and Great Britain important concessions both in Europe and in the Far East. A large part of Eastern Europe was acknowledged by the Western powers as a Soviet sphere of interest. In the Far East, the Yalta agreement gave the Soviet Union Dairen, an important warm-water port on the Pacific Ocean, as well as gains in Manchuria, and confirmed the "independence" of (Soviet) Outer Mongolia. All these were of course clear losses to China. But the realisation of the European and Far Eastern gains in the immediate post-war period depended on continued correct relations between the USSR and the Western powers, and even with Chiang's government. If the independent line of any European or Far Eastern Communist Party compromised the USSR in the eyes of the Western powers and Chiang Kai-shek, they might regard it as a breach of contract, invalidating those clauses of the Teheran and Yalta agreements which were profitable to the USSR.

Chiang was the ally of the Western powers. The aggressive line of the Chinese Communists might persuade Chiang that Mao was prompted by Stalin, and lead him to denounce the Yalta agreement.* This was the reason why Stalin insisted on a peaceful settle-

---

* "The real peril to Soviet aims in the Far East, as they were defined in Yalta, lay in the possibility of a fresh outbreak of civil war between the Communists and the Kuomintang. . . . No matter how discreetly the Soviet Union might behave in any clash between the Communists and the Nationalists, it could not avoid Chungking's charges of complicity

ment between Chiang and Mao and was angered by Mao's aggressive policy.

3. The resolutions of the Chinese Communist Congress not only threatened the renewal of the civil war but also doggedly insisted on the correctness of Mao's unorthodox method in reaching the orthodox Communist aim.

Stalin represented the orthodox Marxist-Leninist line when he insisted that the Chinese "bourgeois revolution" (under Chiang) would produce capitalism and that only then, once the capitalists had developed modern industry, the industrial proletariat would lead the Socialist revolution. The supreme textbook of the Party taught at the time that "in spite of the numerical preponderance of the peasantry and the relative weakness of the proletariat, it was on the proletariat and on its growth that the revolutionaries should base their chief hopes".[13]

Marx, Engels, Lenin and Stalin taught that only the proletariat— the industrial workers—of the cities could be the vanguard of the Communist revolution, not the peasants.

The Chinese Communists, in agreeing on their official Party history, not only reasserted the correctness of the Mao line, but denounced "Li Li-san and others" who had in the past represented Stalin's line:

> These comrades . . . considered . . . that the major cities should take the lead so as to form centers of the revolutionary upsurge, and hence, slanderously labelled as "absolutely erroneous" and "localism and conservatism of peasant ideology" Comrade Mao Tse-tung's idea that for a long time we should employ our main forces to create rural bases . . . to expedite the nation-wide revolutionary upsurge.[14]

4. In Mao's works and in the Chinese Communist Party's pronouncements there were too many hints for Stalin's liking about the importance of the "Chinese road" as a model for semi-colonies and colonies. In references to the semi-colonial or colonial situation of China, there was the implication that the Chinese peasants did not differ from colonial natives, and that the techniques developed

---

because of its ideological identification with Yenan. An embattled Kuomintang, angered by this suspected perfidy . . . could be expected in due time to denounce the Yalta agreement, which favoured Russia" McLane, *Soviet Policy and the Chinese Communists*, p. 180.

[13] *Short History*, p. 10.

[14] *SW*, Vol. IV, p. 178.

for their revolutionary upsurge might serve as a blueprint for other colonial revolutions. To the ears of a Marxist scholastic, like Stalin, this statement of Mao's must have sounded suspect:

> In the Chinese revolution, because semi-feudal and semi-colonial China is a big, loosely knit country which lacks democracy and where industry is poorly developed, armed struggle is the main form of struggle and an army composed mainly of peasants is the main form of organisation. . . . The indispensable, vital positions for the Chinese revolution are located in the vast rural areas which are the home of the broad masses of peasants . . . and that armed revolutionary bases *can* and *must* be built in China as a starting point for winning national victory.[15]

Stalin wanted no complications for his Soviet Party, such as might arise from coloured Communists attempting, like the Chinese, to lead the coloured Communists of the world.

It was in vain that the minutes of the Seventh Congress offered bouquets to Stalin, like this:

> Comrade Mao Tse-tung, *in line with Comrade Stalin,* pointed out not only that the task of the Chinese Revolution at the present stage is to fight imperialism and feudalism, but, in particular, that the peasants' fight for land is the basic feature of the anti-imperialist and anti-feudal struggle.[16]

This and similar pronouncements failed to convince Stalin. In his eyes, Mao and his colleagues were not real Communists, because they were not blindly subservient to Moscow; they were deviationists—and in addition they represented a potential danger to Soviet interests. In the Eastern European countries Stalin's men were by now returning from their Moscow sojourn to their respective countries and making preparations for the Communist takeover. Stalin no doubt hoped for similar Communist régimes at a later date in parts of China, possibly in Manchuria and Sinkiang. But in the spring of 1945 he wanted no Communist régime in China, not even one led by his own satraps, let alone an independent and deviationist one.

At that time little credence was given to Stalin's sincerity when he told the US Ambassador, Harriman, that "the Chinese Communists are not real Communists. They are 'margarine' Communists."

---

[15] SW, Vol. IV, pp. 193-4. (Italics in the original.)
[16] Ibid., p. 190. (Emphasis added.)

Other American diplomats and statesmen reported Stalin as describing them as "radish Communists—red outside and white inside" or as "cabbage Communists". Harry Hopkins reported on May 28, 1945, that Stalin made a "categorical statement that he would do everything he could to promote unification of China under the leadership of Chiang Kai-shek. He further stated that this leadership should continue after the war, because no one else was strong enough. He specifically stated that no Communist leaders were strong enough to unify China."[17] At the Potsdam Conference Stalin stated again that "Chiang Kai-shek's Government was the only possible Government in China and that the Chinese Communists were not real Communists".[18]

The US Ambassador Hurley later told the Senate Foreign Relations Committee: "Russia . . . does not recognise the Chinese armed Communist Party as Communist at all. Russia is not supporting the Chinese Communist Party."[19]

These statements were not taken seriously, as everyone had ample reason to doubt Stalin's veracity. It did not occur to those who doubted Stalin's words that, in his eyes, only his obedient tools were "real Communists". The question why Stalin did not denounce other Communist parties was never asked. Why was it that he always belittled the strength and significance of Communist armies not under his direction? His statements and actions were consistent in this respect. Churchill noted at the Teheran Conference that "the rôle of Yugoslavia in the war was dismissed by Stalin as of minor importance, and the Russians even disputed our figures of the number of Axis divisions" tied down by Tito's partisans.[20] Similarly, he had no faith in the Chinese guerillas and even when the Soviet press started to criticise certain Kuomintang generals for their reluctance to fight the Japanese, no credit was given to the Red forces.

IV

Mao's essay, *On New Democracy*, written in 1940, had outlined the general principles for the ensuing period. Now, in 1945, on the threshold of power, in his political report to the Party Congress, he gave the programme in detail: *On Coalition Government*. He

---

[17] R. E. Sherwood, *The White House Papers of Harry Hopkins*, Vol. II, London, 1949, pp. 891-2.
[18] J. F. Byrnes, *Speaking Frankly*, London, 1946, p. 288.
[19] Herbert Feis, *The China Tangle*, Princeton, 1953, p. 410.
[20] Winston S. Churchill, *The Second World War*, Vol. V, p. 413.

demanded the abolition of the Kuomintang one-party dictatorship and the establishment of a democratic coalition government:

Some people wonder whether the Chinese Communists, once in power, would follow the example of the Russian Communists and establish a proletarian dictatorship and a one-party government. Our answer is that a new-democratic state based on an alliance of several democratic classes is different in principle from a socialist state under proletarian dictatorship. Beyond doubt, our system of New Democracy will be built under the leadership of the proletariat, of the Communist Party, but throughout the stage of New Democracy, there cannot and therefore should not be in China a system of one-class dictatorship and one-party government. We have no reason to refuse co-operation with any political party, social group or individual, so long as their attitude towards the Communist Party is co-operative and not hostile. Russian history has shaped the Russian system. . . . Similarly Chinese history of the present stage will shape a Chinese system for the present stage, and for a long time to come there will exist in China a particular form of state and political power, i.e. New Democracy based on the alliance of several democratic classes, a system which is distinguished from the Russian system and which is perfectly necessary and reasonable for us.

We Communists propose to . . . establish coalition governments and unite with the representatives of all classes and political parties willing to join us in order to fight on a democratic common programme for the victory of the war against the Japanese invaders now and the building of a new China in the future.[21]

The ultimate Communist aim was not denied, but the other "democratic classes" were reassured that the transition period would be a long one. According to Mao in April 1945:

In China the fight for democracy will be a protracted one. It would be sheer illusion to try to build socialism on the ruins of the colonial, semi-colonial and feudal order, without a united new-democratic stage, without the development . . . of private capitalist and co-operative enterprises . . . without the liberation and development of the individual initiative of hundreds of million people.[22]

[21] SW, Vol. IV, pp. 277-8, and p. 285.
[22] Ibid., pp. 274 and 275.

This programme was published in Yenan soon after the Congress.

The then unpublished resolution on Party history which served as a textbook on Party tactics, would have been less reassuring: ". . . Comrade Mao always demands the utilisation of every conflict inside the reactionary camp by taking active steps to widen its cleavage. These tactical principles of 'capitalising on contradictions in order to win over the majority, oppose the minority and crush the enemies separately' were applied and brilliantly developed under his leadership. He also proposed to transform the Party's open organisations of the 1924-7 revolution into underground organisations.

"Comrade Liu Shao-chi maintained that, in utilising the contradictions within the enemy camp and winning over temporary allies, the Party should

precipitate an open conflict of these contradictions and form a temporary alliance against the principal members in the enemy camp with those of their colleagues who may co-operate with us or who have *not yet* become our principal enemies;

and that it should

make necessary concessions to allies willing to co-operate with us, to draw them to unite with us and take joint actions and then to exert our influence on them and win over their rank-and-file."[23]

The theoretical works, political speeches and actions of Mao Tse-tung, Liu Shao-chi, Chou En-lai, Chu Teh and the other fifteen supreme leaders (who are still leaders in 1962) show that they were in perfect agreement on what we, in the West, would call a policy of dual standards. The ruler from the Yenan caves and his chief associates always made it quite clear to the Party faithful that they never meant to carry out their United Front pledges or any agreement made with the other "democratic classes" or with the Kuomintang. In their conspiratorial speeches and instructions to Party functionaries there are innumerable passages similar to this one from Mao's pen:

An important part of the building of the Chinese Communist Party is that the Party develops and steels itself in the course of both uniting with the bourgeoisie and struggling against it. Unity here means the united front with the bourgeoisie. Struggle

---

[23] Ibid., pp. 198-200. (Emphasis added.)

means "peaceful" and "bloodless" struggle waged along the ideological, political and organisational lines when we unite with the bourgeoisie, a struggle which will *inevitably* turn into an armed struggle, when we are forced to split with the bourgeoisie.*

All Party members were warned constantly "to differentiate strictly between the public and secret work of the Party". And although much of the secret work entailed the breaking of the United Front and coalition agreements, Mao and his associates were genuinely shocked and indignant when the other side also broke them.

They constantly denounced the Kuomintang press censorship, though their own press was completely under the Party's direction. They denounced the secret police system of the Kuomintang, although their most complex and highly developed intelligence and security forces were just as ruthless as those of Chiang, only better camouflaged.

During the Yenan years Mao personally supervised the organisation and development of his security police network. It was mainly due to the complete isolation—and often to the blockade—of the Yenan régime, that the rest of China learnt so little about this most important basis of Mao's power. Mao's iron grip, through the security forces, was most evident to Party members, first of all to the "cadres", that is to Party members having Party, government or army functions. It was only after a decade or so that the outside world could learn about the various "personnel", "social", "political defensive", etc., departments which, from the Yenan period on, permeated the Chinese Communist Party, its army, government, its mass organisations and front organisations, the guerilla base areas and the Kuomintang territories.

In addition to every Party member's duty to report every disloyal, "anti-Party" or deviationist statement or action of Party or non-Party people, the central cadres department had its watchdogs everywhere and so of course did the security branch itself. How many victims there were in the 1942 Party rectification campaign cannot be documented. It is likewise difficult to tell how many deviationist Communists there were among the Japanese, puppet or Kuomintang spies executed by the army's counter-espionage

* This was originally written for *The Communist* (an *internal* Party journal published in Yenan) in October 1939. In the collected works published in Peking after the take-over, the word *inevitably* was omitted. (SW, Vol. III, p. 59.)

corps. There were rumours that Party deviationists were sent into hopeless skirmishes or were charged with secret work in enemy territory—so that the enemy should liquidate them. Many statements were made during the "Hundred Flowers" period which indicate that the Communist Party was already a Party of fear in the Yenan days.

In the "anti-Japanese government areas" the Red Army's counter-espionage or security force dealt with the non-Communist enemies or potential enemies. No one could ask for proof if the army stated that a spy or saboteur had been caught.

A special branch of the security police was trained to "manipulate the masses". These plain clothes men posed as peasants, students, or workmen. They were taught to study a village, find out about grievances, prompt some local peasants to call an indignation meeting and then, with cleverly applied slogans, "get the masses infuriated" with the person or persons whom the Party wanted to liquidate.

Yet another branch learnt the art of "remoulding" captured Kuomintang or puppet soldiers. The first step was to get them to "speak bitter". These prisoners of war were asked if they had any grievances in their army, in their village or town? Had they been treated badly by a landlord, a government functionary or an officer? They were then encouraged to tell each other about their grievances, to unleash their hatred. "To speak bitter" was one of the hundreds of slogans which Mao produced during this epoch. In reality, it was a step in "cleansing people's minds", in "preparatory thought-exploring" for the later "surrendering one's heart" and complete "self-remoulding".

What the rest of China heard about this was not frightening. People were told, that this was needed to produce good anti-Japanese fighters. Mao said:

> The Kuomintang soldiers are the worst fighters, but as soon as we liberate them, and they have some class education and take part in the *speak-bitterness* movement, and they understand why they are fighting and who they are fighting for, they immediately become good fighting soldiers."[24]

The rest of China only heard that Mao instead of cutting off the heads of his prisoners of war, *changed the contents of their heads,*

[24] Quoted by Yen Chang-lin, "Great Man of a Glorious Era", in *Chinese Literature*, Peking, January 1, 1961, p. 42.

in making them good patriots and valiant fighters. This, in a way, was true. But it was also true that the Yenan period also served to build up a terribly efficient security police organisation and test those methods which the outside world later called "collective brain-washing". In the name of patriotism and liberty a vast machine of mind-seduction and oppression was built up.

The outside world was told by various Western journalists—who reported it in good faith—that in Yenan they personally had not met a Chinese Communist who drivelled "our great leader" phrases. This was of course entirely possible. But especially in the second part of the Yenan period there most certainly was a ritual of hero-worship of Mao Tse-tung, Chu Teh and the other leaders. Mao was treated as the greatest of them all. Of course, it was good policy to emphasise the modesty and simplicity of the Chairman, compared with the feudal haughtiness of the Generalissimo.

But the Yenan city walls and cliff-sides had many slogans inscribed on them in praise of Mao; many Mao-quotations adorned the red paper banners on the walls of theatre-tents and meeting places. These were of course written in Chinese and the foreign visitors did not notice them. But the famous slogan—"In his mind a million bold warriors . . ."—was first inscribed on the Yenan walls.[25]

A careful analysis of Mao's works, of his style and of his actions during the Yenan period (1936-48) gives the impression that he was genuinely unaware of his own hypocrisy, of his own bad faith and cynical Machiavellianism. In this too, his chief associates were just like him. For decades of bitter struggle they regarded themselves as the builders of a happy-day-after-tomorrow for China and mankind alike. For decades they believed that in accelerating the "inevitable objective process of history" by *any means*, they were serving the best interests of everyone concerned, even if those concerned disagreed violently. It would be a very primitive mistake to think that they acted in the spirit of "the end sanctifies the means". It never occurred to them that the means needed sanctifying or excuse. They had remoulded *themselves*: their "human nature" was effectively changed into "class nature" and class nature exists on quite a different plane and level of reference from what we in the West would call common sense and common decency.*

[25] Yen Chang-lin, *Chinese Literature*, Foreign Language Press, Peking, January 1, 1961.
* Tolerant liberalism was always anathema to Mao. In September 1937 he issued a Party directive to combat this type of liberalism which "negates ideological struggle and advocates unprincipled peace", which

So far Mao and his associates had achieved everything through the support of the peasants. They had based their entire strategy for coming to power on the peasants. They had learnt to live and, in a way, even to feel like peasants. Yet from the outset they meant to and did in fact abolish the peasant way of life. They meant to regiment and transform the peasantry, to deny them their millennial dreams of owning a house, a plot of land, even the right to live under the same roof with their families.

They offered alliance to the non-Communist intellectuals, to the "nationalist bourgeoisie", even to capitalists, repeating the promise that the transition period would be a protracted one, that it would last through an "entire historical period", while in fact they did everything to ensure that this period should be as short as possible.

During their last four years in Yenan, an ever-growing number of non-Communist Chinese visited the Red capital or had first-hand evidence of life there. In this way most of China heard about the very simple, frugal and strenuous life of the Red leaders, about their caves, long working hours, ragged uniforms and all. Millions of non-Communist Chinese came to be convinced that the Red leaders were genuine revolutionary patriots. The absence of all luxury, all corruption, all forms of "leader adulation" gave an impression of thorough honesty. And subjectively—within the Communist framework and in the mental and emotional climate of Communist double-morality—Mao and his associates were genuine.

There was a further development in the electronic brain aspect of Mao's mental processes (and of those of his leading associates). By the end of the Yenan period in 1948, just before taking over the whole of China, they exercised over ever-growing territories those methods in political and military tactics and strategy for which they had "programmed" themselves at the outset. To his Yenan cave, information poured in from every corner of China. Through daily contact with the millionfold reality of China, and through the successes of their political and military operations, these "mechanical brains" grew more and more convinced of the correctness of their basic principles, of their tactical and strategical policies, i.e. their "programming". Everything was "proved by practice". In

---

makes one behave "as if a Communist were merely an ordinary person". Such deviation results in some Communists not even reporting "counter-revolutionary opinions on hearing them". "Liberalism is extremely harmful. It is corrosive which disrupts unity. . . . It deprives the revolutionary ranks of compact organisation and strict discipline." (SW, Vol. II, pp. 74-75.)

directing thousands of offensives and guerilla campaigns, in setting up tens of thousands of local political organisations, they acted like the central guiding system of a fully automatised factory. Their thinking mechanism became like an electronic brain in another important respect too. Given its programming of equations and system of solutions, an electronic computer operates without regard for any subjective human aspect. Electronic brains have no feelings, no morality, and once set on their courses, they cannot commit mistakes within their own terms. Mao and his colleagues were similar in this respect too.

Being almost completely isolated from other ways of thinking, disregarding hostile bourgeois views, they progressed strictly in their own pre-set direction. Their isolation from the rest of China and from the entire outside world was complete. The rulers of a mighty state had on their office walls only maps of China, none of the world.

At the end of the Yenan period, Mao Tse-tung knew the actual Chinese situation as fully and completely as humanly possible. He insisted on and received factual reports from all the functionaries. He insisted on knowing Chinese reality. At the same time he had a most primitively dogmatic, elementary Marxist-seminar picture of the world. Robert Payne who visited Yenan in 1946 recounts how Mao told him that the "English socialists" were imperialists. "They will never let India free". When Payne insisted that this would happen sooner than he believed, Mao "looked incredulous, almost as though he was talking to an ignorant child and changed the subject".[26]

Mao and his associates had the same primitively dogmatic views on the absolute impoverishment of the Western working classes, on the contradictions in "dying capitalist society". To them, all Western governments were the organs of the dictatorship of monopoly-capitalists, and most non-Communist intellectuals and scientists were the "lackeys of capitalism", etc.

His China-centred thinking, his disregard of the outside world, his utter dedication, his absolute lack of scruples, his ever-growing popularity among the masses, the complete loyalty of well-tested and extremely able associates, the discipline and conspiratorial excellence of his Party machine—all these convinced everyone who observed him from close quarters that, after the defeat of Japan,

[26] Payne, *Mao Tse-tung*, London, 1951, pp. 219-20.

Chiang's Kuomintang would be no match for him. Only a strong, efficient and honest democratic régime could stop him from conquering China.

In August 1945 the atom bombs were dropped on Hiroshima and Nagasaki.

XII

FOUR YEARS TO VICTORY

I

The A-bomb on Hiroshima was dropped on August 6, 1945, that on Nagasaki followed on August 8. The same day the Soviet Union declared war on Japan. On August 14 the Emperor announced Japan's surrender. The Soviet forces disregarded the surrender and went on to occupy the whole of Manchuria, concentrating on the cities, ports and mining districts and securing the railway lines. Mao's local guerillas, self-defence corps and militiamen, under the guidance of Communist organisers from Yenan, hurriedly "liberated" large tracts of the countryside.

Soon after Marshal Malinovsky had created order in the Manchurian cities, the civilian advisers, experts and administrators arrived from Moscow, among them a group of Chinese Communists who had lived in the USSR for a good many years. The group was led by Li Li-san, Mao's erstwhile opponent and rival, and most members of his group were Chinese "Muscovites", opposed to the Yenan leadership.

The Chinese CP's resolution on Party history passed three months previously had given a great deal of space to Li Li-san's very grave mistakes. As Li Li-san had committed them more than fifteen years earlier, it was curious that a Party resolution in April 1945 should mention him by name twenty-three times in connection with his erroneous line, and devote more than 5,000 words to proving how nonsensical it was to insist that the Chinese Communists could succeed only by proletarian uprisings in the big cities.[1] Li Li-san was attacked as if he still represented a concrete political force. This was true in the sense that in Moscow in April 1945 he was regarded as one of the Chinese Communist leaders. It is perhaps not too rash to suppose that the aim of the resolution was to try to persuade Stalin to drop Li Li-san.

Li's arrival in Manchuria had portentous significance for Yenan. There were the examples of Poland, Hungary, Roumania, Czechoslovakia, East Germany, etc., to show that the Communist func-

[1] SW, Vol. IV, pp. 171-218.

tionaries brought back to their respective countries from Moscow by the Soviet occupation forces were taking over the leadership of their parties. The fact that Li Li-san was acknowledged by the Soviet command as the Number One Chinese Communist in Manchuria, indicated that Stalin meant him to lead the "real Chinese Communists".

Had the significance of Li Li-san's arrival been properly understood at the time by Chiang Kai-shek and the Western governments, the relationship between Moscow and Mao's Party would have seemed less enigmatic in retrospect, and subsequent events would also have seemed less puzzling.

In 1945 and even later the true relationship between the USSR and the Chinese Communists was misunderstood and disregarded. Those few Western diplomatists and journalists, American generals and other officials who reported the real situation, were ignored or attacked. Two sets of contradictory misconceptions clamoured for acceptance. According to one, all Communists any time and anywhere are always centrally directed from Moscow by the wonderfully far-sighted and extremely cunning Stalin; while the other school saw Communists as all sorts of different individuals and believed that Mao's unorthodox means in realising the most orthodox Communist ends made him a "national-Communist", a "peasant rebel", a "leftish patriot" with whom it was both possible and necessary to negotiate for formal "democratic compromises".

General MacArthur as Supreme Commander of the Allied Powers issued a General Order on August 15, 1945, instructing the Japanese to surrender to the Soviet forces in Manchuria, and to Chiang Kai-shek's forces elsewhere in China. The General Order emphasised especially that *no other Chinese forces* were permitted to accept the surrender of Japanese troops. Next day Chu Teh ordered the Red forces to accept the surrender of the Japanese puppet armies surrounded by them. Chu's order was sent to the American, British and Soviet Embassies in Chungking. But the three powers, *the USSR included,* reaffirmed Chiang's monopoly over the acceptance of Japanese surrender. The Allies made Chiang Commander of the "China Zone", so that American troops were placed at his disposal.

The Pact of Friendship and Alliance between the USSR and Chiang Kai-shek's China was concluded on August 14. Article V of the Pact provided for "non-interference in the internal affairs of the other contracting party", and in the subsequent exchange of notes the USSR pledged "moral support and assistance" to China, "such support and aid to be entirely given to the National Government as the central government of China."[2]

Both before and after the signature of the pact Mao Tse-tung criticised and attacked *the Americans* for supporting only Chiang Kai-shek. On July 12, 1945, the Yenan news-agency published this comment written by Mao:

> Ambassador Patrick J. Hurley . . . bluntly declared that the United States would co-operate only with Chiang Kai-shek but not with the Chinese Communist Party. . . . If Hurley's policy continues, the *US Government will fall hopelessly in the deep, stinking cesspool of Chinese reaction.*[3]

The fact that the USSR continued the same policy was, of course, obvious to everybody.

During the last four months of 1945 America gave massive help to Chiang Kai-shek in the process of taking over from the Soviet occupation forces in Manchuria. During these months the US Army transported three Kuomintang military detachments to east and North China by air and over 400,000 Kuomintang troops by sea. In addition, 50,000 US Marines were airlifted to North China where they held key railroads, bridges and coalmines for the Kuomintang.[4] "With this and other American assistance Chiang Kai-shek's troops were able to accept the capitulation of a great majority of the 1,200,000 Japanese troops in China proper. By the end of 1945 . . . Chiang Kai-shek's forces had been able to . . . obtain control of Peking, Tientsin and the lines of communication to the Manchurian border."[5]

Chiang Kai-shek, who later accused the Soviets of helping the Chinese Reds, seemed at the time to be quite satisfied with Soviet behaviour. On September 18, 1945 he declared:

> With the military assistance of our ally, Soviet Russia, the Cairo and the Potsdam declarations have been realised, and our north-

---

[2] Texts of Pact and notes in *United States Relations with China*, pp. 585-96.

[3] *SW*, Vol. IV, pp. 328-29. (Emphasis added.)

[4] *US Relations with China*, pp. 311-12.

[5] R. C. North, *Moscow and Chinese Communists*, Stanford University Press, 1953, p. 223.

eastern Provinces [Manchuria] liberated, and our countrymen there brought back in the fold of the fatherland.[6]

Chiang was also pleased because the Allied Supreme Command did not interfere in a curious move of his. All those Chinese puppet forces which had served the Japanese till the last days of the war were permitted and encouraged by Chiang to declare themselves for the Kuomintang. Hundreds of thousands of the collaborationist troops were promptly incorporated into Chiang's armies. In many cases Chiang instructed the commander of the puppet garrison by telegram to accept the surrender of the local Japanese forces in his name.

Many books on China assert that the Soviet Army in Manchuria contributed greatly to Mao's coming to power by giving his troops Japanese equipment and by training and transforming the Chinese guerillas and Red Army men into regular soldiers. These accounts disregard the fact that the Chinese Reds had built up their army in two decades of fighting and that tens of thousands of Red officers were trained in the Yenan Military College between 1936 and 1945. As to Japanese arms and equipment, no documentary evidence has been adduced to prove that the Soviet forces in Manchuria ever gave Japanese arms or other material aid to the Communists. On the other hand, the USSR gave 300,000,000 US dollars worth of aid to the Kuomintang up to 1942, and from then on until 1945 the United States gave a 500,000,000 US dollars loan to Chiang and, in addition, very massive aid in war equipment as part of the lend-lease agreement. According to both American and Kuomintang official accounts a significant part of the Kuomintang Army was American trained. Documents since published bear out General Marshall's statement that *there was absolutely no evidence to suggest that the Chinese Communists were being supported by Russia.*[7]

On November 15 the *New York Times* reported from Chungking that the USSR had agreed that the Kuomintang government should fly daily 1,500 troops to Manchuria. The same paper reported a Chinese Communist statement on November 26, that the USSR was "very friendly" towards the Kuomintang government and that Soviet forces were holding key cities and railway points pending the

[6] *The Collected Wartime Messages of Generalissimo Chiang Kai-shek, 1937-1945,* compiled by the Chinese Ministry of Information, New York, 1946, Vol. II, p. 867.
[7] *New York Times,* January 12, 1947.

arrival of the Kuomintang troops. On November 27, the Soviet command in Manchuria agreed with the Kuomintang in ordering a Communist withdrawal from the Manchurian cities of Mukden and Changchun. According to the *New York Times*, this agreement was carried out.[8]

While Mao and the Yenan radio and press protested violently against the American support given to Chiang Kai-shek, emphasising all the time that it was most difficult to come to an agreement with this "fascist chieftain", the international organ of the Soviet Union, the *Novoye Vremya* (published in several languages—*New Times, Neue Zeit,* etc.), wrote in its editorial of the September 1, 1945, issue:

> It is no secret that the progressive development of China up to now has been hindered in no small degree by discord between the Kuomintang and the Chinese Communist Party. Abroad there are many dubious well-wishers who from time to time shout loudly of the inevitability of civil war in China. There can be no doubt that such a war would be a catastrophe for the country, which now more than ever needs peace in order to liquidate the devastating results of the long Japanese occupation.

On September 28, Moscow Radio announced, contrary to all the facts, that "unity in China has been established" and that China now had a "completely unified central government".

We know now that after the victory over Japan Stalin asked the Yenan Border Region Government (not the Chinese CP!) to send representatives to Moscow. On certain stages of the negotiations we have on this occasion only indirect and circumstantial evidence, not accepted by many authorities on Sino-Soviet relations. The present chronicler, however, tends to believe that Stalin attempted to persuade Yenan to accept Li Li-san and some other "Muscovites" into the Party leadership and to change or at least modify its "peasant strategy". In this way Stalin probably hoped to oust Mao from leadership. One aspect of the talks is, however, generally accepted as historical fact: *Stalin tried to convince the Chinese Reds that their strategy had no hope of success and that they should dissolve their army and join the Kuomintang government as junior partners.*

Before the complete break with the Yugoslav Communists in 1948, Stalin tried to stop them from helping the Greek Communist

[8] Ibid., November 28, 1945, p. 1.

partisans. (Incidentally: at that time many Western authorities believed that the Greek partisans were being helped and encouraged by Stalin!) On this occasion he told Kardelj, the Yugoslav representative:

. . . we do not agree with the Yugoslav comrades that they should go on helping the Greek partisans. In this matter, we think we are right, not the Yugoslavs. It is true, we also have made mistakes. For instance, after the war we invited the Chinese comrades to come to Moscow and we discussed the situation in China. We told them bluntly that we considered the development of the uprising in China had no prospects, that the Chinese comrades should seek a *modus vivendi* with Chiang Kai-shek, and that they should join the Chiang Kai-shek government and dissolve their army. The Chinese comrades agreed here in Moscow with the views of the Soviet comrades, but went back to China and acted quite otherwise. They mustered their forces, organised their armies and now, as we see, they are beating Chiang Kai-shek's army. Now, in the case of China, we admit we were wrong. It was proved that the Chinese comrades and not the Soviet comrades were right. But that is not the case with you in the Balkans. It is not the case with the Greek partisans, and the Yugoslav comrades should stop helping them. That struggle has no prospects whatsoever.[9]

This statement was never denied in Moscow or Peking; on the contrary, since 1956,* the Chinese Communists have often mentioned Stalin's "bad advice" about dissolving their army. The Chinese delegates evidently promised Stalin that they would try to establish a *modus vivendi* with the Kuomintang. After the delegation's return, Mao and his colleagues repeatedly attacked the *American reactionaries* for suggesting the dissolution of the Communist armies!

[9] Vladimir Dedijer, *Tito Speaks*, London, 1953, p. 331.
* After the anti-Stalin pact read by Khrushchev which mentioned that *Stalin was prepared to break with the Chinese Communists*, the satellite press published several allusions to this incident. Sample: Janos Kadar, the Hungarian Communist leader, after his return from an official visit to Peking, told Hungarian Party activists: "The Chinese comrades said that they had received much good advice from Stalin and had followed it with good results. Comrade Stalin also gave *bad advice*, and by not accepting some of it, the Chinese had also achieved good results" *Nepszabadsag*, Budapest, October 16, 1957. (Emphasis added.)

Stalin was displeased by reports about the strength of the Red forces, which he disbelieved. The American Secretary of State, James F. Byrnes, reported that during the Foreign Ministers' Conference in December 1945, Stalin laughed when he was told that the Chinese Communists claimed to have an army of 600,000 in the Tientsin area. Stalin remarked that all Chinese were boasters who exaggerated the forces of their opponents as well as their own.[10] As a matter of fact Mao's forces (regulars, guerillas and militia), were well over 600,000 at that time in the Tientsin area.

Painstaking analysis of the material available in 1945 (or even in 1943) could have shown the West that Stalin was biased against and misinformed about the Mao leadership in Yenan; that he did not believe in the possible success of Mao's peasant armies; that he had another set of Chinese leaders in Moscow whom he intended to entrust with the leadership of the Chinese Party.

A situation arose in which all the protagonists acted on false premises. Stalin, Chiang Kai-shek, and at times Roosevelt and Truman, misjudged Mao's power and significance. Both Chiang and the American Government misunderstood the relationship between the Soviet and the Yenan Communist parties. Chiang distrusted Stalin during a long period when Stalin truly wished him every success against Mao, who was striving to be the leader of the Communists in the non-white world. While some Western quarters sadly underestimated Mao's forces, others overestimated them because they were firmly convinced that Mao, as Stalin's Number One agent, was enjoying very massive actual support from the Soviet Union. Mao's statements strengthened the latter misconception, since he pretended that all was well between the Soviet and the Chinese Communist parties.

The fact that the American and certain other Western Communists also misunderstood the Stalin-Mao relationship helped to mislead non-Communist observers after 1945. The American Communists *assumed* that it was their duty to give propaganda backing to the Chinese Reds, and did so, even at times when the Soviet press was silent, or actually friendly to the Kuomintang. Later, when the presence of American troops in China convinced Stalin that they might endanger the security of his Far Eastern frontier, the Soviet press also objected to their continued presence. The fact that both the Moscow and the Yenan press objected to the presence of US

[10] J. F. Byrnes, *Speaking Frankly*, p. 228.

troops was taken as proof that they were centrally directed by Stalin. A closer reading of these articles would have shown that Moscow objected to the *presence* of the US troops, while Yenan resented their *activities* in helping Chiang.

In Manchuria Soviet operations had one aim only: to further Soviet interests and collect as much booty as possible. Mao's armies on the other hand were serving the interests of Red China. Many foreign observers, however, were convinced from the outset that they were acting in unison, according to a prearranged plan. If Soviet troops in Manchuria seemed to stay longer than had been agreed with Chiang Kai-shek, this was taken as proof that Stalin wanted to help the Chinese Communists in this way. Those Western observers who thought that Soviet forces were withdrawing too early also believed that Stalin was helping the Chinese Communists—that by prematurely withdrawing his troops he was giving the Chinese Communists their chance. Granted this prejudice, almost anything the Soviet forces did could serve as proof that Stalin was backing Mao.

The personal representative of the American President, Edwin W. Pauley, investigated the amount of war booty carted away from Manchuria by the Soviet forces. In his report the direct loss in goods, dismantled factories, railway rolling stock, etc., was estimated at 858,000,000 US dollars, while with the value of indirect damage, cost of replacement, etc., the total loss was estimated to be 2,000,000,000 dollars. The Soviet forces *destroyed* a great deal of machinery and equipment which they could not take to the USSR. The contents of the Mukden arsenal were destroyed. All this was rightly taken as a further example of Soviet ruthlessness. But Western prejudice was so undiscriminating at the time that official policy did not benefit from this clear demonstration of the actual situation. Stalin, in swiftly destroying the industrial and military potential of Manchuria, demonstrated:

1. that he believed that this most important industrial and strategic region of China would fall into the hand of enemies of the USSR, or at least into those of unfriendly neutrals:

2. that he did not want to help Mao Tse-tung to establish a strong Red puppet state in Manchuria.

True, Stalin made a thorough job of plundering the East European satellites too. But Manchuria was supposed to serve "Stalin's Mao" as the strong base from which he could promptly conquer the rest of China. Had this been the "far-sighted" Stalin's aim, he would not have been in quite such a hurry to cripple Manchuria's industry, nor would he have given the Manchurian cities to Chiang Kai-shek's forces.[11]

II

Clarification of events in Manchuria during the Soviet occupation and of the real relationship between the USSR and Mao's Party is especially important for any attempt to fathom the further development of what is called in China "Mao Tse-tung Thought".

The American Ambassador Hurley flew to Yenan after Japan's surrender and persuaded Mao to accompany him to Chungking for peace talks with Chiang Kai-shek. On August 28, 1945, Mao flew for the first time in his life over China. The famous poem[*] of his, which was inspired by this flight, the vision of the vastness of Chinese lands and of Chinese history, ended with the realisation that all the great conqueror emperors of China from Chin to Genghis Khan, were "alas, short of stature" . . . "for the towering figure watch the scene today."

This "towering figure" had a well-known public *persona* in the original Latin sense of the word—player's mask.

[11] See: C. P. Fitzgerald, *Revolution in China*, London, 1952, p. 93 and Max Beloff, *Soviet Policy in the Far East, 1944-1951*, p. 44.
[*] In Chungking he met Liu Ya-tse, who asked him for a poem. Mao then wrote his famous *Snow*. In a free translation the concluding lines read:

> ". . . *These lands, these rivers, their bewitching charm*
> *Inspired the conqueror-emperors of Chin and Han,*
> *Tang and Sung in splendour striving to expand.*
> *Alas! All short in stature! And Genghis Khan*
> *Knew only how to shoot a hawk for play.*
> *For the towering figure watch the scene today."*

More revealing is the clumsy but literal English translation published by the Peking Foreign Language Press in 1958:

> "*Such great beauty like this in all our landscape*
> *Has caused unnumbered heroes to bow in homage.*
> *But alas these heroes! Chin Shih Huand and Han Wu Ti*
> *Were rather lacking in culture;*
> *Rather lacking in literary talent*
> *Were the emperors Tang Tai Tung and Sung Tai Tsu;*
> *And Genghis Khan, beloved Son of Heaven for a day,*
> *Only knew how to bend his bow at the golden eagle.*
> *Now they are all past and gone:*
> *To find men truly great and noble-hearted*
> *We must look here in the present."*

Both the Yenan press, and Mao in his public appearances, in his speeches and writings, and in his behaviour when he met foreign authors and journalists, were intent on emphasising a rather large number of character traits, abilities, habits and attainments.

He was supposed to be a simple, serene, unassuming man, careless in personal habits but most meticulous in his work. A great revolutionary leader, a far-sighted statesman and military commander, an original Marxist philosopher, a genius of tactics and strategy. One of the masses of the Chinese people, their embodiment and representative, who at the same time had mastered everything that is best in classical Chinese culture; a scholar and poet. A warmhearted and good man in his thinking of and dealings with people, an extremely tough and dangerous fighter against the enemies of the people.

Much of the mask of course fits the face behind it. But what else lay behind the *persona* at this stage of his career? The content and style of his writings afford at rare intervals glimpses of other traits, other patterns, other moods. For some time there were signs that the non-personal megalomania of the cause-addict was only cloaking his great conceit. The occasional reports of his violent temper, of his uncouth outbursts when encountering basic criticism, of his cantankerous moods are borne out by occasional sentences in his essays and speeches. Although these have been carefully edited, enough has been left in to indicate his fierce pride in his achievements; his impatience and burning anger for not being sufficiently acknowledged and appreciated by the "outside"; the nagging sense of monstrously unjust treatment by the "outside world"; his petrified distrust, hate and contempt for everything non-Chinese.

Mao was of course, like everyone else, a man of many moods and many talents. But the long years of his cave-existence, boycotted, attacked, ignored, belittled by Chiang and his men, by the West, and by the leader of his own ideological camp, Stalin—made these moods stronger and more prevalent. Psychologists would no doubt have relevant comments on the possible effect of many years spent within cave walls. Even laymen can feel that these years could not have had an altogether healthy effect on a gigantically ambitious man, who for two decades could not break through the walls of isolation and non-recognition.

The Chungking visit was the first formal recognition by the outside world of his person and power. He was about to negotiate directly with Generalissimo Chiang and the representatives of the American government.

He was received politely enough at Chungking airport by Kuomintang officials and during the first few days of his visit he was invited to dinner by the Generalissimo, with whom he also had a series of informal talks. During the negotiations that followed, Mao Tse-tung behaved with dignified reserve. Some reporters gathered that he was politely ironic.

Knowing from his own lips how he despised and hated "unremoulded" leftish intellectuals, we have no difficulty in imagining how he reacted to Generalissimo Chiang's imperially haughty manners and to the luxury of his residence.

The talks lasted forty days. During this time Mao met a number of Chinese writers and intellectuals. He had a chance of impressing them with his ability to improvise poems, his knowledge of the Chinese classics and with his "democratic tolerance". He insisted that the Chinese Communists were sincere in wanting a democratic coalition régime. The encounters gave him first-hand impressions of the attitudes and mood of the anti-Chiang "democratic conservatives", liberals and non-Communist radical intellectuals.

His first-hand impressions of American representatives and of Kuomintang leaders did not correct his distortedly one-sided and extremely prejudiced picture of "American imperialists and their lackeys in Chungking".

Chiang wanted to strengthen his power, to dissolve the Communist armies and incorporate the Communist territories. The Americans wanted a democratic multi-party state with a strong central government and proposed that the Red Armies should be incorporated in the army of the republic. For Mao this meant Chiang's army. He believed that the American proposal for a multi-party democracy cloaked their striving for a multi-party system in which only one party, Chiang's Kuomintang, would have its own army.

Mao's writings, speeches and actions after these talks give not a single hint that his simplified Marxist textbook picture of the Western world had changed in one iota. The "outside world" for its part continued its hostility to him and he was still not recognised.

During the negotiations Mao avoided an open breach. He did not want to be accused of sabotaging a negotiated solution, neither was he willing to allow the Kuomintang authority over the Red Army and the Communist-controlled territories. The official communiqué issued on October 11 announced that the two parties had agreed on the early convocation of an all-party Political Consultative Conference to settle outstanding problems. The two parties agreed to strive for the early establishment of a constitutional government and that "peace, democracy, solidarity and unity should form the basis of the nation's concerted efforts". Chiang promised to legalise all political parties, to release all political prisoners. Mao Tse-tung promised to reduce the strength of the regular Red Army to twenty divisions, that is, to one-fifth of the projected strength of the peace-time Chinese army.

Mao Tse-tung then flew back to Yenan. Two days after the communiqué was issued, there were already clashes between the Kuomintang and the Communist forces, each side accusing the other of attacking first. Soon, however, Chiang Kai-shek issued a new *Manual on Bandit Suppression*, and in the second part of October 110,000 of his troops were attacking the Red areas in North China.

In December General Marshall arrived in Chungking as President Truman's representative and mediated a cease-fire agreement which was signed in January 1946. During this cease-fire period, Chiang Kai-shek occupied further cities, while Mao's forces enlarged their rural areas. In agreement with the Soviet command, Chiang's forces took further important Manchurian cities and ports, while the Communists withdrew to the countryside. Chiang airlifted more troops to Manchuria and, with the approval of Marshal Malinovsky's headquarters, started conscripting Manchurians into his Peace Preservation Corps.

During these events the first (and last) Political Consultative Conference took place in Chungking and decided on the convocation of a National Assembly at a later date. A few days after this conference there were large-scale anti-Communist and anti-Soviet demonstrations in Chungking. Soon the demonstrators also turned against the conservatives and liberals and all other adherents of a multi-party system.

The civil war broke out again on many fronts. In June 1946 General Marshall succeeded in bringing about a new cease-fire agreement which lasted for a month. But by this time both sides were even less willing to compromise. The deterioration in Soviet-American relations raised Chiang's hopes for American aid on an even larger scale. Mao and his colleagues were also confident, seeing that the Generalissimo had in no way profited from the lessons they had given him in the art of waging civil war in China. He went on fortifying cities which were completely surrounded by Red "liberated areas" or guerilla areas. In effect, Chiang held scores of urban islands surrounded by the hostile sea of rural China. In May 1946 the Soviet forces withdrew from Manchuria. Chiang took over most

of the cities—where the factories had been effectively crippled by
Soviet removals. Some of the Kuomintang cities had to be supplied
by air, because Mao's forces were systematically cutting the north-
south and east-west railways.

For a time General Marshall set his hope on other political parties, mainly the "third force" represented by the Democratic
League, a party of adherents of the Western-style parliamentary
system. The growing popularity of this party, and General Marshall's evident approval of it prompted Chiang to turn against it.
The Democratic League had the backing of the middle classes and
of all those who had had enough of Chiang's corrupt and terroristic
dictatorship, yet did not want to live under Communist rule. The
League was led by some of the most outstanding intellectuals of
the country and most of the educated class including the bulk of
the students supported it.

General Marshall was probably right when he estimated that in
a free election the Democratic League would have gained millions
of votes. But the League had no army, and Chiang Kai-shek was just
as intent to destroy the democrats as the Communists. At first,
Chiang's secret police arrested only lesser adherents of the League,
and to begin with only administrative measures were taken at the
universities against League-supporting professors and students. But
while General Marshall was still seeking to establish a coalition in
which the Democratic League should play a major rôle, Chiang
stepped up his campaign against the League, both overt and covert.
Arrests multiplied, offices were raided, publications were confiscated, and those who propagated parliamentary democracy were
sent to the concentration camps. And as if all this were not enough
the assassin took a hand. Professor Wen Yi-to of Kunming University, who was the League's representative in the National Assembly,
was mysteriously assassinated; a few days later another leader, Li
Kung-po, was murdered by "unknown persons", and so it went on.

The fate of the "third force" was sealed by the fact that it could
be regarded as the nucleus of a non-Communist alternative government to Chiang's dictatorship. After the spate of arrests and assassinations, some of the leaders went into exile or escaped into Communist areas.

Thanks to Chiang's secret police and concentration camps, a new
and very large stream of intellectuals and students began to wend
its way to Yenan, including democrats who now realised that there
could be no "third force". A very large part of the educated class
had good reason to fear Chiang's régime. Mao Tse-tung stepped up

propaganda among the intellectuals. In the cities and universities, constantly threatened as they were by Chiang's secret police, Mao's agents spread the information that "democratic brain-workers" were more than welcome in Yenan.

No doubt many intellectuals were attracted by the doctrines of Chinese Marxism. But at this time far more saw in the Red territories the lesser of two evils. If Mao had only himself to thank for winning the peasants, he was greatly indebted to Chiang for winning him further thousands from the intellectual cream of China.

When at the end of 1946 General Marshall gave up in despair his attempt to bring about a peaceful solution, the civil war turned into an all-out war between White and Red China. In his official report in January 1947 General Marshall rightly blamed both the Kuomintang reactionaries and the "dyed-in-the-wool Communists" for the failure to achieve unity.

As American arms, tanks, aeroplanes and all sorts of military supplies came pouring in, Chiang proceeded with his largest-ever Communist extermination campaign. He always thought in terms of cities, the capture of which is most impressive to the outside world. As before, Mao's instructions to his generals were to retreat if attacked by superior force, to leave the cities to the enemy, and to concentrate on annihilating or capturing enemy troops, whenever and wherever their force was not superior. One of the Generalissimo's spectacular successes was the taking of Yenan, the Red capital. By this time Yenan and the entire Border Region had lost its great strategic value. The Reds had the Manchurian countryside and also held important cities including Harbin. They also had most of the Shantung province and many large areas in other parts of China. When Chiang attacked Yenan, with a very large force, Mao decided to evacuate it. He did not move to Harbin, but set up his headquarters in the guerilla district of North China, and spread his power over ever-widening regions of China.

The American representative on the spot saw the situation clearly; in 1947 General Albert C. Wedemeyer was sent by President Truman on a fact finding mission to China. He reported in September 1947:

> Notwithstanding all the corruption and incompetence one notes in China, it is a certainty that the bulk of the people are not disposed to a Communist political and economic structure. Some have become affiliated with Communism in an indignant protest against oppressive police measures, corrupt practices and mal-

administration of National Government officials. Some have lost all hope for China under existing leadership and turn to the Communists in despair. Some accept new leadership by mere inertia. . . . Adoption by the United States of a policy motivated solely toward stopping the expansion of Communism without re- gard to the continued existence of an unpopular repressive gov- ernment would render any aid ineffective.[12]

The Red armies and guerillas were reminded of an order which Mao had issued in December 1936:

Our basic directive is to rely on the war industries of the imperial- ist countries and of our enemy at home. We have a claim on the output of the arsenals of London as well as of Hanyang, and, what is more, it is to be delivered to us by the enemy's own transport corps. This is the sober truth, not a joke.[13]

This time it was the American arsenals that were producing for the Red forces and the arms were being delivered by Chiang's disheartened troops. Chiang kept pouring American arms into the besieged Manchurian and North China cities. The American Consul General at Mukden reported on May 30, 1947:

There is good evidence that apathy, resentment, and defeatism are spreading fast in Nationalist ranks, causing surrenders and desertions. Main factors contributing to this are the Communists' ever mounting superiority . . . the Nationalist soldiers discourage- ment over prospects of getting reinforcements . . . their growing indignation over the disparity between officers' enrichment and soldiers' low pay, life, and their lack of interest in fighting far from home among "alien" unfriendly populace.[14]

Although most American politicians, diplomats and generals re- ported on the corruption and inefficiency of Chiang's dictatorship, America went on giving support to the Kuomintang in the belief that this was the way to contain "Soviet Communism". At first this aid was based on the belief that there was no other way to stop Mao from handing Manchuria over to the Soviet Union. In the grow- ing cold war atmosphere, less and less attention was paid to the realities of the most complex Chinese situation. From 1945 (VJ

[12] United States Relations with China, p. 768.
[13] SW, Vol. I, p. 253.
[14] US Relations with China, p. 317, quoted by North, Moscow and the Chinese Communists, p. 238.

Day) to the middle of 1948, 1,600,000,000 US dollars worth of aid was given to Chiang, mainly in all sorts of military equipment. From the summer of 1948 onwards, thanks to the American arms captured from Chiang's forces, Mao's armies won many victories, yet from then on until his total defeat, Chiang was given a further 400,000,000 dollars worth of aid, bringing the total for 1945-9 to over two thousand million dollars.

III

On December 25, 1947 there was a meeting of the Communist Central Committee in northern Shensi. In his report Mao Tse-tung announced that the Red Army, renamed People's Liberation Army (from now on PLA) *had now passed from the stategic defensive to the strategic offensive.* In the future, positional warfare must also be stressed. The army was to learn the art of storming fortresses in preparation for taking cities.

Cities were to be taken step by step and with discrimination— first the small and medium-sized ones, then the big ones; first those cities where the enemy defence was weak, then, at the opportune moment, those where the enemy defence was fairly strong, and finally, when conditions became ripe, those where the enemy defence was very strong.[15]

After admonishing his functionaries not to antagonise the middle peasants, Mao announced the "correct urban policy" in the cities to be liberated. He emphasised that while the property of Kuomintang millionaires ("bureaucrat capitalism") was to be confiscated, national industry and commerce were to be protected.

Mao's urban programme served both short-term tactical and long-term strategical aims. In the cities he wanted to show the middle classes, the merchants, industrialists and bankers that the Communists were fighting only against the Kuomintang monopolists and meant to liquidate only the immense economic might of the "Four Big Families" (all closely connected with Chiang Kai-shek), but the small and medium capitalists had nothing to fear from them.[16]

Finally Mao reasserted the importance of the revolutionary united front after Communist victory. The Communists were prepared to form a coalition with all democratic parties and groups

[15] *A History of the Modern Chinese Revolution,* Peking, 1959, p. 507.
[16] Ibid., pp. 508-9.

accepting Communist leadership. This new programme, widely publicised by the Communists, helped to weaken the resistance of the
Kuomintang territories.

By early 1948 the territory north of the Yangtze, with the exception of the besieged cities, was virtually in Communist hands. This
made it necessary for Mao to set up the "Government of the Liberated Areas". Yet it was at this time that Stalin again made an attempt to interfere in the affairs of Mao's Party and Red armies, by
advising the continuation of the guerilla war, without aiming at
swift final victory.

Mao's Party leadership had had no official contact with the Soviet
Communist Party since 1935. In 1948 Stalin was still not prepared
to recognise the Mao leadership as that of *the* Chinese Communists.
He still hoped to replace Mao with some "Muscovite" Chinese
Communist. This time he sent a semi-official invitation to Mao's
government to dispatch a representative to Moscow for preliminary
talks with the Soviet Government. Mao sent Liu Shao-chi who was
just as staunchly *Chinese* Marxist, as he was himself.

In Moscow Stalin tried to convince Liu that it was quite hopeless
to aim directly at total victory. On the other hand, the continuation
of the guerilla warfare would greatly weaken America and would
best benefit the Communist camp and ultimately the Chinese Party.

At a conference in South Hopei in July 1948, Mao and his colleagues decided instead to press on with the strategic offensive. In
besieged Mukden, Chiang had a well-equipped army of more than
100,000 men, and he was about to land his best armoured divisions
in South Manchuria to lift the siege. Both forces were soon wiped
out. In the second part of 1948 Chiang lost twenty-five American-
equipped divisions and thirty other divisions. Mao's PLA captured
more than 200,000 American-made rifles and proportionately large
numbers of other weapons and military vehicles.

Stalin showed his anger that his advice was disregarded. He
could not permit the existence of disobedient Communist régimes.
After Mao's great victories the USSR took the initiative in prolong-
ing the Kuomintang-USSR non-aggression treaty for a further two
years. The victories won by the Chinese Red armies in the autumn
of 1948 were barely mentioned in the Soviet press, and on the
November 1948 anniversary of the Russian Revolution Molotov
caused quite a sensation in Communist quarters when, speaking at
length about the development of the "liberation movements" in Asia,
*he did not devote a single sentence to the successes of the Chinese
Communists.*

(This was after the Tito affair. On June 28, 1948, the too independent Yugoslav Party was expelled from the Cominform, and the Yugoslav Communists and the Yugoslav people were told to force Tito and his colleagues to recant, and if they refused, to throw them out. More than a year earlier, Gomulka had written his famous article on the "Polish road to socialism" in the April 1947 issue of *Nowe Drogi*. After the expulsion of Tito, he was forced to recant and was in his turn expelled from the Party. His arrest came only in 1951, but his fall was complete in 1948. By this time there were already many direct and indirect attacks against Mao's "Chinese road".)

Peking, the capital, Tientsin and many other cities in the north were by now closely surrounded by the Red forces, while the Red guerillas behind the Kuomintang lines were enlarging their areas, using the fighting and organisation techniques evolved during the eight years of war against Japan.

In Kuomintang territories chaos, corruption, police terrorism, enervation and defeatism increased, in pace with the leaping inflation. The everyday life of the population became a nightmare as they carried basketfuls of money, the value of which fell every half-hour. By 1948 prices had risen three million times as compared with the pre-war period. In 1948 the Kuomintang exchanged three millions of the old currency units to one new "gold yuan", with an international value of four yuans to the US dollar. But the "gold yuan" lost purchasing value with the same alarming speed as the old currency. Inside a year, instead of four yuan to the dollar, it was five or even ten million yuan to the dollar. Middle-class savings and medium capital were wiped out. Want, illness, misery prevailed. At the same time enormous fortunes were made by speculators, mainly by those who got all sorts of monopolies and concessions from Chiang's entourage. While some Kuomintang generals fought heroically in a hopeless situation, others were working the black market and were busy sending their newly won fortunes to foreign banks. The Generalissimo himself was believed in China to have amassed fabulous fortunes during this period.

As the tidal waves of the Red armies rolled over the vastness of China, which had suffered forty years of incessant war and civil strife, Mao's organisers were instantly on the spot. Many of them had one or even two decades of practice in finding representatives of the other "democratic classes" and setting up village councils. The "new-democratic" pattern, developed and perfected over the years by Mao and his associates, was well known to these Communist cadres who arrived in the wake of the armies. They had the method. Mao had even worked out to the last detail possible adaptations of the pattern to fit the wide variety of possible local conditions. The technique of first inspiring, and then utilising and meeting, seemingly quite voluntary, even impromptu local demands, produced quick results. The cadres aimed at convincing the local population that what they had to offer was order and safety after decades of chaos and danger; honest administration instead of Kuomintang corruption; and economic consolidation after years of terrible inflation.

By giving important public functions to non-Communists who offered their services in their patriotic zeal, they succeeded in creating the impression of a broadly based multi-party régime. Great care was taken that there should be no visible secret police activity. All the executed anti-Communists were denounced as Japanese spies or wicked landlords. Mao's newly developed urban policy was also put into practice, and the functionaries did their best to advertise it by taking dramatic, picturesque, interesting action. In giving instant help to independent factory owners, merchants and other "small and medium capitalists", they made sure that this news should spread into territories still held by the Kuomintang. Those Kuomintang generals and officers who were responsible for peaceful mass surrenders (called "agreement for peaceful reorganisation") were respectfully treated. They were given a chance to "save their face".

These actions of Mao's civilian administration proved to be quite effective in the psychological offensive, which was in many cases the chief factor in the swift surrender of a Kuomintang division or a Kuomintang-held town.

Kuomintang strength was swiftly crumbling. By the end of 1948 the Communists had not only the massive backing of the entire countryside and the growing support of the intelligentsia and the middle classes, but they also had an army of over three million, partly American equipped. Early in 1949 the most important northern cities surrendered, or were taken by force. Tientsin, the main industrial and commercial city of North China, was taken on January 15. The more than 200,000 defenders of Peking surrendered without much fighting on January 31. In the Peking-Tientsin campaign Chiang lost 520,000 troops.

The Red armies avoided bombarding the cities they meant to take. In Peking they shelled only the headquarters of Chiang's secret police. The population was not harmed.

Peking saw Mao's troops long before the great one himself appeared in person high above the vast multitude thronging the Tien An Men square.

The date was February 3, 1949. A cold dust-storm made the people shiver. The Red troops entered the city in the morning, column after column with machine-like precision; a huge stream of infantry, artillery, cavalry, tanks, transport troops.

> The long columns . . . took all day to pass through the great south gate . . . and then file—deliberately—through the old Legation Quarter, to humble the last shreds of the foreigner's pride. . . . The troops, veterans, instantly recognisable to all who saw them as real soldiers, not the ruffians in uniform who had so long disgraced the name of China, were under a firm and rigid discipline. Their weapons were well-kept and clean, and they were of Japanese or American make in almost equal proportion. To the surprise and disappointment of some observers, who had fixed ideas on the subject of Communists, no Russian weapons and no Russians were to be seen.[17]

On New Year's Day, 1949, Chiang proposed peace talks. As the Communist conditions in the changed situation were even stiffer (they proposed a coalition government led by them, which would instantly take over from the Kuomintang), Chiang announced his retirement on January 21, and gave over his duties to Vice-President Li Tsung-jen. The peace talks held with the new President in April 1949 broke down, as the Communist conditions aimed in effect at acceptance of their complete power. From then on Mao's generals were permitted to sign "regional peace agreements" with Kuomintang governors and generals who accepted "peaceful liberation".

Li Tsung-jen had more success in negotiating with the Soviet Ambassador. According to the official *US Relations with China* (p. 293), the new Kuomintang President made a tentative agreement with the USSR. They agreed on Chinese neutrality in any future war, on elimination of US influence from China and "real co-operation between Kuomintang China and the Soviet Union". Li Tsung-jen sought American approval for this agreement, in the hope that the Soviet Union would succeed in restraining Mao and his colleagues. The US Government, however, did not agree. That Stalin, true to his behaviour in the nineteen-thirties, was again seeking to make a

[17] C. P. Fitzgerald, *Revolution in China*, London, 1952, pp. 114-15.

deal with the "left-Kuomintang", is made probable by several facts. He initiated talks with the Kuomintang regarding Sinkiang as late as March 1949. The Soviet consulates were instantly closed down one by one in all the cities taken by Mao's forces. Other consulates remained. When Mao Tse-tung made his triumphal entry into the nation's capital, Peking, on March 25, 1949, he was still not recognised by Stalin as the real ruler of China. Nanking was captured on April 23, nearly a month later. Only then did the Kuomintang government move to Canton, yet Stalin instructed his Ambassador to follow! Unlike the American Ambassador and all his other colleagues, the Soviet Ambassador to Chiang's China was the only one to follow the beaten Kuomintang Government to its last foothold on the mainland of China, to Canton.

So the USSR seemed to support Chiang to the last. It was only after Mao's armies began to advance over a huge front south of the Yangtze that *Pravda* suddenly announced the collapse of "the reactionary Kuomintang régime".

XIII

AIYAYO! HE IS THE PEOPLE'S GREAT SAVIOUR

I

The clothes he wore were still those of a peasant. The crumpled cloth cap was the same too. Yet the man wearing them was not standing in his solitary cave but on top of a famous and colossal building overlooking a vast square filled with a multitude of tiny upturned faces—the people.

They were singing songs about him, they were shouting with a rhythmical roar, wishing him to live for 10,000 years.

He himself was barely visible to the multitude. But on the historic wall, right under the place where he stood on the terrace, hung a gigantic picture of his smiling face.

That picture, that cloth-capped head, that simple happy smile was seen during this year of victory in hundreds of cities. On tanks and on the boilers of railway engines, spread over the walls of tall buildings, on tiny flags in the hands of millions of children, on peasant carts bringing grain to the cities, on the first page of newspapers, over the stages of theatres, on books and pamphlets—everywhere—the happy smile of this giant of a "no one".

> *. . . With him, we shall build a new China,*
> *Aiyayo, he leads the people into the future.*

The hundreds of thousands of tiny heads swayed to the gaily lilting rhythm of this famous song. Victory marches. Songs of the guerillas. The victorious flag song:

> *O, you are the bright sun and the flag of victory*
> *. . . .*
> *We will follow you and enter a new world. . . .*

Tientsin and Taiyuan, Nanking and Shanghai, all the cities of China were singing these songs and holding their celebrations, and now the people of Peking were wildly welcoming the greatest event of all, the formal birth of the new China, the end of chaos and humiliation, the end of non-recognition and isolation.

"The greatest victory the Chinese people ever had."

"The greatest turning point in history."

"Mao Tse-tung, the great architect of our victory."

Communists and non-Communists alike were eager to learn about the great one. From the hundreds of thousands of pamphlets and booklets published during the last three years, they had learnt the official view of the Chinese Communist Party:

> Mao can be truly regarded as a genius such as has never before appeared in Chinese history . . . the truest and most perfect representative of the Chinese people and a leader of the people of the world.[1]

. . . The same clothes, the same cap. . . . Was he the same man? Would he be remoulded by his victory, by the tremendous power he had now won over China, by all this adulation, by getting used to the constant spectacle of a human sea undulating far below under him?

Was it for all this he had thirsted through the hard, dangerous and bitter decades of struggle? Was it his impatience for acclaim and recognition that prompted his Party to print hundreds of thousands of pamphlets about his genius, about his being a great leader of the people of the world?

Only time would tell. Only time did tell.

The date was October 1, 1949. The place was Peking, the Tien An Men, the Gate of Heavenly Peace, from the top of which Chairman Mao Tse-tung issued a message to the entire world, solemnly proclaiming the establishment of the People's Republic of China and its Central People's Government. He formally notified the governments of the world:

"The Central People's Government is the sole legal government representing all the people of the People's Republic of China. This government is willing to establish diplomatic relations with any foreign government which is willing to observe the principles of equality, mutual benefit and mutual respect of territorial integrity and sovereignty."

And then came the fighters. Red Army men in captured American tanks; Red Guards with their Japanese rifles; peasant guerillas with their home-made bombs; artillery, cavalry, Red sailors, armoured cars; men and women of the Red Army theatre troops; the dancers and propagandists; the medical corps, the nurses; young-

[1] Chang Ju-hsin, *On Mao Tse-tung*, first published in Yenan, reprinted in Peking, 1949.

sters and veterans of the Long March. The reality and the legend of two decades marched through Tien An Men square.

History and legend were also there on the terrace high above the roaring square. On each side of the "great saviour" stood the other leaders: Chu Teh, Chou En-lai, Liu Shao-chi and the rest, who had shared with Mao the decades of danger, hardship and struggle. They all emerged from the Yenan caves, from illegal quarters, from army tents—and already during this year of victory they had all stood more than once above jubilant multitudes in various great cities. They all faced the same sort of remoulding which awaited Mao.

Now they were full of their victory, full of expectations, eager to build up the most populous country of the earth into a great power in the international arena; eager to be acknowledged as real Communists by the Communist parties of the world.

Chou En-lai, Premier and Minister of Foreign Affairs, notified the governments and the United Nations that the Chinese People's Republic was ready to play its due part in international affairs.

The speeches, articles and actions of these days show how strong was the belief that October 1, 1949, was the day of the *great breakthrough*.

Ten days previously, at the opening of the Political Consultative Conference which was to set up the Republic, Mao Tse-tung said:

Our work will be written down in the history of mankind, and it will clearly demonstrate the fact that the Chinese, who comprise one-quarter of humanity, *have from now on stood up*. . . . We have united ourselves and defeated both our foreign and domestic oppressors by means of the People's War of Liberation and the people's great revolution, and we announce the establishment of the People's Republic of China. *Our nation will from now on enter the large family of peace-loving and freedom-loving nations of the world.* It will work bravely and industriously to create its own civilisation and happiness and will, at the same time, promote world peace and freedom. *Our nation will never again be an insulted nation. We have stood up.*[2]

For many years in the past there had been in their own Shanghai the park to which "Chinese and dogs" were not admitted. Now— they felt—the days of monstrous humiliation were over, once and for

[2] Quoted by Liao Kai-lung, *From Yenan to Peking*, Foreign Language Press, Peking, 1954, pp. 114-15. (Emphasis added.)

all. Now their China had achieved admission to the world on equal terms.

Mao and his colleagues experienced not one but two shatteringly great and bitter disappointments during these months. They were not recognised as real Communists by Stalin and the Cominform, and their China was not admitted to the international arena as one of the great powers.

The UNO and the governments of the world were asked in formal notes to recognize the Chinese People's Republic. The Communist Parties of the world were given a far more massive and elaborate notice that the Chinese Communist Party, having brought its revolution to victory, now asked to be recognised as a true Marxist-Leninist Party. This "notice" was given in a series of actions and declarations intended to show that the Chinese CP was as disciplined, as orthodox and as loyal a Party as the other "fraternal parties"; that it accepted the leadership of the Soviet Party and marched in step with the other parties even before recognition.* Mao declared that the Chinese CP had had no official contact with the Soviet CP since 1935. Now it wished to establish official relations between the two parties and with the other Communist parties of the world. Before recognition and inclusion in the Cominform (which never came), the Chinese CP denounced Tito as soon as the Cominform expelled him.

Mao's essay *On People's Democratic Dictatorship* published on July 1, 1949, made it quite clear that the Chinese CP would build a socialist country on orthodox lines, based on the proletariat of the cities and the development of heavy industry, and that internation-

---

* In March 1949 the Plenary Session of the Central Committee announced that after the nation-wide victory the Chinese Communist Party would base itself on the proletariat of the cities:

"Since the failure of the First Revolutionary Civil War in 1927 the Party, under the leadership of Comrade Mao Tse-tung, had *temporarily* transferred the centre of its work from the cities to the countryside and set up revolutionary bases and accumulated revolutionary force . . . for encircling and eventually seizing the cities. After over twenty years of arduous struggle, this task was now accomplished. *Henceforth . . . the cities would lead the countryside.* It is . . . imperative to *rely whole-heartedly on the Party's own class.* . . . The political leadership of the Chinese Communist Party and *the working class,* and the leading position of the State-owned socialist economy controlled *by the working class,* would ensure China's steady transition to socialism" *History of the Modern Chinese Revolution,* pp. 524-7. (Emphasis added.)

ally it would stand on the side of the Soviet Union and the Cominform countries.

An article written by Mao in June 1949 was published in the July 15, 1949, issue of the Cominform journal: "For a Lasting Peace, For People's Democracy". This article contributed greatly, of course, to the conviction that Mao was Stalin's Number One agent in the Far East:

> We are told: "You incline toward one side". This is precisely what forty years' experience of Sun Yat-sen and the twenty-eight years' experience of the Communist Party has firmly convinced us of: that in order to achieve and consolidate victory we must follow one side . . . the Chinese people must either side with imperialism or with Socialism. There can be no question of remaining between them, there is no third path. . . . Internationally we belong to the anti-imperialist front headed by the Soviet Union, and for genuine friendly aid we must look to this front and not to the imperialist front.[3]

This was all in vain. The Stalinist attacks against the Chinese leadership went on.

In July 1949, the Editorial Board of the Bombay *Communist* attacked those Indian Communists who wanted to follow Mao's path. Mao—according to the editorial—co-operated with the rich peasants and neglected the hegemony of the working class. The editorial went on to say:

> Some of those who advocate what they call the Chinese way formally stand for the hegemony of the proletariat. But they suggest that the Chinese experience shows that it is exercised through the Communist Party . . . which in reality reduces itself to the assertion that a Communist Party, basing itself on the ideology and political platform of the proletariat, can successfully lead the revolution without setting the working class itself, the mass of the workers, in motion . . . we must state emphatically that the CP of India has accepted Marx, Engels, Lenin and Stalin as the authoritative sources of Marxism. It has not discovered new sources of Marxism beyond these.[4]

All through 1949 Chinese Communists were invited only to the meetings of the Communist-led International Trade Union confer-

---

[3] "For a Lasting Peace, For People's Democracy", July 15, 1949.
[4] *Communist*, Bombay, July 1949.

ences, but there was no question of their admission to the Cominform. Stalin kept himself free to recognise a "real Chinese CP" at some later date.

Mao Tse-tung had already written his article "For Lasting Peace", when on July 3, 1949, *Pravda* and *Izvestiya* reported the arrival in Moscow of a delegation of the "Manchurian People's Democratic Authorities", under the leadership of Kao Kang. This delegation concluded a one-year trade agreement between the two countries. This was many months after the establishment of Mao's "Liberated Areas Government". Kao Kang, once the commander of the Red forces in northern Shensi, before the arrival of Mao's Red Army, had been a supporter of Mao until 1947. Since taking over leadership in Manchuria, however, presumably under the influence of the Soviet Command, and the "Muscovite" Li Li-san, he had become increasingly Stalinist. After his return from Moscow, Kao Kang, who was secretary of the North-East (Manchurian) Bureau of the Chinese CP, became Chairman of the "People's Government for the North-East" (Manchuria). On his inauguration he promised to follow the Soviet example as closely as possible.

Mao Tse-tung, anxious just then to avoid any friction with Stalin and the Soviet authorities, gave his official blessing to the Soviet-Manchurian agreement and to Kao Kang's election, and appointed Stalin's man, Li Li-san, Minister of Labour in his first government. Only Mao's later actions betray his real attitude at that time. After Stalin's death, Kao Kang and his entourage were accused of many crimes, among which figured their separationist tendencies: they were charged with plotting to set up an "independent kingdom". Kao Kang, according to Mao's press, committed suicide in 1954, while several members of his entourage were executed. The same fate awaited the Stalinist anti-Chinese leaders in Korea and the pro-Soviet separationists in Inner Mongolia and Sinkiang. The purges in these border regions and the settling there in subsequent years of millions of Chinese, clearly showed that Mao was intent on defending China against Soviet encroachment in Manchuria, Sinkiang, and Inner Mongolia.

Stalin threatened Mao through both governmental and Party manipulations. The separationist régimes in these territories, comprising more than one-third of China, were led by Stalinist Communists, loyal to the Stalin way and neutral or hostile to the Mao way.

Although the USSR and the East European satellites accorded governmental recognition to the Chinese People's Republic, and Stalin at last withdrew recognition from Chiang's régimes on October 5, he still very conspicuously refused to recognise the Mao leadership as "real Communists". Despite Mao's declarations, the Soviet Party's theoretical organ, *Bolshevik*, in its October 1949 issue officially defined Mao's Chinese Republic as:

An anti-imperialist, also anti-feudal and anti-bureaucratic régime, transitional to a non-capitalist or more accurately to a socialist development of the country.[5]

It was made quite clear that despite its name, the Chinese régime was not regarded as a real People's Democracy, like the régimes in Eastern Europe.

Mao and his colleagues answered this and similar statements by reaffirming their Marxist-Leninist stand and repeating that *the Chinese road was a separate road to Communism*. They even chose this time to make a formal challenge to the Soviet Party, with the assertion that the colonial and semi-colonial countries should follow "the way of Mao Tse-tung".

When the World Federation of Trade Unions held a conference of Asian and Australasian trade unionists in Peking, the opening address on November 16, 1949 was delivered by Liu Shao-chi:

The way taken by the Chinese people in defeating imperialism and its lackeys and in founding the People's Republic of China is the way that should be taken by the peoples of the various colonial and semi-colonial countries in their fight for national independence, and people's democracy. This is the way of Mao Tse-tung.[*6]

While Western observers debated for a decade whether there ever was a "Mao way", or "Chinese way", the Chinese leadership always insisted on it. Lu Ting-yi gave its Chinese definition during the thirtieth anniversary celebrations of the Chinese CP:

The classic type of revolution in imperialist countries is the October (Russian) Revolution. The classic type of revolution in colonial and semi-colonial countries is the Chinese Revolution.

[5] *Bolshevik*, No. 18, October 1949.
[*] The Cominform organ, *For Lasting Peace, For People's Democracy*, in its December 30, 1949, issue, carried a slightly different version of Liu's speech. After stating what path was followed in China in winning victory, the Cominform version says: "This path is the path of Mao Tse-tung. It *can* also become the main path of the peoples of other colonial and semi-colonial countries . . . *where similar conditions prevail*." (Emphasis added.)
[6] Text of speech in *Mao Tse-tung on the Chinese Revolution*, by Chen Po-ta, Peking, 1953, p. 86.

II

It is not too much to say that Mao and his colleagues felt that
the world was again taking the "Chinese and dogs not permitted"
attitude towards them. No other Communist Party in the world had
come to power after such a long and bitter struggle as theirs. The
East European Communist leaders were in power thanks to Soviet
occupation troops. Yet these were the acknowledged leaders of the
Cominform which was not prepared to admit China. Mao, Liu,
Chou and the others knew that in their final aims they were at
least as orthodox as Stalin, if not more so, yet their Communist
faith was in doubt. Similarly the UN refused to admit China, though
not only such Soviet satellites as Czechoslovakia and Poland had
been UNO members since 1945, but also the Byelorussian SSR and
the Ukrainian SSR, which could scarcely be regarded as more independent of Moscow than the Chinese People's Republic!

"Our nation will never again be an insulted nation. We have stood
up", said Mao on September 21. But as the months passed, it became obvious to him that the outside world was bent on continuing
its insulting attitude towards China. During these months Mao Tse-
tung achieved in China everything he ever dreamed of or planned
for. He was the leader of a united China. His solemn announcements of China's emergence as a great independent nation expressed the intense nationalism of the Chinese people. During the
"hundred flowers" period in 1957, when the Chinese Communist
press printed thousands of bitter denunciations of Mao's régime,
peasants, workers, businessmen, students and professors, and the
leaders of the other parties risked their necks to tell the truth, but
they all stated that in the autumn of 1949, they admired Mao Tse-
tung, as one bringing peace, national greatness, order and new life.

It should be mentioned here that the Political Consultative Conference which founded the People's Republic preserved some façade of democratic coalition. Out of the 142 delegates of political
parties there were sixteen Communists. The Revolutionary Committee of the Kuomintang and the China Democratic League had sixteen delegates each, and many other parties and political groups
were also represented.* Seventy-five specially invited personalities

* China Democratic National Construction Association (12), Non-party
Democrats (10), China Association for Promoting Democracy (8),
China Peasants and Workers Democratic Party (10), Chinese People's
National Salvation Association (10), Three People's Principles Com-

were present headed by Soong Ching Ling, the widow of Sun Yat-sen. This list included all the members of the former Kuomintang peace delegation which had refused to return to Nanking when the Kuomintang government rejected the Communist terms.

Among the Vice-Chairmen of the Central Government elected in 1949 were Soong Ching Ling, the (then) most popular non-Communist personality in China, the Chairman of the Democratic League and the Chairman of the Revolutionary Committee of the Kuomintang. In the absence of elections all this helped to give the impression of nation-wide representation in a real democratic united front.

After decades of war, civil war, chaos and misery, the majority of the people were eager to believe that at last China had achieved peace and unification. Speaking with boundless national pride and arrogance, Mao Tse-tung won the grudging approval of many of his class-opponents in China. His hatred and distrust of the foreigner, and first of all of Anglo-American imperialists, was welcome even to the former right-wingers of the Kuomintang. In this, Mao did not differ greatly from Chiang Kai-shek, whose xenophobia is manifest in his principal work, *China's Destiny*.

Before the establishment of the Republic, Mao Tse-tung made a policy statement which makes many of his later actions in the international field less puzzling. He quoted the maxim of a Sung philosopher: "Apply to anyone the method he has first used on others!" Then he went on to say: "This is what we are doing. That is, to apply to imperialism and its lackeys . . . the same method with which they treated others. Simply this and nothing else!"[7]

For a very short period Mao really was the popular leader of an intensely nationalist, righteous China craving for peace and order. He promised the workers and peasants a better livelihood, the intellectuals and the nationalist middle classes a chance to help in reconstruction, and the former people's enemies a chance to live and work—*after thorough remoulding*. During the mass-celebrations

---

rades Association (10), China Kuomintang Association for Promoting Democracy (8), China New-Democratic Youth League (10), three smaller political groups together (17).

There were 102 delegates from various regions, 60 from the army, 206 delegates from the All-China Federations of Trade Unions, Democratic Women, Democratic Youth, Students' Federations, Artists, Writers, educationalists, natural scientists, social scientists, etc.

[7] Quoted in *China—New Age and New Outlook*, by Professor Ping-chia Kuo, London, 1960, p. 223.

in Tien An Men square, he was not deluded by pride when he felt that he was popular, that he was respected as a tremendously successful war-lord and a great statesman about to realise China's national aspirations.

While United China—so he felt—was acclaiming his leadership, the outside world—Communist and non-Communist alike—withheld recognition. He meant to treat the non-Communist world as it treated China. To the Communist world he and his colleagues wanted to prove that they were better Marxist-Leninists than any other group of leaders. To Stalin and the Russian leaders they were intent on proving that they meant to copy loyally and thoroughly, everything from the theory and practice of Soviet Communism which was at all applicable in China. Subjective feelings had little to do with this. The past and the following decade amply showed that the frictions, intrigues and controversies between Peking and Moscow were meant to be "within-the-family" tensions. Both sides were always careful to avoid an open split in the Communist family. But to dismiss these frictions as *only* family quarrels, is misleading. There are no more burning hatreds than between members of the same family.

When Mao Tse-tung arrived in Moscow on December 16, 1949, he and his Party were not yet recognised as members of this Communist family. After his arrival, Mao made it quite clear that the intended negotiations would take place between the Chinese and Soviet governments, not between the two parties. He made this statement because he had been given to understand that Stalin was not prepared for inter-Party negotiations. It would take too much space to set out the circumstantial evidence to show that while Mao originally wanted Party negotiations, Stalin's willingness to give some degree of international backing to China was only because it was a safely anti-imperialist régime, not because he regarded it as Communist.

Mao was received by Stalin a day after his arrival. The result of the inter-governmental negotiations seems to indicate that Stalin was not very friendly to Mao and his government. The Treaty of Friendship, Alliance and Mutual Assistance, signed on February 14, 1950, was similar in many respects to the Stalin-Chiang treaty of 1945. It was in fact a military alliance in which the contracting parties pledged mutual assistance, not only against Japanese aggression, but also against any other state which might unite with Japan, directly or indirectly, in any act of aggression.

In Manchuria the USSR promised to return Port Arthur, Dairen and the Changchun Railway to China by the end of 1952. This promise was not kept!

Stalin drove a hard bargain. He got Mao to agree to the "independence" of Outer Mongolia, to the separate economic agreements with Manchuria and Sinkiang régimes led by Kao Kang and other Stalinist Communists. In return Mao got political backing as an "anti-imperialist" power and a loan of the monetary value of 300,000,000 US dollars spread over five years. This was less than the USSR had previously lent to the Chiang Kai-shek government. The year before Poland had received a 450,000,000 dollar loan. The Chinese had to pay an annual interest of one per cent on the loan, the value of which was decreased almost at once by about one-fifth, by the revaluation of the rouble on February 28, 1950.[8]

The separate Soviet treaties with Manchuria and Sinkiang were anything but helpful. While Soviet troops were stationed in Port Arthur and Dairen, Kao Kang's Manchurian Regional Government was conspicuously kept apart from the Chinese People's Republic. Manchuria kept its special currency, and its economy was also largely autonomous. In Sinkiang, two mixed Soviet-Sinkiang companies were established for the exploitation of oil and non-ferrous metals. Both the Manchurian and the Sinkiang economic pacts were signed after the departure of Mao and his delegation.

In his farewell speech on February 17, 1950, at the Moscow railway station, Mao said that the treaty would "inevitably bring its influence to bear, not only on the prosperity of the two great countries, China and the Soviet Union, but on the future of humanity and on the victory of world peace and justice". Chinese-Soviet solidarity would "be everlasting, indestructible and inalienable". Molotov spoke later in the same manner but he also pointed out that

After the October Revolution in our country, the victory of the people's liberation movement in China is another tremendous blow against the whole system of imperialism.[9]

So it was not the Communist Party but the "people's liberation movement" that was accorded recognition!

[8] Beloff, op. cit., p. 75.
[9] *Pravda*, March 11, 1950.

III

The Mao Tse-tung of 1949—after these bitter disappointments—
was very like the isolated ruler in the Yenan caves. He could rely
only on his own resources. But these were now tremendous. The
Party apparatus, the army, the great security police network on the
one side, and the absence of any sort of organised military or political opposition on the other, made it possible for him to use as much
naked force as his own prudence and tactical instinct permitted.

In his statement "On the People's Democratic Dictatorship", Mao
said on July 11, 1949:

> We are told: "You are setting up a dictatorship!" Yes, my friend,
> you are right. We are indeed setting up a dictatorship. . . . This
> means that the reactionaries must be deprived of their right to
> express their opinion, and the people alone have the right to vote,
> to express their opinion. . . .
>
> . . . We are told: "You are not benevolent!" Exactly. We defi-
> nitely have no benevolent policies toward the reactionaries or the
> counter-revolutionary activities of the reactionary classes. Our
> benevolent policy does not apply to such deeds or such persons,
> who are outside the ranks of the people; it applies only to the
> people. . . . To hostile classes the state apparatus is an instru-
> ment of oppression, of coercion and not "good will".
>
> . . . *At the present time* the "people" in China are the working
> class, the peasant class, the petty bourgeoisie and the national
> bourgeoisie. These classes have united under the working class
> and the Communist Party in order to form their own State and
> select their own government to establish dictatorship over the
> lackeys of imperialism—the class of landowners and bureaucratic
> capital. . . . These two aspects, democracy among the people
> and dictatorship over the reactionaries, comprise the dictatorship
> of the people's democracy. (Emphasis added.)

In 1950 when Mao Tse-tung and his handful of colleagues set out
to remould China, they had their general blueprint ready for the
next decades. Their statements and actions from 1936 to 1949 show
that after the take-over they envisaged a shorter period of transition
to complete socialist transformation than that of their Soviet model.
This despite the fact that China in 1949 was far more backward in
every respect than the Russia of 1917. The events of 1950-60 show
that in their great hurry and impatience they disregarded even their

own over-ambitious plans and used naked force to speed up the various transitional stages. They were impatient to build up a powerful China with a well-equipped army, securely based on her own heavy industry and with a hardened and disciplined population. They were also impatient to show that they were real Communists and that the Mao Tse-tung way was the way for the Communists of the non-white world. And just as Chiang Kai-shek's annihilation campaigns had forced them to rely entirely upon the countryside, during the next decade their international isolation was to force them to have international ties only with the Soviet orbit and with the revolutionaries of the non-white world. Internationally the coloured peoples were to play the same rôle in Mao's thinking as the peasants had during the preceding decades.

This international position also tended to influence them towards extremist solutions and towards a crudely misinformed and hostile attitude to the outside world.

The first example of this came after the British recognition of China on January 6, 1950.

> H.M.'s Government . . . observing that the Central People's Government of the People's Republic of China is now in effective control of by far the greater part of the territory of China, have this day recognised the government as the *de jure* government of China. In these circumstances H.M.G., in response to Chairman Mao Tse-tung's proclamation of October 1, 1949, are ready to establish diplomatic relations on the basis of equality, mutual benefit, and mutual respect of territory and sovereignty, and are prepared to exchange diplomatic representatives with the Central People's Government.*

Mao's government refused to implement the British recognition by exchanging ambassadors and appointing a Chinese Communist diplomatic mission to London! However, they accepted a British Embassy in Peking, with a large staff headed by a *chargé d'affaires* in the absence of an Ambassador enjoying the usual diplomatic privileges, as well as British consulates in all the main ports. It is of course obvious that this one-sided diplomatic relationship gave Peking no advantages. With a large Chinese Embassy in London, they could have established a propaganda and listening post in

---

* Indian recognition came on December 30, 1949. During the first three months of 1950 the following countries recognised China: Pakistan, Ceylon, Norway, Denmark, Israel, Afghanistan, Finland, Vietnam, Sweden, Switzerland, Holland, Mongolia.

one of the great Western centres. They could also have established Chinese Communist consulates throughout the then British colonial empire from Malaya to Africa, in support of their bid for leadership in the colonial world. They could have impressed Moscow more with their importance; and lastly, by making full use of their diplomatic ties with Britain, they could have attempted to exploit "the contradictions between the British and American capitalists", in the existence of which they so firmly believed.

Instead, Mao Tse-tung chose "to apply to imperialism the same method with which they treated others!" This, of course, was not a rational act, and did not further Chinese Communist aspirations. It was an act of senseless anger. Internally, much was made of the fact that the Chinese People's Republic could "slight" the British imperialists. How illogical all this was, can best be seen from the continued attempts to get Red China admitted to UNO.

Mao could not forgive the world for not trembling after his announcement: "China has stood up". His full fury was turned on those in China who might stand in his way in making *his* China quickly so powerful that the world would be forced to recognise it.

His full fury turned on the Chinese people.

XIV

"TERROR BY FANFARE"

"In reasoning, we must begin by administering a shock and shout-
ing at the patient: 'You are ill!', so that he is frightened into a
sweat, and then we persuade him gently that he needs treatment."
(Mao Tse-tung.)
"Two ways are open to all counter-revolutionaries: the way of death
for those who resist, and the way of life for those who confess. . . .
To confess is better than not to confess."
(Lo Jui-ching, Mao's security chief in 1949.)

Before we can chronicle Mao Tse-tung's development during his
first decade in power, we must establish what in fact happened
during this decade.

In a police state, in which it is mortally dangerous not to show
conspicuous enthusiasm for every order of the régime, the unsus-
pecting foreign visitor is often misled. Personal impressions are of
great value—but not in a country in which even facial expressions
are regimented. This account of developments in the fifties is therefore based mainly on Chinese Communist sources. Much can be
documented from the statements of Mao and his colleagues, from
reports and resolutions of the Party Central Committee and other
Party bureaux, from articles published in the totally controlled Chinese Communist press and from similar sources. This, plus the astonishing material that appeared during the "hundred flowers"
period, gives a sufficiently clear and conclusive answer to the question—what really happened during Mao's first decade in power.[1]

[1] The chronicler wishes to emphasise his indebtedness for being able
to quote Chinese Communist sources to the library of the Royal Society
of International Affairs, Chatham House, London; and to historians
and economists, whose painstaking research helped to fill many gaps,
specially to Mr. Richard L. Walker (*China Under Communism—The
First Five Years*, London, 1956); Robert C. North (*Moscow and the
Chinese Communists*, Stanford, Calif., 1953); Ygael Gluckstein (*Mao's
China—Economic and Political Survey*, London, 1957); Roderick Mac-
Farquhar (ed. *The Hundred Flowers*, London, 1960); last but not
least, to the staff of the American Consulate-General, Hong Kong, for
their immense translation service of all significant articles in Chinese
Communist dailies and magazines.

A war-lord gets used to sending thousands into battle day after day knowing that many will die. For two decades Mao and his chief associates were such war-lords. In 1950, when they set out to remould the Chinese people, they cherished very few illusions. All over the country there were pockets of guerilla resistance. There were millions belonging to the "hostile classes" and their lackeys. Lo Jui-ching, the security-police chief, said in 1949 that resistance to Communism "lay not in the rifles of the guerillas, but in millions of hearts". Hence came the later battle slogan: "Surrender your hearts!" The country was taught that "politics took command". Political war was declared against all those who resisted or were liable to resist remoulding. It was planned according to Mao Tse-tung's teachings on tactics and strategy.

A grand strategical plan was formulated by which resistance would be beaten stage by stage through a series of large-scale offensives, until in the end Mao's ideal state would be established. Each offensive had its detailed tactical plan; to each stage a certain time limit was set in advance. The tactical principles were still those promulgated years ago by Mao: *capitalise on contradictions to win over the majority, oppose the minority and crush your enemies separately.*

But in this case the enemies were the various classes, segments and age-groups of the Chinese people.

The Chinese Communists knew the security-police system evolved by Stalin. Mao perfected the system and applied it to Chinese conditions. As a writer equally conversant with the language of the peasants, the workers and the intellectuals, he perfected his technique of producing effective battle-cries, stimulating catch phrases, general slogans and brutally simple "Party-demands".

With his perfected Pavlovian shock-tactics, he sought to disorganise the psychological defences of the entire Chinese people. By mixing promises of a quieter and easier life with threats of forced labour, prison or execution; by allowing a state of high tension to alternate irregularly with reassuring relaxation, the Chinese people (weakened by insufficient food and sleep and too much hard work) were kept in a constant state of near-hysteria.

This was the strategy of "no political rest". This was the strategy of "no rest at all" or, in Mao's terminology, the strategy of "uninterrupted revolution". The main weapons of its realisation were as follows: new movements, campaigns, drives; new slogans; the sudden announcement of great crimes committed by counter-revolutionaries or foreign imperialists, necessitating a new campaign of hate, vigilance, or longer working hours; the purges, the rectification and remoulding campaigns; the constant reorganisations; the economic plans and the declarations that they must be speeded up; the voluntary movements to give up your farm, your factory or your scientific convictions; the upsurges and high tides; the ever-changing new eras —a hundred flowers blooming, poisonous weeds being annihilated; kill the flies, the sparrows, the rats, the dogs; kill the people's enemies; the constant redefinition of "the people". . . .

La Rochefoucauld said: "A man is like a rabbit, you can catch him by the ears." In the morning, when the loudspeakers at every street corner blared out their string of slogans, the words caught the Chinese people by their ears. Everybody had to learn these strange new words which meant life or death. More and more words in this new Chinese language triggered off instant reactions of fear and terror.

The decade started with promises and reassurances. The workers were told they were the most advanced class, the vanguard of the revolution. Their exploitation was over. The leaders of New China would be recruited from their ranks. The poor peasants were given land, the title deeds presented to them with ceremonial fanfare. The intellectuals, the businessmen, the "national bourgeoisie", were reassured that all true democrats would be given a chance to take part in the building of New China. Members of the "hostile classes" were told that with the exception of incorrigible criminals among their ranks, they would all have a chance to cleanse themselves through honest work so that, at some time in the future, they could be admitted into the ranks of "the people".

Hopes were raised. People dared to hope because the war and the civil war were certainly over.

And then the shock treatment started.

I

When on June 30, 1950, the Land Reform Law was promulgated, most of China had already heard alarming news about it from Manchuria, North China, where the campaign was nearly over. The land reform not only implied the confiscation of estates of "landlords" with everything found on them; it was also a "struggle against the landlords", a concentrated drive to punish the "bad landlords" and other rural reactionaries.

In his June 6, 1950, report to the Central Committee Mao outlined the tactics of the land-reform movement. This was to be a class-struggle against the landlords, *who formed about eight per cent of the rural population!* In order to isolate the landlords, the rich and middle peasants were to be left alone for the time being.

On the completion of the campaign, it was officially reported that 450 million people had been examined. With Mao's eight per cent as a basis—and the Chairman's word was already law—there were about thirty-four million "landlords" in China, several in every village.* Although there were variations according to districts, any better-off peasant was in danger of being branded a landlord if he had more than nine acres of land. Even less than nine acres was dangerous if he had family ties with "landlord elements", was against the Communists, engaged in small trading, or had earned the hatred of this or that poor peasant. The formal instruction on "How to Analyse Class Status In the Countryside" were rather vague; and the friends, "lackeys" and political followers of local landlords were also dealt with.

Three hundred thousand Communist cadres were trained to unleash the "tornado of peasant revolution" all over China; for the land reform was meant to be exactly this. Apart from the new instructions, these cadres prepared for their work by studying Mao's famous report on the Hunan peasant revolt written in 1927. This document, which challenged Communist orthodoxy at that time, became one of the sources of the new Maoist orthodoxy. The Chairman, in giving instructions for his great land reform, evidently hoped that the scenes which had left such a deep impression on him in 1927 would be repeated in every village of China in 1950. Mao wrote in 1927 that the peasants do not "allow the landlords to have their say and make a clean sweep of all their prestige. This is tantamount to trampling the landlords underfoot after knocking them down." The cadres, as we shall see, prompted the peasants to do exactly this. Mao had written, nearly twenty-five years earlier, that "scores or at least a few . . . notorious local bullies and bad gentry are to be found in every county, and the only effective way of suppressing the reactionaries is to execute in *every county* at least those of them whose crimes . . . are most serious." . . . According to the Agrarian Reform Law of 1950 (Article 32):

A people's tribunal shall be set up in every county in the course of agrarian reform to ensure that it is carried out. This tribunal

* The Communist functionaries (cadres), who carried out the land reform, did not want to risk being denounced as "soft-rightwingers", by finding less than eight per cent landlords in every village.

shall travel to different places and try and punish, according to law, hated despotic elements who have committed hideous crimes, whom the masses of people demand to be brought to justice, and all such persons who resist or violate the provisions of the Agrarian Reform Law or decrees.

The law assumed that there were hated, despotic elements in *every* village. The tribunals could sentence people to prison or to death, and death sentences approved by the people were to be carried out on the spot.

The Party cadres moved from village to village. Each village was sealed off for the duration of the campaign. The peasants were told that everyone's property in land, animals, farm implements, money, stored grain, etc., had to be listed. The people were to be classified. Rich and middle peasants could keep their "surplus land", but that of the landlords was to be confiscated and given to the poor peasants. According to law, the "non-criminal landlords" were to be left as much land as the average poor peasant received. By this law, Mao made doubly sure of real class struggle in the villages. It was naturally in the interests of the poor peasants that there should be plenty of "landlord land". The more "criminal landlords" there were to be executed, or imprisoned and totally expropriated, the more land for them.

While the lists were being compiled and argued over, the cadres had to ferret out hatreds, frictions and jealousies in the village. The poor peasants were summoned to denounce, at first privately, the landlords, usurers, former usurers and "bad reactionary elements". Everyone in the village was visited and encouraged to "speak bitter". Later, smaller impromptu accusation meetings were held. People were given a chance to denounce their personal enemies, cantankerous old gossips "to wag their tongues". The peasants were lectured about the crimes of the landlord class. The classification lists were prepared, shown, corrected. People were prompted to quarrel. Those rich, middle or poor peasants who disliked this unleashing of hate and jealousy, were admonished for their reactionary sentiments. As the atmosphere of hatred, fear, suspicion and tension deepened, preparations were started for the mass-trial.

At the climax of the campaign the judges arrived, the People's Tribunal was organised, and a mass-meeting was called. The presiding judge solemnly declared that hated despotic elements and those whom the people wanted to see punished would presently be tried. If the peasants did not speak up, or failed to shout down the defence of those who protested that they were not landlords, the Communist cadres intervened:

> We are instructed by our leaders to scatter among the crowd at the meeting. Our tasks are: when the peasants are at a loss how to argue with the landlord, we should give the peasants some ideas how to speak up: when the peasants become incensed and want to resort to rough measures, we should exhort them to be calm.[2]

The Land Reform Law itself warned against *indiscriminate* beating or killing of people, and the Peking *People's Daily*, in its July 21, 1950, editorial, also warned that, though the peasants understandably hated the landlords, this feeling "must not be allowed to take its natural course, or it will lead to indiscriminate beating and killings". The cadres were themselves the unwitting victims of the psychological warfare unleashed by their leaders. They were first taught to exploit the land-greed of the poor peasants and fan their hatred for the landlords; to prepare carefully for "accusation meetings" and for the grand session of the People's Tribunal, and then they were asked to prompt the masses, when they were too soft, but control them when they were in too violent a mood. This was of course impossible, as the leaders well knew. As in lynchings, the public trials also bred anxiety and a feeling of guilt in all participants, passive or active alike.

There were many reports of mass-executions in the villages in the Communist dailies. In 1950, when the campaign was just starting in most of China, books and pamphlets appeared describing the mass-executions. One of these, written by Hsiao Ch'ien was esteemed so highly that the Foreign Language Press of Peking published it in English translation in 1951. The following account is taken from it:

> With raised fists, the audience below shouted in one voice: "Down with reactionary landlords!" . . . "Down with criminal landlords who hide and disperse their properties!"
>
> . . . It had started raining. . . . By four o'clock over twenty peasants had poured out their grievances from the platform. Mass sentiment surged to boiling point. . . . Not one person left or took shelter in spite of the terrific downpour. . . .

[2] Feng Yu-lan, "Lessons of My Participation in the Land Reform", *Hsüeh-hsi* (Study) Peking, April 1, 1950.

"Peasant comrades," the Judge's voice was grave. "We have just heard some of the accusations made by the local peasants. From these . . . it ought to be clear to everyone how the *landlord class* has always worked hand in glove with the enemy of the peasants . . . to oppress the peasants themselves. The same motive has prompted them to act as fawning lackeys to American imperialism, since American imperialism is directly opposite to the people's interests too . . ."

"Our verdict on the three criminal landlords . . . death . . . death. . . . Do you all agree?"

The sound of applause that came from below the platform was deafening. . . . The prisoners were escorted to the graveyard south of the temple. From the back of the graveyard came the sound of several shots. . . . Sighs of relief were heard as justice was meted out to the convicted.

"Down with reactionary landlords!"

"Long Live the Communist Party!"

"Long Live Chairman Mao Tse-tung!"[3]

The documentation of this period is made easy by Mao's policy of "terror with fanfare". In December 1950 and January 1951 the Peking *People's Daily* and other newspapers all over the country urged the cadres to explain to the "backward peasants" that suicide was a "reactionary and illegal activity". The cadres were warned against "warm-feelingism" (the official term for bourgeois sentimentality) which makes one pity the enemy. Some cadres were arrested and their cases widely publicised as a warning not to be too soft on the landlords. Other cadres got into trouble because they tried to leave the land-reform campaign and get employment in the cities. In the villages, the cadres had to publicise the doctrine that class status is hereditary and that, consequently, children of landlords and other reactionary elements had to work their passage home into the ranks of the people by denouncing their parents. (See below: denunciation movement.)

As soon as the mass-trial was over, the cadres called for meetings in celebration of the victorious land reform. The villages had to be decorated, feasts prepared. At these meetings, the poor peasants were solemnly and ceremoniously given the deeds of their newly won lands which were to be theirs for the next long period of

[3] Hsiao Ch'ien, *How the Tillers Win Back Their Land*, pp. 74-80. (Emphasis added.)

transition. The local activists thanked Chairman Mao and the Communist Party for the land.

A few days or weeks later, however, it turned out that *new counter-revolutionaries had turned up among the poor peasants*. All China learnt about a poor hired farm labourer, Liu Ssu-hsi, who became the symbol of the "backward, selfish, conservative, complacent and politically shortsighted peasants".

His case was described and used to start an all-China campaign by the central theoretical organ of the Party, *Hsüeh-hsi* (Study) in its September 16, 1951 issue:

Liu Ssu-hsi . . . has worked for over ten years and all the time suffered bitter hardship. Only after liberation did he marry and have a son. During land reform he was extremely active, and was elected secretary of the youth corps branch. But after he had obtained land, he did not want to go on working but wanted to go home *to devote himself solely to production*. When the cadres admonished him, he cried out with passion: "All my life I suffered hardship and had no land. Now I have land and am completely satisfied. Why still carry on revolution? What for?"

There were nation-wide campaigns against "Liu Ssu-hsiism", against peasants who said that after living so long in unrest, they would now like to be left in peace. This was not to be. Shock after shock came in quick succession. There was the land-reform-re-examination campaign. This too started in the north in the "old liberated territories". It was found that even in the close vicinity of Peking, where government control was more effective, a large percentage of people had been "erroneously classified". In three villages for instance where twenty-six families were expropriated and tried "only four families were landlords (one family came under the heading of despotic landlord), while the rest consisted of four families of rich peasants and eighteen families of middle peasants".[4] Summaries were never published for the whole of China, but according to a report on 124 counties (out of over 2,000 counties in China) the People's Courts had to deal with 143,761 cases of wrong classification between November 1950 and April 1951.[5]

The re-examination campaign unleashed a new wave of unrest, quarrels, bitterness and fear in the villages. Poor peasants had to

[4] "General Report of Peking Municipal People's Government on Agrarian Reform in Peking Suburban Areas", Peking, November 21, 1951. Quoted by Ygael Gluckstein, *Mao's China*, London, 1951, p. 92.
[5] *NCNA*, Peking, November 14, 1951, quoted by Gluckstein, op. cit.

give land back to wrongly expropriated rich and middle peasants. The rest of the confiscated land had to be redistributed, each poor peasant receiving less. In view of the fact that by this time Mao had already ordered a campaign of enlightenment in the country-side with the aim of preparing the peasants for the transition to agricultural co-operatives, the re-examination campaign seemed to be pointless at that time. It seemed to be even more so, when it turned out that the indefinite period for individual ownership of land was not to be reckoned in decades, but in years.

The peasants who had helped Mao to power were also exposed to a great many other campaigns in the period 1950-2. The mass-accusations in the villages had come to stay. The various drives, movements and campaigns which mainly hit the urban population were not without their effect in the countryside.

As with all other mass-drives, the campaign to suppress counter-revolutionaries and reactionary elements started a long time before Mao Tse-tung promulgated the extremely severe "Regulations for the Punishment of Counter-revolutionaries" on February 21, 1951. In Manchuria, and North China, the campaign had been waged since 1948-9. In July 1950 the Government Administrative Council issued instructions to the effect that counter-revolutionaries sentenced to death had no right of appeal.

China was divided into six large administrative regions. The chairmen of the Administrative Councils of four of these reported that 1,176,000 counter-revolutionaries were liquidated between October 1949 and October 1950.[6] This was *before* the great campaign was unleashed! And some months later Mao warned that the courts should stop "showing boundless magnanimity" to counter-revolutionaries.

The 1951 February regulations made it possible to sentence people to death for "conducting counter-revolutionary propaganda and agitation, fabricating and spreading rumours, alienating and splitting the solidarity between the Government and the nationalities, democratic classes and groups". The fact that one could be executed for spreading rumours would not perhaps have conditioned everybody into total outward conformity with the régime had not these executions been carried out "with a fanfare". All over China "accusation mass-meetings"* were organised, public trials and public executions staged.

[6] The Chairmen's reports, in *CB* 39.
* One of the Current Affairs Handbooks (No. 12, April 5, 1951, Peking), had this title, *How to Hold An Accusation Meeting*.

The first widely publicised mass-trial was held in the Peking Central Park on March 24, 1951. The accusations lasted for five hours, then the Mayor of Peking, who presided, asked the multitude:

"Comrades, what should we do with all the criminals, bandits, secret agents, evil landlords, heads and organisers of reactionary Taoist sects?"

". . . Shoot them!" . . . "Should we have mercy on them?" . . . "No! No!". . . .

". . . We are here representing the people," concluded the mayor. "It is our duty to do the will of the people. We suppress the counter-revolutionaries. This act we perform according to the law. Those who have to be killed, we kill. In cases where we could kill or not, we do not kill. But when it has to be killing, we kill. . . . Now you all want them *suppressed*. Tomorrow the Court will pronounce judgment and they will be executed."

This is taken from the report published in the Peking *People's Daily* of March 25, 1951. Next day the same paper reported that the executions outside the city walls were witnessed by masses of people and were broadcast over Peking Radio Station.

The newspapers of Shanghai, Nanking, Canton, Tientsin and other large cities of China carried similar reports during the following days. Everywhere the executions were broadcast; loud-speakers were installed at street-corners, in public squares, in factories, everywhere, so that the masses should know what was afoot. In Shanghai, the Bund on the Whangpoo River was roped off, roofs of tall buildings were guarded day and night to prevent attempts at suicide and people hardly dared to walk on pavements near the tall buildings for fear of falling bodies.

The army, while annihilating the last remnants of the Kuomintang troops in China, dealt also with war-criminals, collaborationists, former Kuomintang security men, gendarmes and the like. In addition it had to liquidate bandits. On September 23, 1951, *NCNA* reported from Peking:

Apart from annihilating the Kuomintang troops, the People's Liberation Army has wiped out more than one million bandits in the past two years.

And the Minister of Finance, Po I-po, wrote: "In the past three years we have liquidated more than two million bandits. Counter-revolutionaries and secret agents have also been put under control and custody."[7]

The Peking *People's Daily,* published on October 11, 1951, one of the most revealing and important documents of the period. The Minister of State Security, Lo Jui-ching, proudly reported in a signed article that the overwhelming majority of the Chinese population was "educated" by witnessing public executions:

> According to the Public Security Bureau of Peking, a total of 29,626 [mass-accusation] meetings were held in Peking with an aggregate attendance figure of more than 3,379,000. In the period ranging from March to July, 21,400 mass meetings were held in Tientsin with an aggregate attendance figure of 2,200,000. . . . According to incomplete figures covering the eight administrative areas and four municipalities of Hopei, 653 trial and accusation meetings had been held with more than 3,900,000 people attending . . . more than 60 per cent of the population of the Central-South region, more than 70 per cent of the population of Fukien Province, and more than 80 per cent of the population of Nanking have *all been subjected to this education.* (Emphasis added.)

It is of course terribly and tragically important whether "only" two million people were executed up to October 1952, as Mao's minister would have it, or fourteen million as the Free Trade Union Council of the AFL estimated on the basis of various provincial and regional reports. But psychologically even the official Communist figure is staggering, as the régime took good care that the majority of the population should be "subjected to this education", that is, to watching executions or hearing over loudspeakers delirious crowds roaring "shoot! shoot! shoot! . . . kill! kill! kill!"—to be followed by the sound of dozens of rifles spitting death.

Education by terror, discipline by terror, production by terror! The Minister of State Security reported in the same article that millions of lesser criminals were being sentenced to forced labour. He wrote:

> The subjection of counter-revolutionaries to forced labour is an indispensable means for the liquidation of the counter-revolutionary class, as well as a basic policy for the thorough reform of the culprits into new human beings. . . . It is up to *all levels of people's government* and *various people's public security organs*

---

[7] *New China's Economic Achievements 1949-52,* Peking, 1952, p. 152.

to pay adequate attention to . . . this aspect of work, which is possessed of the *greatest political and economic importance.* . . . Compulsory labour will produce wealth for the government.[8]

Mao's government did not publish overall figures of people doing forced labour at various times. From diverse Communist reports, however, we can form a rough idea of the numbers involved. The Ministry of Water Conservancy reported in October 1952 that "in the past two years 10,370,000 conscripted workers participated in water conservancy work throughout China under the supervision of 320,000 armed police."[9]

Article 31 of the "Regulations Governing Labour Service for Reform" states:

Production of labour service for reform shall be subject to the unified leadership of the committees of financial and economic affairs of the People's Governments at *all levels,* and also to concrete guidance by the relevant agricultural-forestry, industrial, financial, communications, water conservancy, and commercial departments.[10]

On the same day, the *People's Daily,* in an editorial comment, emphasised that eighty-three per cent of the forced labourers took part in "agricultural or industrial production, or have been organised into various engineering corps for the felling of trees, construction of buildings, restoration and construction of conservancy works and the building of railways and roads."

If water conservancy took up more than ten million forced labourers, it is easy to estimate that the equally or even more urgently necessary road and railway buildings and all the other branches of agricultural and industrial production took many tens of millions more. *People's China*[11] reported for instance that in 1951-2 a total of 4,600,000 workers and peasant "volunteers" worked on the project to harness the Huai River. They dug the equivalent of two Panama Canals or one Suez.

The tens of millions of forced labourers spent their nights in concentration camps. There was hardly a county in China without one.

[8] *PD,* October 11, 1951. (Emphasis added.)
[9] *FEER,* October 30, 1952, p. 572, quoted by Walker, op. cit.
[10] *PD,* September 7, 1954.
[11] Peking, February 1, 1953, pp. 13-15.

II

By this time, Mao's cult had started to surpass the adulation Stalin accorded himself. The public appearances of the Chairman were theatrically magnificent. In 1952, the newspaper *Ta Kung Pao* printed an article by a "model worker" who was honoured by an invitation to a banquet given by Mao Tse-tung:

> We walked into the Faijen Palace of royal splendour. The dining hall was beautifully furnished and decorated. Food was plentiful and lavish. With a great number of red candles in gold candelabras, the hall was as bright as sunshine. Fresh flowers were abundant. Waiters clad in white moved to and fro. . . . Suddenly music started. Everyone applauded. Chairman Mao entered the hall! When the clapping died down, Chairman Mao drank a toast. We all emptied our cups. Cameras flashed . . . Chairman Mao stood in the centre of the platform . . . he looked strong and healthy . . . I stared at him: his green uniform, his dark hair, his stout figure, his benign smile.
>
> Then there were shouts: "May Chairman Mao live ten thousand years" and the banquet began.

China Youth, the official organ of the Young Communist League published on February 20, 1953, an article on a surprise visit of Mao to a ship. Mao appears:

> . . . a fatherly smile on his face, looking at us with his saintly eyes, that had the warmth of the sun. . . . The comrades were overwhelmed with joyous surprise . . . their eyes began to get wet as they looked at their respected leader.

Similar articles by the hundreds showed how overwhelmed with love and adoration the people were whenever they set their eyes on "the sun that never sets". Of the hundreds of odes to and poems about Mao Tse-tung that were published in this period, one stands out especially. It was written in 1952 by a famous poet, Hu Feng:

> . . . *Mao Tse-tung*
> *Standing erect on the mountain's topmost peak*
> *Looks like one turning to himself and to the world,*
> *announcing:* . . .
> *High over the sea*

Would I be magnified—
Magnified that I may be able to embrace the whole world—
Magnified that I may be able to flow into eternity. . . .

By a curious sequence of events, we know from Mao's press how
Hu Feng really felt about the Chairman some time after he wrote
this poem. During the purge among intellectuals, Hu Feng was arrested in 1955 as an anti-Party criminal. The Chinese press
launched a violent campaign against him, and the Peking *People's
Daily* published excerpts of his private letters which the Security
Police had found in the flats of his friends. One of these letters Hu
Feng wrote in 1952 not long after the quoted poem. It appears
that Hu Feng was ordered by the Party to write a commemorative
article on Mao's celebrated Yenan lecture on literature delivered in
1942. Hu Feng—still in jail in 1961—wrote in 1952:

I have tried to gather material to support Mao's Yenan address.
. . . Before I started, I felt disgust at the work. After I had set to
work, I could not help crying. *How came there to be such an
imbecile, such a rotten beast?* . . . Mao's address is essentially not
realism, I now feel it won't do. Under present circumstances, it is
liable to kill people.[12]

During the "hundred flowers" period the Chinese press published
many similar demonstrations of the fact that by 1952 Mao's popularity was swiftly disappearing and that there were some people
in almost every city of China who detested the great leader. Discerning observers could not help seeing Mao's hand in all those
drives and campaigns which intensified bureaucratic despotism. The
campaigns were always launched by copious quotations from Mao's
earlier works, showing that it was he who planned and directed
everything. No one could pretend that the general developments
were not in harmony with "Mao Tse-tung thinking". Although the
Chairman interfered from time to time to stop "excesses", it was
obvious to a growing number of people in China that these excesses
were caused by Mao's impatience to have China remoulded.

Mao was quoted when a *denunciation drive* (officially so named
by Mao's authorities) was started all over China, concurrently with
the campaigns against landlords and counter-revolutionaries.

---

[12] *PD*, May 13, 1955. (Emphasis added.) On this date and on May 24
and June 10 *PD* published excerpts of 169 Hu Feng letters.

During the denunciation movement, many instances . . . occurred of counter-revolutionaries being denounced by their family members and relatives.[13]

The *Current Affairs Handbook* for popularising the Party line in its February 25, 1952, issue published an appeal to women to denounce their relatives:

Sisters, if your own father, brother, husband or child has committed any of the above-mentioned crimes, you must rid yourselves of any scruples and courageously prevail on them to confess or you must report them. . . . Everybody must understand that it is a glorious thing to induce your own relatives to confess or to report your own relations, the only shameful thing is to protect them.

China Youth encouraged young people to denounce their relatives. In its May 8, 1951, issue the paper published the open letter of denunciation written by a student girl:

Lu Hsu, when I write out this stinking name of yours, I feel ashamed and intolerably insulted. In the past I looked upon you as my father, but now I have seen your true face. . . ."

The press published accounts of model children who demanded the execution of their father; and the imprisonment of fathers, mothers, sisters, brothers for *not having denounced their next-of-kin.*

A campaign was started to eradicate bourgeois attitudes to parents, teachers and elder people. Private bourgeois love was to be replaced by the *Five Loves:* love for the fatherland, the people, labour, science and public property. The drive was not yet directed against such bourgeois sentiments as love between parents and children, and between people of opposite sex, so long as it did not go to the excess of "warm-feelingism".

The Five Loves were supposed to prompt people to take part in the patriotic emulation drives, to buy State Saving bonds, to donate money to the Aid Korea campaign.

[13] *NCNA*, Mukden, June 4, 1931.
* The *NCNA* reported from Nanking (June 1, 1951) the names of model children demanding the death sentence for their father. The Chungking *New China Daily* (October 2, 1952), reported with satisfaction that 134 Youth League members had denounced their fathers, elder brothers, uncles and other relatives for "unlawful behaviour" during a local campaign against "bourgeois" individuals.

This period also witnessed several specific purges, drives and
other movements. The drive to establish Party control over art and
literature started in May 1951,* when the Central Committee attacked an "erroneous" film. In September 1951 the "Ideological
Remoulding Movement" was started on a nation-wide scale. Intellectuals were organised into meetings for discussion, thought-
cleansing, thought revelation; they had to attend "criticism and self-
criticism" sessions, confess their deviations and "cut themselves
away" from bourgeois ideology.

October-December 1951 saw the start of the "Three-Anti" and
the "Five-Anti" movements. The "Three-Anti" campaign was directed against "Corruption, waste and bureaucratism" and aimed at
eliminating wavering Communists, and administrative and judicial
personnel carried over from Kuomintang times. The "Five-Anti"
drive was against "Bribery, tax evasion, fraud, theft of State property, and divulging State economic secrets". This was directed
against businessmen, merchants, employees and better-off members
of the middle classes.

The small and middle capitalists were repeatedly promised safety
by Mao in 1949. One of the 1950 May Day slogans was: "Members of the Chinese working class! Consolidate your ranks and unite
with the national bourgeoisie!"

These promises and tactics proved effective. The owners of small
and medium industrial or commercial enterprises were hopeful that
for a long time to come they were going to be able to work and
prosper in peace. This was not to be. The cadres conducting the
Five-Anti campaign descended on their factories, shops or offices,
encouraged workers and employees to "speak bitter", to expose
cases of bribery, tax evasion, fraud, etc.

The Five-Anti campaign led to the expropriation of thousands
of "criminal capitalists". In 1950 the State owned an estimated
twenty-three per cent of the retail trade, for instance. This grew
to thirty-two per cent by the end of 1952 and to eighty-two per
cent by 1955.[14] This is not surprising, since Minister of Finance,
Po I-po reported that out of 450,000 private industrial and commercial enterprises investigated, seventy-six per cent were found
guilty of various illegal actions.[15]

* See chap. XVI below.
[14] Bulletins by the State Statistical Bureau, Peking, and the last figure
reported by *NCNA*, Peking, June 14, 1956.
[15] *New China's Economic Achievements*, pp. 152-3.

The Three-Anti and Five-Anti campaigns were carried out through a long series of accusation meetings and public trials. Hundreds of thousands of middle-class people were arrested, including "opportunists of middle-class origin", who had "wormed their way into the Communist Party". These two campaigns lasted through 1952.

1950 was the first year of the Resist America and Aid Korea campaigns, culminating in the formal establishment of the Chinese People's Volunteer Army in Korea. During 1950-2 this campaign served to intensify all the other campaigns, increase vigilance against spies and counter-revolutionaries and underline the necessity for harder work and a more austere life. Food rationing was introduced in many provinces. In "Aid of Korea" there was the campaign for "voluntary" contribution of money and unpaid overtime work.

The workers—"the leadership class of Chinese society"—had their shock treatment too. The Provisional Procedure for Settlement of Labour-Capital Disputes[16] outlawed strikes for workers in *capitalist-owned industries* too. To strike in State-owned factories was of course banned as a crime against New China.

In 1952 the trade unions were purged of those officials who were alleged to be inspired by the ideology of "bourgeois trade unionism" and by "tailism" (being "on the tail of the workers", i.e. led by workers) and of those who had committed "mistakes of economist and syndicalist tendencies". (Economism: too much preoccupation with the welfare of the workers; syndicalism: too much insistence on workers' rights.)

Hsu Chih-chen in presenting the new Constitution of the T.U. Federation said that, while in the past it had been the task of the trade unions "to wage legal and economic struggle" in order to overthrow capitalism, this was no longer the case. To follow the same policy of economic struggle, Hsu said, would be "to oppose the working-class régime led by the working class itself."

The immediate and sectional interests of the working class must be subordinated to the long-term and overall interests of the State, that is, *the interests of the State led by the working class.*[17]

"Struggle meetings" were organised during which cadres turned their onslaught against workers who failed to understand that

[16] *NCNA*, Shanghai, September 7, 1949.
[17] *The Seventh All-China Congress of Trade Unions*, Peking, 1953, pp. 52-54. (Emphasis added.)

strikes and labour discontent, though permissible and necessary in capitalist states, are impermissible and unnecessary in a socialist state. In 1953 a new campaign was started against "excessive slackness in labour discipline". In 1953 Workers' Courts were set up in the likeness of People's Tribunals but with additional powers. This meant in effect that the Party secretary and security official of the factory or mine pronounced final sentences without any right of appeal. The August 12, 1953, issue of the Peking *Daily Worker* exposed "some cadres" who were beating and torturing workers in the factories, and added:

> It must be made clear that, in the work of strengthening labour discipline, we must determinedly prevent the occurrence of this method of punishment, but this does not mean that the adoption of necessary punishment measures is rejected.

By this time, China had learnt the "some cadres" technique. In Mao's China, as in Stalin's Russia, the great leader and "the Party" never made mistakes. Difficulties were always due to enemy agents, reactionary saboteurs, or too slack or over zealous minor officials, the "some cadres" or "some comrades" mentioned in the reprimands.

The cadres themselves had their difficulties. They had to carry out their instructions on pain of arrest or worse. Hence, one of the endemic diseases of the Chinese CP throughout the 1950-60 decade: "commandism". Instead of "patiently explaining" to the workers that they should accept less wages for more work, they simply "commanded" and tortured or beat up those who resisted. In the early days of the decade the workers had not learnt what the word "voluntary" really means in the Party language. Some believed it was up to them to volunteer or not to volunteer. Hence commandism and beating.

The workers were paid on the basis of the piecework system, with severe "norms", or labour quotes. These were constantly raised, i.e. workers had to produce more for the same wages. Soon it turned out that

> some comrades are afraid of discussing with the workers the elevation of existing norms for they consider existing norms very high already. Such a conservative view of norms is not the Marxist view. Norms always go forward. Norms which are advanced today may possibly become backward ones tomorrow.[18]

[18] *NCNA*, Shanghai, December 14, 1953.

Norms had to be raised constantly in order to raise productivity. This was difficult because of the need for an exceedingly large bureaucracy to exercise control over the workers. As each citizen in Mao's China has to carry an internal passport; as the workers have to have their own workers' cards; as a change of job requires a permit; as the government and Party offices and the various planning bureaux demand a large number of reports—the managerial staff in the factories and mines grew tremendously. The security police and the Party cadres and personnel departments also have their representatives in the management. The result is a bureaucratic elephantiasis. Already by 1954 this had grown to such an alarming degree that the Peking *People's Daily* (March 11, 1954) had to issue a general warning.

The paper commented in its editorial on a sample survey of 195 factories. *In 138 of these the managerial staff was from twenty to fifty per cent of the number of workers,* in fifty factories the percentage was between ten and twenty and only in seven factories was it less than ten per cent.

Privately-owned industry had to be abolished for the simple reason, among others, that these factories were more efficiently run and required far fewer bureaucrats; hence they could pay better wages. It was the gravest insult to the régime when workers from State-owned and Communist-run factories streamed to the "last remnants of capitalism". The Shanghai *Liberation Daily* attacked private industrialists for luring away skilled workers from State-owned factories. The attack ended with the remark that "employees and workers accepted new offers chiefly because they wanted better wages and welfare provisions."[19]

For years the Party press attacked the private capitalists for paying better wages to workers. Some factory owners were sent to jail for this offence. Enticing workers by offering them better pay was called hijacking.* At the same time the private capitalists were constantly denounced for exploiting the workers.

The inherent characteristic of the bourgeois class is to make money through the exploitation of the working class. . . . Instead

[19] *Liberation Daily,* October 11, 1951.
* *Ta Kung Pao,* Tientsin, June 11, 1954, reported that the "profiteer Tsou Shu Tang, proprietor of the Chunghua Auto Repair Shop enticed seven workers from the State-owned Auto Repair Plant, who entered his shop through the back door so as not to be seen. His sentence: three years."

of resting content with legitimate profits, they seek excessive profits, they undermine the progress of the economy of the State enterprises, and thus undermine the Common Programme.[20]

Thus, private capitalists went on to seek excessive profits, and exploited the working class *by paying higher wages than the State, and selling at lower prices than the State.*

The secretary of the New Democratic Youth League complained about capitalist competition:

In private enterprises, lawless capitalists are trying to disintegrate the working class by bribing and enticing their workers with higher wages, increased welfare benefits and various corrupt bourgeois ways of living.[21]

And finally, when the time came for the State take-over in the form of "joint State-private" enterprises, the workers had to be reprimanded editorially by the *People's Daily* for disliking the idea of "socialist" ownership:

There are some office employees and workers of private enterprises, who, *receiving higher wages and better amenities in private enterprises,* are afraid of reduction in wages and amenities and afraid of the rigorous labour discipline after the private enterprises have come under joint operation. Consequently, their attitude is not active enough towards joint public-private operation. These office employees and workers mainly lack the collective idea of the working class; they cannot see the collective and long-range interests of the working class for their immediate and insignificant interests.[22]

As to the working hours in State-owned enterprises, an article in the Peking *Daily Worker* (May 27, 1955) gives some idea:

There has been no limit to the prolongation of working hours, individual workers have worked continuously for 72 hours through additional shifts and working hours. . . . As a result of exhaustion, sickness and casualties have been serious. There are quite a few cases in which owing to exhaustion, workers have fainted, vomited blood or even died.[23]

[20] Editorial, "Refuting the Ridiculous Views of the Bourgeois Class", *Hsüeh-hsi* (Study), March 1, 1952.
[21] *China Youth*, November 1, 1954.
[22] *PD*, January 17, 1956. (Emphasis added.)
[23] Quoted by Gluckstein, *Mao's China*, p. 275.

"Struggle meetings" were at first organised only against anti-people elements but soon workers were also being victimised by such meetings. The Peking *Daily Worker* wrote on January 21, 1955:

A few enterprises even held struggle meetings against workers who were injured while performing public duties, demanding that the workers confess how they were injured and allowing them to give only subjective and not objective causes.

. . . production accidents are frequent in many enterprises . . . some units, instead of investigating and analysing the causes of accidents, frequently shifted the blame to the workers and penalised workers without checking up the responsibility of the leadership, without rectifying matters.[24]

III

All this was not terror for the sake of terror.

It was simply a great shock administered to the patient to frighten him with his illness so that he should accept the cure without a murmur. Mao's speeches and actions during this period show that his first preoccupation was with production. He stated at the outset, in 1949, that the damage wrought by war and civil war had to be repaired in the next three years, so as to make the country ready for the first Five Year Plan of "national construction". His preoccupation was with national economy:

Some of the things we are familiar with will be laid aside, and we will be compelled to tackle things with which we are not familiar. This means difficulties. The imperialists count upon our not handling our economic problems well. They stand on the side-lines and wait for our failure.[25]

To restore the economy in a *Communist* manner was also most important in order to impress Stalin and his followers, who—if they were not standing on the side-lines awaiting Mao's failure—certainly acted as if they would be pleased to hand over the direction of affairs in China to Mao's arch-rival of the day, Kao Kang.

Mao's attitude to economic plans—as to all other problems under the sun—was that of a warrior. Two of his definitions are relevant in this context:

[24] Quoted by Gluckstein, p. 278.
[25] *On People's Democratic Dictatorship*, pp. 24-25.

"Social science is knowledge of the class struggle"; and, "Natural science equals knowledge of the production struggle."

His grand strategic plan aimed at making China the strongest power on earth. He learnt from Marx, Lenin and Stalin everything that he thought was relevant to China. He also learnt from the great ones in the millennial history of China.

It was written in *The Book of Lord Shang*:

A country where the virtuous govern the wicked, will suffer from disorder, so that it will be dismembered; but a country where the wicked govern the virtuous, will be orderly, so that it will become strong. . . . A country which is administered by the aid of odes, history, rites, music, filial piety, brotherly duty, virtue and moral culture, will, as soon as the enemy approach, be dismembered. If he does not approach, the country will be poor. But if a country is administered without these eight, the enemy dares not approach. . . . A country where uniformity of purpose has been established for one year, will be strong for ten years; where uniformity of purpose has been established for ten years, it will be strong for a hundred years; where uniformity of purpose has been established for hundred years; it will be strong for a thousand years . . . and will attain supremacy. . . . He, who can create order in one day will attain supremacy. . . .[26]

Figuratively speaking, he wanted to create order in one day.

In every way possible in China, he copied the methods of Lenin and Stalin. Conscious as he was of having far greater power and far more popular backing than Lenin had at the outset, he meant to compress decades of Soviet development into as many years.

The "terror with fanfare", announced by his security chief, was necessary for a wide range of tasks, all of them connected directly or indirectly with production.

He had to forge an extensive and powerful Party apparatus to direct and control all public and private activities. Millions of new cadres had to be taught, disciplined and hardened in the terror campaigns. The cadres had to know that if they failed, they themselves would be "suppressed". Only with a steeled and blindly obedient Party apparatus could he force the people to accept ever larger sacrifices and go on increasing production.

He knew from experience that Lenin was right in saying that all

[26] Translated by J. J. L. Duyvendak, in *Probsthain's Oriental Series*, London, 1928, Vol. XVII, pp. 199-200.

peasants are village-capitalists at heart, and that the workers, left to themselves, instinctively follow the "bourgeois trade unionists", that is, they want a better life *now*. If—as he intended—peasants and workers were to produce more and more for less and less incentives, than the great Stalin principle had to operate: people had to be forced to work by terror.

The campaign against the traditional Chinese family, against the various religious sects, against "warm-feelingism", individualism, against private aspirations, private ties, private life and all—aimed at destroying all public and private bases of resistance to the relentless production drive. People had to be remoulded into completely conditioned human machines, as similar as possible to such biologically conditioned insects as the ants or the bees.

In his vast country where the regional despot or war-lord was not the exception but the rule, Mao had to create unity and a centralised power in the hands of his Politbureau. This he achieved to a great extent during the first two years, but only a new terror wave helped him to gain complete power over Manchuria.

In order to be a mighty world-power in modern conditions, China had to match the rest of the world in science and technology. This was the greatest problem of all in Mao's strategy for remoulding human beings. What he wanted was to harness the human spirit to his gigantic production drive, without those conditions of freedom which render the human spirit truly creative. His many harangues to scientists, writers and artists show that he was fully aware of the dangers. Terror again promised to bring the required results, until he could produce new generations of intellectuals brought up on "Mao Tse-tung Thought". (This was of course before the lessons of the Soviet "thaw", the Hungarian revolution and the Chinese "hundred flowers" period.)

Terror then, was a tactical method. Originally, Mao and his associates did not mean the terror to get out of hand. Not because of moral considerations (this would mean accusing them unjustly of bourgeois "warm-feelingism"), but because too much indiscriminate killing harms efficiency of production. That the terror got out of hand during 1951 was in the nature of the Party system and Party ideology. In 1953 Mao relaxed the pressure when it became evident that production was suffering.

Seen from his residences in Peking's moat-girt South Lake Park, and in the outskirts, in the Jade Fountain Pagoda, the mass-executions in the cities and villages seemed far less monstrous. There were in fact thousands (but not millions) of bad landlords, collaborators, war-criminals, heartless profiteers and Kuomintang agents. There were also real bandits. After two decades of warfare, not only Mao and his top associates, but millions of Communists and non-Communists alike, approved of the shooting of Kuomintang secret police personnel, of arch-collaborators, of notorious usurers and their like.

For Mao and his associates the first three years in power meant a tremendous amount of difficult work on unfamiliar terrain. They had to increase the Party apparatus tenfold as they went along. They had to build up the Soviet-type State apparatus, to be guided by the Party apparatus. They had to stop inflation, start industrial and agricultural production, restore the communications network, reorganise the educational system on Communist lines, rebuild factories, houses, hospitals, schools, and train their economic general staff for coping with the thousandfold problems of the first Five Year Plan.

In asking and allowing private enterprise to help in reconstruction, Mao took a leaf from the Soviet book—Lenin's brief relaxation of terror during the so-called NEP-period.

The initial popularity of the régime, the high hopes entertained that after a few hard years life would become pleasanter, the enthusiasm and the national pride of the people, no doubt helped with the success of the reconstruction. Because, on the whole, it was successful. Inflation was stopped, the land reform was carried out, industry got going. Private industrial and commercial enterprises also benefited from the restoration of railways, roads and river transport. The vast internal market was opened up and private businessmen were confident that in spite of the heavy taxation, they would profit by the fact that costs in all State enterprises were much higher than in the "private-sector". The cautious confidence of private industrialists and merchants—who never dreamt that the period of New Democracy would be so short—contributed greatly to the initial successes in reconstruction.

The task that faced Mao and his chief associates was truly gigantic. They meant to build from a poor, war-ravaged agricultural country a strong industrial power. Although the eulogies that poured forth about Mao and the other leaders became ever more sickening in their insane adulation, there is no reason to doubt the often repeated statement that in this period the leaders often worked sixteen or even twenty hours a day.

The internal problems of this country of six hundred million people were paralleled by most complex external problems.

Korea was a great problem for Mao long before she became a grave international issue. The Russian troops occupying the northern half of Korea in 1945 brought with them a group of Communists from Moscow, led by Ho Kai Ye, a Soviet citizen born in Siberia. Ho Kai Ye was put into a leading position by the Soviet command in 1945.

While the Soviet forces thoroughly crippled Manchurian industry, carting away or destroying the most important plant, *North Korean industry was not harmed.* In Manchuria, an integral part of China, the pretext was that the industries there were in Japanese hands, and they constituted war booty. Yet in North Korea, where industry was completely Japanese property, the factories were left intact. If this did not make it clear to the outside world that Stalin trusted the North Korean régime more than he did Mao's in China, Mao and his colleagues had no illusions. It meant that the North Korean Reds had been immediately recognised by Stalin as real Communists, and were treated as the leaders of a trusted Soviet satellite.

For Red China a Communist North Korea on its borders was infinitely preferable to a Korean régime allied to the United States. Moreover the North Korean power plant at the Yalu River, on the border, supplied electric power for a large part of Manchurian industry. In the initial stage of her reconstruction Mao's China wanted many things, but an immediate war was not among them. It may be argued that the Peking leadership would have felt safer had there been Communist rule over the whole of Korea at a later date, but there was certainly no earthly reason for (and no indication of) their wanting a war at that time.

The North Korean armies launched their attack against the South on June 25, 1950. In China, the entire Party and State apparatus was preparing for the promulgation of the Land Reform Law on June 30. And it should be mentioned in this context that one of the main reasons for the drive against landlords was to secure the régime's rear against possible anti-Communist revolt. The declared class-enemy, the landlord class, was the natural potential and in many cases the actual ally of Chiang Kai-shek's exiled régime and of all groups from which organised resistance against the Communists might be expected. It is hardly likely that Mao should want a war on the eve of launching this campaign for effective power over the countryside, and when the country as a whole had not even started to recover from the ravages of decades of fighting. In fact, for Mao, this war could not have come at a worse time.

It is equally clear that the North Korean régime was wholly subservient to Moscow, and that it could not decide on a military campaign without getting large shipments of Soviet arms during the previous months. There was little doubt at that time that the attack against South Korea, and its exact timing, were planned and ordered by Stalin. Subsequent events did nothing to alter this general impression. As is usual in Communist affairs, the historians of the Korean war have to engage in detective work and piece together circumstantial evidence in support of their suppositions. This chronicler believes that Stalin hoped to embroil the United States in a long-drawn out military conflict, localised to Korea and the Chinese mainland; and hoped to use this opportunity to replace the Mao-group with his own nominees. In 1950, Stalin had ample reason to count on the following general sequence of events:

1. The United States would assume Red China's complicity in the Korean invasion and would support both South Korea and Chiang Kai-shek.

2. South Korea with US support would advance so far to the north that Mao's China would have to join in the war.

3. Chiang Kai-shek's Formosan régime would seize the opportunity to launch a general attack against South China.

4. The war would cause such disruption in China that the Mao leadership could be dislodged and replaced, possibly by the Kao Kang group. (It should be borne in mind that Stalin still had a poor opinion of the strength of the Mao régime.) In any case, such a war would make Mao's régime more dependent on Russia.[27]

On June 25, 1950, the North Korean forces made a surprise attack across the 38th parallel against South Korea. Moscow Radio and the Soviet press at once reported the North Korean version, alleging that the attack came from the South and stating that the North Korean Army had immediate orders to repel the attack on a large scale. But during the first day after the attack, Mao's radio stations and newspapers gave every sign of being completely unprepared for these events.* Conflicting reports were broadcast, implying various and conflicting attitudes of the Chinese leader-

[27] Cf. Gluckstein, op. cit., p. 411.

* "The disarray of the Chinese Communist press during the first twenty-four hours of the Korean War is an interesting and suggestive fact" (C. P. Fitzgerald, *Revolution in China*, London, 1952, p. 220).

ship. Only next day did Peking hurry to walk in step with the Moscow propaganda-line; but there was no hint of armed intervention either by volunteers or by regular troops.

The events which led to the Chinese intervention were these: President Truman made a unilateral declaration, undertaking defence of Chiang's Formosa against Communist Chinese attack during the Korean war. The United Nations sent troops to Korea, and General MacArthur, the UN Commander in Chief, opened military consultations in Formosa with Chiang Kai-shek. American military aid was again extended to Chiang, *before* Mao's intervention in Korea. These actions convinced Mao that the Korean war was only part of a general offensive to be launched against Red China. When during their initial successes, the UN troops advanced through North Korea towards the Yalu River, the Chinese-Korean frontier, Chinese armies intervened, and on October 25, 1950, the Chinese Volunteer Army was formally established in Korea.

At first Mao backed a peaceful solution. On July 5, Sardar K. M. Panikkar, the Indian Ambassador in Peking, obtained the approval of Mao's government for a peace move to be made by Nehru. On July 13 Nehru in a private message to Stalin and the US Secretary of State, Dean Acheson, proposed that with the co-operation of the US the USSR and Red China, the Korean problem should be settled peacefully. Stalin, by ordering the publication of this exploratory and confidential approach on July 18, effectively sabotaged this peace move.

Stalin started the Korean war and was unwilling to end it. Mao at first supported a peaceful settlement and was forced into the war only through his own bias and by the developments of the ensuing months.

The Chinese People's Volunteers were in fact divisions of seasoned regular troops under the command of one of Mao's best generals, Peng Teh-huai. All through the war, however, Peking stressed that they were volunteers, who were only backing the heroic North Koreans. It was not Mao's design to seek all-out war with the United States. The Moscow propaganda-line was quite different. Attempts were made to hint that the Korean war was Mao's affair. In November 1950, the UN and US forces suffered their first defeats, due to Chinese intervention. In this situation, when American public opinion turned even more bitterly against Communist China, Stalin used not very subtle methods to goad the US into more aggressive action against Mao's régime.

For instance, *Pravda's* official commentator, *Nablyudatyel* (Ob-

server) wrote on December 3, 1950, that the victorious offensive
had been planned and timed by Mao Tse-tung. It was also most
significant that *Pravda* gave the North Koreans almost no credit
for the victories; they were won by the Chinese alone. The word
"volunteer" was not mentioned at all, although it was most important for the Peking line that they should be regarded as volunteers.[28] There were indications that Stalin would not mind if the
Korean war spread over the Chinese mainland. Mao, on the other
hand, from the moment the Chinese North-Korean forces had again
reached the 38th parallel, was ready for peace. In December 1952,
with Mao's knowledge and approval, India again made a peace
move which was again promptly turned down by the USSR.

It is also instructive to note how Stalin timed his recognition of
Mao Tse-tung as a great Communist theoretician. The first volume
of Mao's *Selected Works* was published in Russian in August 1952.
Pravda not only acknowledged Mao as a real Communist, but
credited him with enriching Marxist theory: "Mao Tse-tung adapted
Marxism-Leninism not dogmatically but creatively, successfully
adapting Marxist theory to China and thus greatly enriching that
theory."[29]

This acknowledgment of ideological identification, withheld from
Mao's China for decades, did not come at a particularly helpful
time. If Mao was already thinking of ending the Korean war, this
conspicuous move on Stalin's part to show solidarity could only
stiffen the Western attitude to him. Moreover, this public gesture
of recognition was coupled with ever more unfriendly behaviour
behind the scenes. In the same month that this gesture was made,
August 1952, a Chinese delegation led by Premier Chou En-lai
arrived in Moscow to negotiate a new economic treaty. The delegation was first kept waiting, and when negotiations started at last
and dragged on for months, they produced no results. Not even
the 1950 promises were kept. The promised increase in material
aid from the USSR was most important for China for two reasons.
The Korean war had heavily taxed Chinese finances, industry and
man-power. Towards these costs the USSR had not contributed.
Even more important, the first Five Year Plan of China which was
about to be launched had to be delayed because the USSR, far
from helping, actually slowed down the construction of the fifty

[28] For a detailed chronicle of Soviet diplomacy and propaganda line
during the Korean war, see Beloff, op. cit., pp. 155-207.
[29] *Pravda*, August 28, 1952.

industrial enterprises for which contracts had been signed. Stalin furthermore went on with his encroachment in Manchuria and Sinkiang and also gave encouragement to Kao Kang who was busy trying to consolidate the semi-independent status of Manchuria.* Stalin's actions made it obvious that he intended to weaken Mao's China into full submission. He could not accept Mao's formula for Sino-Soviet relations: complete solidarity between independent states.

The sequence of further events is also most instructive. On March 6, 1953, Stalin dies. On March 30, a diplomatic move by Chou En-lai makes the ending of the Korean war possible. This time, the Kremlin leaders, engaged in their personal struggle for power, make no more difficulties. August 1953: purge in North Korea. Nine top Korean Communists, all of them Stalinists belonging to the Ho Kai Ye group, are executed. Stalin's Number One Korean favourite, Ho Kai Ye is said to have committed suicide. (His latest positions had been Vice-Premier and head of the Secret Police.) North Korea becomes a joint Soviet-Chinese satellite.

In fact, the Korean war, started by Stalin's Russia, was brought to an end by Mao's China.

The Korean war, the renewed American backing given to the Chiang régime, and American determination to exclude Red China from the UN, all prompted Mao to transform the Resist America campaign into the Hate America drive. America became "the most deadly enemy of the peace-loving people of the world", and there was no crime under the sun with which the American "imperialists" were not charged. Americans were accused of cannibalism, of waging bacteriological warfare by dropping containers with plague and pest-carrying insects. At mass-trials thousands of class-hostile elements had to insert an additional clause into the long list of their crimes, describing themselves as American agents, saboteurs or spies. The Hate America campaign was linked to a general anti-Western campaign. Western missionaries were accused of the murder of thousands of Chinese children in their mission hospitals and orphanages.

Some relaxation came in 1953, thanks to many factors. First of all, three years of violence and regimentation had resulted in an alarming drop in production. In the atmosphere of general suspicion, anxiety, bureaucratic despotism, and forced "voluntary shock-work",

* For which crime, Mao, after Stalin's death, drove him to suicide and executed his entourage.

both industry and agriculture threatened catastrophic breakdown. A contributory factor to relaxation was Stalin's death, which decreased the danger from Moscow to the Mao leadership. Lastly, the first Five Year Plan began officially on January 1, 1953 (although it was not published in concrete form until July 1955).

An attempt was made to reassure the population that no nasty shocks awaited them and that there would be less bullying and interference. Even the fund-raising drives were allowed to slacken. Naturally the relaxation was announced and conducted in a series of campaigns, this time against "commandist" and "bureaucratist" Communist functionaries. The press was suddenly full of reports about cadres who had ordered people to be beaten up and tortured or who had driven them to suicide. "Chairman Mao and the Party" now conducted a severe drive against such persons.

> Fifty-seven cadres of the bank of Chiahsing in Chekiang, were repeatedly guilty of beating up the masses and as many as 174 peasants became victims. When collecting debts . . . bank cadres bound and imprisoned the peasants who were unable to repay their debts. . . . Cadre Chiao Ho-shien forced peasant Yuan Chien-ying to repay his cattle loan, and Yuan was forced to go to a hill at night and hang himself.[30]

The Second Secretary of the Shantung Party, reported that some cadres in the villages

> cruelly oppress the masses, fined farmers at will, raped women and even young girls at the point of bayonet, and beat up, insulted, detained, put under surveillance and assaulted families of service men and workers. As a result seventeen families were detained and put under control, two persons were forced to commit suicide, and four persons died of injuries from beatings.[31]

Cadres, whether representing the police, the State, a bank or a newspaper, used their position as Party members to use naked force. The case of subscription salesmen is enlightening. They were under such pressure from above that

> they had to resort to forcible methods in order to fulfil their task. Consequently, they forced the aged to subscribe to the China Youth journal and the illiterate to buy Study (the Party

[30] Ta Kung Pao, Tientsin, March 24, 1953.
[31] PD, February 23, 1953.

theoretical journal). They even compelled a factory with only 161 workers to subscribe to 443 copies of newspapers.[32]

In June 1953 the "Five-too-many" movement was started against the following grievances: too many assigned tasks, too many meetings, too many organisations, too many concurrently held posts, and too many official documents and forms.

Mao Tse-tung's Politbureau was driving China through Party decrees, Government orders, "voluntary" movements, campaigns and slogans. The extremely large and clumsy Party apparatus—like a gigantic steam-roller—rumbled as it ground to a halt and suddenly turned in a new direction. Relaxation this time took the form of a terror drive against too terroristic Party cadres. Again it was terror with fanfare.

[32] *Chung-kuo Ch'ing-nien*, March 1, 1953.

XV

THE DEMAGOGUE-ORACLE

There is no Jade Emperor in Heaven
There is no Dragon King on Earth
I am the Jade Emperor!
I am the Dragon King!
Make way for me, oh! ye mountains.
I'm coming.
                    (A "folksong" of New China.)

Mao drew his own portrait as a ruler: his features are seen in his actions and inactions. In a way the best portrait of Mao Tse-tung is provided by the chronicle of his first decade in power, just as we know far more about Stalin from those actions of his which are matters of hard historical fact, than from the impressions of his eulogists, his enemies or his casual and neutral observers. In Mao's case, the first decade of his rule offered enough evidence of the extent and limitations of his power to make it clear that ultimately he was responsible for everything that happened to the Chinese people. We know moreover—as this chronicle will show—that whenever he disagreed with any decision taken by a majority of his most important associates, he could and did come forward and record his massive dissent by brutally overruling them.

If we had reliable details about his private life—as we most certainly do not—they would no doubt round out his portrait, but they would not change its main outlines. If for instance—as some observers believe—it was true that for periods of several months he simply withdrew to one of his private residences because he had had a terrific row with his own highest associates and felt like sulking, or because he was working on one of his "epoch-making" theoretical works; or again, because he was ill and felt miserable and did not want to see anyone—all this would not change the fact that, by his own decisions, he unleashed an avalanche of misery on the Chinese people. His great ambitions, the goals towards which he was working, are obvious and were repeatedly stated by him. His character as a ruler, and as one of the most important statesmen of the contemporary world, can be portrayed on the basis of these ambitions and goals, and the way he strove for their realisation. For writers of historical novels the lack of intimate details about his everyday life would make it impossible to write a novel about Mao Tse-tung, the flesh-and-blood human being. For historians, he has fully revealed himself as a statesman in those policies for which he alone was responsible.

The fact that as soon as he came to power the Mao cult speedily developed to puzzling extremes, shows his own tremendous conceit. His sycophants emphasise his habit of "conscientiously" reading and studying the Chinese dailies. These newspapers wrote about him as the Saving Star of China, the Sun That Never Set, the Great Helmsman of the Revolution, the great political scientist "who is always right". In the early nineteen-fifties, most public utterances already had the ritual ending "Long Live Chairman Mao". His portraits adorned public buildings and were present in all offices and most homes, where they replaced the former Kitchen God. The land-reform meetings in 1950-2 started with the singing of the national anthem; "then everybody took off their hats and bowed to the national flag and to the portrait of Chairman Mao." At other meetings, Mao's portrait was brought in on a sedan chair.[1]

Nothing was ever done to stop people writing and speaking about him as omnipotent, omniscient and infallible, or as the great genius who, with a few simple words, could give guidance in their own professions to surgeons, novelists or hydraulic engineers. The Mao cult was not toned down even after the brief anti-Stalin campaign in the Soviet Union, when in other parts of the Communist world the fight against the "personality cult" was the order of the day.

Many of the Chairman's speeches and reports were only published several months or even years after he had delivered them. Other results of this will be examined later, but one must be mentioned here. When outer-Party members and non-Communist functionaries had had no opportunity of learning Mao's view on a given subject, they often unwittingly committed the crime of disagreeing with him, whereupon they were immediately persecuted as right-wing, reactionary or anti-Party criminals. In checking the dates of Mao's temporarily unpublished speeches and the onset of such campaigns, it becomes evident that Mao could not suffer opinions differing from his own. The same was the case when anyone made a factual report on some question. If the facts reported ran

[1] Hsiao Ch'ien, *How the Tillers Win Back Their Land*, Peking, 1954, p. 27.

counter to Mao's (unpublished) contentions, the reporter was suddenly attacked in the press or demoted, or simply vanished.

Circumstantial evidence of this kind bears out the accounts of
those Communist and non-Communist functionaries who later escaped from China. Chow Ching-wen, for instance, former Assistant
Secretary-General of the Democratic League (one of the window-
dressing coalition-parties in the government) met Mao off and on
for seven years at various government meetings. In his book, Chow
describes a scene when another Democratic League politician
called Liang displeased Mao by reporting that the peasants had a
heavier burden to bear in China, than the workers:

> Placing a microphone before him, Mao proceeded to engage in a
> verbal battle with Liang.
>
> Mao said: "You may think yourself very pretty, prettier than
> such famed beauties as Hsi Shih and Yang Kuei-fei. But I think
> you are a skunk."
>
> Liang was dumbfounded. He could not continue his speech.
> At the same time the atmosphere in the assembly became more
> tense. Pointing at Liang, Mao continued: "The Taiwan Radio
> praised you as a man of integrity and determination. I think you
> smell rotten, rotten to the very core of your bones."
>
> Standing on the rostrum, Liang looked as if lightning had just
> struck without any warning. He could not understand what had
> made Chairman Mao so very angry. He made a gesture to con-
> tinue his speech; but now roars from the audience overtook him.[2]

Liang became "an enemy of the people", and disappeared.

Liang was, of course, a nonentity. But Mao Tse-tung behaved
in the same contemptuous manner when he disagreed with his
own chief associates, and with the considered decision of the highest
organs of his own State and Party. In July 1955 his own chief associates, indeed the entire Chinese Communist Party "looked as if
lightning had just struck without warning", when Mao turned
violently against them, and overruled their decisions.

This event was so significant, that the developments leading up to
it must be examined in detail.

---

[2] Chow Ching-wen, *Ten Years of Violent Storm*, Hong Kong, 1959,
quoted by Professor Richard Walker in "Chairman Mao", *Encounter*,
London, June 1960, p. 39.

I

In January 1954 the government promulgated the "General Line of the State for the Period of Transition to Socialism". This meant in practice—if not fully so in theory—the end of the "long historical period" of New Democracy. The Chinese people were asked to prepare for austerity, hard work, and strict obedience to the central authority.

For the peasants, the liquidation of New Democracy had started even earlier. The last group of poor peasants had just ceremonially received the title deeds of their freehold land in South China, when Mao's Central Committee passed its "Decisions on Mutual Aid and Co-operation and Agricultural Production" on February 15, 1953. The plan called for the organisation of mutual-aid teams "with an embryo of socialism". These were supposed to pave the way gradually for the formation of "lower grade agricultural co-operatives" in which most of the land is pooled and worked as a unit, small plots being retained for private use, while the peasants remain the owners of their freehold land and have the right to leave the co-op whenever they choose. In 1954, when Party leaders were envisaging that one-third of the peasantry would be in co-operatives by the end of 1957, the first step was already taken for further development; "higher stage co-operatives" were set up, in which land, tools and animals were owned in common and the amount of profit and food received by the members was based on units of work performed. The press published accounts of the solemn and happy occasions when the peasants deposited the deeds of their freeholds in the common till. From then on, again for "a long period", the peasants were promised they would collectively own their land.

Mao's régime had not yet started to cure the two chronic causes of the Chinese food shortage—the general backwardness of agriculture and the seasonally recurrent floods, droughts and consequent famines—when its measures provoked the peasants' dogged resistance to "the road to socialism". Each year the press carried reports about various famine-stricken areas.*

---

* In 1951 for instance, it was reported that in North China more than ten million people were affected by "a serious famine situation". In 1952 and 1953 floods, droughts and sudden frosts caused famines in very wide areas. On February 10, 1954, *People's Daily* reported that grain had to be given in large quantities to help "famine stricken peasants

It was quite natural that the Ministry of Agriculture, the Central Planning Commission and various Party bureaux concerned with food production and consumption, were against too speedy collectivisation, since the peasants' response to it was resistance, active or passive. In many areas the peasants simply slaughtered their livestock or abandoned their farms to look for work in the cities. *New China Daily* (Chungking), reported on March 2, 1953: "The reason why the majority of peasants abandoned their spring farming is due to their loss of self-confidence and their mistaken belief that farming is no longer profitable." The Central Government issued orders to prevent mass migration of peasants to the cities and to prevent the slaughtering of draught-animals and young animals. In the more fortunate and fertile areas the peasants protested against Party interference in farming methods. *NCNA* reported from Nanking on April 19, 1953, the following typical complaint of peasants: "You people simply come to give us trouble and waste our time. You live on public grain and fear no starvation. Who is going to make up our losses should your method result in failure?"

The Chinese Party and Government functionaries who advised a more prudent advance in collectivisation could quote the Soviet example. In September 1953 Khrushchev gave an alarming report to the Russian Central Committee concerning the state of Soviet agriculture, comparing the 1916 and 1928 (pre-collectivisation) situation with that of 1952.*

It was during the winter of 1954-5 that the highest organs of the Chinese Party and the State were working on the final draft of the first Five Year Plan which, according to a temporary blueprint, had already been in operation since January 1, 1953. Subsequent events proved that during this period, and even up to the end of July 1955, Mao Tse-tung did not succeed in persuading his Party and State apparatus to adopt his own extremist line. This was all the more puzzling as, according to the new 1954 Constitu-

---

constituting about ten per cent of the rural population", that is, some sixty million people. On July 5, 1955, *NCNA* reported "great floods . . . in 1954 such as had never been seen for a hundred years".

* Although the Soviet population had increased by nearly fifty million and world agricultural technique showed a great advance over 1916, there was less livestock in Soviet Russia in 1952 than in 1916. Grain production in comparable areas could only show an increase of barely five per cent since 1928. Such were the consequences of forced collectivisation.

tion, the most powerful man in the country was Mao Tse-tung. In September 1954 the National People's Congress elected him as Chairman of the Republic, Chou En-lai became Prime Minister (Chairman of the State Council), while the other Party leaders occupied the rest of the most important government posts.

According to the Constitution, the Chairman of the Republic, in accordance with the decisions of the National People's Congress or its Standing Committee, promulgates laws and decrees, appoints or removes the Premier, the Ministers and heads of Commissions; commands the armed forces, and is Chairman of the Council of National Defence.

And, since the State is directed and controlled by the Party, Mao Tse-tung as head of the State was directly responsible to himself, as Chairman of the Central Committee, the Political Bureau and the Central Secretariat of the Communist Party.

As head of the Party, Mao directed the organs of State security, the various mass-organisations and the other "democratic parties", which by definition had to accept Communist Party guidance.

Yet in spite of all this power—as subsequent events showed—Mao did not get official Party and Government backing for his extremist peasant-policy.

At the beginning of 1955 the Chinese Central Committee called a halt to the over-hasty expansion of co-operatives. A *People's Daily* editorial on February 28 stated that "the idea of emphasising the numerical increase in co-operatives and neglecting the work of consolidation was a harmful one". The State Council directive on spring cultivation, of March 3, emphasised that the attempt "to expand the scope of the co-operatives rapidly 'had created' suspicion and misunderstanding of the co-operative movement among some peasants."

In February 1955 the Central Committee, and in March the National Conference of the Chinese CP, examined the final draft of the first Five Year Plan and resolved that it should be submitted to the supreme organ of State power, the National People's Congress. The NPC met in July. Li Fu-chun, the Chairman of the State Planning Commission, submitted the plan which aimed at organising about one-third of the peasants into co-operatives by the end of the plan period in 1957. The Plan was formally adopted by the NPC on July 30.

The very next day the lightning struck!

On July 31, Mao Tse-tung, in a speech made to a meeting of the secretaries of Provincial Municipal and Area Party Committees,

hurled astonishing accusations against all those who were responsible for the decisions of the highest organs of the Party and the
State. The printed text of this speech was handed to all the par-
ticipating delegates. The opening sentences were as follows:

> Throughout the Chinese countryside a new upsurge of the So-
> cialist mass movement is apparent. But certain of our comrades
> are tottering along the way like old women with bandaged feet,
> constantly moaning that the others go too fast. They imagine that
> by clutching at straws, by groaning without reason, by making an
> endless din and by issuing innumerable taboos and orders they
> are guiding the socialist movement along healthy lines.
>
> No, this is not the right way at all. It won't do!

Mao criticised the March decision of the State Council (under
Chou En-lai) to slow down the tempo of collectivisation and to
concentrate on the consolidation of the existing healthy co-operatives. This decision—according to Mao—led to "the repetition of the
1953 mistake of mass-dissolution of co-operatives". He accused those
comrades who "think that the present situation of the co-operative
movement is critical" of right-wing tendencies and also those who
think "that several hundred thousand small semi-socialist agricultural producers' co-operatives that have sprung into being have
'gone beyond practical possibilities'".

These comrades were of course the majority of the Politbureau,
the Central Committee, the State Council and the National People's
Congress.

He called for class struggle against rich peasants and against
all those who wished to remain outside the co-operatives. He firmly
rejected the view of "some comrades . . . who advise us to get off
the horse and pause on our journey along the road to co-operation".
Only by carrying out the Socialist transformation of agriculture
would the Party "put an end to the system of rich peasant and
individual economy in the countryside". Mao suggested that with
the help of the "active elements" among the poor and middle peasants "vigorous struggle should be waged against the rich peasant
tendency" and against individual farming.

"The Central Committee,"—Mao went on—"decided to increase
the number of co-operatives by fifty per cent . . . I consider that
this increase is too modest. . . ."

He demanded a hundred per cent increase![3]

[3] Text of Mao's speech in *People's China*, November 1, 1955.

This shows that in the March-July period Mao Tse-tung had not succeeded in persuading his colleagues in the Political Bureau to adopt his extremist line. He had not contradicted their proposals, based on a painstaking analysis of the real situation and of future dangers, when they were discussed at the plenary sessions of the Central Committee, the National Conference of Communists and in the National People's Congress, for had he done so, it is hardly likely that these proposals would have been carried. Yet, the day after all these bodies had set their seal on a decision affecting the lives of 500,000,000 peasants, he turned against this decision and appealed to the lower Party apparatus, and the local Party secretaries from all over China! These naturally took Mao's words as a command. The text of his speech was read at Party meetings all over China, and Party headquarters in Peking received an avalanche of reports on how enthusiastic the cadres were not to "totter along the way like old women with bandaged feet".

The conspiratorial nature of the Communist Party is such that the lower apparatus was convinced that it was the Chairman who was carrying out the Party's real policy. All Mao had to say was "I consider this too modest", and his associates were presented with a *fait accompli*. Forced collectivisation went on at a break-neck speed. In July 1955 16.9 million peasant families (fourteen per cent of the total) were in co-ops. By next June more than 108,000,000 families (90.4% of the total) were collectivised. Moreover, the planned gradual development was also cast aside on Mao's prompting: 73,000,000 families were already in higher stage co-ops and only 35,000,000 in lower grade producer co-operatives.

The press did not publish Mao's speech until the middle of October. There were only indirect signs to suggest that some secret decision must have been taken on speeding up the agricultural revolution. Finally the Central Committee held an enlarged session between October 4 and 11, 1955, and adopted Mao's revision of the Five Year Plan. The fact that the Central Committee session had been enlarged by more than 300 other Party delegates shows that *someone* could not rely on the Central Committee alone. The fact that the debate lasted eight days shows, furthermore, that the adoption did not go any too smoothly. The ministers and Party leaders, however, who tried to reckon with the real situation, had to give in to Mao, since both Party reports and press accounts spoke about boundless enthusiasm for "the high tide of socialist transformation", and since the Security Police was in Mao's hands. In the

middle of October, the entire press published Mao's July speech
and the October decisions of the Central Committee.

The campaign was on against "rightist elements within the Party
. . . who did not lead the masses to take the road to Socialism, but
rather dragged the masses away from the road of Socialism."[4]

The Party and State leadership, reluctant to jeopardise food production, decided to avoid a new all-out terror wave over the countryside. Mao—in a speech which betrayed his rage—demanded that
a vigorous struggle be waged against "rich peasant tendencies",
knowing full well that this was a command to his cadres to be mer-
ciless with all those poor and middle peasants who did not wish to
enter a co-operative. For, by sticking to individual farming, these
too manifested "rich peasant tendencies".

The publication of Mao's July speech in October 1955 led very
swiftly to the changing of the Five Year Plan in other most important aspects too. The socialisation of industry and commerce
was greatly accelerated. The Government had already announced,
a year earlier, the establishment of "joint public-private enterprises".
These provided the State with expert knowledge, managerial skills
and seventy-five per cent of all profits. According to the original
Five Year Plan about eighty per cent of private industry and commerce was to be organised into "joint public-private enterprises".
Yet in November, the organ of private capitalists, the All-China
Federation of Industry and Commerce, appealed "voluntarily" for
immediate "socialisation". NCNA reported on January 21, 1956, that
during the previous ten days "all private industry and commerce
in Peking, Tientsin, Shanghai, Canton, Wuhan, Shenang, Sian and
other major cities switched over to joint State-private operation".

These astonishingly speedy results were due to the new wave
of terror personally unleashed by Mao. The cadres were driven
to the most violent methods. The Security Police, the voluntary
security teams, the Household Police and "good Communists"
worked overtime. In China, where hospitality was a most precious
tradition, people had to obtain police permission for anyone to
stay overnight under their roof. The campaign was on against personal love, family ties and ties of friendship.

The July 31, 1955, incident gave an alarming glimpse not only
into the actual workings of Mao's rule, and the contemptuous way

<hr />

[4] Vice-Premier Chen Yi, PD, November 13, 1955.

he treated his entire Party and government leadership, but also into his own state of mind.

In Kiangsi, before the Long March, he had resisted the dogmatic demands of his Stalinist Party leadership for class struggle against the rich peasants in the Red areas, by simply pointing out that he could not endanger the food supply of the Red districts by alienating the peasantry. During the Kiangsi and the Yenan periods he gave the impression that he was not isolated from reality, and that if he had to choose between dogma and practical possibilities, he chose the latter. Why then did he endanger China's food supply in 1955—although no one forced him to do so? Why did he disregard Khrushchev's report in 1953 on the consequences of collectivisation in the USSR? Why did he disregard the advice of his own associates and experts?

It is possible that his actions from 1955 onwards cast a new light on his own past. Discerning observers have to consider the possibility that much of what appeared to be a demonstration of Mao's prudence and talent as a political strategist was largely due to pressure of events: the Chiang Kai-shek offensives against his forces, the developments of the Second World War, and Stalin's moves against his policy. To put it briefly, in the 1927-49 period Mao was to a large extent under "the dictatorship of reality" and it seems that the moment he was free from this dictatorship he became a most dogmatic and imprudent ruler, increasingly more isolated from reality.

The 1955 July incident also laid bare the real pattern of Mao's power. All Party and Government functionaries learnt that if they did not want to risk demotion, prison or death, they had to obey Chairman Mao's wishes, they had to fathom, even anticipate, his views on the necessary development of events. Long before the great campaign was launched to make everyone in China get down to studying "Mao Tse-tung Thought", the Party and Government functionaries were doing everything in their power to divine the slightest change in Mao's views to read between the lines, to be the first to spot any intimation in his speeches of some sudden new "upsurge", "high tide" or "leap into the future".

We have no direct evidence as to how his chief associates reacted at first to this situation. But they must have realised quite soon that, given the immense Mao cult they themselves had helped to build up, they could not use Party statutes, Politbureau votes, or State decisions, against the infallible leader whose forecasts were taken by the Party organisations as commands and promptly "over-fulfilled". Mao Tse-tung himself became, through this process, even more convinced of his grasp of the real situation, his closeness to the masses, the infallibility of his judgment.

Mao's power had then—and possibly still has in 1962—a dual character. With his associates he had built up an enormous apparatus of bureaucratic despotism. As the Chairman of this apparatus and as the leader among the six or seven men who in fact govern the Party and the country, he was something of a dictator-in-chief in the coalition of Communist dictators. But whenever the system of bureaucratic despotism failed to carry out his policies to the letter, the Chairman at once deserted the "coalition" of leaders (in Communist terminology, the collective leadership) and turned against it. At this stage he would fall back on his other and perhaps basic source of power: that of *a demagogue-oracle*.

The long years of terror with fanfare have so conditioned the Chinese people that at a word from the demagogue-oracle they leap in any direction he wants them to.

II

More than once between 1950 and 1956 Mao Tse-tung disappeared for considerable periods from the public eye. On such occasions the Western press reported the rumours reaching Hong Kong —that Mao was incurably ill, had been purged, was in Moscow, or even that he had probably died. There were weeks in 1951 and 1952 when Mao did not appear at events which it was his routine to take part in. In the spring of 1953 he was missing for a fairly extended period and there was a further "disappearance" of his in the winter of 1953-4. A Central Committee meeting was held without his participation. The 1954 New Year greetings to the nation were delivered by Chu Teh instead of Mao, who at that same time also missed important diplomatic receptions. During a protracted absence in May 1955 it was again reported that he was suffering from a fatal illness. He was missing again in January of 1956. At other times, when his public appearances were fairly frequent and regular, it was nevertheless often left to Liu Shao-chi, Chou En-lai or Chu Teh to perform political or purely ceremonial functions which are normally the Chairman's prerogative.

Although circumstantial evidence makes it probable that at least two of his more protracted disappearances were due to illness (certain undoctored pictures taken by press photographers show signs of a recent illness), some of his absences must have had other reasons. The Chairman is known to have interrupted his seaside holi-days and flown to Peking or Shanghai for occasions which were important for him, so frequent and prolonged holidays cannot ex-plain his absences. The hypothesis, or rather rumour, that at least one of his longer disappearances signified an attempt by his col-leagues to oust him, has not been substantiated and all the material available at present makes it most unlikely. It is much more probable that Mao's interest in the day-to-day running of Party and State affairs was uneven. It is possible that, as his habit had been in Yenan, he liked to retire for a while when those matters in which he was most interested seemed to be in a satisfactory state.

A listing of his significant appearances on the other hand is more revealing. The occasions when Mao Tse-tung personally initiated campaigns, promulgated laws, announced political decisions or emerged suddenly to override the policies of his associates, show a most characteristic pattern. Most of his significant political ac-tions were aimed at speeding up the process of remoulding the Chinese population to his ideal of fully conditioned rational termites; at increasing the discipline of the Party, the efficiency of the Security Police, and the intensity of terror against the enemies of socialist transformation. It goes without saying that in his view these were the prerequisites for the rapid transformation of China into a mighty industrial and military power.

For many details of Party and Government affairs which did not seem to him to have direct bearing on his main aims, he showed a singular lack of interest. So this too may account for his absences.

The text of his announcements also shows some disregard for reality on the whole and for details in particular. As he grew more and more convinced that he knew how to "liberate the immense energies latent in the revolutionary enthusiasm of the masses", he often tried to, and did in fact, govern China with campaigns and slogans. In his extremist impatience he tried to move China with simple slogans and catch-phrases, similar to those with which in his youth he had induced village peasants to follow his lead.

Mao's outward prestige grew as China's industrialisation seemed to proceed satisfactorily. His régime succeeded for the first time in Chinese history in imposing on a united China an all-powerful central government. The 1954 census revealed that China had a population of nearly 600,000,000 and that it was growing by a rate of ten to fourteen million people a year.

In 1954 Premier and Foreign Minister Chou En-lai and Premier Nehru signed the Sino-Indian treaty on Tibet and they jointly promulgated the "Five Principles of Peaceful Co-existence". In 1955 China emerged as one of the leaders of the Afro-Asian Conference at Bandung. China's growing importance as a world power was attested by the constant stream of foreign delegations and by the visits of important personalities, among them the Indian Prime Minister and the former British Prime Minister Attlee.

In the Communist world, for the first few years after Stalin's death, Mao Tse-tung was "the towering figure of today". First Malenkov and later Khrushchev eagerly sought his backing. In October 1954 Mao was host to a Soviet delegation headed by Khrushchev, Bulganin and Mikoyan. Khrushchev obtained Mao's good will and support in his fight for power by handing back Port Arthur to China, by restoring the Sino-Soviet Joint Companies to Chinese ownership, and by giving China a new loan of 500,000,000 roubles.

Mao was now in a position in which even important foreign visitors humoured him or changed the subject in embarrassment when the Chairman betrayed his astonishing ignorance of the non-Communist world as he did to Premier Nehru or to members of the Attlee mission. In speaking to members of the Attlee mission for instance, he mistook the Scandinavian countries for Belgium and spoke about Scandinavian colonies in Africa. Others noted how firmly Mao believed in the "absolute impoverishment" of the Western working classes, and that his picture of the capitalist countries in the second half of the twentieth century was based on the situation described by Marx in the nineteenth century.

Apart from China's internal developments, Mao was taken up with developments in the USSR and its European satellites since Stalin's death. The Russian intellectual "thaw" had started in 1953 and there was a grave danger that China would be infected with the partial relaxation in Russia. The 1953-6 Russian "thaw"—with its criticisms of security police terror, of bureaucratic despotism, of the stifling of the creative spirit in art, literature and science—could be kept a secret from the Chinese masses, but not from the Chinese intellectuals, tens of thousands of whom had been forced to learn Russian.

Although it was Mao Tse-tung himself who had started the ideological remoulding of Chinese intellectuals in 1951, when he subjected them to "struggle meetings" of collective brain-washing, to various thought-control and thought-rectification campaigns, and also to unconcealed security police purges—he could not be sure of them, nor of the Party functionaries.

The Party grew enormously and was constantly purged. The

Secretary-General of the State Council reported late in 1955 that *over forty per cent* of the personnel of Government agencies and *forty-seven per cent* of the personnel of Party agencies had been discharged. Hundreds of thousands of these had been sentenced to corrective labour or prison.

The accelerated tempo of social transformation engendered resistance in all sectors of Chinese society. In 1954 People's Courts and Tribunals, Workers' Courts and Procuratures were instructed to step up the struggle against "concealed enemies", reactionaries, and violators of labour discipline in the factories and co-ops. "Educational terror" was again the order of the day:

> The people's courts . . . should dispatch circuit courts and procurator's teams to the countryside to dispose of cases of disturbances of social order and agricultural production. Serious typical cases should be disposed of with publicity in order to . . . educate the masses and cadres and heighten their revolutionary vigilance.[5]

Workers were sentenced to long prison terms for absenteeism; peasants and merchants were executed for "sabotaging" the State food monopoly.

In February 1955 a new campaign was opened against "bourgeois and idealistic thought in literature and art". The writer Hu Feng and his "accomplices" were arrested. In the summer of 1955 the security chief ordered a new wave of struggle and a punitive campaign against reactionaries, counter-revolutionaries and bandits. The security authorities extended the network of "people's supervision correspondents" and the number of boxes for the mailing of denunciations was greatly multiplied.

Since forty to forty-seven per cent of Party and Government functionaries had been found untrustworthy, and as workers and peasants were constantly being warned against bourgeois trade-unionism and "rich peasantism", it was not surprising that Chou En-lai should announce at the January 1955 Conference of Intellectuals in Peking that the majority of Chinese intellectuals were either unwilling to support Communism or were actively opposed to it.

In these circumstances, the relaxation, if not the actual discontinuation, of police terror in the Soviet Union came at a particularly unfortunate time for the Chinese régime, while the anti-Stalin revelations read by Khrushchev at the Twentieth Soviet Party Congress

[5] *PD*, April 28, 1954.

in February 1956 came as a terrible and most unexpected shock
to Mao.

From 1950 to 1953 he had been treated as "the Chinese Stalin",
and after the Soviet despot's death had been frequently described
as "the Stalin of today". He wrote of Stalin's death with "boundless
grief":

> Stalin [was] the greatest genius of the present age, the great
> teacher of the world Communist movement. . . . All his writings
> are immortal. . . . The victory of the Chinese revolution is in-
> separable from the continual care, guidance and support of Com-
> rade Stalin . . . dearest friend and great teacher of the Chinese
> people.[6]

The Twentieth Congress of the Soviet Communist Party between
February 14 and 25, 1956, began with Khrushchev stressing the
loss suffered by the Party when "death tore Josip Vissarionovitch
Stalin from our ranks". Next day Marshal Chu Teh read the telegram from the Chinese Central Committee signed by Mao Tse-
tung. The telegram was worded in the spirit of the Stalin-cult; and
at the beginning of the Congress Khrushchev spoke of the "enemies
of the people" in approved Stalinist manner. On the last day of
the Congress, however, on February 25, he read to the closed session of delegates the famous anti-Stalin tract, calling the "greatest
leader of all ages and peoples" a sadist, a mass-murderer, a coward,
a military bungler, a falsifier of history. He said:

> Stalin originated the concept "enemy of the people". . . . This
> term made possible the use of the most cruel repression, violating
> all norms of revolutionary legality, against anyone who in any
> way disagreed with Stalin, against those who were only suspected
> of hostile intent. . . . The formula "enemy of the people" was
> specifically introduced for the purpose of physically annihilating
> such individuals.

There were two theses of the anti-Stalin tract which were not
at all to Mao's taste. Firstly a Marxist-Leninist refutation of the
ideological pretexts for one-man dictatorship, for terror and mass-
repression. Secondly, the assertion that without democratic majority
rule in the Central Committee and the Praesidium (Politbureau),
and without Socialist legality, there is no defence against "the
wilfulness of individuals abusing their power".

[6] Mao's article in *PD*, March 9, 1953.

Mao could have had no warning from Khrushchev of this most dramatic turn of events, since *Khrushchev himself did not know on the first day of the Congress that eleven days later he was to read the anti-Stalin tract.** He was forced to read it by the pressure of events and that of some of his associates. It is unnecessary to elaborate what a shock this was to Mao at a time when the cult of his own personality had reached deification level and when he was forcing his régime to extremes of bureaucratic despotism.

Like all other Communist parties in power, the Chinese Party Centre received the official Russian text of the anti-Stalin tract and it was translated in a limited number of copies so that the higher cadres should be able to study it.

Subjectively Mao Tse-tung did not have many reasons to fret because of Stalin's demotion from historical greatness. Mao did not need the Khrushchev tract to be apprised of Stalin's colossal political blunders, or the Soviet despot's narrow-mindedness, prejudices, conceit, isolation from reality. He knew very well that Khrushchev's statement about Stalin's willingness to break with the Chinese Communists was an extreme understatement.

Objectively, however, the de-Stalinisation campaign, the ferment of freedom in Russia and in East Europe, and the massive assault on the cult of personality, were all most dangerous for his personal position, both in the present and as a historical figure after his death.

The thought that years after his death he too might be denounced as Stalin now was, certainly entered his head. In his speeches during the ensuing period he reminded China that it was he who had initiated the periodical purges against "commandists", terroristic and inhuman officials. He could not turn against Stalin openly, he could not even hint at his own difficulties with the dead Russian despot, but he could take steps to go down in history as a Communist ruler vastly different from Stalin.

III

The prevailing wind in the Communist world was now against police terror and bureaucratic despotism, and in favour of relaxation of thought control. As a good tactician Mao decided to move with this prevailing wind, to appear in China as the exponent of

* For an analysis of this most controversial event, see my *Khrushchev, The Road to Power*, London, 1960, pp. 182-209.

the "thaw" or, better still, to permit and prompt it, and at the same time control and canalise it. Still convinced of his popularity, of his supreme understanding of the masses, he announced the slogan of the period: *"Let a hundred flowers bloom, let diverse schools of thought contend."**

With his usual technique, this slogan was gradually revealed to the Chinese people. Although there are signs that Mao mentioned it some months earlier in higher Party circles, it was only on May 2, 1956, that he offered it as a campaign slogan at a *closed session* of the Supreme State Conference. The text of this speech is not yet published (1962!). China learnt about it at that time from various articles and speeches in which other leaders mentioned or expounded the guidance given by Mao, without committing him to exact directions or precise formulations.

This technique of gradual revelation is one of the reasons why Mao had his speeches and reports published months or even years after their actual delivery. The effects of a campaign launched by a Mao speech could be studied for months—the speech could then be edited, the text changed, so that its publication should furnish further proof of the Chairman's infallibility.

In January 1956, before Khrushchev's anti-Stalin speech, Mao announced that in China "the Socialist revolution, in the main, could be completed on a national scale within about three more years. . . . China at present . . . is in the high tide of Socialist revolution." In other words he intended to increase, not decrease the terror.

At the same time there were reassuring signs in the Chinese press, before the anti-Stalin speech, that the Party meant to exercise stricter control over too terroristic cadres and intended to correct abuses and make the life of the people somewhat easier. Intellectuals were reassured; China needed them and the Party intended to help them to raise their professional skill.

The Party's main newspapers printed letters to the editors, exposing cases of "commandism", "meetingism", "bureaucratism", etc. The letters always complained about one or "some districts", a single factory or office, for "globally" and "on the whole" the situation was supposed to be most satisfactory.

China could now read letters complaining that "female comrades" had no time to handle their family affairs, being forced to remain

* These are two old Chinese sayings. The word "hundred" does not mean literally the number as such, but simply "numerous".

long hours on duty even if there was nothing to do, and to attend pointless meetings. "When all participants have only their crying children and the sad looks of their husbands at heart, how can a meeting be expected to end in success?"[7] In one letter, a father wrote that his wife left at 6 a.m. when the children were asleep, and returned at 11 p.m. when they were asleep again:

When they stumble, they cry for their papa, but not mama. I also have very little spare time. The children want to hear stories, so I have to sacrifice some of my resting time to give them satisfaction. Because of this I am criticised by some leadership cadres for "liberalist distraction in departure from the masses". . . . My eldest child . . . learned to use different kinds of foul language . . . his face was smeared with dirt all day long. He ate irregularly and was always in rags. My wife wept with grief a number of times over this.[8]

Articles appeared with titles like "Why is there no rest all the year round?" "Why rob workers of their rest for the sake of long meetings?" and "Agony of having no time to educate one's children."

Similar letters and articles tried to reassure peasants, workers, intellectuals and writers that "Chairman Mao and the Party were intent on rectifying the mistakes of 'some cadres'". At the same time any general criticism of the Party was denounced as rightist, reactionary, counter-revolutionary and criminal activity. Criticism of mistakes was encouraged, but to talk of freedom in general or to demand freedom from Party control was still a crime.

One of the Party writer-functionaries, writing in the Tientsin *Ta Kung Pao*[9] stated with moronic frankness:

Chinese intellectuals who have recognised their own future will no longer think of the question of freedom, a term in vogue before liberation.

The high tide of socialist revolution, the first uneasy steps towards relaxing terror over the intellectuals, was interrupted by the effects of the anti-Stalin revelations, which started to spread all over China. At the same time, the food situation was again catastrophic. On March 23 the State Council issued a directive on famine

[7]*China Youth*, January 12, 1956.
[8] *PD*, January 15, 1956.
[9] March 26, 1956.

relief which said that in certain areas, largely owing to petty official callousness, "there are signs of some peasants suffering from
food shortage, while others are running away from their homes to
escape famine."[10]

Nature and some minor officials were again blamed, and the
minor officials punished.

Officially the Chinese general public heard nothing about Moscow's degradation of Stalin for more than five weeks. On March
30, the *People's Daily* reprinted a ten-thousand-word article from
the March 28 issue of *Pravda*, entitled: "Why is the cult of personality alien to the spirit of Marxism-Leninism?" This gave the Moscow Party line on what was to be praised and what blamed in
Stalin's career. From subsequent articles it appeared that Mao's
leadership deplored the pointless and economically wasteful bru-
talities which Stalin brought to socialist transformation, while of
course fully approving of the process itself.

In April, *People's Daily* articles emphasised that Communism does
not deny the great rôle of leaders in history. The Party line as to
the leader was confirmed on the Eighth Congress of the CCP
in September, by Liu Shao-chi:

> Our party's principle of collective leadership does not in any
> way negate the necessity for personal responsibility or the im-
> portant rôle of a leader. . . . The reason why the leader of our
> Party, Comrade Mao Tse-tung, has played the great rôle of helms-
> man in our revolution and enjoys a high prestige in the whole
> Party and among all the people of the country is not only that
> he knows how to integrate the universal truth of Marxism-Lenin-
> ism with the actual practice of the Chinese revolution, but also
> that he firmly believes in the strength and wisdom of the masses
> . . . and steadfastly upholds the Party principles of democracy
> and collective leadership.[11]

Although on May 26 the country was told about Mao's "hundred
flowers" campaign and in June the rectification drive began among
Party and Government personnel to eradicate terroristic, inhuman
and economically wasteful methods of leadership, the majority of
Communists and non-Communists alike did not dare to criticise.
The central organs of the Party and the Youth League had to
furnish examples. It is very important not to confuse the criticism

[10] *NCNA*, March 25, 1956.
[11] *NCNA*, September 16, 1956.

published between May 1956 and April 1957 with the real "hundred flowers" period. During these twelve months, the Party prompted some officials, some enthusiastic Communists and non-Communists, to expose vile and economically wasteful trends in the Party and Government bureaucracy.

Chiang Ming in *China Youth*[12] wrote an article under the title "Do not criticise indiscriminately and restrict the activities of youth." The article revealed that certain cadres of the Communist Party and of the Youth League at the universities were leading a concentrated campaign against talented, industrious and ambitious students who were being prevented from perfecting their knowledge and developing their powers. One undergraduate student of mathematics was so sternly criticised for having the "ideology of seeking fame and profit", that he did not dare to publish his highly original solution of a problem in higher mathematics.

The habit of spare-time reading and study outside the curriculum was persecuted as "bourgeois individualism", as "personal quest for fame and profit". According to *China Youth* some cadres held the belief, announced by one of them at a student meeting that "students should not become markedly prominent in their studies."

> Some comrades look upon efforts at study as the manifestation of individualism. . . . If differences between man and man are obliterated, if everybody is made to conform to the same pattern, it will not only violate the laws of objective beings, but also be detrimental to the cause of Communism.

Communists writing in the Party's own organs complained against the too wide application of the drive against "bourgeois individualism". They put the question: Why try to arouse the enthusiasm of the people for socialist emulation, why institute the system of "advanced workers", "model workers" and "labour heroes" if afterwards the Party organisations start to question their motives, conduct meetings against them, and make their life miserable?

China Youth[13] in an article entitled: "Why question the motive of our youth?", dealt with these questions and also with the experiences of enthusiastic Communists who were sincerely concerned with the problems of production and the life of the masses. "A Youth League member, seeing that the leading personnel of the mine

[12] May 16, 1956.
[13] September 16, 1956.

paid little attention to the hardships of the miners . . . brought
the matter up." For this he was instantly persecuted and became
a suspected person. Why is it, the paper asked, that if someone is
enthusiastic, courageous, original, the Party organisations promptly
say: "Let us see his motives!" "Is he seeking fame as a hero, as a
model worker, or a model Communist?" Why say that such people
have individualist, or even counter-revolutionary tendencies, why
say that they are "accusing the leadership" when they want to improve a concrete situation?

People's Daily in a July 16 article deplored the persistence of
wrongful punishment of members in some co-operatives as a result
of which "work is falling behind more than ever; it is obvious that
co-operatives will soon be ruined if members are punished continuously."

Some articles during this period of official "blooming" sounded
sincere. A professor of Physics at Tsinghua University attacked
"excessively rigid control of youth":

> Some people think that "education" is rules and regulations, put-
> ting youth within enclosures . . . abide by rules, be conservative
> and careful. . . . The methods they employ are also too severe,
> applying on youth pressure, and even corporal punishment. . . .
>
> I have seen for myself active and lively youth being gradually
> turned into silent and dull persons. Young friends who had
> grown up together, have separated for fear of being accused with
> the formation of small cliques. Proper living conditions and talent
> have all been restricted. . . . Proper love affairs . . . have been
> suppressed.[14]

The revelations during this period of carefully controlled "blooming" were quite shattering. But the criticism did not get out of
hand. Minor officials, cliques, bad districts were exposed, not the
general situation, not Mao Tse-tung and the Party. The other aspect
of this period produced some gems of wisdom:

> The themes and scope of literary works should be unlimited. *One
> may either praise the new society or criticise the old.*[15]

Peking Radio on July 11 defined the Party line concerning the
famous Mao slogan:

[14] *China Youth*, August 15, 1956.
[15] Chang Hen-hsui, at the Chinese Writers' Union Conference as reported by *NCNA*, July 17, 1956. (Emphasis added.)

The practical procedure of "let diverse schools contend" is the ideological remoulding procedure of the intellectuals; through contention a correct outlook . . . may be formed, enabling those who still held idealist views to see the truth.

It was not surprising that Chinese intellectuals did not dare to contend and that the masses of people were reluctant to "bloom". From the criticism voiced by Communists, however, it was clear enough to Mao and his associates that some of the government methods had to be rectified.

Mao's "let a hundred flowers bloom, let diverse schools of thought contend" slogan had, however, very great effect in the Soviet Union and the East European satellites. There, the intellectual ferment was nearing its climax when the Mao slogan was reported to the world at the end of May 1956. It was immediately taken by the "freedom writers" as proof that the greatest living Communist personality, Mao Tse-tung, was a leading exponent of the de-Stalinisation drive. It encouraged those Communist functionaries who hoped for a moral rejuvenation of Communism, it prompted opportunist commissars to join the anti-Stalin ferment, and to a certain extent it contributed to the Hungarian revolution and to the bloodless revolt of the Polish intellectuals.

But after more than six years of terror with fanfare, the Chinese people did not dare to "bloom and contend". They had to be prodded, cajoled, tricked and ordered into "blooming".

Mao no doubt also hoped to trick hidden enemies into revealing themselves, but all his actions before the real blooming began show that he thought the hidden enemies were in the minority. Like the gullible foreign visitors, who went to China "to see for themselves", the Chairman thought that on the whole his régime was immensely popular.

And then came Judgment Day.

XVI

THE VERDICT

I

The news of the Hungarian revolution shook Mao Tse-tung far less than had Khrushchev's unexpected anti-Stalin revelations eight months earlier. After the Soviet Government's declaration on October 30, 1956, about the withdrawal of Soviet troops from Budapest and about its willingness to open discussions on the general position of Soviet troops in Hungary, the Peking régime was almost jubilant.

Next day the State Council announced that it was "following attentively the Polish and Hungarian people's demand for democracy, independence and equality, and a rise in the standard of living based on the development of production".

"These demands are fully justified", Mao's government declared, and went on to call for firm opposition to "great-power chauvinism", which "inevitably results in serious damage to the solidarity and common cause of the Socialist countries".

Coming after Mao's "hundred flowers" slogan, this declaration of his government's support for the Polish and Hungarian people in their *just* demands for democracy and independence, convinced the Hungarian revolutionaries that they had Peking's full backing.*

The extreme hurry with which the Chinese government hastened to dissociate itself from Soviet "great-power chauvinism" was unprecedented in the six years' practice of the Mao régime. The prompt stand taken was, after all, not against the "imperialists", but against the Soviet Union.

In the absence of direct evidence the motives behind this astonishing and momentous move are still open to various interpretations. Considering the past experience and behaviour of the Mao leadership and its subsequent actions up to 1962, it would seem

---

* The editorial "With Arms at Rest" of the revolutionary *Irodalmi Ujsag* (Literary Gazette), published in Budapest on the morning of November 2, 1956, contained this sentence:

"West and East are on our side. America has just as clearly proclaimed her faith in our cause as have the mighty countries of China and India."

that they were not so much prompted by an imprudent thirst for revenge as desirous to attempt a breakthrough into the wide comity of nations.

Mao and his associates had ample reason for wanting to avenge themselves on the Russian Communists for their persistent and catastrophic interference in Chinese affairs and their manifest readiness to make deals with Chiang Kai-shek, the Japanese or anyone else likely to harm the Mao leadership. If it is true that Stalin started the Korean war to involve the Mao leadership in a war with the USA, while the USSR intended to remain a "friendly neutral", Mao had every reason to welcome the possibility of a Russo-American war over Hungary, which would have given a neutral Red China the chance to become stronger while the two world powers weakened each other.

All Mao's speeches and writings on the Western powers show that he believed in the fundamental unity of the "imperialists" when their supreme interests were at stake. He believed that the imperialists always and inevitably exploit every weakness of their opponents. Knowing how much the West was prepared to risk for Korea a few years earlier, Mao, Chou En-lai and the others, had every reason to expect the West to give prompt and massive diplomatic, economic and even military support to the Hungarians who had declared their independence and *neutrality*. It was, after all, not ludicrous to imagine that Eastern Europe was at least as important for the West as Korea. After the emergence of Yugoslavia as an independent Communist state, after the Polish events and the Budapest victory of the Hungarian revolution, prompt Western-United Nations intervention, the arrival of a UN mission in Budapest and a US guarantee of Hungarian neutrality and independence had a chance of success. And the establishment of an independent and neutral Hungary could have led, if not to the crumbling, at least to the weakening of Russia's satellite empire.

Only such reasoning, some such conviction, could have led Mao and Chou En-lai to their prompt declaration of solidarity with Polish and Hungarian aspirations for independence. It seems probable that they were convinced that the "imperialists" would promptly act in their own interests, that they would help Hungary, weaken Russia and open the first fissures in the satellite empire—as a consequence of which there would be every chance of solving the German and Berlin questions too in a way advantageous to the West. Being reasonably certain of some such sequence of events,

they had grounds for believing that while their declaration could
not now damage the Communist cause, it could yet greatly improve
China's international position.

All through the years from 1927 to 1956 the Chinese CP and,
since 1949, Red China itself had been isolated. The Soviet Union
was a member of the United Nations, Red China stood alone. China
was not in the Cominform and was isolated from the West. For
the first time, by declaring her solidarity with the Hungarian revolution, Red China was sailing with the prevailing wind that was
moving the whole world—except Russia. This was the chance for
a great breakthrough, with Red China declaring the same sentiments, taking the same standpoint as America, India, and the whole
world. Red China in the comity of all people—the Soviet Union in
isolation. Whether they expected an international war over Hungary, in which they could remain neutral, or a peaceful victory for
the West, this stand of theirs could have led to their admittance to
the United Nations, to Western aid, to the end of their isolation.
With the power of the Russian leaders over the Communist world
broken, China could have at once become the leading power of the
independent Communist countries, and Mao Tse-tung the great
new leader of international Communism—Mao, the real "anti-Stalin", who would thus have shown himself to be a more consistent
destroyer of Stalinism than Khrushchev.

But the "imperialists" were not so logically "imperialistic" as Mao
and Chou supposed them to be. The Suez affair led neither to a
great war nor to a localised one—as they hoped. At dawn on November 4, 1956, Khrushchev's mechanised divisions moved into
Budapest to crush the Hungarian revolution. By the evening it was
obvious that America and the UN were not going to stop Khrushchev. So on November 5 the Peking *People's Daily* (not the
Chinese Government!), announced a hundred per cent turn about.
The banner headline read: "CELEBRATE THE GREAT VICTORY OF THE
HUNGARIAN PEOPLE!" The editorial gave full endorsement to the
crushing of the Hungarian revolution. Instead of the Hungarian
people's "fully justified demands for democracy, independence and
equality", it turned out that "dollar-fed diversionists", "fascist beasts",
and "misled masses" had taken part in a "counter-revolution",
hence Khrushchev was right in giving brotherly help to the "Hungarian people".

As the declarations of Mao and the Chinese Government were
to show during the next few months, this *People's Daily* article was
a hasty improvisation, the result of confusion due to the unex-

pected turn of events. For once it was amply proved what a great crisis the Hungarian revolution had caused in the Communist world, Mao went back to the "great-power-chauvinism" line.

The Soviet Twentieth Party Congress and the Hungarian revolution had destroyed a large part of the Communist theoretical edifice. There was no current international Party line. Now Mao Tse-tung stepped into the breach and made his first major bid for ideological leadership of the post-Stalin Communist world.

On December 29, 1956, the *People's Daily* published the Chinese Politbureau's and Mao Tse-tung's "theses" on the fundamental contradictions inherent in the capitalistic system and the "non-fundamental contradictions" occurring within a Communist Party, between Communist parties, between Communist states and *between the peoples and governments of a Communist state*.

The *People's Daily* article went on to say that the Soviet Union was guilty of great-power chauvinism and the satellites of excessive nationalism. But Soviet intervention in Hungary was justified. The Soviet CP had taken commendable steps to eliminate past mistakes and to restore the solidarity of the Communist camp. It remained the "centre and core" (but not the "sole leader" as hitherto) of the Communist movement.

This was the theoretical preparation for an important move: *the first case in history of Chinese intervention in European affairs*.

It was most dramatically staged. Chou En-lai was on an Asian tour when Mao suddenly decided that the unity of the Communist camp must be saved through a prompt intervention. Chou returned unexpectedly from India on January 2, 1957, to consult with Mao, then flew to Moscow, and later to Warsaw and Budapest. The tour strengthened Khrushchev's position in the Soviet CP and the Soviet position in East Europe. Chou declared the Chinese Party's complete backing for the USSR and its determined hostility to all those threatening the unity of the Communist camp. He denounced the Hungarian revolutionaries in violent terms.

On February 27, 1957, Mao Tse-tung read to the enlarged session of the Supreme State Conference his exceptionally long tract "On the correct handling of contradictions among the people". Among the 1,800 participants there were several hundred non-Communists: leaders and deputies of the window-dressing political parties and representatives of the non-Party intellectual élite. In accordance with Mao's usual technique, the text of his speech was not published although it gave detailed guidance on handling "contradictions" (i.e. conflicts) among the Chinese people—between the Party and the Government on the one side and the people on the other. The speech repeated the slogans on "letting a hundred flowers bloom", "letting diverse schools of thought contend" and permitting "long-term coexistence and mutual supervision" between the Communist Party and the other parties in the government.

This speech led to the shattering six week period of "blooming", but its amended text was published only after the "blooming" had been brutally suppressed. When the *NCNA* released it on June 18, 1957, it was stated that "Chairman Mao went over the transcript and made certain additions". In fact, we have ample reason to know that as was his usual custom, Mao cut and altered important passages to show that events had not taken him unawares and that he had foreseen everything.

But the day after the speech was delivered the 1,800 members of the Communist and non-Communist élite who had heard it started to discuss it and went on debating it in public sessions— amply reported in the press—for the next two months. In March and April, the *People's Daily*, which can be regarded as the Chairman's personal organ, published dozens of articles on the correct handling of contradictions and, lastly, the Russian and East European Communist parties received either the complete *original* text, or authoritative extracts from it, some of which got into print. So we have a fairly full knowledge of what Mao said originally, and what he later changed.

For the non-Communists living in Communist countries, the original Mao speech was full of most hopeful signs. Mao stated that while the "methods of dictatorship" were to be used in dealing with external and internal enemies, contradictions among the people should be solved by the "method of democracy": education and persuasion instead of compulsion. "Crude coercive methods should not be used in this struggle, but only the method of painstaking reasoning". The formula for resolving contradictions among the people was that of "unity-criticism-unity" in which "struggle and criticism" would ultimately bring unity. The speech invited non-Communist individuals and parties in China to criticise Communists and the Party itself and commanded cadres to *rectify* their dictatorial, terroristic, coercive, bureaucratic methods in dealing with non-Communists. Below we first quote parts of the speech which we can be reasonably certain were contained in both the February and June versions:

Never has our country been as united as it is today. . . . The days of national disunity and turmoil which the people detested have gone for ever . . .

While we stand for freedom with leadership and democracy under centralised guidance, in no sense do we mean that coercive measures should be taken to settle ideological matters and questions, involving the distinction between right and wrong about the people. Any attempt to deal with ideological matters or questions involving right and wrong by administrative orders or coercive measures will not only be ineffective but harmful. . . .

After liberation, we rooted out a number of counter-revolutionaries. Some were sentenced to death because they had committed serious crimes. This was absolutely necessary. . . . Since 1956, however, there has been a radical change in the situation. Taking the country as a whole, the main force of counter-revolution has been rooted out. . . . As regards the suppression of counter-revolution, the main thing is that we have achieved successes, but mistakes have also been made. There were excesses in some cases and in other cases counter-revolutionaries were overlooked. Our policy is: "counter-revolutionaries must be suppressed whenever they are found. Mistakes must be corrected whenever they are discovered". . . . *Decisions on exoneration and rehabilitation should receive the same measure of publicity as the original mistaken decisions.*

. . . The policy of letting a hundred flowers blossom and a hundred schools of thought contend is designed to promote the flourishing of the arts and the progress of science; it is designed to enable a socialist culture to thrive in our land. . . . Questions of right and wrong in the arts and sciences should be settled through free discussion in artistic and scientific circles. . . . They should not be settled in summary fashion. A period of trial is often needed to determine whether something is right or wrong. In the past, new and correct things often failed at the outset to win recognition from the majority of people and had to develop by twists and turns in struggle. Correct and good things have often at first been looked upon not as fragrant flowers but as poisonous weeds. Copernicus' theory of the solar system and Darwin's theory of evolution were once dismissed as erroneous and had to win through over bitter opposition. Chinese history offers many similar examples.

In 1956, small numbers of workers and students in certain places went on strike. The immediate cause of these disturbances was the failure to satisfy certain of their demands for material benefits. . . . But a more important cause was bureaucracy on the part of those in positions of leadership.

. . . We do not approve of disturbances . . . but this does not mean that in our country there is no possibility of the masses creating disturbances. . . . *If disturbances should occur as a result of bad work on our part,* then we should guide those involved in such disturbances on to the correct path, make use of these disturbances as a special means of improving our work and educating the cadres and the masses. . . ." (Emphasis added.)

Five days before the amended text of the Mao speech was published in China, Sidney Gruson, the Warsaw correspondent of the *New York Times,* reported extracts from the original Mao speech which was at that time being hotly debated in Polish Communist circles. These extracts, published on June 13, 1957, when compared with the statements of those who heard the original text, have a very strong flavour of authenticity:

The opinions against the policy of a hundred flowers are the result of a fear of criticism, fear of losing the monopolistic position. They are an example of dogmatism. Marx never said that he should not be criticised. To those who do not follow that teaching of Marx, I would address an old saying: "He who does not allow himself to be criticised during his life will be criticised after his death". . . .

There need be no fear that the policy of a hundred flowers will yield poisoned fruit. Sometimes it is necessary even to have this poisoned fruit to know what it is that we are fighting against. For this reason, too, it has been decided to publish the full works of Chiang Kai-shek and even a volume of some of the Voice of America broadcasts. It is not enough to attack reactionaries. We must know exactly what the reactionaries want and what they represent. . . .[1]

The old saying—"He who does not allow himself to be criticised during his life will be criticised after his death"—could of course have been addressed to Stalin too, and may be taken as an indication of one of Mao's motives for the "hundred flowers" slogan.

Both the original and the published text contained exhortations to criticise Communists and their theory. A *People's Daily* editorial

[1] Sidney Gruson, *New York Times,* June 13, 1957, quoted by Mac-Farquhar, op. cit., pp. 275-6.

(April 17) emphasised that no one, *however exalted*, should be immune from criticism and self-criticism. The promise that the suppression of counter-revolutionaries would be re-examined and that unjustly sentenced people would be rehabilitated, while cadres and officials would be punished for criminal deeds, was tremendously encouraging. In both versions Mao urged freedom of speech among the people with certain reservations. We have good reason to think that in the original version the reservations were far fewer in number and far more vague than in the published version, when it was already too late for all those who had overstepped the (as yet unpublished) limits of permitted free speech.

A *People's Daily* editorial of April 1 urged the people that Mao's offer to "bloom and contend" should be acted upon. On the 13th this paper wrote against "seriously bureaucratic" individuals who have "rudely suppressed the opinions and demands of the masses and have impaired the rights and interests of the masses". Another article told "such cadres" that they should not be alarmed if the masses "got together and created disturbances!" If this was not an open invitation to stage strikes and demonstrations against bad cadres, then nothing was. Similar official incitements were very often repeated until the very day the avalanche started. It looked as if Mao had decided to incite turbulent meetings and demonstrations like those staged in Budapest by the members of the revolutionary Petofi Club.

A *People's Daily* editorial on the 23rd called for a nation-wide rectification campaign among Government functionaries. On April 27, the Central Committee of the CP issued a directive launching the campaign "to rectify the working style within the Party".

The people, however, still did not dare to "bloom and contend".

In his article, "Why is there a feeling of 'early spring'?" Chien Po-tsan wrote:

The intellectuals are still at the stage of groping their way at the moment. *They have to speculate for example whether the call for flowers to bloom forth is sincere or just a gesture. They have to guess to what extent, if the call is sincere, flowers will be allowed to blossom forth and whether the call will be recalled after the flowers are in bloom.* They have to guess whether the call for flowers is the end or just a means and whether the call is made for the sake of bringing prosperity to culture and science or of unearthing thoughts and rectifying individuals. They have to guess which are the problems that can be brought up for discussion and which are the problems which cannot be discussed.[2]

Everything was done to encourage "blooming" and to dispel doubts. On April 25 Voroshilov, the then nominal head of State of the USSR, arrived at Hangchow airport. While Chou En-lai waited for his arrival with the Soviet Ambassador to China, Yudin, and other Soviet officials, he had a "humorous and intimate chat" with the Soviet functionaries. Curiously enough, the *People's Daily* correspondent was not only permitted to eavesdrop on this conversation, but also to report it to his paper, which published it prominently next day:

The conversation started with Premier Chou En-lai introducing the guests to the scenery of Hangchow's famous West Lake. Holding a map of Hangchow in his hand, the smiling Premier told the guests: "I have been to Hangchow twice this year already so I can tell you something about the place." Comrade Rashidov observed: "It's usually hard for a leading Communist to find time to get around to different places." "Yes, one should get around more," the Premier said, "bureaucratism will develop if one always stays in Peking. The high city walls of Peking are likely to separate the leadership from the masses." Jokingly, Rashidov said: "These city walls have their advantages, too. They keep bureaucracy within bounds." "There's still another advantage," quipped Premier Chou En-lai, "if people oppose bureaucracy the city walls will keep them off for a time. But they cannot be a certain guarantee," he said. "Walls can be breached. Nearly forty years ago, we Peking students broke into Peking's ancient city to oppose the bureaucrats and war-lords of that day." He pointed to two children who had come to present flowers to Comrade Rashidov and Ambassador Yudin and said: "*If we don't change our bureaucratic ways, some day they will break through the walls. . . .*"
Ambassador Yudin said: "Oh yes. People think that since they have the support of the people, they cannot be bureaucratic." "Here lies the tragedy," Rashidov joined in, "one gets bureaucracy without being conscious of it. This work China is carrying on now is of great significance." At this moment, Premier Chou En-lai pointed to the two children and said: "If, ten years from now,

[2] *NCNA*, April 21, 1957, quoted by MacFarquhar, op. cit., pp. 27-28. (Emphasis added.)

there is still bureaucracy in the leadership, you should oppose it."[3]

In spite of all this prompting and cajoling, the great majority of the Chinese were still reluctant to use the opportunity for free speech, demonstrations and strikes, most personally offered to them by the "great Saving Star" of China. Whereupon the Party stepped in with direct commands. The Party Central Committee has a "United Front Work Department" which guides and controls the other democratic parties of the nominal coalition. This party department organised open "blooming and contending forums" on which leading non-Communists had to participate. The first forum was held on May 8, 1957, in Peking and soon in all the major cities of China. The press was ordered, as we shall see, to give the verbatim text of any criticism directed against Mao and his Party, to quote typical passages from other criticisms and also to report any instances of those disturbances, demonstrations or strikes to which the Party had now been urging the people for so long.

Khrushchev, in one of his unusual understatements, remarked about the Hungarian revolution that "none of this would have happened if a couple of writers had been shot in time". Mao too wanted to trick a few thousand (not a couple by any means!) hidden or potential enemies into showing their hands. He thought they *were* only a few thousand. As we shall shortly see, the Chinese Party later proudly proclaimed that the period of free speech was a trap set for potential enemies. But this was not quite true: not at least for some months. Between January and May 10, 1957, this was only one of the several motives behind Mao's actions. He really wanted to give the people a chance to let off steam. He really believed that a period of free criticism could act as a safety valve. He really believed that public debates between Marxists and anti-Marxists would strengthen the Marxists and would demonstrate the vast superiority of their creed. In February he said: "Fighting against wrong ideas is like being vaccinated—a man develops greater immunity from vaccine after it takes effect."

During this period he also wanted to demonstrate to the Communist world that his régime was popular and could afford extensive relaxation of control. It was so taken by anti-Stalinists and Stalinists

[3] *PD*, April 26, 1957, emphasis added, quoted by MacFarquhar, op. cit., p. 31.

alike in the European Communist countries. Gomulka told the Polish Central Committee on May 15:

> An expression of the great strength of the Communist Party of China and of its close unity with the nation is the introduction . . . of new methods in solving non-antagonistic contradictions. Similarly, the thesis about the hundred blossoming flowers is a bold step forward, so far unknown in the practice of socialist construction in other countries.

It is also quite certain that Mao wanted to weed out from his Party and Government apparatus the too bureaucratic, too terroristic, inefficient functionaries. Aware that so far people had not dared to criticise the cadres, he thought that in an atmosphere of frank criticism the régime would learn about anomalous aspects of its own apparatus hitherto concealed from it.

Between May 8 and the middle of June 1957 China and the world witnessed the astonishing spectacle of a Communist dictatorship opening wide the gates to an avalanche of pent-up fury, hatred, and desperation. This was not "blooming and contending" but a tidal wave. A mysterious tidal wave, because it was both controlled and uncontrolled at the same time. If it was a terrific shock to Mao in certain respects, in others he was fully prepared for it. For a time this tidal wave confused, bewildered and bewitched thousands of loyal Communists, and took quite unawares the security organisations that were supposed to be prepared for its arrival.

The flood of criticism was a mixture of most sincere outbursts on the one hand and the example set by cadres on the other. Some high-ranking Communists believed that the régime really would change and made violent attacks on the system of bureaucratic despotism, for which they later paid with their lives. Students all over the country were in a violent mood. They hoped to stage a "second Hungary". For Mao, the students—the products of his own régime —were the greatest shock, as they had been to his Hungarian colleagues who witnessed thousands of Communist students fighting wildly against Soviet tanks.

For a brief six weeks, the truth came out. The people judged. The Chinese Communist press produced massive documentation of the fact that Mao Tse-tung was the most hated man in the country, and that his Party was detested by the people.

Before giving an overall picture of this period, a few items must be quoted at some length to give an impression of the prevailing tone:

Ko P'ei-ch'i (lecturer, China People's University, Peking, in physics and chemistry):

When the Communist Party entered the city in 1949, the common people welcomed it with food and drink and looked upon it as a benevolent force. *Today the common people choose to estrange themselves from the Communist Party as if its members were gods and devils. . . .* The Party members behave like plain-clothes police and place the masses under their surveillance. The Party members are not to be blamed for this for the Party organisations instruct them to gather information. . . .

If the Communist Party distrusted me, the distrust would be mutual. China belongs to 600,000,000 people including the counter-revolutionaries. It does not belong to the Communist Party alone. . . . If you carry on satisfactorily, well and good. *If not, the masses may knock you down, kill the Communists, overthrow you.* This cannot be described as unpatriotic, for the Communists no longer serve the people. The downfall of the Communist Party does not mean the downfall of China. . . .[4]

From a 10,000-word open letter to Chairman Mao:

Our Constitution provides that citizens "enjoy freedom of residence and freedom to change residence." In fact, we have not given any of the 500 million peasants the freedom to change their residence to a city. . . .

Again, our Constitution provides that "freedom of the person of citizens is inviolable." During the campaign for the suppression of counter-revolutionaries in 1955, an untold number of citizens throughout the country were detained by the units where they were working (this did not happen to myself). A great many of them died because they could not endure the struggle. No matter how strong the "reasons" were for detaining these citizens, to conduct struggles against them, this was, after all, a serious violation of human rights.

This is tyranny! This is wickedness! . . .

We have applied to intellectuals methods of punishment which peasants would not apply to landlords and workers would not apply to capitalists. During the social reform campaign, unable to endure the spiritual torture and humiliation imposed by the

[4] *PD*, May 31, 1957. (Emphasis added.)

struggle . . . *the intellectuals who chose to die by jumping from tall buildings, drowning in rivers, swallowing poison, cutting their throats or by other methods, were innumerable.* The aged had no escape, and pregnant women were given no pardon. . . . Comparing our method of massacre with that adopted by the fascists at Auschwitz, the latter appeared more clumsy and childish (at any rate, they hired executioners), but more prompt and "benevolent". If we say that Comrade Stalin has not escaped from condemnation in history for his cruel massacre of comrades, then our Party, in my opinion, will also be condemned for our massacre of intellectuals who had already "surrendered" themselves to us. Our Party's massacre of intellectuals and the mass burying alive of the *literati* by the tyrant, Ch'in Shih-huang, will go down in China's history as two ineradicable stigma. This cannot but make us feel utterly heartbroken![5]

Two Communist professors against Party dictatorship:

Chang Po-sheng and Huang Chen-lu at a "contention" meeting of the faculty members of the Shenyang Normal College on June 10, jointly made a long speech lasting about three hours . . . Chang Po-sheng is head of the propaganda department of the Communist Youth League in the Normal College and Huang Chen-lu is editor of the school paper. . . .[*]

The central problem brought up in the joint speech by these two men was "doing away with the absolute leadership of the Party".

Huang Chen-lu said: "Since the founding of the Republic, particularly in the last one or two years, the Party has become superior to the people and has assumed privileges, praising itself for its 'greatness, glory and correctness' and placing itself above the State, above the people. . . . The Communist Party has 12,-000,000 members, less than 2 per cent of the total population. *The 600 million people are to become the obedient subjects of these 2 per cent of people.* What sort of principle is this? The absolute leadership of the Party must be done away with. The privilege of Party members must be done away with!"

---

[5] Yang Shih-chan, member of the Communist Party, Professor of Accountancy, Central-South Institute of Finance and Economics, date of letter May 17, 1957, published by *Hankow Ch'ang Chiang Jih Pao*, July 13, 1957. (Emphasis added.)

[*] The official organ of the Communist Youth League Committee of the college.

Supplementing this point, Chang Po-sheng said in his speech
. . . "The Constitution is a scrap of paper and the Party has no
need to observe it. Outwardly we have democratic elections, a
united front policy and non-Party people exercising leadership;
actually the Party exercises dictatorship and a few persons of
the Political Bureau of the Party Centre exercise absolute power.
. . . As to freedom of assembly, association and publication, that
is just something written in the Constitution; actually citizens
can only become obedient subjects or, to use a harsh word, slaves.
*The Party is the emperor and an august and sacred body. Who
dares to oppose it when it holds the bible of Marxism-Leninism
in the one hand and the sword of State power in the other?*
You would either be labelled an anti-Marxist-Leninist or hand-
cuffed with 'unfounded charges'". . . .

"The Communist Party, if it really represents the people, will
not be kicked out; if the Communist Party is kicked out, it means
it no longer represents the people. Is it pitiable to have such a
Party kicked out?"

Chang Po-sheng went on: "The National People's Congress is
nothing but a mud idol while all power is in the hands of the
Party Centre. . . . All kinds of important questions are decided
upon by six persons—Chairman Mao, Liu Shao-chi, Premier Chou
En-lai and those above the ranks of the secretary-general of the
Party Centre. . . . The destiny of 600 million people is dictated
by the pen of these six persons. And how can they know the
actual situation? At best they can make an inspection tour of
the Yellow River and swim in the Yangtze."*

"Even if they talked with the peasants, the peasants would not
tell the truth and could only say: Chairman Mao is great. . . ."[6]

Yen Wen-chieh, the director of a research unit in the Ministry
of Foreign Trade, had joined the revolution at Yenan in 1938 and
had been a Party member since 1942. His speech made at the
"contending session" of his ministry in June was only quoted when
criminal proceedings were opened against him. All those foreign
visitors to China, who have seen for themselves "how enthusiastically
the Chinese supported Communism", and who dismissed what
refugees in Hong Kong had to say about the horrors of the struggle
meetings as "biased accounts of reactionaries", should read what a

* A reference to Mao Tse-tung's famous swim across the Yangtze in
May 1956.

[6] *Shenyang Daily,* June 11, 1957. (Emphasis added.)

high-ranking Communist who had spent fifteen years of his life
in the Party told his own comrades in Peking about these "struggle
meetings". *NCNA* reported:

> "People who have gone through these movements themselves will
> remember the terror and even the thought of them causes their
> hearts to flutter and their hair to stand on end. . . . At that time,
> everyone felt that he might be the next victim and there was
> general terror in society. . . . *The scenes of struggle were more
> unbearable than prison* . . . I feel that these struggles might
> force some people who originally had no intention of becoming
> counter-revolutionaries to join the counter-revolutionary camp.
> . . . We must demand that the Government lay down a stipula-
> tion to the effect that the ordinary organs and organisations may
> not inaugurate any struggle meetings unless they have obtained
> the approval of the Procurate-General and that such meetings
> must be conducted under the auspices of a court of law. . . .
> Death to those whose false charges led to the death of other
> people. . . . Imprisonment for those whose false charges led to
> the wrongful imprisonment of other people. . . ."

He asked for fewer movements, so that people may put their
mind at ease, *instead of living in a tense state of mind from
dawn to dusk*. . . . Concerning the articles written by the
leader, he slanderously and maliciously said: "It looks as if one
article (Mao's) on how to handle contradictions is enough to
solve all the theories and work problems in the world. . . . If
the things written by a man have to be explained in numerous
ways before they can be understood by other people, we can very
well go without them."[7]

From May 7 until May 25 the impression given to the Chinese
people by government actions, by the press and radio, and also by
the conspicuous *inactivity* of the Security Police, Household Police
and similar bodies, was that for some reason or other, Mao Tse-
tung, Chou En-lai and some other Party leaders were *ordering*
free speech and bitter criticism and encouraging demonstrations
and strikes. The press also gave the impression that many dogmatic cadres were resisting these orders and trying to sabotage their
realisation.

The "forums" of the coalition parties were reported everywhere.
All over China "blooming and contending committees" were set up.

[7] *NCNA*, July 23, 1957.

Some high Party officials gave the initiative by boldly criticising certain evils of bureaucratism and even permitting themselves a few general remarks on the system as a whole. At this stage, of the thousands of non-Communists who spoke up, or wrote critical articles, the majority were quite prudent. Only some hundreds wrote in the spirit of the above mentioned specimens. Some outer Party members criticised boldly, hoping to reform the Communist Party "in the spirit of Mao Tse-tung". These simple souls believed—as Mao believed in his childhood about the Emperor—that the great ruler himself was good, and only some of his officials were bad. "Are you with the doctrinaires or with Chairman Mao?" some enthusiastic young Communist reformers asked their opponents.[8] Even high-ranking Party functionaries were misled about Mao's position. Writing about the June riots, NCNA (July 22), reported that at Tsinghua University "important bases of the Party's ideological front . . . had reached a state of disintegration and paralysis" and the First Secretary of the Party Committee had even spread the rumour that "Chairman Mao is under pressure" to stop the rectification movement against the cadres.

Some disenchanted Communist intellectuals turned violently against the dictatorship of the Politbureau. But the general picture drawn by the press gave the impression that these were isolated instances. This was not true. It turned out later that the editors were guided by the Party about what proportion of "poisonous weeds" to publish without any comment and what anti-Party excesses to publish with comment. And they were instructed, as was later admitted, to withhold the majority of the bitter attacks. At this stage, Mao did not want to discourage potential critics.

As the atmosphere of tolerated free speech gathered momentum, the Chinese press published quite sharp attacks on various aspects of bureaucratic despotism—coming from all sections of the élite. Ministers of the Central Government, Marshals and Generals of the Army, senior civil servants, university professors, famous writers, opera singers, actors, painters, physicians, sociologists, economists, historians, engineers, heads of industrial and commercial enterprises of the State—all attacked dogmatism, Party dictatorship, Security Police terror and the colossal mistakes committed in planning, in running industry, agriculture and commerce. But very few of the published attacks during this period were directly against Mao Tse-

[8] *Tsingtao Daily*, giving a summary of the June 2 riots in its July 18 issue.

tung or his régime as a whole. The critics exposed only the situation in their own profession, in their own branch of economy or
industry, in their own city or village. But read together, day after
day, the sum total of these exposures constituted a surprise for the
general public and a great shock to the simple credulous Communists who till then had felt that although there were many mistakes, on the whole everything was going well. For the people it was
of course no surprise to learn how monstrous the terror régime was.
It came as a surprise, however, to learn from cabinet ministers,
great economists, industrial and agricultural experts, etc., how
thoroughly inefficient and wasteful it was, that many famous "production victories" existed only on paper; that due to bureaucratic
muddle hundreds of waggons of food rotted in a starving country;
that factory workers were driven to long bouts of "shockwork" only
to find out that their products were then left for months in the
rain and snow because of lack of storage space, and so on. For
the believing simple Communists, outer Party members, it was a
terrible shock to realise that the extreme sacrifices of the population were largely in vain, that *because of* bureaucratic despotism
China did not produce more, but rather less.

These Communists then tried to save their Party by reforming
it; they joined the ranks of courageous critics.

The last to believe in the possibilities of free speech, and consequent basic reforms, were the students, the workers and the
peasants. But when they moved the storm broke out.

The great wave of revolt among the students started only on
May 19:

> Peking University has all along been ahead of the other institu-
> tions of higher education in the capital in "blooming and con-
> tending". . . . Students . . . have started a "Democratic Wall"
> on the campus in front of the dining hall and through the medium
> of large-character newspapers many views have been put forward
> directed against the "three evils". . . . Students themselves . . .
> thought that this was carrying on the democratic traditions of
> Peking University at the time of the May 4th Movement.[9]

The May 4th (1919) Movement was of course the first great
revolutionary demonstration against the oppressive régime of that
time. The fact that Peking students felt they had to agitate in 1957

[9] *Kuang Ming Daily*, May 26.

in the spirit of the May 4th revolutionaries, was certainly an ominous sign for Mao and his associates.

The Peking correspondent of the Shanghai newspaper, *Wen Hui Pao* was obviously in sympathy with the ferment in Peking. His report fanned the flames of revolt in Shanghai:

> Not long ago the sound of spring thunder was only indistinctly heard. But within a few days, all the flowers blossomed overnight. . . . The first critical bulletin appeared on the wall of the dining hall on the morning of May 19 . . . recommending the development of a *garden of democracy,* to develop a campaign for free debate. . . .
>
> The atmosphere of free debate at once engulfed the whole University. On the square in front of the dining hall (at Peking University), *like in Hyde Park,* thousands of students were listening to one heated debate after another. The Student Association announced that the period from 5 p.m. to 10 p.m. would be given to debates, and two classrooms were allotted for the purpose, while platforms were also erected and loudspeakers installed on the square to facilitate the holding of debates.
>
> In Peking University with its glorious revolutionary tradition, more than 8,000 young people had become inflamed with enthusiasm.[10]

The Peking students founded the "Hundred Flowers Society", the "Free Tribunal" and the "Hundred Flowers Tribunal". Without Party consent they published new magazines called *Public Square, Accusation,* etc. At Peking Normal University, two new students' papers were called *Voice of the Lowest Stratum* and *Bitter Medicine.*

The Peking Hundred Flowers Society sent teams to the universities in many other cities, carrying the "relay baton of democracy". These "relay batons" were in fact collections of mimeographed political tracts and memoranda. Students all over China were asked to discuss them, add to them, and pass them on. As in the revolutionary turmoil in Mao's youth, students and intellectuals produced hundreds of new magazines, with most revolutionary titles. In the various universities the students formulated their seven-, nine-, twelve-, sixteen-point demands, directed against terrorism, the security police, the oppression of workers and peasants. The "relay baton" memoranda asked the people to discuss the *sources* of the

[10] *Wen Hui Pao,* May 27. (Emphasis added.)

three vices so that people should realise that "not the working style has to be rectified but the State system itself".

In a matter of a few days, the atmosphere of free debate changed into a raging storm—so named later by the Party itself. The revolutionary storm was directed against Mao Tse-tung and the Party, and against the Communist system in general.

In some provinces, the rebellious students and intellectuals were in contact with similar groups of workers or peasants. At many universities and other higher institutes of learning, the rebellious students were led by disenchanted or "revisionist" Communists. As this storm raged on in Peking and other cities, high-ranking Communist intellectuals joined the movement. Party headquarters lost control over scores of Communist newspapers and periodicals for days, in some cases for weeks. For some days the Chinese press was not the precise instrument on which Mao's high command could play at will, mixing the proportions of various types of criticism, preserving the semblance that although there were anti-Party criminals, rightists and some misled people, the country as a whole stood solidly behind him.

Precisely because the press got out of control, Mao Tse-tung was forced to realise that in such a "freedom atmosphere" he could lose his tremendous power as the demagogue-oracle who in "normal times" (i.e. in a China completely terrorised by him), only had to speak one word to bring people instantly to heel.

So on May 25 he tried to stop the storm sweeping from the universities all over the country. On that day he told the delegates to the Communist Youth League Congress that *all words and actions that deviate from socialism are completely mistaken*".

As everyone in China knew that the word "socialism" meant in fact the dictatorship of Mao's Politbureau and the Communist Party, this was a command to stop the general attacks on himself and Communism.

He spoke the word and, most astonishingly, people did not obey instantly. Many did not even know it had been spoken.

The Communist editor of the *Current Events Handbook* (published by the Central Propaganda Department of the Party!) later confessed his "rightist" crime; that the *Handbook* edited by him had reported Mao's address to the Young Communist League "in brief", on the back page, without quoting what Mao said.[11] Many dailies reproduced Mao's speech in small type, *not fully*, and did

[11] *NCNA*, July 15.

not reproduce in a conspicuous place *People's Daily* leaders dealing with it. For all this, proceedings were later started against them.[12]

The real eye-opener for Mao came between May 25 and June 18. It was during these weeks that he had factual demonstration of the real situation—that the greatest danger to his régime came not from the frightened ex-capitalists, but from the students, workers and peasants and from an unknown but very large percentage of Communist Party members.

During the Party-ordered forum of non-Party people, many leading politicians had bitter things to say about the "saving star of China". On May 8, for instance, Chen Ming-shu, former Prime Minister of the anti-Chiang Fukien revolutionary government and NPC deputy, was imprudent enough to criticise Mao for being "hot tempered", "in love with greatness", "over-confident about the false reports and dogmatic analyses presented by his cadres" and "impetuous in making decisions without making a careful study of facts".

This was of course reported to Mao, but not to the general public which heard about it only when Chen made his tearful self-criticism.[13]

Lo Lung-chi, Mao's own Minister of Timber Industry and a member of the Standing Committee of the NPC, said at the same May 8 forum: "Chairman Mao is a very shrewd and crafty man, *much more ruthless than any other ruler in our history*". This again was only reported to the public when Lo had to answer for his crimes.[14]

These were non-Communists, old radical revolutionaries. But it was quite a different matter when on June 11 students posted on the main street of industrial Hanyang posters like this: "The Communist Party is going down and Chairman Mao will have to vacate his seat."[15] At the neighbouring Wuhan University, students spread their anti-Party movement to factories and rural areas and mobilised the masses to stand up to fight for "democracy", "human rights", and "liberty".[16] The Tientsin students pasted up posters in the streets "describing present society . . . *as a place of total darkness*". Another poster was more explicit: "Exterminate the Communist bandits". "*They also argued that Mao Tse-tung's thought was designed*

---

[12] *NCNA*, July 10 and 13.
[13] *Peking Daily*, July 28; *NCNA*, July 29.
[14] *NCNA*, August 10.
[15] Reported by *NCNA*, August 6; *PD*, August 8, 1957.
[16] *PD*, August 17, 1957.

to mislead the people."[17] Nanking University students on their "democratic walls", "demanded the termination of courses in Marxism-Leninism" and . . . "the establishment of real democracy."[18] Linchuan Normal School (Nanchang) students

slanderously described the leaders of the people and the State as "persons who ride in sedan chairs" who formed a "feudal dynasty imposed on the people". They also declared that "the power of the Party is in the hands of only Mao Tse-tung and Chou En-lai" and did everything to discredit them.[19]

The *Chinese Youth Newspaper*, in denouncing the large-scale revolt against Mao and the Party leadership *within* the Communist Youth League, gave no details. It reported only a summary:

The rightists inside the League wildly attacked the leadership of the Party, promoted the mood of distrusting the Party, did not execute the directives and policies of the Party, and *detached* the League from the leadership of the Party.[20]

Miss Lin Hsi-ling, a Communist Party member, twenty-one years old in 1957, a student of the People's University, at an open-air forum in Peking on May 23:

maligned the members of the Chinese Communist Party as mostly being "rotten eggs", intellectually stagnant and useless, with comparatively few true Bolsheviks among them. . . . She arrived at the conclusion that present-day China is not socialist. She loudly demanded a search for "true socialism" . . . and the reform of the present social system . . . she called [it] a class system [which] had already entered all aspects of life.[21]

Ke Yang, one of the editors of *New Observer*, a Communist Party member said:

In the past, to be a Party member one had to regard oneself *as either a lunatic or a corpse*. One could speak one's own mind only in the privacy of one's own bedroom.[22]

A correspondent of *NCNA* who joined the Party in 1944 was charged with planning to organise a "Revolutionary Committee of

---

[17] *NCNA*, June 29 and 30.
[18] *Wen Hui Pao*, June 29; *Hsin Hua Daily*, July 6.
[19] *Kiangsi Daily*, Nanchang, September 6, 1957.
[20] *CYN*, August 2, 1957. (Emphasis added.)
[21] *PD*, June 30, 1957.
[22] *NCNA*, July 26, 1957.

the Communist Party" to overthrow the present leadership and
eradicate the special privileged class of the upper cadres. He had
started in November 1956 with a 10,000-word letter "attacking the
Central Committee and Chairman Mao". In July 1957 he refused
stubbornly to criticise himself and he was ready to go to jail.[23]

During these three weeks and during the punitive campaign that
followed, it transpired that students of universities, colleges, normal
schools and middle schools all over the country took part "in the
anti-Party storm". Bombs were thrown (Peking Medical School, on
June 17, NCNA, June 20), "democratic walls" came into use at all
universities. On June 27, NCNA reported that at the end of May
"*a mad attack has been launched against the Party and socialism*".
A student of the Physics Department at Peking University had the
audacity to call Marxism an "obnoxious weed", others suggested at
a public discussion that "the Party Committee be removed from
the throne". The *People's Daily* was called "the Great Wall that
shuts out the truth".[24]

Rioting students in Peking, Tientsin, Shanghai, Nanchang,
Wuchang, Hanyang, Futan, Canton and other cities announced their
intention of staging another "Hungarian incident". They said that
"a mere call would make the peasants rise". They sent delegations to
factory workers in the cities and to the peasants in the countryside.
They beat up Party officials, security police officers, wrecked Party
bureaux and newspaper offices, and were suppressed only when the
"masses were mobilised".[25]

Middle school students were in similarly violent mood. For instance, about a thousand students of the Hanyang First Middle
School staged a rebellion which they themselves called a "Hungarian
incident in miniature". Between June 11 and 14 they organised
demonstrations; abducted and beat up Communist Party and Government officials; tried to rob the arsenal and open the county jail to
free political prisoners; drafted "A letter to the people of the country" denouncing bureaucratic despotism; besieged the Military
Conscription Bureau; tried to occupy the post office and were over-
powered only after four days by "the masses".[26] The three ring-

---

[23] NCNA, August 7.
[24] NCNA, June 20, 1957.
[25] NCNA, July 17-August 31; PD, July 24-August 8; Kiangsi Daily,
September 6; Tsingtao Daily, July 18; Changtu Daily, July 9; Hsin
Hua Daily, July 6; Wen Hui Pao, July 3-August 23, etc.
[26] NCNA, July 17, August 5 and 6; PD, August 8.

leaders were later executed before a mass-meeting of 10,000 people and more than a hundred others were sent to prison.

The reports of strikes and "incidents" in the factories and of rural unrest all over the vast country are too numerous for even a summary treatment. The newspapers reported "violent assaults" upon cadres by peasants from several counties of *each* province. Peasants left the co-operatives by tens of thousands. It was reported from all corners of China that rioting peasants shouted: "We are starving".

Reports from the provinces did not vary very much. The Vice-Chairman of the Kwantung Provincial Advisory Bureau for instance reported:

> The people of Kwantung Province are living on the verge of starvation. . . . The people of Hainan Island live wretched lives; the standard of living there is as low, if not lower than it was before the liberation. *Everybody is worrying about survival.*[27]

Similar reports came from most of the provinces. It was quite natural for the peasants when they learned they could do something to improve their situation, to start attacking the Party officials and village cadres.

As for the workers, the weeks of "blooming to order" started with the declaration of Lai Joy-yu, president of the TU Federation, that the trade unions had "lost the confidence of the masses" because in labour disputes they "always stood on the side of the government".[28] After a nation-wide investigation of the labour situation, it was officially stated that the workers distrusted and hated the trade union officials because the latter did not resist the factory Party committee and did not dare to speak up for the workers.[29]

During its "erroneous period", Peking Radio, reported on May 19 that in one factory 56.1 per cent of the workers lived barely above, at, or below subsistence level. Also in its erroneous period, *People's Daily* on May 29 suggested the gradual introduction of the system of workers' congresses in State-owned enterprises, so that "the workers' views should also be heard".

That the overwhelming majority of the workers and peasants betrayed their total hostility to Mao's régime during the hundred flowers period, was not only stated in so many words by Mao and the

[27] *PD*, June 28. (Emphasis added.)
[28] Peking, *Daily Worker*, May 7.
[29] Peking, *Daily Worker*, May 29.

régime's mouthpieces; it was brutally demonstrated by the campaign of total suppression that Mao ordered against them in the days that followed.

We have a great deal of circumstantial evidence that in June and July 1957 there were large-scale armed revolts in Honan, Kwangsi, Liaoning (Manchuria), and in most other provinces of China. Peasant guerilla armies, led by students and by disenchanted Communist officers, took to the hills. The Chinese Communist press, however, published only sporadic direct reference to these and similar revolts. Between August 7 and 10, *NCNA* reported the unmasking of two large-scale revolts in Central China, both in the Hunan-Hupeh area. The armed revolts in these areas were led by "The Central Headquarters of Mid-China Generals" and by "The Third Regiment of the Chinese Anti-Communist Army for the Salvation of the Country in the Hunan-Hupeh Border Region". In Yunan Province, south-west China, the "counter-revolutionary bandits were broken up and driven into the hills".[30] In Tsingtao, the "China Liberty Party" had armed bands and tried to establish branches in all the cities.[31] In Tsinghao Province, adjoining Tibet a "Government By All The People" was set up and crushed.[32]

Professor Fei Hsiao-tung, a former student of Professors Malinovski and Firth, an eminent anthropologist, whose *Peasant Life in China* and *Earthbound China* were translated into many Western languages, took part in a conference in Peking on June 6. It was called by the non-Communist intellectual leaders to discuss the revolutionary situation. Professor Fei Hsiao-tung was reported as saying:

> Once the students are aroused to action, the situation is likely to deteriorate. The students are looking for leaders everywhere. If teachers join in, there will be bigger trouble. Of course, it is easy to put it down. *Three million soldiers would put it down,* but public support would evaporate and the Party's prestige among the masses would be finished.[33]

Circumstantial evidence seems to support the eminent professor's forecast. "Bigger trouble" broke out all over China. And at least three million soldiers were used to squash it.

[30] *NCNA,* August 8.
[31] *NCNA,* July 27.
[32] *NCNA,* July 24.
[33] *PD,* July 4.

III

In his great confidence that contradictions in his China were really "non-antagonistic"—that they were not basic and dangerous for his rule, that the régime was popular and the nation united—Mao had insisted on having a period of free speech. Doing so, he had overplayed his hand. The first open forums of the Communist and non-Communist élite showed that in these circles the situation was far worse than anticipated. The first shock was the high proportion of Communist Party members among the bitter opponents of the dictatorship of the Politbureau. Then, and only then, did the trapping of hidden enemies become the main motive in Mao's action. But on May 15 he issued his warning that he would not permit basic criticism.

Knowing then that the writers, scientists, intellectuals, civil servants and many Party functionaries were against bureaucratic despotism, he anticipated that when the masses started to "bloom" there would be far more potential leaders of local revolts than he had imagined in February. So he made very large-scale preparations.

City by city, county by county, the "masses" were made ready for the possibility that some demonstrations might threaten to get out of hand. When student riots began in earnest in any city, the "masses" turned up promptly. In the cities the "masses" were dressed as workers, peasants and minor officials. They were supposed to represent the overwhelming majority of the population, loyal to the régime. These "masses" in fact were mostly Security Police officers and men in mufti, helped by employees of such auxiliary bodies of the security network as personnel departments, village and factory security teams and similar Party stalwarts, brought in from neighbouring districts. In the villages, the "masses" were soldiers on leave, students on their way to visit their relatives, factory workers passing by. The best proof that, even in the middle of May, Mao and his high command did not anticipate eruptions everywhere and on such a very large scale, is furnished by the fact that in many places the "masses" were not present in sufficient number to overpower a few hundred students. In the Wuhan industrial area, according to official reports, the number of rioting students was not over three thousand. And although Wuhan is one of the greatest industrial centres of China, with hundreds of thousands of factory workers, it took the "masses" a week to subdue the students. The real masses of Wuhan of course had no share in it. Thousands of them were themselves on strike. Later many of them were arrested and carted off to forced labour, for *their* counter-revolutionary activities.

The "masses" however could and did arrest many of the leaders everywhere. From June 16 onwards security police in uniform went into action. In the vastness of China the thousands of local rebellions were soon isolated from each other, encircled and thoroughly crushed.

The signal that *real blooming* was a crime punishable by death came on June 18, when the amended text of Mao's original "contradiction speech" was finally published. From newspaper reports we know that the original speech took four hours to read, but when the amended text was read to Peking functionaries it lasted only two and a half hours. Mao had cut out all those sections which events had shown to be too imprudent, and introduced a lot of retrospective wisdom meant to show his own Party that he was not too rash. He inserted the statement that to turn against one's own Party is a great crime. Only now did the country learn from Mao that "not to have correct political views is like having no soul".

And what Mao Tse-tung had learnt from the brief hundred flowers period was that the whole people was without a soul. Over the decades he had made his plans for remoulding the Chinese people. In Yenan in 1942 when his plans for this remoulding were already mature he told the intellectuals to become like workers and peasants. It seemed he truly believed that the majority of workers and peasants were not hostile to Communism. The bitter disillusionment caused him to order the remoulding of entire China.

While previously only intellectuals, bourgeois and petty bourgeois elements had to be remoulded by unity-criticism-unity debates (i.e. mass meetings for mutual brain-washing, or struggle-meetings against incorrect political ideas), he now said:

> We want all our factories, co-operatives . . . in a word, all the six hundred million of our people to use [this method] in resolving contradictions among themselves.[34]

But what he really had in mind was revealed by his next command. He ordered a nation-wide "Socialist education campaign" to solve the *"contradictions between the tasks of the State and the demands of the masses."*[35]

[34] *NCNA*, June 18, 1957.
[35] *PD*, August 5.

This was an open and massive admission that the masses do not "clamour all the time for a speedier advance on the road to socialism" (as he so often asserted himself) but have demands contrary to "the tasks of the State", that is, to Mao's one-man decisions.

The Central Committee directive on this campaign confirmed that it would take the form of debates (struggle meetings) in which workers and peasants would be "persuaded" of the superiority of the co-operatives, and the workers would be "convinced" that their short-term temporary interests conflict with their own "basic, long-term interests". Failure of persuasion, the Central Committee announced, might mean "disintegration".[36] There was no great risk of failure, since the Party repeatedly stated that "only bad elements cannot be persuaded". And "bad elements" were given over to that great educational institution, the security police.

But even before this great "educational campaign" was announced, Lu Ting-yi, Mao's Party propaganda chief, told the NPC delegates that "opposition to the Chinese Communist Party is *treason*".[37]

The rectification campaigns, originally directed against bureaucrats, were now turned against the entire nation. Once more it was terror with fanfare for everybody. The giant security police apparatus rolled over the country. Millions were carted off to forced labour camps. Tens of thousands were executed. Other millions were put under "public surveillance" as rightists. Everybody had to confess, everybody had to take part in self-remoulding.

The urgent task was to "prove" that the riot, revolts, strikes, and the attacks on Mao and the Party had been instigated, organised, led, and in most cases even carried out, by a "handful" of former landlords, capitalists, people of bourgeois origin, thieves, murderers, lechers and other thoroughly "rotten elements". The "people"—according to this particular Big Lie—were soundly on the side of the régime. Some, but very few, had been temporarily misled. But at the same time all 600 million of them had to be remoulded and re-educated.

What the people themselves thought about this when they were alone with the terrified beating of their hearts, the reader may imagine. Publicly they confessed. Publicly the peasants, in a Hupeh co-operative, "after a debate decided to *eat less*, to be frugal and

[36] *PD*, August 8.
[37] *NCNA*, July 11, 1957.

to sell *surplus grain* to the State".[38] In May and June peasants had
been reported as shouting everywhere that they were starving; now
they "discovered their erroneous stand" and reports streamed in from
all parts of the country that peasants decided to "conserve food
through reduced eating".[39]

The new campaign misled very few people. But Mao seems to
have been one of them. His own Security Police "found out" that
everywhere the "mad attack against the Party" had been financed
by the US imperialists, by Chiang Kai-shek or by "capitalists" and
other "bad elements". Thousands of agents, spies, former landlords
and capitalists confessed their crimes publicly, and were executed
for them—what more proof could anyone want? Mass-meetings were
held all over China in which everybody—students, intellectuals,
workers and peasants—bowed before Chairman Mao's picture, and
whenever his name was mentioned went on applauding wildly for
so long that often the leader of the meeting had to command them
to stop. There was "boundless enthusiasm" for the great leader and
for his "glorious Party".

Everyone who had a chance confessed. The editor of *China Youth
Daily* said in a speech on May 16, that Chinese newspapers were
"the notice boards, gramophone records and the reprinting presses
of the Party". Two months later he published his self-criticism for
"confusing the contents of propaganda with its technique . . .":

Because as far as the contents are concerned, what is wrong with
becoming gramophone records or reprints of Marxist-Leninist
ideology and the Chinese Communist Party policy?[40]

In May General Lung Yun, Vice-Chairman of the Defence Council, had criticised the Soviet Union for dismantling and shipping
away the machinery of Manchurian factories without ever compen-
sating China for it. He thought that "it was unreasonable for China
to bear all the expenses of the Aid Korean war, without any Soviet
financial help" (*NCNA*, June 18). On July 19, he publicly confessed
"although I erroneously believed that my motive for making
speeches in the past stemmed from my love of the country, actually
the objective results . . . have proved that they were anti-Socialist,
anti-Party, and anti-people". He now realised that what he thought
his "patriotic motive" was nothing but "reactionary nationalism".[41]

---

[38] Peking Radio, August 23, 1957.
[39] *NCNA*, August 7-17.
[40] *NCNA*, July 10.
[41] *NCNA*, July 20.

Professor Ku Chih-chung said on May 27 that "the freedom of the person as provided by the constitution has not been respected by certain people. Although citizens had the right to appeal against State personnel for unlawful acts . . . yet no one had ever exercised this right" (*Kuang Ming Daily*, June 3). A month later, the professor attempted suicide while being publicly "criticised":

He beat his chest and stomach and hurled himself against a stone pillar wildly yelling: "I cannot live on". . . . He was warned to be honest and to "remove his trousers".[42]

From July onwards the press published the texts of recantations and confessions. Some sample titles:

I Bow My Head and Admit My Guilt before the People, by Chang Po-chu.
A Review of My Mistakes and Crimes, by Huang Shao-chung.
Request for People's Forgiveness, by Huang Chi-hsiang.
Why Have I Committed Such Serious Errors? by Tan Ti-wu.
I Admit Guilt to the People, by Fei Hsiao-tung (the world-famous anthropologist quoted earlier).

The Chinese writers were the guiltiest of them all. More than half of the membership of the Writers' Union (to which all writers *must* belong) were sent to be remoulded through manual labour. *Pravda* published a Peking report on November 20:

As a result of reorganisation taking place in the literary journals and organisations of the Chinese Writers' Union, about fifty per cent of the members will be released for work at the grass roots level. Many Chinese writers have already declared their intention of living and working in factories or on the land.

But in November the campaign against writers had just been started. The punishment for them, as for all other deviators, went according to categories. Those labelled "counter-revolutionaries" were executed or imprisoned. The "rightists" were put under public surveillance. They were demoted from their former jobs, and given the lowliest of tasks to perform, had to report daily to the police, had no right to speak to anyone save their relatives, and were under "the constant vigilance of the Household Police". They were the lucky ones among the rightists. The rest were sent to do their self-remoulding through physical labour.

[42] *NCNA*, July 5.

The number of the worst category, that of counter-revolutionaries, was staggering. Before the end of July 1,300,000 counter-revolutionaries were discovered. Of the 1,880,000 intellectuals within the Communist Party more than 5,000 were counter-revolutionaries and more than 250,000 rightists.

In the Communist Youth League, 3,000 counter-revolutionaries and more than 180,000 rightists were found. The number of plots and conspiracies during the May-June period was not at once revealed. The investigations went on for a year before it was found that there had been over 3,600. In November it was reported that 810,000 Party and administrative cadres had been demoted.

One of the last anti-Party groups to be unmasked was the Communist leadership of Honan Province, in the heart of China. This group was led by the Communist commanding the province: Pan Fu-sheng, First Secretary of the Honan CP, and Political Commissar of the Honan Military Command. The charge against his group was:

they made publicly such utterances as "famine has occurred continuously" . . . "we are sitting on a volcano, the peasants will revolt and reject the leadership of the Communist Party" . . . "the problem of food production will not be solved in 10 years, mechanisation will not be achieved in 10 or 20 years" . . . "the peasants are beasts of burdens, human beings are harnessed in the fields, girls and women pull harrows with their wombs hanging out."[43]

The Communist governors, Vice-Governors, or other leading Communists of the following provinces were charged with similar crimes: Kansu, Chekiang, Tsinghai, Yunnan, Hopei, Kwangsi, Shantung, Liaoning, Kiangsi, Fukien and Hunan. Ministers of the Central Government, Generals of the Army, members of the Supreme Court and similarly high-ranking people shared the fate of innumerable students, peasants and workers, who all had to make false confession that they were former landlords or capitalists, spies and foreign agents.

These examples give a rough idea of the scope of this new campaign for the suppression of rightists and counter-revolutionaries. The Government never published full statistics. This would have been almost impossible in any case as the "criminals" of the 1957 hundred flowers period had still not been publicly indicted when a

[43] Report on the ninth enlarged session, CCP, Honan Provincial Committee, Kaifeng, *Honan People's Daily,* July 4, 1958.

new campaign was started against the opponents of the Commune movement.

The first campaign had barely got under way when it was announced that Chairman Mao next intended "to change man himself":

> In 1956 the Socialist transformation of the economic system was on the whole—though not finally—carried through to completion, but the *changing of man himself has not yet been completed.* . . . Time and again the Party has pointed out the need and possibility of transforming men, but no way has been found to convince the reactionary bourgeois rightists. . . . But men have to be changed. . . . If we do not win this battle, there is no hope for Socialism. . . .[44]

*   *   *

The British edition of this work was criticised by the London *Observer, Sunday Times,* etc., for the assertion that "tens of thousands" were executed for their participation in the revolts, uprisings and violent demonstrations during the hundred flowers disturbances. It was pointed out that there are no documentary proofs of these executions. This is true. But it is also true that opposition to the Chinese Communist Party was declared to be *treason* (page 310) and that Hanyang middle school boys were publicly executed for their deeds, although they had killed nobody. The present chronicler sees no reason to suppose that leaders and members of the "Third Regiment of the Chinese Anti-Communist Army", or those of the "Central Headquarters of Mid-China Generals" and many similar armed bodies were not executed, although schoolboys were. It ought to be remembered that until the 1956–62 Soviet revelations there were no documentary proofs, either, for the mass executions of the Stalin era.

[44] *PD,* September 18, 1957. (Emphasis added.)

XVII

SURRENDER YOUR HEART!

Mao Tse-tung: "If a person really takes an attitude of equality to others, they will feel so grateful that they will give their hearts to him."

(*Ta Kung Pao*, March 5, 1958.)

I

While the "poisonous weeds of thought-resistance" were being weeded out and trampled underfoot to "be used as fertilisers", the author of this suggestive sentence emerged from his Olympian seclusion to descend among the masses. He wanted to see for himself. From Court proceedings and from reports of mass trials when the people themselves screamed against the counter-revolutionary criminals, he had already received some reassurance that his original idea about contending and blooming was right. He had begun his speech on how to solve contradictions with the statement: "Never has our country been as united as it is today". The reports streaming in from every corner of the country were most reassuring. The new provincial Party Centres, once they had been properly purged, all reported that, although many errors and shortcomings had been discovered, things on the whole were going well, the people were enthusiastic and eager to progress towards socialism. They could report that "the great saving star of China" had never before been so popular. The people worshipped him.

But the great one wanted to see for himself. From July 1957 onwards whenever he could, he left for one or other of the provinces. With a very small retinue of bodyguards, he visited co-operatives, factories, kindergartens, schools, and the "masses" everywhere greeted him with boundless enthusiasm, with tears in their eyes—"tears of gratitude to fate that they could set eyes on him". In Shanghai, he called at a machine-tool factory. The workers were "beside themselves with joy":

Chairman Mao . . . had a stout build, a swarthy face with a red-dish glow, greying hair; wore a half-new grey-coloured uniform and black cotton shoes. He had in his hand an ordinary black folding fan. What could be more appealing to human emotions?[1]

[1] Shanghai, *Lao Tung Pao*, August 3, 1957.

He asked the workers, while their beloved Party secretaries and trade union officials stood by with a benign smile, if they were satisfied. "Do not be afraid to speak frankly," Chairman Mao said. And the workers frankly and sincerely told him, with beaming faces, that they were satisfied, that "the great wisdom of Chairman Mao" gave them inexhaustible strength and that they wished to be led into even greater "production battles". They realised—some workers added—that evil elements had played on their worst instincts of selfish greed.

The Chairman—as the papers constantly reported—moved along among the masses like a beloved father. The peasants told him sincerely and frankly how happy they were to work in the co-operatives.

And the Chairman travelled on. His appearance everywhere "liberated even more of the latent creative enthusiasm of the masses" —so all the papers reported, and so the production sheets showed which were sent to his secretariat. Everywhere the Chairman found some mistakes. He was told about bad bureaucratic cadres who wormed their way into the Party and managed affairs with "brutal commandism". Curiously enough, these were in most cases the very same cadres who had to be executed for their counter-revolutionary crimes.

As the Chairman travelled on, he was comforted to see that his formula "unity-debate-unity" was a sound one, that his people were now more united than ever before.

The speeches he made during these visits were never published. But wherever he was, the local papers criticised those waverers within the Party who advocated an erroneous "anti-rashness" policy, and who thought that the hundred flowers campaign was a rightist mistake. These waverers were afraid that the too leftist economic policy of accelerated socialisation was "adventurism", and would lead to troubles in production.

In the autumn of 1957 the situation was normal again. The blue-uniformed sexless millions (girls and boys, women and men wore the same blue cotton blouse and trousers) worked with "boundless socialist fervour". The loudspeakers at street corners, in village squares, factories, mess halls, trains and parks blared Chairman Mao's battle cries, slogans and wisely, simple formulas, which everyone could understand. The editorials of his very own Peking *People's Daily* were broadcast by the radio, read in study circles, explained at "blitz-meetings" in the fields and factories. Once more everyone from schoolchildren to dotards knew by heart the language of the day. Foreign visitors could truthfully report that aged peasants in godforsaken villages and children in the seaboard cities voiced the same opinions as Mao and his newspapers. Foreign visitors were solemnly told by old women in the sewing brigades and by university students how grateful they were to the Party for the All-China struggle-meetings which gave everyone a chance of self-remoulding and thought-cleansing. The intellectuals again spoke to foreigners through interpreters, once again they knew no foreign language. No one any longer complained, as the Peking Professor Fang Chung-chih had on May 14, that "when foreign visitors came to the university, the professors were forced to use Chinese and were not permitted to speak in a foreign tongue".[2]

Writers and intellectuals were silent. They were either using shovels to remould themselves in the interior or in the far North, or were in prison, or were taking part in struggle-meetings. The idea of individual talent was again under fire. Ting Ling, the famous woman novelist, who once in 1942 had had to exercise self-criticism in Yenan, was now unmasked as the leader of an anti-Party clique among writers. Ting Ling was the most famous among Chinese Communist writers and her novel *The Sun Shines Over Shangkan River* had received the Stalin Prize in 1951. A Party member for twenty-six years, she was now attacked by the entire press. *China Youth* (September 1, 1957), for instance under the title "Liquidate the evil influence of the soul-corroding master, Ting Ling" reported the general indignation in the country when an author forgets that the "literary calling is merely a nut in the overall Party machine. . . . We are against the bourgeois idea of the writer as a special sort of person, with individual ambition and even against the idea of individual genius."

Ting Ling was deposed from all her functions. In order to remould her evil genius she was ordered to scrub the steps and act as a charwoman in the Peking Writers' Union Building. There was to be only one genius in the country. His infallibility, the inevitable accuracy of all of his forecasts, the universality of his genius were praised all the time—things really had returned to "normal".

When Mao went to Moscow in November 1957 to take part in the anniversary celebrations of the Russian Revolution and the meeting of all the Communist parties in power, he was most confident. He was no longer overshadowed by Stalin. During the past year Mao had twice intervened to save Khrushchev's position, and

[2] *Kuang Ming Daily*, May 15, 1957.

this gave him an added stature among the Communist leaders. The more militant tone of the "1957 Moscow Declaration" was mainly due to his influence. In his parting speech he confidently told the Communist world: "It is now the East wind which prevails over the West wind."

For China a passage from his opening speech was far more significant:

> We are now carrying forward the people's self-education campaign among our 600 million people, stage by stage and section by section, and it is probable that in another few months nationwide success will have been achieved. *In future we aim to conduct a rectification campaign every year or every other year.*

China learnt that the struggle-meetings were here to stay, and that everyone had better behave all the time with an eye to avoiding the culprit's place on the platform at struggle-meetings.

The Khrushchev-Mao line of overtaking the imperialists in production was promulgated. China was to overtake Britain in fifteen years.

During his stay in Moscow Mao visited Chinese students, who greeted him with the customary "Long Live Chairman Mao", "Live for ten thousand years", etc. Mao was reported as remarking: "Please, do not say that. I am making only a five year plan for my personal future." If this remark—not reported in the Chinese press— was really made, and if Mao meant what he said, some of his actions become more understandable. Some observers think that this is one of the reasons for the insane speed of the drive towards Communism that Mao has forced on his associates and on his country.

Whatever were the reasons, he certainly did force the pace. He again ruled the country—and overruled the highest organs of his Party and his State—by slogans, battle cries, formulas, "basic equations" and campaigns. These slogans, formulas and equations were, however, not composed in 1957 when he is said to have realised that he might die soon, but years and decades earlier.

Ever since his Kiangsi days Mao has asserted in various formulations one of his favourite axioms, which in 1940 he put in this way:

> The deepest source of military strength lies in the masses of people. Weapons constitute an important factor in war, but not the deciding factor. *The deciding factor is man not material.*[3]

[3] *On the Protracted War.*

The Chairman taught his people that "the deciding factor is man" not materials—as much in "production battles" as in guerilla war. The deciding factor is the enthusiasm and the muscle power of the properly commanded masses.

After his Moscow visit Mao continued his travels in the country, trying out the effect of his axioms and slogans "at the grass root level". Most of these were first launched without fanfare "among the masses", and it was from the newspapers that the Central Committee and the State Council learned that the meetings between Chairman Mao and the "simple, toiling people" had produced a new campaign, hit upon a new task, found a new solution for China's problems.

These problems were many. The rate of population growth was fourteen million a year and the first Five Year Plan could not even keep pace with this population increment, let alone tackle the further development of agriculture and industry. The pressure of the population grew enormously, and agriculture could not produce "surplus value" enough to finance the most necessary industrial constructions. Only the properly commanded masses could save the situation. It was in March 1958 that all China started to learn what the solution was.

1958 was a tremendous year. The Chinese population reached 682 million. It was one of the years of the glorious Mao Tse-tung era. It was also the first of the three bitter years, announced by the Chairman:

Build up work enthusiasm, work bitterly for three years and promote industry and agriculture.[4]

Although Liu Shao-chi and his faction in the Politbureau were advocating a policy of consolidation, Mao's travels created the necessary atmosphere to enable him and his principal supporter, Chou En-lai, to overrule the "anti-rashness" faction.

Mao found a new formula: "balance-imbalance-new balance" as the basis of "positive planning". A *People's Daily* editorial, quoting the Chairman, wrote that the way to success was to upset old targets, turn balance into "imbalance" and constantly organise a new balance in all sectors of the economy. Instead of consolidation, Mao advised constant and dynamic tension in planning and production. This was one of the new miraculous Mao-formulas. The Party, and even the very influential Liu Shao-chi faction, had to concur.

[4] *PD*, February 18, 1958.

The Central Committee directive of March 3 on the rectification campaign was full of quotations or paraphrases of Mao's earlier speeches. The directive tried to reconcile the "two urgent tasks of production and rectification", because "some comrades" felt them to be contradictory:

> During the campaign miraculous surprises will occur constantly . . . advanced targets, hard to reach ordinarily, will also be reached with the establishment of good examples and miracles. . . .
> . . . Some existing regulations and systems which are no longer favourable to the growth of productive forces will be broken constantly by the creativeness of the masses. . . . Already some people demanded that unreasonable wage and welfare systems be cancelled or changed.[5]

The Chairman, this infallible oracle, forecast new miracles. He also forecast that peasants and workers would demand more work, less pay and less welfare amenities. And by March 15, a *People's Daily* editorial could already report meetings at which workers asked for *higher* work norms and the discontinuation of "unreasonably" high wages.

The Great Leap Forward was announced.

Mao told the world: "The great liberation of the productive force of the labour people has the same effect as the smashing of the nucleus of an atom."[6]

For days China heard this wonderful thesis expounded, repeated, developed, extolled and repeated over and over again. "H-bombs and American space satellites are paper tigers. (Maybe even Soviet H-bombs and Sputniks are paper tigers too?) The Chinese people whose liberated enthusiasm for work equals nuclear energy can and will perform miracles. Given the necessary battle cries they will win all the production battles."

The immediate tasks were great. According to the Chairman "the supreme target [was] turning 600 million people into a force that is not only 'Red' but also 'expert' ".

But woe to those who are more expert than Red. In remoulding China, the balance-imbalance-new balance formula also held true. The Chairman said: "Continuous self-transformation, even for Communists", is necessary to ensure that everyone continues to be "Red";

[5] *NCNA*, March 3, 1958.
[6] *PD*, March 16, 1958.

whoever ceases transformation is faced with the danger that his colour may "fade".[7]

But quick self-remoulding and the "liberated productive force" of 682 million people were not enough to speed up industrialisation and the progress towards Communism. A more efficient method of regimentation had to be found to "liberate completely" the energy of the people. The formula for this method Mao had found long ago in his youth, when he learnt parts of the *Communist Manifesto* by heart. Marx and Engels, writing their *Manifesto* in 1848 set ten tasks for proletarian dictatorship after taking over power. Two of these were

1. Combine agriculture and industry and facilitate the gradual elimination of distinction between town and country.

2. Combine education and material production.

These two measures were the ingredients of the Mao-formula for the communes, which resulted in the worst miseries the long-suffering Chinese millions have ever experienced:

> The communes . . . combine industry, agriculture, commerce, education and the militia within each unit, thus facilitating leadership.[8]

> When the system of communes is fully established the differences between workers and peasants, between town and country, as well as mental work and manual work—these remnants of the old society . . . will gradually disappear.[9]

Mao did not launch the commune campaign openly, since the majority of the Party leadership was against further "adventurism". But the first large Communes were organised during his rural travels in March and April 1958. The first communes were established in Honan as early as April, yet the second session of the Eighth Congress of the Chinese Communist Party held in May did not adopt any resolution regarding the establishment of communes. The Congress was opened by Mao, but his speech was not released to the press. The Central Committee's official report was presented by the Vice-Chairman of the Party, Liu Shao-chi, who praised Mao's leadership; but the general line of the Central Committee report was still that of consolidation of "socialist" ownership and the carry-

[7] *NCNA*, March 26, 1958.
[8] *NCNA*, August 11, 1958.
[9] *NCNA*, August 31.

ing out of a technological and cultural revolution, thus "completing
the socialist revolution on the economic, political and ideological
fronts". Liu repeated the Mao slogan "Build socialism by exerting
our utmost efforts to achieve more, faster, better and more economically". It appeared that the Central Committee fully endorsed the
other Mao battle cry: "Hard work for a few years, happiness for a
thousand." In the name of the Central Committee Liu gave full
backing to the "great leap forward" policy but by praising Mao Tse-
tung for it twelve times in his report, he underlined Mao's responsibility for it.

But there was definitely no talk of communes or of leaping forward straight into Communist utopia. According to all the basic
tenets of Marxism, even to start to proceed from socialism to Communism a country has to have fully achieved socialism and the
highest possible grade of industrialisation. The Chinese Communist
Party, when it closed its Congress on May 23 agreed only to speed
up the progress *towards* socialism and industrialisation.

At Mao's personal instigation, however, hundreds of thousands of
peasants had been already herded into communes, which are the
units to facilitate the leap into Communism.

In May the word "commune" was not yet used as a campaign
slogan. But there were scores of other campaigns going on simul-
taneously. The overall rectification movement included the special
drive against "conservativism and waste" in production, and the
great "ideological remoulding campaign".

During the end of April and the beginning of May there were
the "kill-the-sparrows" days all over China. As sparrows consume
food, which is scarce, it was decided to exterminate them. Literally
the entire population had to take part in the "anti-sparrow" drive.
In the capital, according to Peking Radio (April 28) three million
people went into battle. At 5 p.m. schoolchildren carrying pots and
pans, ladles and spoons, students, civil servants, workers—all with
their noise-producing instruments took up their positions. Then
bugles sounded, factory sirens howled, cymbals clashed, rattles rat-
tled, whistles trilled and the swarms of bewildered sparrows flew
helplessly hither and thither until, exhausted, they dropped down
to be exterminated. In the cities and all over the countryside people
were ordered to give no rest to the sparrows, until they were all
liquidated. The command was given and 682 million people
obeyed. Even foreign embassy staff were asked to take part in the
anti-sparrow drive.

But before launching the drive for communes, and the "everybody-produce-steel" campaigns, the wise Chairman discovered that if he treated people as equals during his brief visits to the factories or the fields they were so grateful that they gave their hearts to him. So now, he simply asked all China: SURRENDER YOUR HEARTS!

These words were uttered at the beginning of the year. Soon the Chinese cities and villages were witnessing the "heart-surrendering ceremony". In Shanghai 10,000 democrats, carrying a giant heart of red cloth and heart-surrendering pledges, paraded through the streets to the Shanghai Communist Party Centre building, to implore Chairman Mao and the Party to accept their hearts.[10] In Tientsin "some 30,000 industrialists and businessmen have pledged to surrender their hearts" in a mass-demonstration lasting for hours. They asked the Party to end public-private ownership, to take over completely their enterprises and to "let them become 'people'".[11]

In Peking, for instance, the street committees which constantly supervise every inhabitant, increased their meetings from one to three a week to bring the rectification campaign to the remaining housewives and elderly persons, who produced thousands of posters with suitable criticism and self-criticism and with "heart-surrendering pledges".[12]

Rectification, self-remoulding and thought-cleansing were "tremendously helped by the millions of large-character posters produced everywhere. . . . The power of the posters lies in the fact that everything is revealed in the sunlight."[13] In order to save paper, the large red characters were printed on old newspapers. On millions of walls all over China these posters quoted Chairman Mao's sayings and exhorted people to everything to which they were supposed to exhort each other that day.

The campaigns went on and people urged each other to work more for less pay; but they still did not know what was in store for them. On May 29 the *People's Daily* wrote that the historical significance of the Party Congress lay in its "determination of the general line of building socialism. This general line is the result of Chairman Mao's creative application of Marxism-Leninism". But still no word about the communes.

Two days later, on June 1, the first issue of the Party's new

[10] *NCNA*, March 21.
[11] *NCNA*, March 31.
[12] Peking Radio, April 7.
[13] *PD*, March 28.

theoretical fortnightly, *Red Flag*, was published with Mao Tse-tung's article:

> Throughout the country the Communist spirit is surging forward. The political consciousness of the masses is rising rapidly. . . . In view of this it may not need as much time as was thought before, for our country to catch up with the big capitalist countries in industrial and agricultural production. The decisive factor besides leadership by the Party, is the 600 million people. The more people, the more views and suggestions, and the more intense the fervour and the greater the energy. Never before have the masses been so spirited, with such high morale and so strongly determined. . . .

> China's 600 million people are: first of all poor and secondly "blank". This seems a bad thing, but in fact it is a good thing. Poor people want change, and to do things, want revolution. A clean sheet of paper has nothing on it and the newest and most beautiful pictures painted on it. . . .

> The posters written in big characters have broken the dull air where "ten thousand horses stand mute". . . . A poem written by Kung Tzu-chen of the Chang dynasty reads:

> "Thunderbolt wake the universe to vitality! Shall, sadly, ten thousand horses stand mute? I counsel heaven to bestir itself anew and breaking set standards, bring forth genius."

China learnt that Chairman Mao was again in thunderbolt mood. He was again intent on breaking set standards, and his great genius was about to paint pictures on the "clean sheet" of the Chinese people.

They were the pictures of life in the communes. To describe these "newest and most beautiful pictures" one has to quote the prosaic words of the Chinese Communist newspapers.

II

> It is obvious that, under the direction of Mao Tse-tung Thought, and at a time when national economy and culture are developing at such a rate that "twenty years are concentrated in one day", one can visualise the transition of our country from Socialism to Communism (*NCNA*, August 30, 1958).

> Our country will enter a new era; from the socialist era based on the principle of "to each according to his work", to the Communist era based on the principle "to each according to his needs" (*Red Flag*, Peking, August 30, 1958).

It was of course the accepted privilege and task of the Soviet Union to lead the Sino-Soviet orbit by "blazing a trail" towards Communism. From the August 7, 1958, *People's Daily*, however, the Red globe learned that the first "basic unit" for the advance to Communism, a "people's Commune" had been fully established in April of that year. It was in Suiping County of Honan Province, it comprised 43,000 members and it was organised after Chairman Mao's visit to the county. It was named Weihsing Commune. "Weihsing" is the Chinese word for Sputnik!

It seemed that after all the real Sputniks circling the globe were "paper tigers", like H-bombs and electronically-guided nuclear missiles. The aim and summit of all human history, for which all Marxists strive—Communism in the literal sense of the word—was to be reached by these far more important "Sputniks" devised by the Great Saviour himself. Britain was to be overtaken in fifteen years. But for all perceptive Communists it was obvious that Chairman Mao meant to overtake the Soviet Union in this very same year of 1958. He wanted to start his country on the transition to Communism, before Khrushchev's Twenty-first Party Congress in Moscow announced in 1959 the same transition in the USSR!

This time it was not only the highest organs of the Chinese Party and State which were confronted with a *fait accompli*, but also Khrushchev and the whole Communist camp. In July 1955, when Mao came out with the thunderbolt of one hundred per cent collectivisation, there had been no press campaign to prepare anyone for it. This time, the leaders of the Mao faction and a large part of the Chinese press conducted a not very subtle campaign to prepare people for the full regimentation of all China into semi-military brigades in which "everyone is a soldier-worker-peasant-student"; for "the emancipation of women from household chores"; for the elimination of the family.

During this preparatory campaign two statements were endlessly repeated: 1. Communes were being formed on the initiative of the peasants themselves and their idea had "caught on"; 2. They were the results of Chairman Mao's "brilliant application of Marxism" to the present era.

The first authoritative reference to the communes as Mao's basic policy came from one of the Chairman's staunchest supporters, Chen Po-ta, who announced that the communes would create the necessary conditions for the transition to Communism.[14]

14 *NCNA*, July 2.

On July 6, *People's Daily* announced that families would be "constituted along revolutionary lines, i.e. with a Government organ, factory, co-operative . . . street or village as a unit. These revolutionary families will, in due course, grow to the size of a city, the whole of new China and even the entire socialist camp."

As the reports came in about the various first "experimental communes", the Chinese people discovered another highly—one might say, deadly—significant aspect of the commune movement. The first communes were formed in Honan, Szechuan and Liaoning provinces. These provinces had all been visited by Mao during his extended inspection tours between August 1957 and April 1958. *And they were precisely the same provinces in which not only the peasantry, but also the Party leadership had revolted in 1957 against bureaucratic despotism.*

The reader should bear in mind that the terrible indictment of Mao's régime, quoted in the last chapter, was voiced by the first Communist secretary of Honan, this huge central province of China. It was here that the Party leaders said publicly: "famine has occurred continuously . . . the peasants will revolt because they are beasts of burden, human beings are harnessed in the field, girls and women pull harrows with their wombs hanging out." These Communist leaders were dealt with at the July 4, 1958, session of the Honan Party Committee, more than three months after the Honan peasants were alleged to be taking the initiative in forming the first peasant commune in the world.

It is a hard historical fact that Mao forced peasants into communes in precisely those territories which were completely encircled and occupied by punitive security police troops where he was on the spot to give direct orders, where the Party apparatus was just then being decimated by his firing squads. And he did this without the knowledge of the majority of his colleagues, and before the policy had been discussed, let alone approved, by the Political Bureau.

On July 22 his *People's Daily* announced that communes would also be formed in the cities where "workers' dependants and city residents will be liberated from drudgery and household chores so that all of them may take part in socialist construction".

It was only after a few hundred articles had given the impression that a large part of China was already organised in communes, that the Party's highest organ, the Political Bureau, which is supposed to initiate all basic policies, was called to a meeting on August 17 to "discuss the question of the communes".

Six days before this meeting Tan Chen-lin, a Maoist member of the Politbureau, summarised Mao's ideas on the purpose and rôle of the communes:

Comrade Mao Tse-tung had said that we should, step by step and in good order, organise industry, agriculture, commerce, exchange, culture and education, the military forces into big communes to form the basic units of our society. Now some places are beginning to merge co-operatives into bigger ones to meet the objective needs of the great leap forward. *This merger follows the guiding ideas of Comrade Mao Tse-tung. . . .* These new events, emerging under the brilliance of Comrade Mao Tse-tung's ideas, represent the great aspirations of 500 million peasants to build socialism rapidly in the country and to march towards Communism.[15]

What could the more prudent members of the Political Bureau do? Their meeting was an "enlarged session"—enlarged by safe Mao-supporters. To attempt to overrule Mao was unthinkable. To do so, they would have had to appeal to the people against the Great Saviour. Such an appeal would have led to a great anti-Communist revolution. And the Politbureau members were all Party stalwarts. But even so, their debate lasted from August 17 until August 29, on which day their decision was published. The Politbureau duly decided to organise all the peasants into communes. It also ordered a nation-wide campaign for steel production in small home-made furnaces.

The day this decision was taken, more than 350 million peasants were already in communes. And a month later, at the end of September, 98.2 per cent of the rural population was in these "basic units" of Chinese society! Mao had pointedly demonstrated to all China that the Political Bureau was a rubber-stamp body, which would be used contemptuously late. He alone was to be given credit for the beautiful pictures of life in the communes.

In Hsinyang Special District of Honan, the people in the communes have become disciplined by the large-scale collective labour system. . . . Tremendous changes have taken place in their moral views . . . and living habits. As a result, public mess halls, nurseries and sewing teams have mushroomed everywhere. At present, more than 37,900 public mess halls have been estab-

[15] *NCNA*, August 11.

lished. . . . In seven centres public mess halls have become almost the only place for people to have meals.[16]

The peasants . . . should act more quickly and with greater
discipline and efficiency, so that, like factory workers and the
army, they can be deployed with greater ease and on a larger
scale.[17]

At Chao Ying commune in Honan assembly bells ring and
whistles blow at daybreak. In about a quarter of an hour the
peasants line up. At the command of company and squad leaders, the teams march off to the fields, holding flags. One no longer
sees peasants in groups of two or three smoking and going slowly
and leisurely to the fields. The desultory living habits of thousands of years are gone forever.[18]

At the beginning it was envisaged that all communes would be
mixed. They would be socialistic in paying wages "according to
work" and Communistic in giving free supplies "according to need".
The trouble was that commune members, graded into six to eight
categories, received less and less wages, and the "according to
need" principle meant not the real need of a person for food and
clothing, but the Party's decision on what that need should be.
Soon, however, a campaign to abolish wages was begun.

All will work together and all will eat together, so it will be
superfluous to talk about "to each according to his work".[19]

Collective living completely emancipates the women and thus
breaks up the family as the economic unit of society.[20]

Children should be under communal education as soon as they
are old enough to be separated from their mothers. This is the
ideal of all Communists.[21]

The peasants have entrusted the power of arranging their way
of life to the Party and the people's commune.[22]

In nearly 500 villages in Kiangsu the peasant houses were de-
molished to use the old material and thatch to erect 10,000 dormitories and mess halls in seventeen "Habitation centres". It was

[16] NCNA, August 21.
[17] Red Flag, September 1.
[18] NCNA, September 23.
[19] PD, September 5.
[20] PD, October 1.
[21] China Youth, October 31.
[22] PD, November 10.

emphasised that concentrated housing enables "organisation along military lines, the carrying out of duties in combat style, and living a collective life. . . . In each centre, the peasants assemble in a quarter of an hour and march promptly off to the fields, thereby raising labour efficiency."[23]

In a speech on September 30 Mao Tse-tung declared that "the organisation of militia divisions is very good and should be prompted. It is both a military organisation and a labour organisation, both an educational organisation and an athletic organisation."[24]

Mao's slogan "everyone a soldier-labourer" was promptly translated into reality. In Szechuan thirty million, in Shantung twenty-five million, and in Honan twenty million people, were organised into the new kind of labour militia. The movement spread like a forest fire.[25] "Everyone a soldier! Everyone drill!" In Hopei, people drill "before going to the field in the morning and before blowing out the light in the evening". In Fukien the thing was sloganised: "Be at drill when the cock crows and when the sun sets; be busy at work during the day."[26]

Mao's régime knew, however, that the peasants should not be trusted with too many rifles. Only part of the drilling was carried out with real rifles, the rest with dummies. During the drill with real weapons there was always sufficient army and security staff around to prevent any nonsense. The Director of Mobilisation of the Chinese General Staff gave this warning: "As our class enemies both at home and abroad will certainly try to sabotage our efforts in extensively setting up militia divisions, we must see to it that the arms of the militia are in . . . reliable hands."[27]

Most of the story of the harvest and steel battles can be told in the then current slogans and battle cries:

"Fight for every single minute or second regardless of night or day, rain or shine!"

"Eat and sleep in the fields, and fight day and night!"

"Work like ants removing a mountain!"

"Take no heed of a broken bone or bleeding head, but ensure the fulfilment of the iron and steel tasks!"

[23] *PD*, November 12.
[24] *PD*, October 1.
[25] *PD*, October 11.
[26] *China Youth*, No. 18, 1958; *Ta Kung Pao*, October 8.
[27] *PD*, October 30.

People were reminded all the time that they lived in the glorious
Mao Tse-tung era when twenty years are concentrated into one day.
They were also told to welcome tension:

> Tension is the feature of the order of life in our present era. If
> we do not live tensely how can we . . . build socialism and enter
> the Communist paradise?[28]

The peasants went into harvesting battles, they built dams, road
bridges in "combat-style", and took part with all other Chinese in
the great battles for home-made steel. Wading knee deep in mud,
pulling tremendous loads, they were exhorted by fat female Party
agitators who screamed Mao slogans at them through loudspeakers.

Scenes like those were reported from all corners of China: in
Szechuan thousands of people were deep-ploughing day and night.
The bugles sounded well before dawn, men and women rushed
from their tents to the river-side to wash their faces, then lined up
in the fields, moving with quick discipline like soldiers.[29] Everybody
in Mao's very own Chingkangshan area in Hunan fought to "harvest
iron-ore. No matter whether the person was an old man with white
hair or a child under ten, whether a worker, a peasant, cadre or
housewife, everybody took a hammer and basket and ran into the
mountain. After dark, there was light everywhere and the sound of
explosions continued throughout the night."[30] In formerly rebellious Kwangsi Province "some 70,000 men and women camped out
in the mountains, insisting on fighting for iron-ore even when they
had no water for two days."[31]

In the capital itself the workers slept in their factories during the
great leap forward. Their slogan was "Do not leave the front before
winning the battles."[32] In Honan "people fought day and night,
shifting all the activities of life—eating, sleeping, office, conference
and even nursery—to the field."[33] Also in Honan, in the woman's
battalion, "not a single member left her post for ten days and ten
nights. Some of them passed the doors of their homes three times
without entering."[34]

[28] PD, editorial, October 20.
[29] PD, October 24.
[30] PD, September 30.
[31] Chinese Worker, Peking, No. 21, 1958.
[32] PD, October 6.
[33] PD, October 20.
[34] PD, October 9.

At this time there were great differences between various communes. In some of them, a member got about fifteen pounds sterling worth of supplies and wages for a year, in others twice as much. In many communes all through 1958 the families still lived together; in many others men, women and children were separated, husbands and wives having bi-monthly "private nights" together. In others, where accommodation was scarce, married couples had to queue up on Saturday nights for their bi-monthly "private two hours".

All rural China was in communes by October 20. This was stated by the Maoist Secretary-General of the Party, Teng Hsiao-ping, who —as the Shanghai *Wen Hui Pao* reported on that day—said that urban communes must be set up as a matter of urgency.

But "some cadres" were already being attacked for committing errors while carrying out Chairman Mao's wise policies. "Some cadres" in charge of mess halls "treat the peasants as beggars rather than hard-working people receiving remuneration in kind."[35] *China Youth Daily*[36] published this peasant poem:

> *At the sound of the cease-work bell*
> *We enter the mess hall to eat.*
> *Taking one mouthful of rice,*
> *We find sand between our teeth;*
> *Helping ourselves to the vegetable,*
> *We find grass stalks in it.*
> *We lay down the chopsticks,*
> *And go to work again.*

In one county in Honan "the majority of mess halls not only have no dining rooms, but even have no facilities to keep the cooked rice and vegetables warm; consequently the commune members always eat cold meals."[37] In Shensi Province, according to the official report, the majority of over 100,000 mess halls "have very simple facilities; there are no dining rooms, and the masses have to take their meals in the open air in all weather."[38]

And not all mess halls could supply sufficient food. In parts of the country, there were "famine situations". On October 22, Peking Radio complained of a "tight food situation" in the cities.

In October, high Communist officials of Shantung, Kwangsi and

---

[35] *NCNA*, October 22.
[36] Peking, November 4.
[37] *PD*, November 9.
[38] *PD*, November 11.

Liaoning provinces were dismissed for "right-wing conservative" opposition to the great leap forward.

On November 9, a *People's Daily* editorial called for prudence:

> We can *now* afford to let people have sufficient rest because of the huge amount of work put in before. . . . The purpose of allowing people to have sufficient rest is that we may achieve forward leaps at greater speed in the future. (Emphasis added.)

This was addressed to commune leaders and factory managers all over the country. The Shanghai Party Committee obeyed and instructed officials to ensure for workers and peasants eight hours sleep a night in the future! The labour movement in the West scored a victory when the eight hour working day was recognised as a maximum. In China, progressing towards Communism, eight hours sleep a night had to be defended. In reporting the Shanghai decision, *The People's Daily*[39] added a special plea for the welfare of young people, expectant mothers and the aged.

Red Flag (No. 12), complained that many cadres "consider the militarisation of labour an excuse for high-handed measures, and take 'debate' as meaning 'struggle', thereby *causing the masses to shudder at the mere mention of debate.*" Commandism became rampant. If members of a brigade had some objection to an order, debate, that is struggle, was ordered against them. Labour brigades of too independent a turn of thought were simply given no food for a day.[40] But still all these warnings had no quick results. In Licheng county, Shantung, many cadres

> ignored the health of the peasants, forcing them to labour 16 hours a day and insisting on it even when they asked for a rest. Consequently many people became so over-exhausted that they fell into a doze right at work, thereby gravely lowering labour efficiency.[41]

The rest of the population fought on the iron and steel front. *NCNA* on October 5 reported from many provinces that "hundreds of thousands of women are . . . co-ordinating their efforts in iron and steel production". In Chenghow, housewives have set up sixty-eight steel plants, ninety-four iron plants and eighteen mining teams.

[39] November 14.
[40] *PD*, November 20.
[41] *PD*, November 19.

In Hunan Province, 600,000 women were engaged in iron and steel production.[42] Mao Tse-tung, however, was not satisfied; he said:

> On the iron and steel fronts the masses had been mobilised, but taking the country as a whole, there are still some places . . . where the mobilising work had not been done so well.[43]

The home-made iron-smelting furnaces often collapsed with the liquid iron flowing in every direction. People who had to produce steel *after* doing their "normal" daily work, and who consequently worked mostly at night, suffered many casualties. Yet everybody worked at building home-made furnaces, gathering iron-ore, smelting iron. City barbers, schoolchildren, the remaining housewives, everybody. Smelting furnaces were built in school yards, squares, on the outskirts of villages. It soon turned out that "definite losses have been sustained because the labourers were not well protected."[44]

During the same period the propaganda about leaping forward into Communism was stepped up. Not only Mao and his closest entourage, but even Liu Shao-chi, implied in speeches that "pure Communism" would be achieved in the near future. The drive for giant communes comprising hundreds of thousands of members had begun.

This propaganda drive was coupled to another, against the "bourgeois idea of wages". *People's Daily*[45] in an article entitled "Don't Allow Banknotes to Take Command" maintained that during the great leap forward labour should be "voluntary . . . without a definite limit and without remuneration conditions". Workers were quoted with approval for saying: "Now politics take command, while banknotes took command in the past". Two days later, the same paper quoted some anonymous workers as saying: "We now work hard for socialism and Communism but not for extra wages".—But China recognised Mao's inimitable style.

On November 17 and 18 Peking Radio, quoting profusely from Chairman Mao's speeches, dealt with the problem of wages. It was authoritatively stated that the principle "to each according to his work" was a *"bourgeois legal concept"*. It had to be replaced in the future by the Communist principle "to each according to his needs".

[42] Peking Radio, October 13.
[43] *NCNA*, October 16.
[44] *PD*, November 29.
[45] October 16.

These new aims and slogans were naturally quoted in millions upon millions of large-character posters, small posters, and giant placards that covered all buildings as high as men can reach. Posters were suspended on clothes-lines, hung out of windows and even pasted up on trees. In addition to all the campaigns, shock-works, production battles, debates, Marxist study meetings, sparrow and rat extermination drives, everybody had to take part in poster writing and pasting campaigns. In this drive too, there was a socialist contest between factories, streets, villages, etc. Those who could write, wrote Maoist slogans on posters; those who could not, helped to stick them up. In the large cities the literate ones could read daily on thousands of posters the same slogans about leaping straight into Communism, about doing away with wages, which the loud-speakers blared at them all the time.

Millions of posters quoted in full or in part these sentences from the October 10, 1958, *People's Daily* editorial:

Today in the era of Mao Tse-tung, heaven is here in earth. Once the party calls, tens of millions of the masses jump into action. Chairman Mao is a great prophet. Through scientific Marxism-Leninism he can see the future. Each prophecy of Chairman Mao has become reality. It was so in the past; so it is today.

And the great infallible went on predicting the great leap into Communism.

Then Khrushchev stepped in.

III

All through the commune campaign the Soviet press was conspicuously and singularly quiet about it. Mao's oft-quoted statement that "the liberated, united and organised 600 million people constitute the greatest creative force in the world, and in comparison the United States and Britain are but dwarfs"—was trebly offensive to Khrushchev. Firstly, if sheer numerical superiority makes up for the lack of modern industry, the Soviet Union with her 200-odd million inhabitants would be a dwarf too. Secondly, if the muscle power of 600 million people can make up for full industrialisation, then the Marxist-Leninist theory of the transition from socialism to Communism is all wrong. Thirdly, the communes were offered by Mao as the way to Communism for all under-developed countries. And Khrushchev felt that the communes would not appeal to the non-white world.

In its October 1958 issue Khrushchev's main ideological journal, *Voprosi Filozofii*, explained the Soviet stand on transition to Communism in an authoritative article. According to Soviet theory, the European Socialist countries, led by the USSR and united into a single economic council, "comprise a particular economic zone and *will be the first to enter Communism*". The "Asiatic Socialist countries . . . comprise another regional zone and will also enter Communism all together."

This was the first sign of the Soviet attitude to China's leap into Communism. The second was when the Soviet revolution's anniversary slogans for November 7, 1958, flatly denied the Chinese claims. Slogan No. 4 read: "Long live the Twenty-first Congress of the Soviet CP—the congress of *the builders of Communism!*" Slogan No. 13 was: "Brotherly greetings to the great Chinese people *building socialism!*"

Mao had not only challenged Khrushchev's ideological leadership of the Communist world several times in the past but also interfered repeatedly in various campaigns of Khrushchev's in the international field.* Khrushchev could not act freely as the foreign-policy maker of the whole Communist world. During the 1958 Middle East crisis, for instance, on July 23, the Chinese press violently attacked the proposal for summit talks in the Security Council as a "deceptive plan" . . . "full of pitfalls and loopholes". Two days later Khrushchev nevertheless agreed to the plan. But he then had to fly to Peking and spend four days there (July 31-August 3) to obtain Mao's backing. Instead he had to give up the Security Council summit idea. Before the issue of transition to Communism arose Mao and Khrushchev had clashed several times. But the greatest clash came when Khrushchev's pressure and Mao's own opponents and critics in the Chinese Politbureau forced Mao to a verbal retreat regarding the communes and the leap into Communism.

The opponents of Mao's adventurous policies in the Chinese Communist leadership could quote the opposition and misgivings of the Soviet Party and of Khrushchev, and also the opposition of peasants and Government and Party functionaries. At the beginning of No-

* Mao's separate Asian policy, his endangering Khrushchev's coexistence —and summit—campaigns by producing the various Taiwan crises; the timing of the Quemoy shellings in 1954, '57 and '58; in 1955 the USSR offered to use its good offices to persuade China to discuss Taiwan (Formosa) in the United Nations, but the Chinese refused, to the evident embarrassment of the USSR; the initial stand over the Hungarian revolution in 1956, etc.

vember, Mao had to call a series of conferences on the Communes. There were numerous reports in the press about peasant resistance to the communes, about slaughtering of livestock, "going slow" in field work, "poisoning the cadres". Opposition to communes was reported as existing not only "among the masses of the people" but "also among the ranks of cadres" . . . "Some cadres seriously oppose the Party's (Communes) policy".[46]

Many Communist cadres could not forget that they were parents too. And they objected to the Mao line as expressed in this truly astonishing article in *China Youth*,[47] entitled "The Patriarchal System and the Family.":

> Children should be admitted to kindergartens and nurseries to be brought up, and to live a collective life from infancy, thereby cultivating the habit of loving labour. There is no doubt that this is better than for the children to be raised by the parents themselves. . . . But parents are reluctant to hand them over, they hold that the children are their "own". . . . Even in the comparatively modern family . . . in which children were not beaten and scolded, they were nevertheless regularly held as precious things, decorated and well clothed, given all facilities for fun and joviality. . . . It would be very difficult for children brought up in this way to become "new people" . . . capable of attending to all tasks.

Mao's drive against the family, against love, against not only human but even animal nature, created a front of opposition ranging from non-Communist peasants to high Communist functionaries. The universal opposition to the communes, the dissatisfaction in the army, caused by the too severe rectification drive among officers and men, the criticism of the industrial and agricultural experts, the danger that the Soviet CP would openly attack the Chinese Communists as "left deviationists", produced a situation in which Mao had to retreat.

As recently as August 1958 the Chinese Political Bureau had been unable to restrain Mao. Nevertheless three months later he had to make at least a temporary retreat and had to give up one of his most important positions, mainly because his power as the "demagogue-oracle" was temporarily diminished. His conferences with lower Party functionaries held before the Politbureau and Central

[46] *Red Flag*, No. 12, 1958.
[47] December 1, 1958.

Committee Sessions showed that these too wanted a relaxation in the great leap forward.

The decision about Mao's double retreat was made in the Standing Committee of the Political Bureau which was and is at the apex of power—limited only by Mao's strength as the demagogue-oracle. This time Mao obviously was in no position to overrule his colleagues, none of whom wanted to oust him, but the majority of whom wanted to avoid an open clash with Khrushchev and the Soviet Party. The majority was also convinced that the commune movement had to be slowed down. The Standing Committee consisted of seven members: Mao Tse-tung as Chairman of the Politbureau and the Central Committee, and the five vice-chairmen of these bodies, Liu Shao-chi, Marshal Chu Teh, Prime Minister Chou En-lai, the economy chief Chen Yun and Marshal Lin Piao. The seventh member *ex officio* was Teng Hsiao-ping, the Secretary-General of the Party. The seven members of this all-powerful body, just like the majority of the other nineteen full and alternate members of the Politbureau, were Mao-men in the sense that they had worked with Mao since the Kiangsi days. Most of them had taken part in one of the Long Marches, or worked illegally in enemy territory as chief representatives of the Mao-leadership. Out of the ten Marshals of the Chinese armed forces, seven were members of the Politbureau, all former commanders of the Red Armies that came into being in the 1927-30 period: Marshals Chu Teh; Lin Piao; Defence Minister, Peng Teh-huai; the former bandit chief, Ho Lung; Foreign Minister Chen Yi; Liu Po-cheng and Lo Jung-huan.

The seven men at the top and their nineteen colleagues in the Politbureau concentrated all the commanding positions in the Party, the State and the army in their hands. Mao was also head of the State and as such Chairman of the National Defence Council which is not responsible, even in theory, to the National People's Congress (Parliament), or the State Council (Cabinet). The other Politbureau members were and are chairmen and vice-chairmen of parliament and cabinet. And as the State is run by the Party, they were and are their own superiors in their State functions. Since 1957 the major government directives have been openly counter-signed by the Central Committee of the Party, in practice by Mao as the head of the Party.

The top seven and the rest of the Politbureau were not divided into two or more factions as far as any struggle for power was concerned. They were a team working together, untouched by purges, for nearly thirty years under Mao's leadership. But there were at

least two factions as to political strategy and tactics. The economic
chief, Chen Yun, represented among the top seven the "anti-rashness" line. Born in 1901 he was, with Marshal Lin Piao, the youngest among the supreme leaders, and the only member of the Politbureau of working-class origin (the others come from peasant or
middle-class families), Chen Yun was the first Deputy Prime Minister, directing affairs during Chou En-lai's absences. The factual
objections against Mao's too rash leap-forward policy were probably
most strongly voiced by Chen Yun. This is demonstrated by his
temporary fall from power. Another influential member of the Politbureau ousted subsequently was Marshal Peng Teh-huai, who was
replaced in 1959 by Lin Piao as Defence Minister. It transpired in
the years to come that the then Defence Minister Marshal Peng
Teh-huai protested in a memorandum handed to Mao against the
excesses of the leap forward, against the commune movement, and
against the lowering of the peasants' living standard. It seems that
the Marshal sent a copy of this memorandum also to Khrushchev.
Chen Yun, Marshal Peng and some others helped Liu Shao-chi, the
second man in the Party, to convince Mao of the necessity for retreat. Chou En-lai, as was his custom in the past, probably acted as
arbitrator between the two opposing lines.

That Mao must have encountered very strong opposition both
within the Politbureau and the Central Committee was indicated
by subsequent demotions, in the government and the army. When
in the autumn of 1959—as we shall see—Mao regained his demagogue-oracle powers, his press carried ominous references to
attacks on the Party leadership with the intention of disintegrating
it.[48] Chen Po-ta, the deputy propaganda chief, wrote that "some
wavering and unreliable elements in the Party" were apt to be influenced by reactionary attempts to undermine the Party "even
from within the core of leadership."[49] Hsin Hunan Pao (November 29), complained that "right opportunists tried to alienate relations between the armed forces and the Party". Lastly, these anti-
Party activities were linked to the "opportunists of the type of Kao
Kang", who was purged in 1954 because he tried to oust Mao with
Soviet backing.[50]

The sixth plenary session of the Chinese Central Committee
was held from November 28 to December 10, 1958, "under the

[48] PD, September 28, 1959.
[49] PD, November 11.
[50] PD, September 28.

guidance of Mao Tse-tung". On December 10, they reached agreement to accept Mao's offer to relinquish his office as Head of State and to renounce as utopian the leap into Communism.

These decisions were published only a week later. The Central Committee statement, issued to the press through the New China News Agency on that day, said quite openly:

The session deliberately postponed publication of the resolution to reduce the impact which such publication might have on the people.

The Committee first called a number of telephone conferences to transmit the highlights of the resolution to the people of various nationalities and circles in China. The statement went on to say:

. . . According to reports from various localities, at the beginning of the discussions a large number of people were unable to determine the logic of the resolution. Emotionally, they all wished that Comrade Mao Tse-tung could continue to be Chairman of the State. Later on, after detailed, patient explanations, the overwhelming majority of the people began to understand the reason. . . .

During the discussions, many persons pointed out that by serving exclusively as Chairman of the CCP Central Committee and not as Chairman of the State, Chairman Mao will be able to devote his mind and energy to questions concerning the principles, policy and line of the Party and State and have more time to engage in Marxist-Leninist theoretical work. This is in keeping with the long-term and fundamental interests of our State and our people as a whole. Furthermore, this will in no way prevent Comrade Mao Tse-tung, as Chairman of the CCP Central Committee, from continuing to assume his brilliant leadership over the work of the State. It was generally felt that although Chairman Mao will no longer serve as Chairman of the State, he will still be a great leader, winning the unanimous love and support of all the peoples of various nationalities of our country. . . .

The highlights of the decisions were these:

Any attempt to negate prematurely the principle of distribution according to work and replace it with the principle of distribution according to needs—that is, *any attempt when conditions are not mature to enter Communism* by over-reaching ourselves—is undoubtedly an utopian concept that *cannot possibly succeed.* . . .

. . . The urgent tasks at present are *quickly to achieve a unity of views on the communes among all members of the Party* and among the people, strengthen the leadership over the communes, check up and consolidate their organisation . . . and improve the organisation of production and life in the communes. . . .

We should not groundlessly make declarations that the people's communes in the countryside will "realise ownership by the whole people immediately" or even "enter Communism immediately" and so on. To do such things is not only an *expression of impetuosity,* but it will greatly lower the standards of Communism in the minds of the people, distort the general ideal of Communism and vulgarise it . . . and adversely affect the development of socialist construction. . . .

. . . Some people, while attempting to "enter Communism" prematurely, have tried to negate at too early a stage the positive rôle of commodities, value, currency and prices. This line of thinking is *harmful to the development of socialist construction and is, therefore,* incorrect.[51]

The theoretical parts of the resolution quoted, sometimes verbatim, Khrushchev's "theses" for the Twenty-first Party Congress in Moscow. Khrushchev had announced that within the next fifteen years the USSR would surpass the US *per capita* production and that then "the material, technical base of Communism" would have been created in the USSR. Indeed, the next seven years were described in the Soviet press as a "great leap forward on the road of development towards Communism".

Retreating from the great leap forward the Chinese resolution used the words *gradual* and *gradually* 111 times in 40 pages. The idea of communes was not given up, but the watchword was improvement and consolidation. The opposition to communes among peasants, Party officials and intellectuals was to be gradually changed to approval by permitting, in some communes, "the living together of men and women and the aged and young of each family" . . . "certain commune members may cook at home". . . . "At present, the system of eight hours work and two hours study should be put into effect. . . . But at any rate eight hours for sleep and four hours for meals and recreation . . . must be guaranteed every day and this must not be reduced". . . . "We . . . should

[51] *NCNA,* December 17, 1958. (Emphasis added.)

not be in a hurry to set up communes on a large scale in the cities."

This, then, was not a great leap forward but a step or two backward. For Mao and his entourage this was more than "loss of face", it was a tremendous slap in the face. There was more to come. Gravest of all was the fact that the Party resolution destroyed the myth that the drive for communes was a mass movement from below, that communes were invented by the peasants and that the "idea has caught on".

An illustration of the fact that the personal impressions of even the most eminent observers can be misleading, was furnished by the Labour leader, Mr. Richard Crossman, who toured China in 1958. Writing in the *New Statesman*[52] nearly four weeks after the retreat-resolution, Mr. Crossman quoted the "idea has caught on" version, and went on to say:

I am inclined to believe this statement and to conclude that the movement for the People's Communes did indeed come not from a remote official stratosphere but from that hard puritan élite of peasant Communists, who have emerged in their tens of thousands through the countryside. If I am right, this episode confirms that Chinese Communism still remains a dynamic mass movement and that its leaders still respond to pressure from below.

Mr. Crossman also wrote: "Of course a foreigner who knows no Chinese must be wary on this subject, but I saw no sign that family life was being destroyed."

Such utterances would not be important were they not multiplied daily in the Western press. When French intellectuals, Australian journalists or retired British Field-Marshals go to "see for themselves", without reading the Chinese Communist documents (to be had everywhere in translation), they often unwittingly paint a far rosier picture than do the Chinese Communists themselves.

The next humiliation of Mao Tse-tung came when, at the Twenty-first Soviet Party Congress, Khrushchev, using the "some comrades" technique, rebuked Mao in no uncertain terms.

Some comrades say that the principles of Communism should be introduced more quickly. But to switch over to distribution according to needs when the economic conditions for this have not yet been created . . . means to inflict damage on the building of Communism. . . .

[52] January 10, 1959, p. 35.

. . . Some scientific workers say that distribution according to work means the application of a bourgeois law in a socialist society. . . . This is confused thinking because levelling would lead to unjust distribution. . . . Levelling would mean not a transition to Communism, but the discrediting of it.

The Maoist golden sayings quoted the year before on millions of posters were thus dismissed by Khrushchev as the result of confused thinking and as damaging and discrediting to Communism!

IV

Mao's power then—at least so it seemed for a short while—was limited. The majority of his Central Committee, backed by Khrushchev and the Soviet Party, by the Party rank-and-file and by the masses of people, was able to restrain Mao Tse-tung and slow down his mad rush to reach his obsessional aims, and could even reduce his effective power. After all, by ceasing to be Chairman of the Republic, who promulgates laws, appoints and dismisses governments, and is *ex officio* the Chairman of the Defence Council—he had given up all effective legal power. He *only* remained Head of the Party.

It was an old principle of Mao's to respect the enemy tactically and to despise him strategically. This is what he did in 1958 in relation to Khrushchev and the majority of the Chinese Party leaders. These, however, were anxious to lessen the impact of Mao's demotion. 1957 had demonstrated on what kind of a volcano they were sitting. They feared eruption again if Mao's prestige suffered too greatly. So they paid what they thought was lip-service to his great wisdom, to his theoretical brilliance and general guidance. This gave Mao ample opportunity to reassert his power as the demagogue-oracle.

At the Twenty-first Soviet Party Congress, Premier Chou En-lai, as head of the Chinese Party delegation, declared that the communes were "the best form of developing socialism under Chinese conditions . . . the best form for China to make the transition from socialism to Communism in the future". This stand, widely reported in China, strengthened Mao's position too.

After several revolts in Tibet, large and small, during the previous years, which went largely unnoticed in the West since they were only discussed in Chinese Party reports and resolutions, a very large-scale revolt broke out again in Tibet in March 1959. Faced with this massive danger, with a second "Hungarian situation" since 1957, the Chinese leadership did everything to enhance Mao's prestige. First, he was built up into a withdrawn figure of Olympian wisdom, and his personality was kept before the people by constant references to him in the press and radio. And although one of the reasons given for his retirement as Head of the State was to free him from too many purely ceremonial occasions, he very often took a leading part on such occasions. In April 1959, Liu Shao-chi was elected as Chairman of the Republic. The press started to feature "Chairman Liu" too, beside "Chairman Mao"—but the latter remained the infallible, omniscient and omnipotent leader. And, as a new departure, the study of "Mao Tse-tung Thought" was given importance equal to and often greater than the study of Marxism-Leninism in general.

There is no need to quote more than a few of the thousands of similar statements showing the extremes to which the Mao cult was raised *after* his resignation as Head of the State. They are just as authoritative as the photo-report from the Chinese press showing with what hysterical joy the masses carry round a giant dummy of a newly published Mao-volume.

> Comrade Mao is . . . the beacon showing the path of Communism on which we are now marching. . . . The over six hundred million of our country trust to him their happiness, hope and future, considering him the embodiment of Communism and truth, and the banner of invincibility.[53]

In September, Central Committee member Liu Lan-tao said, that Mao was "the most prominent Marxist-Leninist revolutionist, politician and theorist among all contemporaries. . . . He is the great Marxist-Leninist theoretician of our times."[54]

Mao was repeatedly described by the Chinese press as the greatest Communist theoretician and leader in the world, thus challenging Khrushchev's claim to be the "Lenin of today".

A talk given on Peking Radio (January 24, 1960), was entitled: "Mao Tse-tung ideology glows 100,000 feet high". According to this talk, Mao's ideology is "invincible". "The higher the Red Flag of this ideology is raised, the greater will be the victory in the revolution. This was, is and will be true."

The March 4, 1960, report of the All-China TU Federation announced:

53 *PD*, September 28, 1959.
54 *PD*, January 15, 1960.

The experience of the Party has fully proved that Mao Tse-tung's thinking, once mastered by the masses, immediately becomes a gigantic material force. . . . From experience the broad masses of workers . . . have fully realised that Mao Tse-tung's thinking is truth, and is the guarantee for continuous victories. . . . Should we once deviate from the Mao Tse-tung ideology, we would assuredly commit mistakes.[55]

The real experience of the Party proved just the contrary. A gigantic material force, the enlarged terror machine had to compel the masses to proceed on the "Mao path", but even this "path" had to be altered. The 8th Plenum of the Central Committee held at Lushan in August 1959 decided that the rural communes should "transfer ownership from the communes to the production brigades". The giant communes remained units as far as political administration was concerned, but the agricultural units were to be the more practical, small "production brigades". Those "rightists" however whose influence contributed to this more realistic policy were denounced with renewed vigour. Chen Yun, the economic chief, till then one of the seven rulers of China, was temporarily shelved, Marshal Peng Teh-huai, arrested, while scores of others ousted or demoted.[56]

Marshal Peng Teh-huai, a Politbureau member, a Mao associate since the Kiangsi days, the successful Commander-in-Chief of the Chinese Armies in Korea, feared that Mao's extremist policies would lead to the weakening of China. He was, besides Chen Yun, the most violent opponent of the communes. At the Lushan Plenum Marshal Peng read a very long and most factual memorandum exposing the shortcomings of the great leap forward which in his view was caused by "petty bourgeois fanaticism". He quoted statistics for all China to prove that *in 1958 the population was getting half as much food as during any average year of the 1933-53 period.* He said that if the food situation were not cured, the 1957 uprisings in the countryside would be repeated.

Marshal Peng's greatest crime however was that he sent a letter to the Soviet Party and that in May 1959, when he met Khrushchev

[55] *NCNA*, March 4.
[56] The oldest member of the Politbureau, Li Po-chu escaped with self-criticism because he was mortally ill, and died soon. The ousted and/or demoted "anti-Party" group included the Chief of the General Staff, two Deputy Ministers of Foreign Affairs, several generals, first secretaries of important provinces and many others.

in Albania(!), *he intrigued with the Soviet chief against the Mao leadership.* (In the closed session of the Twenty-second Party Congress Khrushchev stated that Mao liquidated Kao Kang in 1954 because the latter was an adherent of "correct policies towards the USSR". In Khrushchev's view the same applied to Marshal Peng and his group.) The Peng affair contributed greatly to the worsening of Sino-Soviet relations.[57]

It should be noted in this context that in the autumn of 1959, after the Peng affair, Western policy was still based on the assumption of a monolithic Sino-Soviet alliance. The fact that during the Quemoy bombardments Chiang Kai-shek received guided missiles from his American allies, while Khrushchev refused to furnish them to Mao, was forgotten, if ever noticed. . . . What a shattering sensation it would have been if a great war hero and Cabinet Minister in Britain had been arrested because he intrigued with the American president against his own Premier. Yet exactly this happened within the Sino-Soviet "alliance"!

Meanwhile in China, by retaining in name (if not in full practice) the rural communes, and by going on with an extreme urban commune movement, Mao's prestige was saved. The adulation campaign was stepped up.

On February 2, 1960, *NCNA* reported a nation-wide upsurge and campaign of studying "Mao Tse-tung Thought". Workers, peasants, intellectuals, soldiers and youth were fervently studying "Mao Thought":

When some 600 million people are armed with Mao Tse-tung Thought, China's construction will push ahead more rapidly and will eventually make *momentous contributions to the world Communist movement.* The most important object of studying Mao Tse-tung's thinking is to understand the world . . . as well, as to transform ourselves in the course of *transforming the world.*[58]

Whatever plans and ideas some leaders of the Chinese Politbureau and the majority of the Central Committee had had about

[57] For a detailed analysis, shedding new light on this affair, see "The dismissal of Marshal Peng Teh-huai" by David A. Charles, in *The China Quarterly*, London, October-December, 1961. According to Mr. Charles, Marshal Peng was released after a course of "intensive reindoctrination". He then sent a letter of self-criticism to Mao, and was given work as superintendent or deputy superintendent of a State farm in Heilungkiang.

[58] *China Youth*, No. 3, 1960. (Emphasis added.)

curtailing Mao's power, in fact they had heightened it to charismatic and even divine proportions.

Leaving the details of foreign and home policy to the brilliant Chou En-lai and the twenty-odd other leaders,* he went on determining the general extremist directions of these policies. He saw to it that tension should be the order of the day in China and in the world. He made his preparations to avenge himself on Khrushchev. The Chinese population, which had by now reached 700 millions was enjoined to "surrender their hearts" speedily and completely. The Chairman had new measures and campaigns ready to transform them into fully-conditioned blue ants.

* He reassured his colleagues in the leadership by dealing leniently with Chen Yun and Marshal Peng Teh-huai. In an official listing at the end of 1960, they both figured as members of the Political Bureau of the Party.

XVIII

"EMPEROR OF BLUE ANTS"

I

As in the past, China was again largely governed by campaigns, slogans and battle cries. More than ever, Mao stuck to axioms, formulas, equations and principles which he had used ever since the Kiangsi guerilla days. Even the most dramatic demonstrations of the failure of these methods left him largely unaffected.

1959 had opened in China with a new campaign for the "planned consumption of food". Chinese peasants were told that "over-eating is harmful to health . . . and will affect digestion and soon cause gastric troubles. Too many calories will also cause one to become fat, and this will affect one's physical strength and labour efficiency".[1] All through the year reports about the "tight food situation" alternated with "eat less" warnings. In July, the State Council stated that: "No matter whether in cities or rural areas, caution should be exercised in the consumption of food."

Anti-rightist rectification campaigns went parallel with very large purges in the army, with the result that in October Mao's Security Minister, Lo Jui-ching, was appointed Chief of General Staff to ensure that "the Party commands the guns". (April 1959, incidentally was the "Love the People month" for the Security Police.)

After its eighth plenary session in August 1959, the Chinese Central Committee announced that the figures published as the miraculous production results in the 1958 great leap forward had been grossly exaggerated, and that the tremendous drive for steel production in home-made furnaces had in fact been pointless. It had provided no steel at all of a quality suitable to industry. Millions of people had suffered in vain during the nightmare months of the steel battle. The Central Committee re-examined the 1958 production results and found that instead of the reported 375 million tons of food-grains, China had produced only 250 million tons; instead of the reported 11 million tons of steel only 8 million tons; instead of 3.35 million tons of cotton only 2.1 million tons. Although there is no proof that the new figures themselves were reliable, the official

[1] *PD*, January 26.

retreat from the previously announced figures astonished even discerning outside observers. That the Chinese Party's Central Committee could calmly announce that food grain production in 1958 was 125 million tons less than previously stated, cast a doubt on all other miraculous results too.

This was a further demonstration of the fact that the Mao-formula—that the muscle power of regimented millions can accomplish anything—was wrong. Yet he went on applying this formula, along with all the others.

From the commune front reports were published like this:

Some mess halls cover too big an area. Commune members have to travel a long distance. In some instances, they even have to cross streams and climb over hills. This is a great inconvenience. Some mess halls serve food in such a manner that commune members have to queue up first. This wastes time, nor are commune members pleased. . . . Some mess halls are staffed by bad personnel who practice corruption and embezzlement. . . . Unless serious attempts are made to overcome the shortcomings . . . the masses will be discontented.[2]

But instead of consolidating and improving the rural communes, Mao pressed for communes in the cities. These were organised throughout 1959. The 1958 decision that "we should not be in a hurry to set up communes on a large scale in the cities" was disregarded. In 1960 under the slogan: "Everything belongs to the State except the tooth-brush", the drive to complete the communisation of the cities was intensified. The Chairman of the State Planning Commission announced on March 30, 1960: "The people's communes have aroused and organised the forces of our peasant masses, over 500 million strong. . . . Now all the cities are setting up communes in a big way."[3]

The first urban communes were either formed around large industrial enterprises, Government organisations or schools, or were established by local street residents on a zonal basis. The "street factories" produce finished and semi-finished goods for the large factories which are able to concentrate on the production of high quality goods. The street factories—often "open-air factories with workshops located in corridors"—"turn useless into useful things". They make use of waste and odds and ends not needed by the

[2] *New China Half-Monthly*, Hsin-hua Pan-yueh-k'an, June 25, 1959.
[3] *NCNA*, March 31.

large factories. The various commune and street committees direct and control all the waking hours of the city dwellers. The 1960 urban slogan was: "The masses are minding the business of the masses. Everything is in charge of somebody or other; everybody is taking care of something or other."

Theoretically "all personal belongings of the commune, including houses, clothing, furniture, household goods, bank and credit deposits still belong to the individual".[4] But the individual is under the control of the local "Committee for Organising the People's Economic Life". If the individual does not want to hand over his flat for a workshop, or is reluctant to buy "peace bonds", the cadres explain to him why he should do so. If he doesn't see reason, they debate. If the individual wants to avoid being the victim of a struggle-meeting, he gives in. Food consumption is controlled through communal mess halls or street canteens called "People's dining rooms". When mess halls or canteens are opened, every family voluntarily donates all kitchen utensils, chairs, brooms and *ration cards*. Only rightists and counter-revolutionaries resist.

According to Government reports, by the end of 1959 400 million rural commune members, and by the end of 1960 more than 35 million city dwellers ate in mess halls. The campaign for communal dormitories went on, although no overall figures have been published. The dormitories caused new difficulties. In the spring of 1960 the Minister of Agriculture announced that "we should stop killing sparrows from now on. In the pest-extermination-campaign . . . sparrows should be replaced by bed-bugs."[5]

After the grave food shortage in 1958 and 1959, great natural calamities hit Chinese agriculture in 1960. Without giving figures, Chou En-lai said that less food grain was produced in 1960 than in 1958 or in 1959. In 1960 the population increased by about 17 million. The gravity of the situation was illustrated by the campaign for introducing chlorella as an edible food for humans. The chlorella is a green unicellular alga which normally grows in stinking stagnant water. It was already being used to make bread, various sorts of cakes, congee and sauce; after being made into powder, it was also used to feed babies.[6]

The rural communes had proved the most effective tools for saving the peasants from the danger of over-eating. Now the urban

[4] Peking Radio, April 10.
[5] *NCNA*, April 6.
[6] *PD*, July 6, 1960.

communes saw to it that the food consumption of city-dwellers
should be controlled too. Commune members had to give up their
ration-cards, without which oil, rice, flour, meat and in some localities even vegetables cannot be bought. The efficiency of this
system was attested by the fact that in proportion as mess halls
opened, the local food shops closed, since individual buying ceased
in the neighbourhood. As the masses ate in mess halls, they could
easily decide to eat less.

In the poorly furnished flats or rooms, such privacy as remained quickly vanished. Neighbourhood Service Centres or "Street
Service Offices" were set up, to take care of washing and mending,
clean rooms, collect refuse, provide dressmakers and barbers and
help with weddings and funerals. On April 11, 1960, *NCNA* reported on the work of 3,700 service centres in Peking:

> Working couples often leave the keys of their homes at the
> service centres as they go to work in the morning. They find their
> rooms neatly cleaned, and washing and domestic jobs done, when
> they return in the evening.

With this system there is no excuse even for mothers with many
children to stay at home. They all have to work. Nurseries take in
babies from two months upwards as full-time boarders. If the baby
is not yet weaned the mother is allowed to leave her work every
three hours. Parents and children have a happy reunion on Satur-
days or every second Saturday.

Meanwhile the propaganda campaign against individualism
"warm-feelingism", parental love, romantic or sexual love, and
against the family, went on. *China Youth* for instance wrote:

> The relations between husbands and wives will be that they will
> live together but eat separately because they may not work and
> study together. Although parents and children will not live to-
> gether all the year round, they will still see each other fre-
> quently. This could be called a new family system. But it is no
> longer a basic unit that organises society. The family will not
> exist as a cell-forming unit after the extinction of its influence as
> a production unit, economic unit and educational unit.

The same article emphasised that people's preferences for the
small family, "so as to love its warmth and enjoy themselves in
natural happiness", was a "stubborn prejudice". As to love itself:

Love is selfish and repellent in nature. Your girl friend needs to possess the whole of you, or at least the whole of your spare time. What are you going to do, if she wants you to be with her alone, and does not like to join collective activities?

In the Hoping commune in Kweiyang:

you can see very little of the way of life of one family cooking for itself . . . or caring only for itself. . . . A completely new Communist atmosphere has been rapidly formed. Nobody cares for the pay of his work, and *all love the commune more than their own home.* . . . People are working not for fame or money. . . . In the past the practice was for one family to care only for itself. Now . . . one cares for oneself and others, and first of all gives attention to the affairs of the street and the commune.[7]
The birth of the urban communes has not only turned the consumers' cities into production cities, but also changed the relations between men. . . . Each and every person is a part of the collective, and works for the collective. . . . *Everyone loves the collective,* and the collective takes great care of everyone.[8]

[People] completely throw away the dirty things of bourgeois individualism in their thoughts, sentiments and living habits, in order to achieve complete transformation.[9]

These were further signs that Mao wants to change not only the "human nature" of his blue ants, but also their "animal nature".
The city women, "liberated from household drudgery", were deeply immersed in the "Three-Not-Afraid Campaign":
1. We are not afraid of washing dirty clothes and doing tiresome jobs.
2. We are not afraid of mending threadbare clothes.
3. We are not afraid of taking pains.
Housewives organised into street Service Centres thus became "the good housekeepers of the people". Freed from family ties, the outstanding leaders of the Three-Not-Afraid Campaign could houseclean, wash and mend for five, six, and later even ten families. The strain on them was considerably eased when most people in the cities ceased to wear anything but the blue cotton blouse and

[7] *Kweichow Daily*, April 5, 1960. (Emphasis added.)
[8] Ibid., April 6. (Emphasis added.)
[9] *Hsin Hua Daily*, February 25, 1960.

trousers which have become the uniform of China. There was less to wash and clean.

The situation was also eased by the campaign for simplicity. Urban women also now learned that ideologically it is wrong for women in the communes to look attractive and well-dressed. Any attempt to make oneself pleasing to the eye is just as reactionary as eating at home instead of in the canteen.

The idea of "at home" itself is of course reactionary. In many cities the Party has "persuaded" the masses to exchange flats and rooms so that the staff and workers of a factory could work and live together next to the factory. In dormitories, people on the same shift at the same workshop live together. Their Party, Youth League, and TU officials live with them, and each commune of course has its Security Police and Household Police personnel whose work has been greatly facilitated by the habit of leaving keys with the housekeeping brigades. The fact that members of a production unit live together makes their daily two-hours political education easier too. There can be no absenteeism from political classes, and people do not have to travel to get ideological education. Ideological mistakes in "spare-time behaviour" can be, and are, promptly detected. Any deviation from the prescribed communal way of life and "collective morals" is promptly exposed and punished. "Everybody criticise everybody". "Security work is carried on at street level".

To the great demonstrations and mass-meetings in the "Hate the imperialists", "Denounce the Anglo-American Colonialists", "All China supports the Cuban Revolutionaries" (or any other current revolutionary campaigns) people of a street or production unit march together, headed by their Party secretaries. These can see whether everybody shouts with sufficient emotion the hate-slogans or the "surrender-our-hearts" pledges. . . . This was indeed a great leap forward. Writing in 1948, George Orwell imagined it only for *1984*:

In our world there will be no emotions except fear, rage, triumph and self-abasement. Everything else, we shall destroy,—everything. Already . . . no one dares trust a wife or a child or a friend any longer. But in future there will be no wives and no friends. Children will be taken from their mothers at birth as one takes eggs from a hen. . . . There will be no loyalty, except loyalty to the Party. There will be no love, except the love of Big Brother!"

II

Some people have ridiculed us as the advocates of the "omnipotence of war"; yes, we are. We are the advocates of the omnipotence of revolutionary war, which is not bad at all, but is good and Marxist. (Mao, *Problems of War and Strategy*, November 6, 1958.)

Chou En-lai proved himself to be one of the most brilliant diplomats of his age. Whether as Foreign Secretary or Premier, he was responsible for carrying out Peking's basic foreign policies as adroitly as possible. But these basic policies were determined by the tactical principles, equations and formulas Mao Tse-tung had been repeating for decades.

In 1926 Mao had seen the world situation as the final struggle between revolution and counter-revolution. "Two huge banners have been raised . . . one is the Red banner of revolution . . . and the other is the white banner of counter-revolution which the League of Nations holds aloft, rallying all the counter-revolutionary elements of the world."[10] His statements on the world situation in 1961 were almost literally identical except that the League of Nations was replaced by the UN. In 1958, he attacked the "Yugoslav revisionists" for "wanting to solve all issues through the imperialist-manipulated United Nations."[11] Khrushchev too, of course, tried to solve many issues through the UN!

In August 1949, Mao determined the basic lines of Chinese foreign policy in these words:

It is impossible to hope that imperialists and the Chinese reactionaries can be persuaded to be goodhearted and repent. The only way is to organise strength and to fight them, as for example, our people's liberation war, our agrarian revolution, our exposing of imperialism, "provoking" them, defeating them and punishing their criminal acts, and "only allowing them to behave properly and not allowing them to talk and act wildly". Only then is there hope of dealing with foreign imperialist countries on conditions of equality and mutual benefit.

The method of "provocation" was not a slip of the tongue. Mao's press was constantly attacking those who opposed the policy of

[10] SW, Vol. I, p. 14.
[11] *Ta Kung Pao*, August 5, 1958.

provocation. In 1958, when Khrushchev had already embarked upon his summit diplomacy, a *People's Daily* editorial observed:

> Some soft-hearted advocates of peace even naïvely believe that, in order to relax tension at all costs, the enemy must not be provoked. . . . But . . . the stand of these peace advocates is useless. . . . If we allow the people to indulge in the illusion of peace and the horrors of war, actual war will fill them with panic and confusion.[12]

Mao was intent on transforming the whole world into a giant "struggle-meeting", similar to those which he initiated in China. The Khrushchev line—that in the present situation war is no longer "fatally inevitable", nor violence in colonial liberation—was totally contrary to "Mao Tse-tung Thought". Khrushchev's summit policy and his increasing concentration of working through the UN in 1959 and in 1960 were regarded in Peking as "revisionism" (of Leninism) and as a too awkward sign of disloyalty towards China. When the USSR gave loans and material aid to a great many Communist and non-Communist countries instead of helping China in her plight, Peking saw this as further proof of Khrushchev's plan to achieve Communist victory in the world through building up Soviet strength and influence, without letting China's enormous possibilities come into full play.

Ever since coming to power, Mao has maintained that, while the Russian revolution is the model for revolution in "imperialist countries", the Chinese revolution is the model for revolution in colonial and semi-colonial countries. Yet, in speaking about Mao's claim to leap into Communism, Khrushchev said: "One should not hurry and hastily apply that which has not yet matured. This would lead to distortions and to our cause being compromised." So, instead of letting him lead the revolutionaries of the non-white world during this epoch of colonial liberation, Khrushchev attacked Mao for compromising the Communist cause. Mao was not long in launching his counterattack.

Early in 1960, when Khrushchev was working for a summit meeting and conducting an all-out propaganda campaign for his version of peaceful co-existence, Mao Tse-tung started an international campaign which was officially called a "New Storm of Struggle". This was ostensibly directed only against "US imperialism", but it soon turned out that it had other important targets too. Mao was

[12] *PD*, August 8, 1958.

"stormily" struggling for the leadership of the Communist camp and of the revolutionary movements in Africa, Latin-America and Asia. He was also struggling against Khrushchev's "soft and unprincipled" policies.

The fact that Peking was working for international tension when Moscow was aiming at a pre-summit relaxation; that Peking called for an intense offensive against the United States when Khrushchev was trying to reach a negotiated agreement with the US; the fact that Peking denounced the non-Communist governments of former colonial countries which Moscow had recognised—showed that, within the Communist world, Khrushchev was the principal target of the "New Storm of Struggle."

The front line of this struggle was everywhere in the more chaotic parts of the non-white world. Apart from the verbal offensive in which Khrushchev was attacked as an opponent of revolution, there was the campaign which aimed at producing "political facts" against Khrushchev. Each disorder, each violent uprising or slaughter was to be a proof in actual practice that Khrushchev was mistaken in saying that violence can be avoided in colonial liberation. Mao wanted to demonstrate to the Kremlin leadership that Khrushchev's softer line was unpopular among the revolutionaries of the non-white world, that Khrushchev's working through UNO and his summit policy could bring no results. That it was indeed Khrushchev and not Mao who was compromising the Communist cause.

In preparation for this complicated "new storm of struggle", Peking has been built up as a mecca of the non-white world, with the most extremist and intransigent non-white political leaders among the pilgrims. Between July 1959 and December 1960, for instance, eighty-seven African delegations visited Peking, not to mention African leaders who came on individual invitations. During the same period twenty-seven Chinese delegations toured Africa. Ties with Asia and Latin-America showed similar intensity. Most delegations were received by Chairman Mao himself. They all were lavishly entertained, promised political support and were given advice as to the technique of mobilising and manipulating the masses by well-organised minorities during times of turmoil, in the spirit of the Mao slogan: "A single spark can start a prairie fire".

The strategy and tactics preached to the African, Asian and Latin-American pilgrims can be fathomed from such public statements as the one made by Mao's spokesman, Vice-Premier Lu Ting-yi, on the April 22, 1960, mass-rally in which many foreign delegations participated:

In the area of imperialism national wars waged by colonies and semi-colonies are not only possible but *inevitable*. . . . The national wars waged by colonies against imperialism will *inevitably* be a continuation of their national liberation policy. All the means of revolution and forms of struggle, including the illegal and the legal, sanguinary and bloodless . . . all these are for constantly raising the revolutionary fervours of the people and achieving broader mobilisation of the masses . . . preparing for victory.[13]

This was before the planned 1960 May summit meeting between the big four. After the new storm of struggle was launched, Peking Radio doubled the length of its English language broadcasts to Africa. Special broadcasts beamed at West, East and Central Africa, two hours daily, preached extremist Maoism all through 1960. There was also in English language news service in morse at dictation speed for Africa with each item repeated. From April to October 1960 they were repeatedly told to disregard the "absurd idea that the African people can pass over to autonomy by peaceful means".

This is not the place to try to trace the activities of those unknown young Africans who studied in Peking or were inspired by the pamphlets sent from China. Peking has thrown many of them into the African turmoil in the hope that they will furnish the sparks that will start various prairie fires. But in the knowledge of subsequent events, it is instructive that the late Patrice Lumumba's secretary, and his defence minister, were Mao's guests before the Congo chaos started. Two extremist Congo personalities, Mr. Mutombo (People's Party), and Mr. Bengila (African Solidarity Party) were received by Mao and took part in their country's independence day celebrations in Peking on June 30, 1960. Mr. Bengila anticipated future events in the Congo correctly, when he declared that day: "Our economy is still in the hands of the colonialists. . . . *The real fight will begin only today.*"

The Congo turmoil was then used by Peking to show the bankruptcy of the Khrushchev-thesis about the possibility of peaceful colonial liberation.

In April 1960, to coincide with the ninetieth anniversary of Lenin's birth, Mao announced the Chinese Communist Party's total rejection of the Khrushchev policies accepted at the Twentieth and Twenty-first Soviet Party congresses.

The fact that in their April speeches Premier Chou En-lai, and

---

[13] *NCNA*, April 23, 1960. (Emphasis added.)

the Party's Secretary-General, Tseng Hsiao-ping, and many other Party leaders all stressed their belief on the inevitability of war, and that the "Leninist principles are definitely not outmoded and never will be", was a virtual declaration of ideological war. The Party's theoretical paper wrote:

> We believe in the absolute correctness of Lenin's thinking: war is an inevitable outcome of exploiting systems. . . . Until the imperialist system and the exploiting classes come to an end, wars of one kind or another will always occur.[14]
> Lenin said: "Modern war is a product of imperialism". . . . Lenin said: "War arises from the very nature of imperialism". . . . Innumerable historical facts have proved these propositions of Lenin to be unshakeable truth."[15]

Mao Tse-tung's revolutionary diplomatic activities during this period cannot be fully traced, but the Chinese press reported the following receptions held by Mao:

May 3. For delegates from fourteen countries and regions of Latin-America and Africa.

May 7. Trade Union, youth and student delegations from twelve African countries and regions.

May 8. "Friends from eight Latin-American countries."

May 9. Delegations from Iraq, Iran and Cyprus.

May 14. Delegations from Cuba, Argentine, Brazil and Japan.

On these and other occasions, using the "some people" technique, Mao reminded the world of Khrushchev's remarks, after his first American visit, that Eisenhower was a peace-loving man. At the May 14 reception, for instance, speaking about the U2 incident, he said that this

> confirmed to the world the following truth: no unrealistic illusions should be cherished with regard to imperialism. *Some people had described Eisenhower as a man who loved peace very much. I hope these people will be awakened by these facts.*"[16]

The attacks against Eisenhower as a warmonger and a butcher became more violent just before the Paris summit conference planned to begin on May 15, 1960.

[14] *Red Flag*, Peking, April 16, 1960.
[15] *PD*, April 22, 1960.
[16] *NCNA*, Wuhan, May 14.

Vice-Premier Lu Ting-yi, in his April 22 speech made a graver attack against Khrushchev. He denounced:

> some people, who pay attention to the imperialist policy of nuclear blackmail and . . . develop from fear of war to fear of revolution, and proceed from not wanting revolution themselves to opposing other people carrying out revolution.[17]

Khrushchev warned against local wars, for they might develop into general nuclear war. For these reasons, he was denounced as the enemy of colonial and other revolutions.

After the summit failure, to which Mao's new storm of struggle certainly contributed, the attack against Khrushchev was intensified. General Hsiao Hua, of the Chinese Army Political Department, said on June 3, 1960:

> Our attitude towards the imperialist threat of nuclear war is that we oppose it and we are not afraid of it. To be afraid of war and so to oppose all wars, even denying support for the just wars, and to dream of begging peace from imperialists will not only sap one's own will to fight, bind one's own hands and feet and weaken the preparations against an imperialist war, but will certainly also help to raise the enemy's war cries.

Mao's offensive forced Khrushchev to defend himself against the charges of opposing "just wars" and colonial revolutions, and that his soft policies force the Communist camp to give in to imperialism. In June 1960, he attended the Roumanian Party Congress in Bucharest to obtain endorsement of his policies. All ruling Communist parties were represented. In his opening speech, Khrushchev said that the thesis of the non-inevitability of war is the core of his peaceful co-existence policy:

> It should not be forgotten that Lenin's propositions . . . were advanced and developed decades ago, when the world did not know many things that are now decisive . . . for the whole international situation. . . . He, who fails to understand this . . . underestimates the power of the socialist camp and does not believe in the great powers of attraction of socialism.

In the open sessions of the Bucharest meeting the Sino-Soviet differences were glossed over but participants of the secret sessions witnessed serious clashes between Khrushchev and the leader of

[17] *NCNA*, April 23.

the Chinese delegation. Khrushchev again attacked the commune policy while the Chinese raised the question of Soviet interference into the affairs of the Chinese Communist Party. Khrushchev countered with the accusation that the Mao leadership persecutes Chinese Communists who are friendly to the Soviet Union. He referred to the case of Kao Kang, the Manchurian Communist leader who was liquidated because of his pro-Soviet policies.

As the outcome of the Bucharest meeting, Khrushchev was forced to adopt a new "tough" line. During the summer of 1960, the Soviet government sent numerous Notes with astonishing accusations to the governments of the West. Mao's first success was that elements of adventurism and "brinkmanship" appeared in Soviet foreign policy. This caused Mr. Macmillan to express in a personal letter to Khrushchev his "deep concern over what now appear to be a new trend in the conduct of Soviet foreign policy . . . I simply do not understand what your purpose is today."[18]

By the time Khrushchev decided to attend the UN session in September 1960, it was clear that most of his actions in the international field in this period were partially or wholly caused by Mao's campaign against his policies and leadership. At the UN session Khrushchev tried to show to the world Communist movement, and first of all to his possible rivals in the Kremlin leadership, that he is the staunchest advocate of colonial liberation and second to none in fighting against imperialism.

Although Red China was still excluded from the UN, Mao's spirit was most definitely there during the September-October 1960 session. Defending himself against Mao's attacks, Khrushchev was forced to compete with Mao in the violence of his style. Having to prove himself to audiences outside the UN a tough anti-imperialist and a staunch advocate of colonial liberation, Khrushchev was singularly unsuccessful within it. Most of his proposals were rejected, and on his return to Moscow he complained that the non-committed countries "sometime echo the imperialists".

The UN session was neither a triumph for Khrushchev's peaceful co-existence policy nor a successful rebuttal of Mao's accusations. The Soviet and the East European Communist press made much of the Soviet leader's "historic attainments" at the UN session. He himself, however, had to prepare for a "Red summit" in Moscow to reassert his leading position in the Communist world.

The "monolithic unity" of the Communist movement has rarely

[18] July 19, 1960.

been endangered to such an extent as during the summer and autumn of 1960. In addition to the Sino-Soviet accusations and counter-accusations in the well-known "some people" style, there was an exchange of far more bitterly outspoken official communications between the two parties, dealing with the disputed ideological questions. These confidential Party documents were circularised among all the leading parties by Moscow. Mao went a step further. He sent copies of these communications not only to "leading parties" but also to many Communist parties in Asia, Africa and Latin-America. In the wake of these communications the Sino-Soviet Party dispute created warring factions in many other parties too, notably within the Indian and the Brazilian CP. Something had to be done to end the dispute.

This was the reason for the Red summit, which started in Moscow after the anniversary celebrations of the Russian Revolution on November 7, 1960. On the eve of this conference, on October 30, Mao's *Red Flag* again attacked "certain bewildered people" who "say that if the people want to safeguard world peace they should not carry out revolution. Such a view is completely absurd, and is contrary to Marxism-Leninism".

Eighty-one Communist Parties of the world attended the Moscow meeting. Many parties sent large delegations, headed by the Party leader. Mao, however, was absent. His Party's delegation was led by Chairman Liu and by the Party's Secretary-General, Tseng Hsiao-ping, the most extremist Chinese Communist after Mao. The conference lasted for three weeks, giving an indication that it was not easy to produce a declaration satisfactory to both sides. In the final declaration and in the propagandistic manifesto, both sides made verbal concessions. It was asserted that the "peaceful co-existence of countries with different systems or destructive war—this is the alternative today. There is no choice." This affirmed the Khrushchev line. The violently anti-American and generally extremist tone of the declaration and of the manifesto increased the difficulties of the peaceful co-existence policy. This was the victory of the Mao line, just as the statement that co-existence is "a form of the class-struggle between socialism and capitalism".

The Red summit, in effect, only glossed over the Sino-Soviet differences. Peking and Moscow proclaimed that unity was achieved —and started promptly to demonstrate that it was not. The ambiguously worded declaration was interpreted differently in Moscow and Peking. According to the Soviet press it was a document for peaceful co-existence, while the Chinese press hailed it for setting forth the "fighting tasks" for Communists and other revolutionaries of all countries. The New Year article of the Chinese *Red Flag* described 1960 as a year of "tremendous storms of struggle" in Asia, Africa and Latin-America and warned against the "tricks" of US imperialists who aim to change "bloody revolution" into "orderly and peaceful evolution."[19]

As the eighty-one Communist delegations returned to their respective countries, the world soon learned about the violent quarrels preceding the Moscow declaration. Instead of accusing "some comrades", Mao's man, Tseng Hsiao-ping, accused Khrushchev with opportunism, "great-power chauvinism", and with deviation from Communist solidarity by giving aid to neutrals and to Chiang Kai-shek type "bourgeois nationalists" instead of to China. Khrushchev in his turn ridiculed Mao's non-Marxist "paper tiger" terminology, attacked his "ultra dogmatic" policies, emphasised the Chinese leadership's alleged ignorance of modern war, and said that Mao is "another Stalin".

On January 6, 1961 Khrushchev had the difficult task of explaining to the Moscow meeting of the leading Soviet Party theoreticians why the Red summit decided to drop the forty-three-year-old principle of Soviet leadership in the world Communist movement:[20]

". . . The formula that the Soviet Union stands at the head of the socialist camp and that the CPSU stands at the head of the Communist movement" was not included in the Moscow declaration because "at the present time . . . when there are eighty-seven Communist and Workers' parties each with its own tasks, it is impossible to lead all socialist countries and Communist parties from a single centre."

Khrushchev told the meeting that to "be called 'the head' spells no advantages for our Party. . . . Just the reverse. It only creates difficulties."

Speaking to the intellectual élite of his own Party, Khrushchev revealed the true situation in the world Communist movement:

The question may arise: will not our international solidarity be weakened by the fact that this proposition (Soviet leadership)

[19] *NCNA*, January 1, 1961.
[20] The meeting of the Party organisations in the Higher Party School, the Academy of Social Sciences and the Institute of Marxism-Leninism of the Central Committee of the CPSU. Full text of speech in *World Marxist Review*, January 1961, pp. 2-27.

is not written down in the statement? No, it will not. *At present there are no rules regulating relations between parties,* but we have a common Marxist-Leninist ideology, and loyalty to this ideology is the main condition of our solidarity and unity. . . . The CPSU is firmly determined to strengthen unity. . . . In this connection I want to emphasise our invariable effort to strengthen bonds of fraternal friendship with the CP of China. . . . The unity of our two parties, the biggest parties in the international Communist movement is of exceptional importance in the struggle for the triumph of our common cause.

. . . When someone's watch is fast or slow, it is adjusted, so as to show the right time. The Communist movement too, needs to set the time, so that our formidable army should march in step and advance with confident stride towards Communism. Putting it figuratively Marxism-Leninism, the jointly prepared documents of international Communist meetings, are our time-piece.

That the Communist movement should be a formidable army, that it should march in step, was no doubt Mr. Khrushchev's earnest desire. In fact, it was *not* an army, it did *not* set its watches, and most certainly did *not* march in step.

The speculations about the possibility of a Sino-Soviet break are quite pointless. The "monolithic unity" of all Communist countries was a propaganda slogan and it was believed by credulous Western observers. Red China never was an integral part of the Western Communist bloc led by the USSR. From 1927 until 1943 when the Comintern was dissolved, the Chinese Communist Party did not carry out Comintern directions. Frictions, clashes and even periods of manifest hostility between the two parties were not exceptional but the rule, as this chronicle has amply demonstrated.

The Soviet bloc consists only of the Soviet Union and the East European satellites. This bloc was formally integrated by such organisations as the COMINFORM, the COMECON and the Warsaw Military Pact. These last two place the bloc under unified military and economic command. But Red China never joined these organisations. Nothing came of the proposed unified Sino-Soviet naval command in the Pacific.

In fact, Red China never joined the Soviet bloc. From 1949 until 1960 Mao and his associates paid lip-service to Soviet leadership for the sake of appearances. At the Red summit meeting it was one of their conditions for signing the declaration that the formula of Soviet leadership should be dropped. They were no longer willing to pay lip-service to it.

The acceptance of Mao's and Red China's leadership in the "colonial and semi-colonial world" was implied by several passages of the Moscow declaration. In the above quoted speech of January 6, 1961, Khrushchev fully accepted Mao's policy concerning these areas. He said:

> There will be liberation wars as long as imperialism exists, as long as colonialists exist. Wars of this kind are revolutionary wars. *Such wars are not only justified, they are inevitable*, for colonialists do not freely bestow independence on the peoples.

During the first months of 1961 the Soviet press went on calling Khrushchev the "most creative developer of Marxism-Leninism . . . a great world leader", while Peking's *People's Daily* continued to state that "Chairman Mao is the greatest Marxist-Leninist of our time".

The 1958-62 Moscow-Peking dispute was only one of the manifestations of the basic "contradictions" between these two allied powers. These contradictions are great enough without the clashing ideologies.

In the world of 1962, a world of affluent societies and welfare states, a world in which the highly industrialised USSR is intent on raising its standard of living, in a world in which India, Egypt and many other developing countries aspire for a better and fuller life—China with its more than 700 million people has to struggle desperately against ever larger famines.

In the spring of 1961 Mao's régime was in its gravest crisis since coming to power. Writing in August 1960 *People's Daily* stated that "if the people's food needs are to be provided for adequately, and sufficient fodder is to be provided for the development of the country's livestock breeding, China's grain output should be at least double its present level. If the population's clothing needs are to be met adequately, cotton output should be at least trebled, in addition to the rapidly growing fibre industry." This means that in August 1960 China could not feed half of its population (350 million people) adequately, and could not clothe two-thirds (450 million people). And 1960 turned out to be the year of the greatest calamities. In 1961 it was revealed that the original production figures for 1960 had been grossly exaggerated, and the country had produced less than in 1958.

China had to shelve the basic Communist principle of the

priority of heavy industry over everything else. In 1960 the "walking on two legs" policy was initiated, proclaiming equal priority for steel and grain. In 1961 this too had to be dropped and the Party proclaimed that "the whole nation must concentrate on strengthening the agricultural front". Factories were closed, development projects dropped, and millions of workers, students and office employees were sent to the countryside to work on the fields, together with the army, which was mobilised for this purpose.

How to ward off ever greater famines when her population is growing yearly between two and two and a half per cent, soon reaching a *yearly increase of twenty millions?*—this is China's problem.

In this period, pursuing Khrushchev's great-power policy, the USSR gave aid to scores of friendly and neutral countries—none of which was in such a danger of mass-starvation as China. In any alliance, whether Communist or not, such a policy must cause friction. Having common aims, Mao would expect Khrushchev to work for their realisation *through China*. By helping to make China a strong power these common aims could be more easily reached. This is Peking's attitude, and in this there is no difference between Mao and his colleagues.

The friction between the two countries shows a sharpening and increasing tendency. If Khrushchev does not want to give up his aim of overtaking the USA by 1970, he cannot give effective help to China. But the nearer the USSR gets in affluence to the USA the larger will be the difference between China and the USSR.

In the USSR the general tendency in 1962 has been in the direction of further relaxations. Khrushchev, with his policy of incentives, offers a gradually easier, more colourful and less regimented life for the Soviet people.

Mao's China is forced by its situation in the opposite direction of growing terror. In no country of the world in 1962 is there such an enormous difference in the situation of human beings as there is in China. Whatever the difference in standard of living between the richest of the rich and the poorest of the poor in the West, whatever the difference between Khrushchev and the poorest kolkhoz peasant in the USSR, it is slight compared to that existing in China between the ruling apparatus and the people. *The Party and Government apparatus and the Security Police are not faced with the constant threat of starving to death, while the Chinese hundreds of millions are.* No greater difference can exist between human beings.

The three-million-strong Security Police can be an effective instrument of total dictatorship only if its members are fed and paid. This fact makes them ultimately defenceless against the starvation-threatened hundreds of millions who at times have nothing to lose but their miseries. This is what the Communist ruler of Honan Province had in mind when he risked his neck in 1957 for the public statement: "We are sitting on a volcano, the peasants will revolt, and reject the leadership of the Communist Party."

Faced with ever more dangerous consequences of the Chinese population explosion, the Mao leadership is less worried by a possible nuclear explosion than any other government in the world.

If present trends continue, China's population may increase, at the most conservative estimate, as follows:

```
1961—700 millions
1966—770    "
1971—850    "
1976—930    "
1981—1,000  "
2001—2,000 and more millions.
```

There are some indications that in the near future the Mao leadership might try to find a way out by launching a new total campaign, this time against the sexual instinct. The 700 million blue ants, safely regimented into rural and urban communes, would be defenceless against such a campaign, ordering the physical isolation of tens of millions of men and women. The propaganda against the reactionary and selfishly individualistic nature of both romantic and sexual love may be the introduction to such measures.

On January 18, 1961, Mao's Central Committee announced a new All-China rectification campaign against all "bad elements". Stating that ninety per cent of the people are behind the Party and Government, they inferred that the bad elements might be about ten per cent. These are to be remoulded through physical work. This means that some seventy million men and women would be segregated in forced labour camps, where they generally stay for two or three years.

A drastic birth-control campaign of this type is one possible solution. The other is nuclear war.

As long as Mao's China is excluded from the UN she will continue to exert her influence on world affairs through her pressure on the USSR and on the Soviet bloc. During 1960 this pressure decreased the prospects of an even temporary *détente*. Early in

1962 it seemed to be fairly obvious, that the more difficulties Mao's régime has, the more extremist this pressure will be. Local wars started by China might trigger off chain-reactions leading to nuclear catastrophe. The problem posed to the world in 1962 is this: should the rest of mankind risk waiting for a possible anti-Communist revolution in China as the *only* means of eliminating the nuclear danger inherent in the Chinese position, or not? Or should the rest of mankind try other means to avert this danger as far as China's influence is concerned?

In 1962 Mao's government was the only régime in the world which continued to deny that a nuclear war endangers all mankind and not only the "imperialist régimes".

Khrushchev was mistaken when he charged Mao during the Moscow meeting with not realising the implications of nuclear war. All his life Mao has been passionately interested in the science of war. His works show that he always kept abreast with military developments. There is no reason to suppose that the Chinese leadership was not fully acquainted with the theory of the so-called "delicate balance of terror" or with the various calculations concerning the consequences of nuclear attack and retaliation. Mao's spokesmen at the Red summit in Moscow, and in lectures and articles in China, went on asserting that the eventual annihilation of two or three hundred million Chinese in a nuclear war would not endanger the ultimate victory of Communism. The surviving four or five hundred million Chinese safely regimented into communes would see to that!

For Western readers the calculations of the various schools of thought on the nuclear situation seem monstrously and madly inhuman. According to one school, the surprise attack, killing fifty or a hundred million, would annihilate a considerable part of the retaliatory force, so that only ten or thirty million people would be killed in the aggressor country. The "safe deadlock" school maintains that whatever the successes of the surprise attack, the retaliation would kill fifty or a hundred million people in the aggressor country. So aggressor and retaliator would suffer the same losses. Both schools of thought predict that most of the principal cities, the industrial and nerve centres of the warring countries would be annihilated.

There is nothing monstrous in this for Mao. If hundreds of ten megaton bombs were to annihilate a considerable part of the population of America and her allies and of the USSR and her European satellites, Red China would remain the largest effective power in the world. Moreover, the Mao leadership is not at all convinced that Red China would or could also be subjected to effective nuclear attack. But even if China's principal cities and two or three hundred million of her people were destroyed, the surviving four or five hundred millions,—according to Mao—would ensure her status *as the most powerful country of the post-nuclear-war world.*

Seen from Mao's Peking, in the post-nuclear-war era, America and Great Britain (the leaders of the Western-democratic world) and the USSR (the leader of the Western-Communist world), would be crippled for decades. They would lose their leading positions. The poorest and least industrialised parts of Latin-America, Africa and Asia would suffer least from fall-out. This is the "non-white world", which Mao intends to lead with the help of his Chinese hundreds of millions.

The Soviet Union and Red China belong to different camps in many respects. The Soviet Union is a leading member of the UN, Red China is excluded from it and fought against UN troops in Korea. The USSR is basically a European power, and highly industrialised. Red China was never under the influence of the European intellectual-moral heritage, and it is the poorest of the agrarian countries. The USSR wants to keep up the "Two Germanys" solution, Red China fights against the "Two Chinas" idea. The USSR moves in the direction of relaxations, individualism, family life, rising living standards; Red China moves the opposite way. But the greatest factor dividing the two countries is their attitude to nuclear war. Khrushchev and the Soviet leadership want to avoid a nuclear war at almost any price, as do the USA and the other Western nations while, under the influence of Mao's Chinese chauvinism and extremist Communism, Red China's government seems to see not only great dangers but also great advantages in a nuclear war.

In their policies regarding nuclear war, Mao's China and Khrushchev's USSR then belong to two opposite camps. Can there be greater difference between two countries than disagreement regarding the ultimate question of human survival?

The extremely simplified and primitive model of the world divided into two hostile ideological camps with some temporary uncommitted or neutral countries on the fringes is just as outdated in 1962 as Mao's primitive nineteenth-century Marxist model of the Western world of exploiters and exploited. There is no point in trying to solve non-existent dilemmas when constantly faced with "multilemmas" of a fortunately pluralistic world. Instead of two

giant monolithic camps, the world of 1962 was already a most
pluralistic world. The "Sino-Soviet orbit" did not exist. The world
Communist movement with its eighty-seven parties and twelve
Communist governments in Europe and Asia, and with its three
main trends and various sub-trends, was developing towards further
diversity. The "free world"; the various groups of newly independent
countries; the scores of pacts and alliances which, due to historical,
economic, military and other factors, divide and unite at the same
time the very same groups—all give a richly pluralistic picture in
which *diplomacy,* in the best sense of the word can and must be
exercised.

In this situation Red China's continued isolation is highly dangerous. The more isolation, the greater the effect of "Mao Tse-tung
thinking".

Some observers, the present chronicler included, hold that there
are far more dangers in the continued exclusion of China from
the comity of nations, than in giving her an equal vote in UNO
with, say, the Gabon Republic or Guinea. Among the hundred-odd
members of the United Nations there are countries represented by
Communist governments with past records proportionally just as
objectionable as Mao's régime. The voting situation would not be
greatly changed by Red China's admission. But admittance to UNO
would be the first step in ending China's isolation. UN membership,
diplomatic, cultural, scientific, economic and other ties with many
countries, would increase a thousandfold China's contact with
contemporary reality. As in the case of the USSR, the tens of
thousands of diplomatic and other official and semi-official representatives who live or travel constantly in the non-Communist
world, would also in the case of China have a normalising and
restraining influence.

The present isolation of Mao's China places her in a situation
similar to that of an outlawed political party which has been forced
to go underground and has to strive for the realisation of its policies
in illegality. By giving China scope for "legal", that is normal diplomatic actions, her leaders will be faced with a choice: negotiation
or the clandestine starting of "prairie fires" in the non-white world,
and in the international Communist movement.

In 1949 Mao and his associates proudly proclaimed that "China
stood up", that the period of her humiliation was over. The fact
that she was not recognised as a respected member of the international community came as a bitter blow. Humiliated and outlawed, kept in ignorance of contemporary reality, the Mao leader-

ship developed on abnormal lines. The end of isolation could offer a cure for this. It also might make possible China's inclusion in the system of civilised mutual aid. No full member of the community of nations would be left to face the starvation of hundreds of millions in a world of plenty. By helping to avert such catastrophes in China, the world might save itself from an ultimate catastrophe.

III

At the time when this chronicle was concluded, Mao Tse-tung reached his seventieth year. The portrait he has painted of himself through his actions, he may alter during the subsequent period of his life. This future character portrait may be changed again during the decades to come by the revelation of facts not known today. In December 1962, when he was in the middle of one of his most desperate battles against reality, he seemed to be completely remoulded by his own obsession with remoulding the world.

He ordered 700 million Chinese to surrender their hearts to him. They went through the ceremony of heart-surrendering, they chanted the almost liturgical pledges, they swore that their hearts beat only for the gigantic aims of their Sun That Never Sets, they carried huge hearts cut out of red cloth. But the only person who really surrendered his heart to these aims, was the former poet himself.

As Mao's Central Committee saw it in 1956, Stalin's mistakes became

> serious, nation-wide and persistent [because] a series of victories and the eulogies he received in the latter part of his life turned his head. . . . He began to put blind faith in personal wisdom and authority; he would not investigate and study the complicated conditions seriously or listen carefully to the opinion of his comrades and the voice of the masses. As a result, some of the policies and measures he adopted were often at variance with objective reality. He often stubbornly persisted in carrying out these mistaken measures over long periods and was unable to correct his mistakes in time.[21]

In agreeing on this statement the 200 top Communists of China obviously meant to warn their own leader. The years from 1956 to 1962 showed how ineffective this warning was.

[21] *More on the Historical Experience of the Dictatorship of the Proletariat*, NCNA, December 28, 1956.

The entire Communist world, his own Party included, tried to
keep him back from his leap into Communism which met with the
universal resistance and hatred of the Chinese people. He disregarded the opinion of all comrades, Khrushchev included, and
pressed towards his obsessional aims.

Time and again he made speeches fulminating against "commandism and bureaucratism" and against all those who show "serious signs of isolation from the masses and from reality". At such
times people had good reason to think privately, as did the unfortunate Hu Feng in 1952.

How can a leader order the execution of thousands of his followers for closely imitating his example in "commandism", "bureaucratism" and in using naked force on people? How can he
accuse others with isolation from the masses and from reality, when
he himself is the supreme example of all this?

In their despair, the Hu Fengs thought that the miseries of China
were the outcome of some monstrous private joke, of some insane
action gratuit.

In this, they were mistaken. There is no earthly reason to
doubt Mao's gigantic ambitions, his determination to make China
the greatest military and industrial power in the world, and then
to remould the world at gunpoint to the image of his version of
Communist utopia. But the question still remains: why then did
he not see that the method of "struggle" and bureaucratic despotism
is inefficient, when life in China daily produced proofs of this fact?
Why did he not see that his own commandism and bureaucratism
and isolation from reality constitutes the greatest obstacle to the
realisation of his dearest ambitions?

The answer lies in the concrete content of Mao's obsession: Marxism-Leninism. By the seventieth year of his life, Mao had become
the most extremist and most dogma-bound Communist ruler among
his contemporaries. In fact the Mao cult did not exaggerate when
it depicted the Great Leader as the embodiment of Communism.
During his years of power Mao carried Marxism-Leninism to its
logical extreme. He differed from Khrushchev and from the somewhat less dogma-bound members of his entourage not in the content and direction of his obsession but *only in its degree*.

Before coming to power he often deviated from Party discipline.
He was not a perfect Party-member, because he refused to carry
out blindly the momentary Party line of Stalin, the Comintern, or
his own Party superiors. This disobedience was caused by his conviction that he was the destined leader, and was made possible by

the fact that, not having absolute power, he was forced to take account of life around him: the realities of the situation. So he deviated by not carrying out orders and gave the impression of a heretic, although he was nothing of the sort. In basic policies, in the strategic aims of Marxism-Leninism he never deviated. On the contrary, he worked quite efficiently and pragmatically for these ends. As far as China was concerned, he was a better Communist than those whose orders he disobeyed.

Since he came to power he ceased to be a realist. He ceased to be efficient and pragmatical, when he was not forced to be so.

Communist rulers, from Lenin and Stalin to Khrushchev and even to a Gomulka, all present the same problem: Why do they not see that their own commandism, bureaucratism and isolation from reality constitute the greatest obstacle in the realisation of their aims?

The answer lies in the very core of Marxist-Leninist theory and in the Leninist Party-system. A series of axioms lie outside the realm of reason for Communist rulers. They are totally unable to suppose that these axioms might be partly or wholly mistaken:

1. Communist utopia will inevitably be reached through the revolution of the working class, led by its vanguard, the Communist Party.

2. The Politbureau (or Praesidium) "headed by" the momentary leader, does not carry out the demands and will of the people, of the workers, of the Party membership but their "real and basic, long-term interests".

3. What these interests are is defined by the Party leader's correct interpretation of Marxist-Leninist theory.

4. Those who follow the leader are "the people". Those who do not, are "anti-people", "anti-Party", "counter-revolutionary" elements.

5. The masses have to be enlightened and persuaded to follow the leader. Those who fail to do so are enemies and have to be liquidated.

As a result, Communist countries are run by an enormously large State apparatus, controlled and directed by an even larger Party apparatus, while this double governing machine is controlled and spied upon by a huge Security Police network, directly under the leader. These three very large bureaucracies, and the trade unions, youth, women and other federations with their tens of thousands of full-time bureaucrats, constitute the endemic bureaucratic elephantiasis of all Communist-run countries. Those engaged in production have to keep a bureaucracy, which is four to seven times as large per thousand heads of the population as that of the average non-Communist state. The system of multiple controls and constant reorganisations hinders production and makes it much more expensive in self-cost and more wasteful than in non-Communist countries.

This situation could be cured only by the elimination of the Marxist-Leninist type of bureaucratic despotism, clearly an impossible proposition for Communist leaders.

Mao Tse-tung differs from them only in his refusal to deviate a single iota from the Marxist-Leninist precepts.

The lack of Christian moral heritage certainly influenced events in China. But if Confucianism made Mao a-moral in the Christian sense, this made it only easier for him to accept fully the Lenin thesis:

> We repudiate all morality that is taken outside human class concepts. We say that this is deception, a fraud which clogs the brains of the workers and peasants in the interests of landlords and capitalists.[22]

Neither is Mao a deviator from this thesis:

> The scientific concept, dictatorship, means neither more nor less, than unlimited power resting directly on force, not limited by anything, not restrained by any laws or any absolute rules. *Nothing else but that* . . . Soviet Socialist democratism does not in any way contradict one-man management and dictatorship; the will of the class is sometimes given effect by a dictator who sometimes does more alone and often is more necessary.[23]

The sentence: "tactics are the future appearing as present", was written and published a year before Mao became a Communist. (See page 136.) Again, all convinced Communists *know* that according to Marxist-Leninist universal truth, Communism is the highest stage of the social forms possible for mankind, and that "inevitable objective processes" lead to it. In this sense, all Communists are fully rational and logical "prophets", "scientific predictors". They all, from such "middle-roaders" as Khrushchev to such right-waverers as Gomulka, *know* that the function of Communist dictators is to accelerate this objective process and to elimi-

[22] Lenin, *Selected Works*, Lawrence and Wishart, London, 1937, Vol. IX, p. 495.
[23] Lenin, *Works*, 4th Russian edition, Vol. XXX, p. 444. (Emphasis in the original.)

nate all "wasteful obstacles" barring its way. Mao, again, differs from them not in the content of their convictions, but in the absolute degree he insists on them.

All Communists by reducing themselves to thinking mechanisms based on a rigid set of principles, formulas and equations, are in a smaller or larger degree isolated from what even they call reality (significantly, they rarely use the simple word: life). Mao differs from all others in carrying out this reduction to its logical extreme. By casting out moral considerations and the possibility that their basic axioms and principles might not represent infallible "universal truth", they aim at machine-like perfection and precision in their thinking.

During the decades when Mao was fighting for power, outside "reality" was not at the mercy of his own naked force. In Kiangsi, during the Long March, and in the Yenan period, he was forced to communicate with the real world. Armies were fighting against him. He had to get peasants to accept his rule by adapting his tactics to their demands and aspirations. As a war-lord, he had to get correct reports about the number of opposite divisions, about the equipment of his own armies, about the facts of a given landscape, where a battle had to be fought. In this sense, he was far less isolated from reality than since 1949. During the Yenan period he could not wage battles and rule people by simple "commandism" and "bureaucratism".

But when he became the divine and charismatic ruler, when his infallibility was enforced by his armies, his Security Police and his great State and Party apparatus—reality started to conform to his own set of formulas, equations and slogans.

The electronic brain analogy was introduced in earlier chapters as a possible way of understanding Mao's "psychology" and thinking mechanism. It seems to be even more relevant an approximation at this stage.

Originally "programmed" by the *Communist Manifesto,* and all the "objective laws" of Marxism-Leninism, profoundly and proudly ignorant of everything outside the Communist bloc, strengthened in the belief in the universal applicability of his own "struggle" method, through his successes in China—he cannot but operate according to his own patterns of thinking to achieve his own predetermined results. All electronic computers are as "intelligent" as their programming. Mao's programming is based on the highly biased and one-sided generalisations of Marx, Engels and Lenin. But these themselves were dogmatic generalisations of the nineteenth-

and early twentieth-century situation. When Khrushchev, as he did at the Twentieth Soviet Party Congress, tried to adapt these generalisations to the situation in the second part of the twentieth century, Mao violently resisted it, as his brain was programmed to do.

Within the terms of this analogy, all Communist leaders are erroneously programmed electronic brains of the "predictor" type. Some of them, like Khrushchev, are somewhat less rigidly programmed. Mao Tse-tung is an extreme example. He succeeded to the greatest extent in the depersonalisation and de-humanisation of his thinking. For such a long period, for nearly twenty-five years he was "proved right" in his predictions, he got so used to thinking in terms of hundreds of millions of people, and in terms of decades and generations, that he got entirely divorced from ordinary human approach. His ambitions for China, for Communism and for his own historical prestige are millennial. Paying attention only to major issues in the process of remoulding the whole of humanity and its world, ordinary everyday life and the fate of the present generation became for him minor issues. Given the obsessional aim, the statement that China can afford to lose 300 million people is entirely logical for a "perfect thinking machine and scientific predictor".

The contemporary situation is complicated by the fact that, although "subjectively" Mao is a thinking machine, objectively he is a charismatic ruler, a demagogue-oracle. Whenever he sees fit to promulgate a prediction, it is immediately fulfilled. His power is absolute in the sense that his will is done, whenever he interferes in the running of the internal or the international policies of his country. He interferes only when the broad development of affairs does not fully conform to his extremist aims. He does not interfere always. When he is inactive, China is run, and the Soviet bloc is run, by the other, less rigidly programmed thinking machines. They all mean to realise the prescription of the *Communist Manifesto*, and the aims of Marxism-Leninism. Mao wants to realise them sooner and more completely.

His machine-like perfection and machine-like primitiveness contains his almost inevitable failure. Professor Dennis Gabor had this to say about electronic predictors:

> I believe that of all electronic inventions now within viewing distance, predictors are likely to have the greatest influence on civilisation. . . . But a warning must be uttered, not to attach

undue hopes to mechanical predictors when applied to human affairs. A predictor, whether man or machine, can remain objective only so long as its forecasts will not influence the processes which they predict. . . . To avoid complicating matters, let us just consider the case that a predictor has built up such a high reputation of being always right, that men will blindly follow its forecasts. The machine, being a learning machine, will soon notice that everything it says goes, and from that moment on there is no guarantee against its going astray. *Absolute power will corrupt not only men but also machines!*[24]

Mao's failure as a thinking machine was evident as far as the current Chinese situation was concerned. At the beginning of 1962 it seemed unthinkable that China could fulfil Mao's aspirations even in several decades *without a very drastic change of his internal and external policies.*

But the Mao Tse-tung of the nineteen-sixties was not only the dictator-in-chief of Red China but also the leading theoretician of the international Communist movement. And in this respect his "programming" was far from leading him to bankruptcy. Indeed, in 1961-2 he was in the midst of the greatest ideological offensive ever launched between warring factions within the international Communist movement. Moreover, his offensive seemed to show some results. Other preoccupations, and a normal revulsion from the impossibly long-winded and turgid language of Marxism, kept the outside world from realising at once the full significance of the clash between Mao and Khrushchev during and after the Twenty-second Congress of the Soviet CP.

This Congress in October 1961 was full of riddles. International Communism had only two previous programmes; that of 1903 for the establishment of proletarian dictatorship, and the 1919 programme drafted by Lenin for the building of socialism. In October 1961, Khrushchev was to present the third programme, that of reaching the highest possible stage of "social forms": Communism. The draft programme was published in the summer of 1961 in more than fifty languages. For Khrushchev it was supremely important that the attention of the whole world should be focused on this most triumphant occasion in the history of the movement and in his own career. Presenting the programme on October 17, Khrushchev said: "Our Congress will go down in history as the . . .

[24] Dennis Gabor: *Inventing the Future.* Encounter, London, May 1960, p. 10.

congress that considered and adopted the great programme for
the building of the first Communist society in the history of mankind."

Yet at the very same congress Khrushchev did everything to
turn away attention from the brilliant Communist future to the
monstrous Soviet past and to the hostile present conflicts within
the Communist world.

Was this, could this have been, Khrushchev's original intention?
Was it in his interest to direct attention once more to Stalin's
murderous purges and to those who carried them out, when he
happened to be one of them? Was it in his interest to reveal to
the Soviet people, and to the Communist parties of the world, that
his policies are violently opposed by the Chinese Party? That Albania, the worst enemy of the Soviet Party and State, is the best
friend and closest ally of Mao's Party and Government?

Subsequently, it became obvious that Khrushchev's actions were
partly premeditated, partly improvised. But among the factors persuading him to an extreme anti-Stalin drive and to violent attacks
on Albania, Mao and the Chinese situation played a significant part.
The failure of Mao's agricultural policies to provide food for China,
and indeed to ward off the danger of ever larger famines, threatened to compromise Communism in the eyes of underdeveloped
countries. In showing his open disapproval of these policies, Khrushchev demonstrated to the world that Mao's version of Communism is not real Communism, and that therefore its failure cannot compromise Marxism-Leninism. During the preceding two years,
at the closed sessions of Red summits, Khrushchev had repeatedly
called Mao "the Stalin of to-day". His all-out anti-Stalinism, then,
was directed also against Mao.

In attacking Albania he hoped to persuade the Chinese leadership to drop Mao's extremist policies. The Chinese refusal to do so
came as a surprise.

It also became obvious that Mao, for his part, wanted Khrushchev to change his soft policies. With the Chinese ideological
attacks, and by intriguing with the Molotov group, he provoked
and manoeuvred Khrushchev into the extremes of anti-Stalinisation.

In 1958 Khrushchev denounced Mao's blueprint for leaping into
Communism. After the publication of Khrushchev's draft programme
for building Communism it was Mao's turn to explain, in confidential
inter-Party circulars, that it is an anti-revolutionary and not truly
Marxist-Leninist programme. Khrushchev's thesis that the dictatorship of the proletariat ceases to be a necessity during the transition

period from Socialism to Communism was denounced by Mao as gross revision of one of the basic tenets of Marxism: in his *Critique of the Gotha Programme* Marx insisted that during the entire period of transition to Communism *"the State can be nothing else than a revolutionary dictatorship of the proletariat"*.

On the eve of the Twenty-second Congress, Molotov sent a circular letter to all members of the Soviet Central Committee denouncing Khrushchev's new Party Programme as "revisionist, pacifist and anti-revolutionary". He did this in the knowledge that his view was shared by Mao and the Chinese Party leadership. Mao's press, the many foreign language publications of Peking included, demonstrated the fact that *the Chinese Party leadership regards not only the new Soviet Party programme but Khrushchev's internal and external policies as opportunistic and anti-revolutionary; leading to the weakening of the international Communist movement.*

Mao Tse-tung did not oppose in principle the practical de-Stalinisation in the present and in the future, but he violently opposed the raking up of the past for the following reasons:

According to Marxists, the Communist Party is the *vanguard* leading the revolution. This vanguard is directed by its Central Committee and its Political Bureau or Praesidium, the decisions of which are final. To oppose these decisions is an anti-Party crime. Khrushchev had demonstrated to the Twenty-second Congress that in the USSR this "vanguard of the vanguard" consisted of monstrous criminals. After Lenin's death in 1924, the Soviet Politbureau had seven members. Six of these—Trotsky, Bukharin, Zinoviev, Rykov, Kamenev and Tomsky—were executed by Stalin as anti-party criminals. Khrushchev in 1961 still regarded these men as guilty, and brought forward massive evidence that the seventh member, Stalin, was a mass-murderer.*

Therefore, according to the Khrushchev-line, the entire Politbureau had consisted after Lenin's death of criminals and murderers. And, as Khrushchev enlarged the list of murderers and anti-Party criminals by adding Voroshilov, Molotov, Kaganovich, Malenkov, Bulganin and others, according to the 1961 Soviet official line *two-thirds of the supreme Party leadership had consisted of criminals during the thirty-three years between 1924 and 1957.* The Soviet Governments did not fare better. All Soviet Premiers between 1924 and 1958 had been anti-Party criminals

* Next year Bukharin, Rykov, Kamenev and Tomsky had been partially rehabilitated.

according to Khrushchev. This is the list: Rykov, Molotov, Stalin, Malenkov and Bulganin.

The working class—and the whole world—was being asked by Khrushchev to follow a "vanguard" which had been directed for more than three decades by criminal and murderous leaderships! Mao Tse-tung first tried to keep Khrushchev back from this whole-sale discrediting of the Soviet past and that of the international Communist movement. But when this proved to be impossible he did everything possible to differentiate his own Party from the Soviet CP. He demonstrated to the Communist movement his complete disagreement with Khrushchev's policies, and that bring-ing the dispute into the open was Khrushchev's responsibility.

For decades the Communist parties all over the world had been asked and even ordered to translate and publish thousands of Soviet works on philosophy, history and economics. But during the Twenty-second Congress, Khrushchev's ideological spokesman, Leonid Ilyit-sov, said that because of the Stalin-cult "for decades no works on political economy, philosophy or history have been published in our country which were in any way significant. The works of Marx, Engels and Lenin were degraded, [and] extremely subjective, ar-bitrary evaluations were given concerning different theses of Marx-ism-Leninism and even concerning entire works".

Mao and his associates were violently opposed to this all-round denigration of the theoretical guidance emanating from Moscow in the past. But when it happened nevertheless, Mao was quick to exploit all these revelations and admissions for the benefit of his own Party. His ideological diplomats emphasised that the Chinese Party had a clean and heroic past. While mistaken or worthless theoretical works had been published in the USSR by the thou-sands, China had produced the great Marxist-Leninist of the age: Mao Tse-tung, whose many works on ideology, on the tactics and strategy of Communist revolution, are most significant and more than ever valid.

The very real monolithic unity of the Communist parties had been based for decades on their blind acceptance of the thesis that *the interests of the world Communist movement are absolutely identical with the interests of the USSR.* Mao is largely responsible for the fact that a growing number of parties refuse to accept this thesis. His propagandists try to convince the revolutionaries of the non-white world that peaceful co-existence is only in the interest of the USSR, a highly industrialised *white* power, which has much to lose in a nuclear war. Not so the peoples of the underdeveloped countries of the non-white world! Mao's line after the Twenty-second Congress was still that a nuclear war could open the way to a "beautiful future" for the Chinese version of Communism, built on the "debris of imperialism".[25] Peking always made it amply clear that it speaks to the non-white majority of the world population.

During 1962 the Sino-Soviet conflict became both more violent and open. The attacks through substitutes were replaced by open denunciations of Chinese policies, notably at the Czech, Bulgarian, Hungarian and Italian CP Congresses.* At a time when Khrushchev started to probe the strength and resoluteness of President Kennedy and America, Mao demonstrated by *actions* that China must not be left out of international affairs. In the autumn of 1962 when Peking foresaw a new Berlin and/or Cuban crisis, Mao made steps to have his own "independent" crisis so that Khrushchev should not be the principal Communist actor on the world stage. Although the Chinese attack on the Indian frontiers was doubtless part of Mao's long-term strategy, its *timing* was conditioned by his anti-Khrushchev tactics. During the developing Cuban crisis the USSR was in sore need of manifestations of Chinese solidarity. Instead, Mao showed again with his actions that "no one directs China", and that moreover Chinese political strategy differs fundamentally from that of the USSR. This is why Mao started his undeclared war against India during the Cuban crisis. While Khrushchev asserted that the Cuban solution was a victory for peace and sanity, Mao's propaganda apparatus denounced violently Khrushchev's "cowardly compromise":

"If one retreats, bows, or even begs for peace from the imperialists at the expense of a revolutionary people, one only encourages imperialism . . . thereby increasing the danger of world war." (*People's Daily*, Peking, November 15, 1962.)

According to Peking the Cuban revolution was third in "world importance" after the Chinese and Russian Communist revolutions, and Khrushchev's retreat weakened the central base of the great revolutionary upsurge all over Latin-America.

[25] *PD*, December 10, 1961. An earlier statement: "The revolutionary people constitute more than nine-tenths of the world population. . . . Anybody can see for himself who in the end will be the master of the world" (*PD*, June 29, 1960).

*"When we mean China we have no need to say Albania." (Signor Pajetta: *l'Unita*, Rome, December 6, 1962.)

In December 1962 Khrushchev greeted his "dear comrade Tito" as his guest in Moscow, at a time when Mao's press went into paroxysms in denouncing that "agent of imperialism". Khrushchev also announced his new line according to which extremist left-dogmatism is at the present time a greater danger to the Communist movement than "right-revisionism" (of the Yugoslavs).*

When Mao Tse-tung made his sudden tactical step in announcing a unilateral decision to stop fighting on the Indian frontier, the USSR reaffirmed her intention to help India with arms. Red China's enemy, then, received and is to receive *both Anglo-American and Soviet arms and planes!*

At this time Khrushchev and the other leaders of the Western Communist world were horrified and angered by Mao's two alternative strategies. Beside the old one of unleashing revolutionary wars all over the non-white world, he went on with preparatory steps for his new *post-nuclear-war strategy*, calmly assuming the disappearance of the effective might of the Atlantic Powers and that of the Western Communist world. Mao's "puzzling" moves on the Indian frontier and elsewhere, are less puzzling as parts of this strategy. In a world for instance in which H-bombs, intercontinental missiles and jet planes were mostly destroyed together with the plants that could produce them, there would be a great advantage in the possession of the *southern* slopes of the Himalaya when invading India.

Khrushchev was able to hit back by isolating China in the Communist world and by decreasing Soviet aid to and trade with China to next to nothing. This was one of the grave shocks Mao received from "reality". The other, one can assume, was even greater. The Soviet Communists announced in 1962 that the basic principle of building Communism is no longer the hitherto inviolable *primacy of heavy industry* but that of *the development of science*. Khrushchev and his associates realised that the old time-gap between a scientific discovery and its practical application by engineers in industry was reduced to almost nil. In the age of automation, guided missiles and electronic computers the key figure in industrial development and production is not the production engineer but the

---

* "The splitters and sectarians . . . are literally ready to tear to pieces the Yugoslav communists . . . although they themselves are now retreating far more from Marxism-Leninism than those whom they accuse. Such morals are deeply alien to us communists." (Khrushchev in a speech to the Supreme Soviet, *Pravda*, December 12, 1962.)

scientist. This also means *the primacy of the exceptionally gifted and exceptionally highly trained individual,* who was always attacked, suspected or at least neglected by the Mao regime (pages 280-82). The Soviet leadership gave priority in practice (if not as yet in theory) already since 1955 to science, to automation, to electronics and cybernetics. The rewards of these decisions made the Kremlin in 1962 confident that the USSR will overtake America. On the other hand the early nineteen-sixties demonstrated the bankruptcy of the Mao-thesis concerning the supreme importance of the muscle power and enthusiasm of the masses. The resistance of the masses resulted in a discreet relaxation of the commune-system, while keeping up its façade. Meanwhile, China was farther than ever from overtaking the USSR, mainly because the Mao regime misunderstood the importance of the exceptionally gifted and trained individual.

There is a very slight chance that the challenge and shock might even be great enough to prompt Mao Tse-tung to get rid of that part of his "programming" which has led to the present failure of his aspirations in China. This chance however is very slight indeed if the Soviet Union and the United States go on punishing the Chinese people for Mao's policies. To withhold not only material aid but also normal trade relations certainly might lead to famines on a colossal scale, but not to a normalisation of Mao's thinking. On the other hand, if China could be a part of the comity of nations and could find a place in world trade, that certainly could lead to a gradual normalisation of Chinese political and economic developments.

The ethics of the case are clear. The Chinese people cannot be held responsible for the acts of Mao and his associates.

As this chronicle is closed in December 1962, it is still an open question whether the future will see Mao Tse-tung's rule as the most portentous event of the twentieth century or as an interlude of pointless mass-suffering soon to be forgotten in the millennial flow of Chinese history. The question will not be decided by Mao alone or the Chinese people alone.

Meanwhile the Chinese people say to the world: "Go ahead, and punish us."

SELECTED BIBLIOGRAPHY

I

Books

Mao Tse-tung: *Selected Works of Mao Tse-tung*, Lawrence and Wishart, London, 1954-1956. 4 vols., 1,240 pages. (Containing the material of the first three volumes of the Chinese edition.) With notes and comments. Edited and prepared by a Commission of the Central Committee of the CCP.

Mao Tse-tung: *Selected Works of Mao Tse-tung*, Peking edition, Vol. IV. 459 pages, Foreign Language Press, Peking, 1961. (Containing the material of the 4th volume of the Chinese edition.)

Mao Tse-tung: *Analysis of the Classes in Chinese Society*, (this work, and all other works of Mao Tse-tung listed below, were published repeatedly by the Foreign Language Press, Peking).

Mao Tse-tung: *Report of an Investigation into the Peasant Movement in Hunan.*

Mao Tse-tung: *Why can China's Red Political Power Exist?*

Mao Tse-tung: *A Single Spark can Start a Prairie Fire.*

Mao Tse-tung: *On the Tactics of Fighting Japanese Imperialism.*

Mao Tse-tung: *Strategic Problems of China's Revolutionary War.*

Mao Tse-tung: *On Practice.*

Mao Tse-tung: *On Contradiction.*

Mao Tse-tung: *Strategic Problems in the Anti-Japanese Guerilla War.*

Mao Tse-tung: *On the Protracted War.*

Mao Tse-tung: *Problems of War and Strategy.*

Mao Tse-tung: *The Chinese Revolution and the Chinese Communist Party.*

Mao Tse-tung: *On New Democracy.*
          Rectify the Party's Style in Work.

Mao Tse-tung: *Talks at the Yenan Forum on Art and Literature.*

Mao Tse-tung: *On Methods of Leadership.*

Mao Tse-tung: *On People's Democratic Dictatorship.*

Mao Tse-tung: *On the Correct Handling of Contradictions Among the People.*

Mao Tse-tung: *Comrade Mao Tse-tung on "Imperialism and All Reactionaries are Paper Tigers".*

Mao Tse-tung: *Mao Tse-tung on Art and Literature.*

Mao Tse-tung: *Nineteen Poems.*

Chang Ju-hsin: *On Mao Tse-tung,* Peking, 1949.

Chassin, Lionel Max: *La Conquète de la Chine par Mao Tze-tung, 1945-1949,* Paris, 1952.

Chen Po-ta: *Mao Tse-tung on the Chinese Revolution,* Peking, 1953.

Emi Siao: *Mao Tze-dun, Chzhe De,* Moscow, 1939.

Emi Siao: *Mao Tse-tung, His Childhood and Youth,* People's Publishing House, Bombay, 1953.

Fromentin, Pierre: *Mao Tse-tung, Le Dragon Rouge,* Paris, 1949.

Mao Tze-dun: *Biograficheskii ocherk,* Moscow, 1939.

Mao Tse-tung, Wang Ming and others: *China: The March Toward Unity,* New York, 1937.

Payne, Robert: *Mao Tse-tung, Ruler of Red China,* London, 1951.

Schwartz, Benjamin I.: *Chinese Communism and the Rise of Mao,* Harvard University Press, 1951.

Snow, Edgar: *Red Star Over China,* London, 1937.

The Autobiography of Mao Tse-tung, Truth Book Company, Canton, 1938, revised ed. 1949. (The same in Chinese language editions.)

Walker, Richard L.: *Chairman Mao,* Encounter, London, June 1960.

A History of the Modern Chinese Revolution, Foreign Language Press, Peking, 1959.

Abend, Hallett: *My Life in China, 1926-1941.* New York, 1943.

Akademiya Nauk, USSR: *Natsionalno-kolonialno problemy, sbornik materialov.* Vol. I. Moscow, 1937.

All Men Are Brothers (*Shui Hu Chuan*), 2 vols., translated by Pearl S. Buck, London, 1933.

Bakulin, A. V.: *Zapiski ob ukhanskom periode kitaiskoi revoliutsii,* Moscow, 1930.

Beloff, Max: *Soviet Policy in the Far East, 1944-1951,* London, 1953.

Brandt, Conrad, Benjamin Schwartz, and John K. Fairbank: *A Documentary History of Chinese Communism,* Cambridge, Mass., 1952.

Brandt, Conrad: *Stalin's Failure in China,* Cambridge, Mass., 1958.

Brieux, Jean-Jacques: *La Chine: du nationalisme au communisme*, Paris, 1950.

Burnham, J.: *First Act in China.*

Byrnes, J. F.: *Speaking Frankly*, London, 1946.

Chandra-Sekhar, Sripati: *Red China—An Asian View*, New York, 1961.

Chao Chung: *The Communist Programme for Literature and Art in China*, Hong Kong, 1955.

Ch'en Tu-hsiu: *Letter to the Comrades of the Chinese Communist Party*, Shanghai, 1929.

Cheng Tien-hsi: *China Moulded by Confucius*, London, 1946.

Chiang Kai-shek, General and Mme Chiang Kai-shek: *China at the Crossroads*, London, 1937.

Chiang Kai-shek: *Revolution and Reconstruction*, New York, 1942.

Chiang Kai-shek: *Collected Wartime Messages*, New York, 1946.

Chiang Kai-shek: *Soviet Russia in China*, London, 1957.

Chiang Kai-shek: *China's Destiny*, London, 1947.

Compton, Boyd: Mao's China: *Party Reform Documents, 1942-1944*, Seattle, 1952.

Chao Kuo-chun: *Agrarian Policy of the Chinese Communist Party*, London, 1960.

China Handbook, 1937-1945, published by the Kuomintang Government, revised ed. 1947.

Chou En-lai; Yen Chien-ying and others: *China's Resistance, 1937-1939*, Chungking, 1940.

Chou Yang: *The Path of Socialist Literature and Art in China*, Foreign Language Press, Peking, 1960.

Chow Ching-wen: *Ten Years of Storm*, New York, 1960.

Chow Tse-tsung: *The May Fourth Movement*, Harvard University Press, 1960.

Churchill, Winston S.: *The Second World War*, Vol. V. London, 1952.

Dedijer, Vladimir: *Tito Speaks*, London, 1953.

Degras, Jane, ed.: *Soviet Documents on Foreign Policy*, 3 Vols. Oxford, 1951-1953.

Degras, Jane: *The Communist International, 1919-1943*, Documents, London, 1956, Vol. I. Vol. II. London, 1960.

Duyvendak, J. J. L.: *Probsthain's Oriental Series*, London, 1928. Vol. XVII.

Emi Siao: *Kitai nepobedim*, Moscow, 1940.

Erenburg, G. B.: *Ocherki natsionalno-osvoboditelniy borby kitaiskovo naroda v noveisheye vremyia*, Moscow, 1951.

Feis, Herbert: *The China Tangle*, Princeton, 1953.

Feng Yu-lan: *Lessons of My Participation in the Land Reform*, Peking, 1950.

Fitzgerald, C. P.: *Revolution in China*, London, 1952.

Forman, Harrison: *Report from Red China*, London, 1946.

Gabor, Dennis: *Inventing the Future*, Encounter, London, 1960.

Gluckstein, Ygael: *Mao's China—Economic and Political Survey*, London, 1957.

Guillain, Robert: *600 Million de Chinois*, Paris, 1956.

History of the Communist Party of the Soviet Union, Foreign Language Press, Moscow, 1960.

How to Hold an Accusation Meeting, Current Affairs Handbooks, No. 12. Peking, 1951.

Hsiao Ch'ien: *How the Tillers Win Back Their Land*, F.L.P. Peking, 1951.

Hu Chiao-mu: *Thirty Years of the Communist Party of China*, London, 1951.

Hughes, E. R.: *The Invasion of China by the Western World*, New York, 1938.

Isaacs, Harold: *The Tragedy of the Chinese Revolution*, London, 1938, rev. ed. Stanford, California, 1951, 2nd rev. ed. 1961.

Kapitza, M. S.: *Sovietsko-Kitaiskie Otnosheniya B 1931-1945*, GG. Moscow, 1956.

Kardelj, Edward: *Socialism and War* (A Survey of the Chinese Criticism of the Policy of Coexistence), London, 1962.

Karol, K. S.: *Krouschtchev et l'Occident*, Paris, 1960.

Khrushchev, N. S.: *Secret Speech*, London, 1956.

Kautsky, Karl: *Karl Marx's okonomische Lehren*.

Lenin, V. I.: *Selected Works*, London, 1937, Vol. IX.

Lenin, V. I.: *Works*, Fourth Russian edition, Vol. XXX. Moscow.

Lenin, V. I.: *The National Liberation Movement in the East*, F.L.P. Moscow, 1957.

Leonhard, Wolfgang: *Kreml Ohne Stalin*, Koln, 1959.

Liao Kai-lung: *From Yenan to Peking*, F.L.P. Peking, 1954.

Liu Shao-chi: *Liquidate the Menshevist Ideology Within the Party*, F.L.P. Peking, 1951.

Liu Shao-chi: *How to be a Good Communist*, F.L.P. Peking, 1952.

Liu Shao-chi: *The Victory of Marxism-Leninism*, F.L.P. Peking, 1959.

Mannheim, Karl: *Ideologie and Utopia*, London, 1960.

MacFarquhar, Roderick: *The Hundred Flowers*, London, 1960.

McLane, Charles B.: *Soviet Policy and the Chinese Communists, 1931-1946*, Columbia University Press, 1958.

Marx-Engels: *The Communist Manifesto.*

Mende, Tibor: *China and her Shadow*, London, 1960.

Mende, Tibor: *The Chinese Revolution*, London, 1961.

Meissner, Boris: *Das Ende des Stalin-Mythos—Die Ergebnisse des XX. Parteitages der Kommunistischen Partei der Sovietunion*, Frankfurt-am-Main, 1956.

Mif, Pavel: *Heroic China; Fifteen Years of the Communist Party of China*, New York, 1937.

New China's Economic Achievements, 1949-1952, Peking, 1952.

North, R. C.: *Moscow and the Chinese Communists*, Stanford University Press, 1953.

North, R. C.: *Kuomintang and Chinese Communist Elites*, Stanford University Press, California, 1952.

Paloczi-Horvath, George: *Khrushchev—The Road to Power*, London, 1960.

Ping-chia Kuo: *China—New Age and New Outlook*, London, 1960.

Rosinger, Lawrence K.: *China's Wartime Politics, 1937-1944*, Princeton, 1945.

Rosinger, Lawrence K.: *China's Crisis*, New York, 1945.

Roy, M. N.: *Revolution and Counter-Revolution in China*, Calcutta, 1946.

Schapiro, Leonard: *The Communist Party of the Soviet Union*, London, 1961.

Selle, Earl Albert: *Donald of China*, New York, 1948.

Segonzac, Adalbert de: *Visa Pour Peking*, Paris, 1956.

Short History of the Communist Party of the Soviet Union (Bolshevik), London, 1943.

Sherwood, R. E.: *The White House Papers of Harry Hopkins*, Vol. I, II. London, 1949.

Siao-yu: *Mao Tse-tung and I Were Beggars*, Syracuse University Press, 1956.

Simon, Paul: *Le Mouvement Communiste en Chine des Origines à nos jours*, Paris, 1939.

Smedley, Agnes: *The Great Road, The Life and Times of Chu Teh*, London, 1958.

Stories of the Long March, F.L.P. Peking, 1958.

Stalin, J. V., Bukharin and others: *Voprosy kitaiskoi revoliutsii*, Moscow, 1927.

Strategia i taktika Kominterna v natsialno-kolonialno revoliutsii, na primere Kitaia (Comintern documents, edited by Pavel Mif), Moscow, 1934.

Sun Yat-sen: *The Triple Demism of Sun Yat-sen.* The Franciscan Press, Wuchang, 1931.

Sun Yat-sen: *San Min Chu I: The Three Principles of the People.* Chungking, 1943.

Tang, Peter S. H.: *Communist China Today,* New York, 1957.

The Chinese Communist Movement, McCarran Hearings, 7A US Government Printing Office, Washington, 1952.

The Seventh All-China Congress of Trade Unions, Peking, 1953.

Trotsky, Leon: *The Stalin School of Falsification,* New York, 1937.

Trotsky, Leon: *Problems of the Chinese Revolution,* New York, 1932.

Tsi C. Wang: *The Youth Movement in China,* New York, 1937.

United States Government, Department of State: *United States Relations with China with Special Reference to the Period 1944-1949,* Washington, 1949.

U.S. Government: *"MacArthur Hearings,"* Washington, 1951.

U.S. Government; War Department, Military Intelligence Division: *The Chinese Communist Movement,* 3 vols. (*Declassified.*) Washington, 1954.

Vandervelde, Emile: *A travers la Revolution Chinoise: soviets et Kuomintang,* Paris, 1931.

Wales, Nym: *Red Dust, Autobiographies of Chinese Communists* (As told to Nym Wales.) Palo Alto, California, 1952.

Walker, Richard L.: *China under Communism—The First Five Years,* London, 1956.

Wedemeyer, Albert C., General: *Wedemeyer Reports,* New York, 1958.

Wilbur, C. Martin, and Julie Lien-ying How: *Documents on Communism, Nationalism, and Soviet Advisers in China 1918-1927.* (Paper seized in the 1927 Peking raid.) Columbia University Press, New York, 1956.

Wint, Guy: *Spotlight on Asia,* revised ed., London, 1959.

Wint, Guy: *Common Sense about China,* London, 1960.

Wittfogel, Karl A.: *Oriental Despotism,* Yale Univ. Press, 1957.

Wu, A. K.: *China and the Soviet Union,* Methuen, London, 1950.

Yang Shang-kuei: *The Red Kiangsi-Kwanyung Border Region,* F.L.P. Peking, 1961.

Yefimov, G.: *Ocherki po novoi i noveiskei istorii Kitaia,* Moscow, 1951.

II

Newspapers and periodicals quoted
(In case of better known journals, only the English title is given)
Journals, 1915-49, in Chinese
  Youth; later *New Youth,* Peking.
  New Tide, Peking.
  Hsiang River Review (edited by Mao).
  Weekly Critic.
  Red Flag, Shanghai.
  The Communist, Yenan.
  Liberation News, Yenan.
  Peking University Daily.

1949-62, in Chinese
  New China News Agency.
  Changtu Daily.
  China Youth, Peking.
  Chinese Worker, Peking.
  Hankow Chang Chiang Jih Pao.
  Honan People's Daily.
  Hsueh-hsi (Study), Peking.
  Kiangsi Daily.
  Kuang Ming Daily.
  Kweichow Daily.
  Lao Tung Pao, Shanghai.
  Liberation Daily, Shanghai.
  New China Daily, Chungking.
  New China Half-Monthly.
  People's Daily, Peking.
  Red Flag, Peking.
  Shenyang Daily.
  Ta Kung Pao, Tientsin.
  Tsingtao Daily.
  Wen Hui Pao.

Druzhba (the Chinese periodical published in Moscow in Russian).
Published by Peking in English: *Peking Review, China Reconstructs, Chinese Literature, China Pictorial.*

Publications of the Communist International (Comintern):

Inprecor (International Press Correspondence), Published weekly first in Vienna and Berlin from 1922 till 1933, and then till 1941 in London; renamed *World News and Views* in 1938.

Communist International (English edition—slightly modified—of the Russian *Kommunisticheskii international*, British edition: 1919-35, American edition: 1935-39.)

Kommunisticheskii international, (Organ of the Executive Committee of the Communist International Moscow, published weekly, later bi-weekly, 1919-1943.)

Kommunismus, Zeitschrift der Kommunistischen Internationale, 1919-1943.

Soviet publications:

Pravda, Izvestiya, Bolshevik, later *Kommunyist*, *"For Lasting Peace for People's Democracy"* (Cominform publication).

Communist (Bombay).
Militant (New York).
Asahi Shinbun (Tokyo).
New York Times.
New York Herald Tribune.
The China Quarterly (London).

INDEX